A HIGHLANDS OMNIBUS

Angus MacVicar

Containing

Rocks in My Scotch
Silver in My Sporran
Bees in My Bonnet

ARROW BOOKS

Arrow Books Limited
20 Vauxhall Bridge Road, London SW1V 2SA

An imprint of the Random Century Group

London Melbourne Sydney Auckland Johannesburg
and agencies throughout the world

Omnibus edition first published in 1991

Printed and bound in Great Britain by
Cox & Wyman Ltd, Reading

ISBN 0 09 985110 5

A HIGHLANDS OMNIBUS

ROCKS IN MY SCOTCH

Angus MacVicar

ROCKS IN MY SCOTCH

Confessions of a minister's son

Acknowledgements

In connection with the story about the Sollas evictions, my grateful thanks are due to John Prebble for allowing me to follow closely the line of his narrative in *The Highland Clearances*. I am grateful also to Captain Jack Broome for permission to use the story about the capture of a German spy which he tells in *Convoy is to Scatter*. For accurate information concerning the wrecks of the *Argo* and the *Dunraven Castle* I have to thank ex-Coxswain Duncan Newlands and the Royal National Lifeboat Institution.

A.M.

To Willie, Kenneth and John
my brothers still, for a' that

Contents

1

The Sealed Loft

It was in the late summer of 1919, when the excitements of the First World War were fading from a boy's short memory, that Archie and Willie and I solved the mystery of the sealed loft above the coal-house.

Archie was seven and Willie five. Rona, our sister, had been born – but only just – while brothers Kenneth and John had still to make their entrances. I was ten, a man of the world, far-travelled, having been to Campbeltown, ten miles away, several times and to Glasgow once.

The rigours of the journey to Campbeltown were considerable. It was by a motor-bus, an Oldsmobile of uncertain temper belonging to Mrs Gibson of the Argyll Arms Hotel, who persisted in calling it, with hazy topicality, the 'Demobilize'. The driver was her nephew, Willie McKerral, whose sister Jean, then only nine years old, I was eventually to marry.

The 'Demobilize' was uncovered. Passengers had to sit side by side on long benches, facing in towards each other like actors in a classic Russian film, unsheltered from rain, sun or tempest. It shuddered and shook along the metalled road, occasionally suffered broken springs and punctures and, when faced by Kilellan Brae (with a full load and the wind against), began to bubble, boil and whine, with the result that old farmers with cloth caps, oilskin coats, well-trimmed whiskers and rose-brier pipes, along with young women and children like my mother and myself, had to get out and walk alongside as it struggled to the top. Today, even in my eight-year-old Morris Oxford, I can surge up and over Kilellan Brae in top gear and scarcely notice it.

On the journey to Glasgow further hazards had to be faced in the *Davaar* or the *Kinloch*, the elegant steamers which ran daily from Campbeltown to Gourock, via Carradale and Lochranza. Even for me, sophisticated traveller though I was, the sight of white-caps in Kilbrannan Sound and of watery turbulence off the Garroch Head were daunting. Queasiness occurred in my stomach, not from seasickness but from anxiety. I comforted myself by remembering a tale often told by my seafaring friend, old Hughie Stewart. Seated on a bollard on the ancient stone jetty under the Rock of Dunaverty, Hughie would pause in the manufacture of lobster creels and describe to us boys, held fast by his 'glittering eye', how, from the deck of the *Kinloch* in Kilbrannan Sound, he had once seen a passing ship raised so high by waves at bow and stern that under her hull he had glimpsed the rocky coastline of Kintyre! I was grateful that conditions on my journey were scarcely as terrible as that.

But, as I afterwards informed my goggling brothers, the supreme test of my discipline and courage occurred on the train which carried us from Gourock to Glasgow. Scarcely had I recovered from the heart-stopping trauma of plunging unexpectedly into a dark tunnel when another train approached with a howl and a roar and, as I thought, almost collided with us. I sat zombiefied as it screamed past, apparently missing us only by inches. The danger receded. I opened my eyes, took a deep breath and – to prove hardihood – remarked to my mother, 'Great drivers in these trains!'

Not only did I venture in public transport: I also rode a bicycle, an important status symbol in a parish where people – even farmers – were then generally poor, with children lucky to own boots, let alone bicycles. On it, during the summer holidays, I explored roads and glens and practised dirt-track riding on the beaches and on the gravelled Manse drive. It was a sturdy second-hand model bought for a pound from my school pal, Bobby Kelly, a nephew of red-bearded Hugh McEachran who was my father's Kirk Treasurer. The same Bobby is now himself

Kirk Treasurer (and still a pal), which shows that family traditions flourish strongly in a small community like Southend at the Mull of Kintyre.

By 1919 my father had been minister of Southend for nine years. One of those years, from 1916 to 1917, he had spent in Greece as a chaplain attached to the Lovat Scouts, which is why he came to be known as the Padre. He and my mother, along with ourselves and Maimie, the sentimental, kind but hard-knuckled little maid, occupied a three-storeyed Manse with nine rooms, a bathroom, a scullery and a large collection of out-houses.

The out-houses included a garden shed *cum* earthen closet at the back, with, in front, between the Manse and the main road, a complex of buildings comprising a hen-house, a washing-house, a stable, a barn, a byre and a coal-house.

There was also, by itself near the front gate, a dark, dank structure which we called 'Peter's Shed', after a neighbouring farmer who used it for storing his reapers, ploughs, grubbers and other agricultural implements. Though no person or document can be found to confirm it, I believe this building to have been the old Manse ('rendered excessively damp by two great trees which overshadow it and suffering from the effects of fire', according to a chronicler of the period), left derelict when the new Manse in which we lived was built in 1818.

All those out-houses were relics of an era when a Church of Scotland clergyman was also a farmer and cultivated the Church glebelands for his own profit, though long before my father came to Southend the glebelands had been rented out to Peter Galbraith (who gave his name to 'Peter's Shed') and most of them were redundant as far as a minister was concerned. Sometimes, however, the byre was used by farmers as a shelter for cattle being driven to and from the market in Campbeltown; and the stable came in handy for churchgoers and visitors to the Manse, most of whom travelled in horse-drawn 'machines'.

At the time, indeed, only one private motor-car existed in Southend – apart from the Dowager Duchess of Argyll's

Daimler, with its studded tyres and uniformed chauffeur. It belonged to one of my father's leading elders, James Hunter of Machribeg Farm, and we regarded it with the awe reserved by schoolboys today for a flying saucer. It rattled on speedy but erratic courses throughout Kintyre. Hens scattered from its path, squawking. In the fields large Clydesdale horses heard it coming, reared, neighed and fled thunderously to far corners. As it hurtled past the school at thirty miles an hour we would rush to climb the high playground wall and, from this safe eminence, cheer its progress.

Stories regarding Jamie Hunter's driving thrilled and delighted us.

Once he reversed into the window of a china-shop in Campbeltown with smashing results. Another time, attempting a dashing U-turn, he destroyed a wooden hen-house in his own backyard and declared afterwards that it hadn't been there in the morning when he left. Directly opposite the junction of Machribeg farm-track with the main road, there is a gateway into a field. One morning, no doubt preoccupied with thoughts concerning milk-yields and turnip crops, he failed to make the turn on to the highway and plunged straight across it and through the gateway into a slough of cattle-churned mud. The motor coughed itself to death. He banged the steering-wheel. 'Who left that dashed gate open!' he complained.

It was James Hunter who first greeted my father on his arrival by steamer at Campbeltown in March 1910 and drove him, my mother, Maimie and me eight miles south to our new home in the Manse of St Blaan. He used a 'machine': his car had not then been purchased. And it was Jamie Hunter who conveyed our furniture from the pier – in long, ladder-sided carts – and organized help among his fellow-farmers to unload and instal it.

His kindness to 'the minister' and to the minister's family never varied throughout his life. After the First World War, when he exchanged his pony and 'machine' for the car, he continued to offer my father 'lifts' to Campbeltown and beyond. Not wishing to hurt a loyal elder and friend my father had to accept a few such invitations; but my mother, brothers, Maimie and I – though willing enough – were never allowed to accompany him. 'One member of the family risking his life is enough,' he used to say.

His most anguished experience, he often told us, was on a return journey from Campbeltown to Southend, in a fog. On Kilellan Brae (which runs downhill in this direction) the fog was so dense that Jamie ordered my father to put his head out of the passenger window and keep a sharp look-out, while he did the same on *his* side. The road was being remetalled and, following custom, small piles of stones had been deposited at close intervals along the verge, ready for scattering. Suddenly the car's near-wheels bumped over one of those and then, in quick succession, over another and another.

'Broken a spring!' shouted the driver, to whom such accidents were not unknown.

'You haven't!' my father shouted back. 'You're bumping on the road metal!'

'No road metal here!'

'Yes, there is! Steer away from it!'

'If I steer away from it I'll hit the other side!'

'Isn't there plenty of room?'

'How do I know, minister! I can't see!'

The crashing and bumping continued. Bones jarring, my father prayed. Near the foot of the hill the piles of road metal came to an end and the fog cleared.

'I told you!' cried Jamie, almost hysterical with relief. 'There's no road metal here. These dashed springs!'

The Padre, breathing heavily, made no further comment.

He seldom took a dram at home. That night he did. I remember him saying to my mother: 'Greater love hath no man than this, that he lay down his life for Jamie Hunter!'

All the same, he – and all of us – loved Jamie Hunter. He had known tragedy in the death of an adolescent son; but bitterness was never allowed to darken his hopeful spirit.

The derelict out-houses at the Manse might have been of little use to a non-farming minister; to a minister's sons they were caves of exciting romance.

An exception was the barn, a high, airy building used by my father as a kind of timber-yard. When trees were felled in the Manse grounds, or branches blown off by a roistering wind from the west, they were stored in the barn for sawing and chopping into firewood. My brothers and I were forbidden to wield the big axe, in case we did ourselves an injury; but from about the age of nine I had to take a turn at helping the Padre with the cross-cut saw. This, for me, was purgatory.

The preliminaries were always happy enough. Under paternal direction Archie and Willie and I would manoeuvre the sawing-horse into position and, with much tugging and heaving, lift the branch on to it. Having learned from experience, Archie and Willie would then stand back, well clear of trouble. My smiling father would take off his jacket, suddenly appearing oddly naked in dog-collar, shirt-sleeves and braces, and say to me: 'Come on now, Angus. See how many blocks we can make before tea!'

He would place the blade of the saw across the branch, the narrow end in my direction. 'Catch!' he'd say, in high good humour. I'd catch the wooden handle as instructed, but from my heart humour would be absent. At the beginning of operations such as sawing, gardening or repairing punctures on bicycles the Padre was invariably happy and carefree. It was later on, when things went sour, that hell might be glimpsed beneath the gates of heaven.

He had an impatient and somewhat irascible nature. One afternoon it happened that the branch we were sawing was young, sappy and tough, and the cross-cut needed sharpening. Each time it stuck he became more annoyed, his wrenching and pushing more savage. I teetered and staggered, trying to lend assistance. My puny efforts were not appreciated. The branch, the saw and I were denigrated in turn, terrible unministerial words issuing from behind clenched teeth. Archie and Willie giggled in the shadows.

At last the saw became so firmly embedded that even my father's frenzied jerks could not move it. He flung up his hands. 'Useless!' he roared at me. 'Useless!' he roared at the saw. Then he drew back a foot and kicked the horse with such force that along with branch and twanging saw it crashed over on its side. At the same moment he uttered a cry of pain and began hopping on one leg, nursing a bruised foot in both hands.

Archie and Willie fled outside, like camp followers from Culloden. As the eldest son I felt it was my duty to stay with my stricken father and, for want of anything better to do, make feeble efforts to raise the horse.

'Let it lie!' keened the Padre, collapsing on a pile of wood. 'Let the blasted thing lie!'

I departed the scene. Collecting my brothers from beneath the gooseberry bushes in the garden (a favourite hiding-place in times of stress), I led them into the hills behind the Manse. By tea-time, as I well knew, my father's passion would be spent and life would have returned to normal. In the meantime we could search, maybe with profit, for peewits' eggs.

Fifty years later, when the Padre was almost ninety, he was in Achnamara, our bungalow in Southend, watching on television a football match between Scotland and Germany. At the turn of the century as a Glasgow University student, he himself had played shinty for Scotland, and ever since had been interested in sport of all kinds. This day, according to him, the Germans were 'savages', kicking the Scots and getting away with it because of 'that blasted referee'. Kenneth Wolstenholme's commentary also enraged him. 'An Englishman supporting the Germans!' he snarled. 'No wonder there's a Scottish Nationalist Party!'

Suddenly, in full view of the cameras, a player was scythed down in a particularly vicious tackle. The victim writhed in agony – as soccer players, those fugitives from amateur drama, are frequently inclined to do. 'There you are!' exclaimed the ninety-year-old, throwing himself back in his armchair. 'They're at it again! That poor Scots boy!'

'But it's a German who's down,' Jean told him.

'Eh?' He peered forward to confirm the fact. 'So it is!' he declared with satisfaction. 'Let him lie!'

The Padre could never have been described as unprejudiced or even fair-minded. And yet, as we grew older, it was revealed to Rona, my brothers and me that he was a good minister.

All kinds of people – 'tinkers, tailors, soldiers, sailors, dons and duchesses and dukes', but mainly, in a country community like Southend, farmers and farm-workers – called regularly at the Manse for advice. Sometimes his advice was curt, if it concerned a material problem; but when men and women came to him weeping in despair he often wept with them, the quick tears of a Hebridean heritage staining his cheeks as he called for my mother to bring cups of tea.

He visited his congregation with tireless zeal, riding the rough roads on his bicycle and ignoring the weather. He made humorous speeches at weddings. With my mother he would often be the first visitor to touch the hand of a new-born child. When a parishioner was ill he would sit for hours by the bedside; and when death became imminent he would be there to say a prayer for the dying, followed by another to support and comfort the living.

He always worked hard in preparing for a funeral. Once, to a young minister, I heard him give this advice: 'Always be at your best at a funeral, because at a funeral you get nearest to the hearts of your people.' His belief was that a minister had to be close to members of his congregation – a part, indeed, of their daily lives – in order to be of any spiritual use to them.

At the beginning we imagined he was far kinder and more tolerant with parishioners than he was with us. When sawing-horses were kicked with violence and bicycles which resisted his efforts at repair were thrown over the bank beyond the back gate, we often wondered what had happened to the benign approach he seemed to reserve for drunk men and for girls who were going to have illegitimate babies. Later on we realized that only in the superficial, unimportant areas of life did the Padre tend to blow gaskets. When serious moral problems were involved he could understand and sympathize, perhaps because he had personal experience of them.

The sealed loft was above the coal-house, the only means of access to it being a wooden door high on one wall of the barn. Since our arrival at the Manse this door had remained locked, with three stout planks nailed across it. As far as we could discover there was no key.

Archie, Willie and I were constantly curious about what lay behind it.

Maimie would say: 'I am sure *I* can't tell you! It's none of my business, nor of yours either. *Chiall beannachd mi*, there are more important things to worry about than a dirty old loft. I shouldn't be surprised if there's nothing at all inside.'

'If there's nothing inside why is it nailed up?'

'To keep inquisitive boys like you out of mischief – and to save you from breaking your necks trying to climb up to it. Now, skedaddle! Let me get on with making the dinner.'

'But, Maimie' – Archie was persistent – 'maybe there's a ghost in there?'

'Merciful goodness, if there *is* a ghost, you'd be wise to leave it alone, safely locked up. So stop asking questions! Outside you go and get some fresh air. Ghosts! Lord preserve us!'

But we knew that by his mention of a ghost Archie had touched a sensitive string in the constantly twanging harp of Maimie's personality. Born in Perthshire, the home of the Picts and the pixies, she had been brought up in a climate of superstition; and, as a legacy from my father's first parish, she had carried with her to Southend some spine-chilling yarns. One of those was about the Maid of Glen Duror, an apparition which, while prowling in the dark, would seem to have lit up like the phosphorescent tree-stump outside the Manse front gate. The idea that another 'Maid' might exist in the loft above the coal-house had obviously occurred to her as well as to Archie; and, despite the brusque manner in which duty prompted her to deal with us, we felt we might have gained a secret ally in our campaign to get that door opened.

My mother parried questions with patience and common sense. She was of farming stock from Appin, a nursery that has always produced more practical and down-to-earth characters than Perthshire, Maimie's homeland, or than North Uist, my father's.

'It was sealed up before we came,' she said. 'Seems that when the Manse was being got ready for us, nine years ago, they threw a lot of old rubbish up there and decided simply to lock it away. At least, so Mr Hunter tells us. There's no key, as far as I know.'

It sounded reasonable.

'What kind of rubbish?' I asked.

'How should I know? Now, don't bother your heads about it any more. There are far more exciting and interesting things to do outside. You haven't caught any tadpoles lately. Here's an old glass jelly-jar. How about trying to find some up at the Carr Loch?'

The diversion was maternally cunning. It was also successful. Tadpoles *were* exciting and, once caught, might turn into frogs before our very eyes. But on this occasion, when they died instead – the glass jar, though full of water and nourishing weed, being, because of our ignorance, without any kind of aeration – our minds returned to the burr-like problem of the loft.

The subject was never fully discussed with the Padre. If one of us dared to mention it he would snort down his nose – with the strong, curling red hairs sticking out of the nostrils – and tell us to mind our own blasted business. 'Away you go now and practise jump, hop and step or something!' (He had spoken nothing but Gaelic until he went to school in North Uist at the age of five. Ever since then he had been troubled by the English idiom. As he himself used to joke, unwittingly, he was always 'putting the horse before the cart'.)

In time our frustration led to an inevitable conclusion. By some means we ourselves must find a way into the loft.

Years later Archie became a teacher of English, Willie a ship's captain, I myself a spinner of tales. The way we approached our problem indicates that we mistook our vocations. We ought to have joined the secret service, or, perhaps, become demolition experts.

From the beginning we recognized that a direct assault on the door, high on the barn wall, was out of the question. Long before we could remove all the planks and force the lock, the operation was bound to be discovered. The barn, as well as being open to the back yard, was often entered by Maimie when collecting logs for the fire and by the Padre when he came to split them. Besides, if we were caught 'damaging property', as my Tory mother liked to phrase it, then the punishment would be dire, a heavy price to pay even for satisfied curiosity. A way of entry, therefore, must be found elsewhere.

At the age of five, Willie already had a navigator's imagination and sense of direction. Casually he suggested that we might try to force an entrance through the wall directly *opposite* the door in the barn. This, he said, could be done in secret from the adjacent loft above the byre, the door to which loomed twelve feet up on an outside gable wall near the back gate.

It was a brilliant idea, and Archie and I became convinced immediately that we had thought of it ourselves. The loft above the byre was already a 'gang headquarters', where on wet days we and other boys in the parish got together to consume secret hoards of liquorice straps and sometimes to wield them violently in dispensing summary justice to erring members of our fraternity. Our parents and Maimie never objected to our use of the household steps to reach the door, though sometimes they made noises of protest when the older ones among us, fired by tales of Everest in the *Boys' Own Paper*, indulged in the practice of hauling up on ropes some of the infants like Willie, who could not quite stretch up to the threshold from the top of the steps. We were lucky to have a childhood uninhibited by physical mollycoddling and, as will be shown, in a moral sense the story was similar. It seemed evident to us, therefore, that visits to the loft above the byre would cause no suspicion and that we might even be able to enter the loft above the coal-house and discover its contents without anybody being the wiser.

One Saturday morning, with rain spattering on a chill wind from the east, we asked Maimie politely if we could have the steps. On receiving her permission, we placed them in position below the outside door of the loft above the byre. From the Padre's incoherent tool-kit in the barn I took a hammer and chisel and secured them with string underneath my jersey. I climbed up, got inside the loft and helped Archie and Willie, suitably roped like mountaineers, in their scramble to join me.

We made a recce of the blank face of stone and mortar which was all that separated us from the sealed loft above the coal-house. The mortar was old and flaking. At one place we found a group of stones from which some had fallen away. Taking turns, we began work with the hammer and chisel to remove more.

The German prison camp at Colditz was still twenty years in the future; a television series was utterly beyond our reckoning. But we were not without ideas. We shut the loft door in order to muffle sounds and hammered and chiselled in the dark, using only a battery torch which had been a Christmas present to Archie from the Dowager Duchess. The mortar debris we placed in a bag – an old jelly-straining bag abandoned some time ago by my mother on a back shelf of the larder – and, at intervals, emptied it out of sight beneath a pile of straw in a corner.

On that first spell, though we laboured tensely until it was time for lunch, we failed to loosen any of the stones. It was a disappointment; but we were confident that another hour or two of work would bring us to the edge of triumph.

Unfortunately, the day was a Saturday. In the afternoon we

had to attend a children's party at a neighbouring farm. On Sunday, on account of holy observances, a visit to the loft would be impossible. On Monday we had to return to school after the summer holidays. Our first chance to resume operations, therefore, would not occur until the Monday evening.

We spent the week-end in a state of anxiety, even though the home-baked iced cakes and sliced sugared oranges at the farm party – and the moment in church, when to everyone's horror and secret delight, the Padre announced his text from *Galatians*: 'But now, after ye have known God, or rather are known of God, how turn ye again to the weak and buggarly elements' – helped in some measure to ease the burden.

A diversion took place on the Monday morning. It was to be Willie's first day at school, and it soon became evident that going to school was the last thing Willie wanted to do. Perhaps he had visions of working in the loft by himself while Archie and I were busy at our lessons. In any case, when the time came for the Padre to convoy us the short half-mile to Southend Public School, whose headmaster was the blond and bristling Mr James Inglis Morton, he was nowhere to be found.

We searched the dining-room, the drawing-room, the attics, the bedrooms: no sign of him. My mother struggled to camouflage tears. Scuttling about in all directions, Maimie let loose imprecations in the Gaelic, imprecations directed not at Willie but at the Padre for his angry shouts. Archie and I were beginning to be afraid that we might be late for school, which would mean the strap. Mr Morton accepted no excuses, not even from parents.

From above there was a faint sound. Archie and I raced upstairs. In the spare bedroom we discovered Willie below the big double bed, cowering beyond our reach against a corner of the wall.

'Come on,' said Archie, 'we'll be late!'

'I don't want to go to school!'

'Don't be stupid!' I said, in a low voice. 'If the Padre finds you in there he'll kill you!'

'I don't want to go to school!'

I went hurriedly downstairs and got my father's long *cromak* from the hallstand. In the kitchen, upset by the commotion, Rona was howling in her pram, being comforted by our distraught mother.

'Have you found him yet?' bellowed the Padre, rummaging in the rhododendrons at the front door.

I didn't answer.

Half-way up the stairs I met Maimie coming down. She eyed the *cromak*.

'You've found him?'

'Don't tell anybody!' I said.

'The poor dear child – hunted like an animal! You should all think black burning shame of yourselves!'

Black burning shame was something of which – as yet – I had small experience; and, in any case, it was clear that Maimie had no alternative plans to offer. I got down on my knees by the bed and poked at Willie.

'Buck up! You're not a baby any longer!'

For a time he suffered the pokes in miserable silence. Archie pled with him, even promising the gift of a whole liquorice strap if only he'd come out.

Willie said: 'I don't want to go to school!'

I began to make long sweeps with the *cromak*. As it struck Willie's legs I felt cruel and guilty. But in the end the new assault proved effective. He crawled out, uttering heavy sobs.

We led him downstairs. 'It's all right,' I told the Padre, whose complexion had become ruddier than I'd ever seen it before. 'He's coming now.'

In a great silence we trudged down the road to the school – the Padre, Archie, Willie and I. We weren't late. Willie's scholastic career began in an atmosphere of sadness and twanging, ill-received discipline.

His next rebellion occurred when he was sixteen, a pupil at Campbeltown Grammar School. Suddenly he announced that he had had enough of conventional education and was going to join the merchant navy. Long afterwards, as senior Captain with the Anchor Line, he himself brooked no soft options among his apprentices. When appointed to his ship they groaned in concert and hastened to get their hair cut.

But on the evening of that first day of Willie's schooling, before we went to work again in the loft above the byre, I happened to approach the window of the study, where I saw and overheard my father and mother talking inside. They spoke quietly. To my astonishment I detected tears in my father's eyes and voice.

'Poor wee soul,' he was saying. 'I can never get used to this terrible first day at school.'

'Neither can I.' My mother's mouth was awry. 'It's heart-rending.'

'It seems all wrong that we should always have to appear hard and unsympathetic. But I suppose it's for their own good in the end.'

I went thoughtfully to Maimie to borrow the steps.

An hour later I had emotional problems of my own. So had Archie and Willie, and the morning's traumatic events were temporarily forgotten. A large stone moved as I twisted with the chisel. It fell away from us into the loft above the coal-house, dustily dragging with it smaller stones on either side. Silent on a peak, not in Darien but in a Manse out-house, we glimpsed the unknown.

The unknown, from our position, appeared to be an empty wooden floor.

I was shaking. In my imagination living creatures lurked in the dark, just out of sight: rats, voles, perhaps even animals about which we knew nothing, like the prehistoric monsters found in a secret cave in Egypt, as described by Captain Charles H. Gilson in his current *BOP* serial. But I was the eldest. Archie and Willie were looking at me: I was the experienced one, the far-travelled sophisticate.

This is the burden of being the eldest. You are an innovation, the object of experiments by apprentice parents. You are expected, on account of seniority, to be an experimenter and innovator yourself, with curious eyes constantly watching how you go. All my life I have hated this role; but all my life I have played it to the best of my ability, as a kind of challenge to a weakness in my character. I suppose it was an important motivation in my becoming a writer. It certainly causes bitter self-denigration and intermittent stomach ulcers – that is, when experiments go wrong and innovations fail. When they succeed, I believe it causes the euphoric vainglory which also afflicts me.

While Archie and Willie waited, I accepted the situation with much the same fatalism as later on I came to know more intimately before leaving home for the university, before joining the army, before leading a platoon ashore on Madagascar, before my first television broadcast.

I said, like a character in a low-budget Western: 'Come on, let's go!'

I pushed and scraped and wrestled a way through the hole, landing on my elbows on the bare floor. Archie came next with the torch. We dragged Willie in beside us.

We stood still, daunted now by silence, while Archie directed light around and into every corner of the loft. No rat stirred. No monster reared or snarled.

There was nothing in the loft except what looked like a pile of rubbish in one corner. The sense of danger passed. Powerful curiosity reasserted itself.

We approached the pile and saw that it consisted mainly of mouldering books, magazines, papers – and empty medicine bottles. There were scores of bottles, most of them of purple corrugated glass. (Not long ago I saw similar ones for sale in a Glasgow antique shop at 40p each.)

I was interested in the books and magazines.

A number of the books were collections of sermons by somebody called Spurgeon. Born of a confusion of ill-digested facts culled from Arthur Mee's *Children's Newspaper*, I had a vision of a fish-headed man curved over a desk, regularly dipping his pen in caviare.

But then, while Archie and Willie scrabbled in the pile for more bottles – they would make excellent targets for stone-throwing practice down in the glebe – I commandeered the torch and began to look through the magazines. Presently it occurred to me that in their damp pages I had discovered the secret of the sealed loft.

Some of the magazines, including about a dozen copies of *Chambers's Journal* dated 1906 and 1907, were not illustrated and so, to my untutored eye, appeared uninteresting. They had advertisements, however, which *were* illustrated; and one of those, for a sparse moment, held my attention. It was headed FREQUENT MICTURITION. Below this intriguing phrase – and above some letterpress and an announcement of price – was a drawing of something like a bag, with straps attached, which defied my comprehension. I had a feeling of inadequacy. Here was I, ten years old and, as I thought, full of knowledge. Here also, staring at me from a slimy page, were a word and an illustration at the meaning of which I could not even guess. The world and my future life in it began to threaten more worries than ever they had done before.

I pushed the *Chambers's Journals* aside and began to look at a set of magazines printed on thick art paper. Those, I found – in a publisher's phrase learned in later years – were 'lavishly illustrated'.

A few of the pictures were signed by an artist whose name I made out to be Aubrey Beardsley. To me they were grotesque, unreal, infinitely disagreeable. Aubrey Beardsley had created men and women outside my experience, hobgoblins who would mock and terrify me if, one day, I should be forced to meet them in the flesh in a world beyond Southend.

Other pictures, unsigned, were even more frightening. One showed a bearded man holding a flimsily dressed young girl in a savage embrace. Another showed a creature with cloven hooves playing what might have been a gigantic mouth-organ, while, near by, a naked man fondled a naked woman beneath a tree. Yet another showed a voluptuous lady reclining on a bed. She was gazing up at the ceiling, where – of all things – a swan was hovering in a kind of cloud.

As I turned the pages with hands which had begun to tremble, I saw more in the same style. Excitingly pleasant thrills invaded my body. My mouth became dry. I wished I had been alone, without responsibility for Archie and Willie.

I felt then what I think Adam must have felt when he smiled at Eve and took the first bite of the apple. Where innocence had been before, now there was a stirring of lusty male awareness, a recognition of the need to camouflage pleasurable feeling in a society with guilt-ridden rules concerning behaviour. This was an end – or a beginning.

I rearranged the pile, so that the art magazines were hidden underneath the books and the bottles. I said to Archie and Willie: 'Nothing interesting here. Take some of the bottles for plunking at. Come on.'

Archie said: 'What were those pictures you got so interested in?'

'Oh, just rubbish. Landscapes and such like.' It was the first lie I had ever told him.

We retrieved the hammer and chisel and squirmed through the hole, back to the loft above the byre. Puffing and groaning we manoeuvred the stones back into the wall. I lowered Archie and Willie down to the steps, then shut the loft door behind me.

In the yard we met Maimie. 'Merciful goodness, the state of your clothes! What on earth have you been doing?'

'Playing in the loft.'

'Go to the bathroom at once and get cleaned up before your parents see you!'

We obeyed. Her eyes were suspicious as she looked after us. But she kept her suspicions to herself.

On the previous day I would almost certainly have asked her about 'micturition'. Now things had changed. But before going to bed that night, taking care to let nobody see me, I looked up the word in *Chambers's Twentieth Century Dictionary*, which had a prominent place in the Padre's big bookcase. What I found made a life which loomed ahead even more complicated and strange.

We told nobody about the hole in the wall or about what we had found behind it. Some years ago, in 1971, when the out-houses were being demolished before the arrival of a new minister, I made a special visit to see what was happening to the loft above the coal-house. It had already been demolished. In the yard lay heaps of rubble, with, here and there, what looked like pages of old books and magazines stuck in the midst of them, discoloured, forlorn, flapping in the wind.

I made no effort to identify them. I was still breaking into sealed lofts and learning about the world; but most of my eagerness and excitement had become diverted into less physical channels.

2

The Irish Connection

Archie, Willie and I were all born before the First World War. Rona, our only sister, was born in 1918, Kenneth in 1921 and John, the youngest, in 1927, when my mother was in her forty-eighth year.

In July 1943, while serving as an officer with the Argylls in the Second World War, Archie was fatally wounded by a German mortar shell during the battle for Gerbini in Sicily. He was an Honours Graduate in English, a teacher at Dunoon Grammar School. Rona was also a teacher, in Campbeltown. In September 1949, less than a year after winning the Gold Medal for solo singing at the Gaelic Mod in Glasgow, she died of cancer.

There is a small Celtic cross to their memory in Keil-colmcille, the graveyard in Southend. It bears an inscription, 'They were lovely and pleasant in their lives.' I can vouch for its truth. Even after so many years, their blond good looks, their patient gallantry, their disciplined eagerness for life can still, for me, buttress spells of unhappiness.

Willie, Kenneth and John remain alive.

After thirty-five years as a sea captain Willie has retired. His first command was a ship's life-boat containing eighty-two survivors when the 9000-ton liner *Britannia*, under charter to the Ministry of War Transport, was sunk by a German raider off the west coast of Africa on 25 March 1941. The desperate journey ended on the island of Corupu, near San Luiz de Maranhão in Brazil, on 16 April. Willie still can't swim, but I am told that his officers and men were never loath to go to sea with him.

Kenneth has been minister of Kenmore in Perthshire since 1950. Like Willie, he also had trouble during the Second World War, when his reconnaissance Hurricane was shot down over Kinbin, north of the Chindwin, on 22 December 1944. He spent a week in the jungle, being harried and shot at by the Japanese, until at last he stumbled into the welcoming arms of a platoon of Gordon Highlanders. His parishioners in Kenmore – and the people of Loch Tayside in general – look upon him with mingled affection and alarm. Like his father, he is a good minister, inclined on occasion to be irascible, authoritarian and unorthodox. But as he understands his people, so they understand him. This is the best testimonial that can possibly be given to a clergyman.

At the age of forty-nine, John is a mere child compared with the rest of us. He is now Professor of Midwifery at the University of Leicester, with so many medical degrees after his name that my unacademic mind fairly boggles at the sight of them. His status as a good doctor, however, may better be measured, I believe, by the remarkable number of children he has brought into the world who have been given his name.

Except for the final and perhaps the most important one, Willie, Kenneth, John and I have opened a great many more sealed lofts than Archie and Rona did in their short lives. But we count ourselves lucky that as we open lofts we are able to judge their contents against a background of faith instilled in us by our parents, by precept and example – a faith which we later tried and tested for ourselves and have never found wanting.

We are also privileged in that we grew up in an atmosphere of 'family', which taught us a recognition of the rights of others, and in that we have roots in the parish of Southend, which, even yet, has not been too much affected by the modern disease of 'material sophistication'.

In Southend we can, I think, recognize our true inheritance. A Scottish inheritance which, in the first place, came from Celtic Ireland.

My study window looks out across the blue flats of the

North Channel. In September, when a north wind blows, I can see on the other side Red Bay's enclosing arms, Garron's Point and Rownabay Head, and, using binoculars, may catch a glimpse of work going on in the high harvest fields. In the background I recognize my constant companions, the round hills of Antrim, which look to me like fairy hills in a Walt Disney cartoon.

From our bungalow, here on the south coast of Southend, the distance to Rownabay Head is approximately seventeen miles. In the *Proceedings of the Royal Irish Academy* (Vol. VIII) Dr Reeves has this to say about my parish: 'The whole district is strongly impressed with social and ecclesiastical features of an Irish character. . . . The traditional associations of the people all look westward, and the titles of nearly all the adjacent parishes are commemorative of illustrious worthies of the Irish Church.'

Southend is a natural pier-head for Irish visitors; and ever since the arrival in Kintyre of the first mesolithic men from Ireland, around 8000 years ago, there has always been a coming – and a going, too – across the narrow sea.

Here, in the early ages, there landed the *Scotti*, the Irish tribe which gave its name to Scotland. Here, in AD 563, there landed Columba, the saint who gave us Christianity – the greatest saint of them all, in my opinion, because his halo, though shining with the Spirit, was also jaunty and even a little crooked.

Here there landed noble lords from Erin with their soldiers, armourers and sennachies (or story-tellers). Here there landed fishermen and farmers from Antrim seeking new and perhaps more lucrative employment – and also William Burke, on his way to body-snatching ploys with William Hare in Edinburgh. Here there landed smugglers, potato-gatherers, thatchers, peddlars of linen goods, whose names and deeds, all of Irish origin, are commemorated in the songs called 'Come-all-ye's' still sung at our local concerts. From here, during the Second World War, there sailed a German spy bearing news of a convoy to his German friends in the Irish Free State.

Here, today, from boats on a summer jaunt, there land men from the Walt Disney hills – men with names like McCambridge and McNeill who come among us to exchange knowledge of past and present and to invite us across to sample the hospitality of the Glynns. Here, not long ago, there landed pupils from an Antrim school who came to meet the children of Southend and make a radio programme. All were wary of each other, suspecting different looks and accents, until somebody mentioned Rangers and Celtic. Then the arguments and the friendships grew.

Two 'monuments' in Southend typify the close affinity between Kintyre and Antrim. The Padre was never too busy to show them off to visitors. Now I have taken his place as an unofficial local 'guide'.

The first is a flat rock above the churchyard at Keil, less than a mile away from Achnamara. On it are carved the prints of two right feet, known to us as 'St Columba's Footsteps'.

I believe the prints were there long before Columba's time; and, indeed, the Royal Commission on the Ancient and Historical Monuments of Scotland shares this opinion, estimating that the one nearer the sea, aligned east and west, is some 3000 years old. Here, I am convinced, is yet another example of the 'fealty foot' once used by a newly elected chief when swearing faithfulness to his tribe.

The custom, born in antiquity, was still being followed by the Clan Donald as late as the fourteenth century; and a MacDonald sennachie has handed down the following description of the ceremony of proclaiming the Lords of the Isles: 'The Bishop of Argyle, the Bishop of the Isles and seven priests were sometimes present with the chieftains of the principal families. There was a square stone seven or eight feet long and the tract of a man's foot cut thereon upon which the ruler of the Isles stood, denoting that he should walk in the footsteps and uprightness of his predecessors, and that he was installed by right in his possessions. He was clothed in a white habit to show that he would be a light to his people and maintain the true religion.

Then he received a white rod in his hand, intimating that he had power to rule not with tyranny and particularity but with discretion and sincerity. Next he was given his forefather's sword or some other sword, signifying that his duty was to protect and defend his people.'

Though the 'fealty foot' was carved in the rock at Keil before his coming, imagination can picture Columba – an astute statesman as well as a churchman – taking his stand in the footprint (or footprints), first facing the east and the rising sun like a new chief, then turning northward to address the people gathered on the steep hillside, a hillside known in Gaelic to this day as *guala na popuill*, 'the shoulder of the congregation'.

Our second 'monument' with an Irish connection is the Rock of Dunaverty. Like the Antrim hills, I can see it from my window half a mile distant across Machribeg Bay, a lump of Old Red Sandstone, ninety feet high. It once boasted a MacDonald Castle, the fighting part on the Rock itself, the living quarters for families and camp-followers on the high dune on its eastern flank. In the *New Statistical Account of Argyleshire* (1843) it says that the Clan Donald always kept the fortifications at Dunaverty 'in good repair and well guarded, as only from this position could the communications with Antrim be kept open and safe'.

There is no doubt that in past ages Dunaverty Castle must have appeared impregnable both from land and sea, a sullen place, offering no point of weakness to an invader. But today, when closely examined, its sparse, overgrown ruins reveal in places the effects of fire and violent assault. This is not surprising, because its whole history was a violent one, providing evidence that in the face of determined enemies no physical bastion is impregnable.

News of the castle goes back as far as the twelfth century. It was held by Somerled's descendant Angus Mor (Big Angus), the eldest son of Donald, from whom all the MacDonalds derive their surname. He lost it for a time to King Alexander III of Scotland, who was jealous of the growing power of the Lords of the Isles and came marching into Kintyre to demonstrate his authority. He, in turn, lost it to King Haco of Norway in 1263. Afterwards King Haco, who seems to have been a much more reasonable and statesman-like 'viking' than many biased chroniclers have made out, restored it to the MacDonalds.

Angus Mor's son, Angus Og (Young Angus), was a stout supporter of Robert the Bruce. After the disastrous Battle of Methven, Bruce fled to Kintyre, where Angus Og willingly provided refuge. The distinguished fugitive was first concealed at Saddell Castle on the east coast of the peninsula, then in the more secure fortress of Dunaverty; and when even Dunaverty became unsafe, he was taken secretly across the narrow sea to Rathlin. There, in another MacDonald Castle whose ruins today distinctly resemble those at Dunaverty, he was at last able to rest secure from his enemies. And have his notable confrontation with a spider.

Though Angus Og was a king's man, in later years the Clan Donald again became disillusioned with 'authority'.

In 1494 James IV brought an imposing army to Kintyre and seized Dunaverty, placing in it a garrison amply provided with artillery and gunners. At that time the representative of the MacDonalds in Kintyre was Sir John Cahanagh, a MacDonald by blood but so named from having been fostered in Antrim with the O'Cahans. Sir John, enraged by the King's actions, secretly assembled an army of his own – in Islay, Kintyre and Antrim – and awaited an opportunity to expel the royal garrison. The Rev. George Hill, in *The MacDonells of Antrim*, now takes up the story: 'The King, not anticipating any opposition to his arrangements, was in the act of sailing away with his personal attendants from the Mull [of Kintyre], when Sir John stormed Dunaverty, and actually hung the governor from the wall, in sight of the King and his departing ships.'

King James was unable to avenge the insult at the time; but years later, through the treachery of a jealous kinsman, Sir John and two of his sons were seized at Finlagan Castle in Islay and taken as the King's prisoners to Edinburgh. There they were found guilty of high treason and 'executed on the Burrowmuir, their bodies being buried in the church of St Anthony'.

From that time the MacDonalds were continually at variance with what today might be called 'the establishment'. Growing numbers of the clan crossed the narrow sea from Kintyre to Antrim, hoping to find there a more peaceable existence. But, being supporters of Mary Queen of Scots, they were natural enemies of Elizabeth of England, and, in consequence, Elizabeth's Irish Deputy, the Earl of Sussex, made sure that peace remained a word unknown to them.

Nor were the activities of Sussex confined to Ireland. He himself submitted to his sovereign the report of a punitive expedition he carried out in September 1558. On the 19th, in the ship *Mary Willoughby*, he 'arrived at Lowghe Cylkerran [Kinloch Kilchiaran, now Campbeltown] in Kintyre. On the same day I landed and burned eight miles of length, and therwith James McConell's [MacDonald's] chief house callit Saudell [Saddell] a fayre pile and a stronge. The neixte day, I crossed over the lande, and burned twelve myles of length on the other side of the Lowghe, wherein were burned a faire house callit Mawher Imore [Machrimore in Southend], and a strong castell callit Dunalvere [Dunaverty].'

(Sussex was a poor speller but obviously a man of action and an exemplar for all future Empire-builders.)

By 1647, however, the MacDonalds were back in Dunaverty; but now, when Cromwell was the 'authority', they had become King's men again. Their ancient rivals, the Campbells, had taken up arms on the other side; and when General David Leslie was ordered to subdue the rebel MacDonalds in the west, the Marquis of Argyle eagerly accepted an invitation to accompany him and to add a large quota of Campbell clansmen to an already considerable army. Boldly they marched through Dumbarton to Argyll and down upon Kintyre.

Sir Alexander MacDonald made an effort to stop them at a place called Rhunahaorine, a few miles south of Tarbert; but his cavalry floundered to disaster in a peat-bog (which is still there) and he and most of his army were forced to retreat 'in small shippes' to Islay. 'Here,' as is recorded in the *Account of the Clan MacLean*, 'the brave MacDonald made his last stand against the enemies of the King, but finding his position in too precarious a state to hope for success by opposition, or for mercy by submission, he immediately passed over to Ireland.'

A small force of 300 men, however, 'consisting mainly of MacDougalls and soldiers from Antrim', was left behind to defend Dunaverty. This was under the command of Archibald Og MacDonald of Sanda, a direct descendant of Sir John Cahanagh, 'traitorously put to death by James IV'.

For six weeks Leslie and Argyle besieged the castle; but in a hot, rainless June the water in the only well ran dry (occasionally it still runs dry in summer), and in the end it was thirst that defeated the garrison. Archibald Og MacDonald and his men surrendered to 'the mercy of the kingdom', and the mercy of the kingdom, as might have been expected, was death. 'Every mother's son,' wrote Sir John Turner, Leslie's adjutant, 'was put to the sword, except one young man, MacCoul [MacDougall], whose life I begged, to be sent to France, with one hundred country fellows, whom we had smoked out of a cave, as they do foxes.'

An account of the massacre given in the *Memoirs of Montrose* (Vol. II) brings a chill to the heart: 'Having surrendered their arms, the Marquis of Argyle and a bloody preacher, Mr John Nevoy [minister of Loudon parish in Ayrshire and chaplain to Leslie's army] prevailed with him [Leslie] to break his word; and so the army was let loose upon them, and killed them all without mercy; whereat David Leslie seemed to have some inward check: For, while the Marquis and he, Mr Nevoy, were walking over their ankles in blood, he turned about and said, – "Now, Mass John, have you not, for once, gotten your fill of blood?" This was reported by many who heard it.'

Before leaving Southend, Leslie and Argyle set fire to the empty fortress, and afterwards the Castle was allowed to crumble into decay. Two centuries later the bones of the dead were gathered by descendants of the Clan Donald and buried in a common grave. A bleak, rectangular monument, it stands on the bare shoulder of an arable field near the Rock. The field is known to us as *machair a caistel*, 'the field of the castle'.

The massacre of Dunaverty is still spoken of in Southend as if it had happened yesterday.

There is a peat-fire legend about the wife of a Clan Donald soldier to whom the Campbells offered amnesty if, with her baby on her back, she could climb the sheer cliff on the east side of the rock. She climbed it. But as her clutching hands appeared on the summit a young Campbell officer slashed them off with his sword and she and her baby fell ninety feet to their deaths. That day the cliff was given a Gaelic name: 'The Cliff of the Falling Woman'.

Next morning, with the Castle burning, Leslie's army began to march away. As the Campbells, in the rear, were passing through the village of Southend (then called Muneroy), the young officer's horse reared and bolted. He was thrown from the saddle, but his foot caught in a stirrup and he was dragged screaming for help along the rough road beyond the village. His men and the villagers who watched – all of them aware of his action on the previous day – gave no sign that they saw or heard. The horse ran free, swerving from side to side, dashing its rider to pieces against the boulders by the roadside.

Another memory is of the plague brought to Southend by Leslie's army. It is said that hundreds of local people died and that at one time, in the autumn of 1647, 'only two chimneys were left smoking' in the parish.

As boys in the Manse, my brothers and I were eager listeners to the savage tales about Dunaverty, some told by the Padre, some by old men and women whose families had been involved. We appreciated their drama and romance and were scarcely aware of the cruelty, greed and utter contempt for human life and dignity which lay behind them. Vaguely we apprehended that St Columba, the disciple of love, would not have approved of them; but it seemed to us, at the time, that during the past few hundred years standards of behaviour in Britain had changed for the better and that such bloody events could now occur only among ignorant foreign tribes. Contemporary writers of boys' fiction encouraged us in this belief. The slaughter of Red Indians, Zulus and other 'lesser breeds without the law' left us proud and reassured, confident in our British rectitude. It was a traumatic experience when we began to realize that the massacre of millions in two great 'white' wars, with the unending political and sectarian massacres in Ireland on the side, demonstrated that our so-called 'western civilization' could produce an even lower level of conduct than that which had once been ascribed to fictional 'wogs'.

But though this particular sealed loft, when we opened it, offered appalling discoveries, it gave us comfort, too, in a story of human kindness which shone clear among the drab and wicked debris of Dunaverty. I have already told it in *Salt in My Porridge*; but I think it bears repeating – as the Padre kept on doing in his sermons – if only because it provides evidence that the bad in human nature is generally balanced by the good.

The wife of Archibald Og MacDonald, the commander of the Dunaverty garrison, had died in the early part of 1647, leaving him with a baby son, James Ranald. James Ranald was with his father in the Castle when the siege began, looked after by an eighteen-year-old Southend girl called Flora MacCambridge.

On the night before the massacre, putting no trust in 'the mercy of the kingdom', Flora made a plan to save the baby. Round him she wrapped a plaid of Campbell tartan which had belonged to a prisoner captured during the siege. Then, carrying him in her arms, she crept down from the Rock and, in the moonlight, began to run across the beach, away from Dunaverty, away from threatening death. But soon, while still stumbling barefoot over the wet, ribbed sand, she was stopped by a Campbell sentry. Her heart thumped in her throat.

'I am the wife of a Campbell soldier,' she said. 'See, my son wears the tartan.'

The sentry lifted a corner of the plaid. 'Strange!' he said. 'A Campbell mother whose baby has the MacDonald eyes! But go your way, girl. I have no quarrel with women or children.'

So Flora went to a cave under the cliff at Keil, and there, feeding him on sheeps' tallow and ewes' milk, she hid and attended to James Ranald until Leslie and Argyle had gone.

James Ranald grew up and eventually, by patient negotiation, brought about a lasting peace between the MacDonalds and the Campbells. He lies buried in the graveyard of Keil-colm-cille, just over the wall from the big cave in which he and Flora found refuge.

The population of Southend has often been described as one-third Lowland, one-third Highland and one-third Irish. The Rev. Kenneth MacLeod of Gigha – the author of 'The Road to the Isles' – used to say that the Padre was one-third Protestant, one-third Roman Catholic and one-third pagan, an opinion with which my mother agreed. Was this a clue to the success of his long ministry in the parish?

There is no doubt that like everybody else in Southend he had a 'soft side' for the Irish and a continuing interest in the history of the 'connection'. History is people, he used to say, and people are still making it.

Our accents and our dialect owe much to Ireland. Perhaps the best example of how we used to talk (how we still talk when the mood comes on us) is found in a 'Come-all-ye' in praise of a girl called 'Flory Loynachan'. (The surname Loynachan has become Lang in more modern times, and Flora Langs are common in Kintyre today.) The 'poem' was written in the early part of last century by a Kintyrean of Irish stock called O'Brol-lochan, who, while studying at Glasgow University to become a minister of the Free Church, changed his name to Brodie. The tune comes from Ireland.

I heard the song for the first time from Willie McKerral, Jean's father, who kept chuckling as my face registered frequent incomprehension. It is often sung at local ceilidhs, when the whisky flows. Here is part of it:

O, it buitie be an ogly thing
That mougres thus ower me,
For I scrabbed at masel yestreen
An' couldna bab an e'e.
My he'rt is a' tae muilins minched,
Brye, smuirach, daps an' gum.
I'm a poor cruichach spalyin' scrae,
My horts ha'e struck me dumb.

Dear Flory Loynachan, if thou
Through Saana Soun' were tossed,
An' rouchled like a shoggie-shoo
In a veshal wi' wan mast;
Though the nicht were makin' for a roil,
Though ralliach were the sea,
Though scorlins warpled my thowl pins,
My shallop wad reach thee.

Were I the laird o' Achnaglach,
Or Kilmanshenachan fair,
Cnockstaplemore, Kilwheepnach,
Feochaïg or Ballochgair;
Did I inherit Tayinraich,
Drumgarve or Ballochantuy,
Christlach or Kerran – daing the bit,
I'd fauchit them a' for thee.

A rough 'translation' of the first two verses:

'O, it must be a terrible affliction that has come over me, because last night I kept scratching myself and couldn't close an eye. My heart is all minced up like meal, like dross or other types of coal debris. I'm a poor creature, staggering about. My hurts, my wounds, have struck me dumb.

'Dear Flory Loynachan, if you were being tossed about in Sanda Sound, shaken as if you were on a swing, in a vessel with only one mast: though the night threatened a storm and the sea was exceedingly rough, though seaweed wrapped itself round my rowlocks, my small boat would reach you.'

The last verse lists a number of farms still in existence and still with the same names in South Kintyre. Even though he became the owner of all these places the anguished lover declares that – damn the opposition – he would give them all away in exchange for Flory.

As they say, 'Whaur's yer Anglo-Saxon noo?'

Our parents, both native Gaelic speakers, found no difficulty in understanding the 'Come-all-ye's'. Many of the apparently outlandish words are derived from the Irish Gaelic. Others, of Lowland origin, were in everyday use in Southend during the whole of my father's ministry, from 1910 to 1957.

When Flory Loynachan was top of the pops in Southend, 150 years ago, cross-channel boats plied regularly between Cushendun, in Red Bay, and Dunaverty. Each had an individual name but, in general, was known locally as the Black Wherry. Passengers were often debtors or petty thieves trying to escape justice; cargoes sometimes contained contraband – salt, soap, hides, horses, wool – and excisemen in Kintyre and Antrim had a busy time of it, keeping an eye on the people and the goods it carried. Burke was one of the criminals who sailed in the Black Wherry and was able to avoid arrest.

A short, thick-set man with round shoulders, at the time in his middle thirties, Burke was the son of a farmer in County Tyrone, who had been, in turn, baker, cobbler, weaver and militiaman. After a quarrel with his family he deserted the militia and crossed the narrow sea to Scotland. Most writers on criminology accept the supposition that he met Hare in Edinburgh in 1826.

About Hare's origins little seems to be known, but a contemporary pamphleteer described him as a long, thin man, physically Burke's opposite. With their prostitute companions, Helen MacDougall and Maggie Laird, the two men 'shacked up' together in Log's Boarding House in Tanner's Close. There –

and later at a house in Gibbs Close – they carried on a trade as 'body-snatchers', opening graves and selling corpses to doctors and medical students. Their most regular customer was Dr Knox of 10 Surgeon's Square, who sometimes paid as much as £7 10s for a fresh cadaver. When they were unable to unearth a suitable body they resorted to murder, picking their victims from the beggars, cinder women, harlots and other flotsam of the Edinburgh streets.

Burke's the murderer, Hare's the thief,
And Knox the boy who buys the beef.

Justice eventually overtook the vicious pair when a beggar couple named Grey, who had been lodging with them at Gibbs Close, found the blood-stained corpse of another beggar woman in Burke's room and informed the police. At the trial in the High Court of Justiciary in Edinburgh, Hare turned King's evidence and, in consequence, was not tried. Neither was Maggie Laird. The case against Helen MacDougall resulted in a 'not proven' verdict; but Burke was found guilty and sentenced to death. Dr Knox was not even asked to give evidence.

During his time in the condemned cell Burke complained continually that Dr Knox had swindled him over payment for some of the bodies. This obsession with money also caused him to demand a fee of sixpence from curious visitors who wanted to sketch him. He was hanged on 28 January 1829.

What happened to Hare is a mystery. There is a story that he went to the Midlands of England to work in a lime-kiln and that when his identity was discovered his workmates blinded him with quicklime. But could this be a Victorian 'morality'? What seems certain is that he died as a blind old beggar in London.

Our Southend legend, which we learnt as boys with ghoulish delight, insists that Burke and Hare came from Ireland together, in the Black Wherry. They stayed the night at the local inn – the Argyll Arms – and in a drunken brawl killed a man whose body they concealed under the ice in the Carr Loch (where we used to find the tadpoles and where our whiskery elders enjoyed winter curling). I once wrote a short story based on this piece of apocrypha. The story itself was bad, but I still think the title I gave it was inspirational: *Frozen Stiff*.

The brave tales of olden times in Southend are matched by more modern ones. Any visitors who come to enjoy a holiday in our 'sleepy little parish' are always surprised to discover just how much goes on. We attract spies, fugitives and unusual characters, the like of which James Bond, in his tiny metropolitan world of blondes and fast cars, never dreamed of.

Our spy scares have been numerous, not without reason. The Mull of Kintyre overlooks the North Channel, the main convoy route out of Britain. In the two wars, any stranger appearing among us with a sketching-block was bound to come under suspicion.

In the first summer of the Second World War, while recuperating after a long illness and awaiting 'call up', I captured a spy myself.

I had enrolled as a special constable, with instructions to maintain close liaison with the Local Defence Volunteers. (Later the LDV became the Home Guard.) One afternoon a friend of mine, an LDV corporal, rang me up with the news that an individual carrying an easel and paints had been spotted on the moors above the Mull of Kintyre. He was now on his way down to the village of Southend. If I got cracking I could intercept him on the road near Keil.

I met him just beyond the graveyard, under the high cliffs. He was broad-faced, clean-shaven, loose-limbed and tall, with blond streaks in his thick, untidy hair. He wore spectacles, heavy brogues and stockings, a khaki shirt and what I imagined was a German-looking pair of short 'shorts'. We exchanged wary words, and though he spoke good English I was immediately suspicious of what sounded to me like a heavy guttural accent. I asked for proofs of his identity. His papers appeared to be in order, but when I looked inside his knapsack and saw the sketches and paintings he had made I came to a decision.

The Campbeltown police had been visiting the island of Sanda that day, examining the body of a sailor found on the shore. They were expected back in the late afternoon; and, indeed, just as I finished interrogating my suspect, their boat swung round the Bow Reef and entered the bay, heading for Dunaverty.

I took my man and handed him over to them. They whisked him away in their car, and, as far as I was concerned, that appeared to be the end of it. The following month I was called up.

Four years later, at Anzio, when at last the Allies had broken out, I was asked to help in arranging a piping programme by the bands of all the Scottish regiments in the area. An officer from the Gordon Highlanders came to see me about it. Into my dug-out descended the tall, loose-limbed figure of Captain Hamish Henderson, wearing German-looking shorts and greeting me in a Caithness accent as thick as mine from Kintyre. We recognized each other at once. He was my 'spy'.

With his poetic genius, his quick humour and love for all the Scottish arts, Hamish has remained my friend. He tells me that my story is a load of rubbish, full of inaccuracies, and that the Campbeltown police never suspected him for a single minute. Maybe not. But, as we both found during our stints as temporary soldiers, life can be complicated for a writer whose capital is his imagination, especially during a war.

But it seems that while Hamish Henderson and I were disporting ourselves in foreign parts, a real German spy did make a brief appearance in Southend. When I became a civilian again I heard part of the story from my neighbour, Archie Cameron the salmon-fisher, who actually met the spy making his way towards the jetty at Dunaverty.

'He was a good-looking young fellow, about six feet tall, with blue eyes and a fresh complexion,' Archie told me. 'He carried a knapsack and wore RAF uniform. I thought he was an airman home on leave. I came across him at the golf-course gate and said hullo, and he mumbled something in reply. I was hurrying to the Post Office at the time, to phone the police in Campbeltown about a tug that had gone aground on Sanda, and I thought no more about him.

'When I returned from the Post Office I noticed that Dick Gillon's old sailing boat was missing from the jetty, along with a pair of oars from one of my own small boats. I looked out to sea, and sure enough there the boat was, heading south towards the Irish Sea. I thought nothing about that, either. I was sure it was Dick, that he had taken a notion to go fishing.

'A few minutes later I got the shock of my life. I saw Dick walking across the shore, approaching the jetty. I remembered the young fellow then all right and alerted the Coastguards, who at once got in touch with the authorities.

'By this time Dick's stolen boat was out of sight and Dick himself was hopping mad. Southend was in an uproar. I kept wondering if I would get into trouble for leaving the oars unguarded in my small boat, because it was a regulation during war-time that oars must be locked away when not in use.'

Much to his relief, nobody since then has ever mentioned oars to Archie. In the meantime, however, high-powered action was taking place in other quarters. This is described in dramatic detail by Captain Jack Broome in his book, *Convoy is to Scatter*.

Captain Broome was in command of Escort Group One, in the destroyer *Keppel*. He had been summoned to Greenock to attend a conference on a troop convoy which his Group was to pick up off Northern Ireland the following morning. This convoy, one of the largest and most important of the Second World War, was due to sail around the Cape, carrying the basic elements of what was to be the Eighth Army.

'When the conference was over,' Captain Broome writes, 'I looked at my watch and found that instead of staying overnight and sailing with the convoy, I had plenty of time to get down the Clyde, into Loch Foyle and up the river to Londonderry, for all to enjoy a final night ashore with wives, families or girl friends, before sailing early to pick up our convoy.'

The *Keppel* cleared the Cumbraes. Her speed increased until she was thundering along at thirty-two knots. The officers chatted on the bridge. Suddenly the radio officer buzzed through to say that a top-priority cypher from the Admiralty had just been received and was being decoded.

In a few minutes Captain Broome was reading the signal aloud: 'ENEMY AGENT KNOWN TO HAVE BEEN IN ALDERSHOT RECENTLY SEEN YESTERDAY IN GREENOCK MINGLING WITH TROOPS EMBARKING OVERSEAS CONVOY. MOTOR BOAT BELONGING LIGHTHOUSE-KEEPER MULL OF KINTYRE REPORTED MISSING 0900 TODAY WEDNESDAY. CONSIDER POSSIBLE AGENT HAS STOLEN BOAT AND NOW MAKING FOR IRISH FREE STATE WITH IMPORTANT INFORMATION ABOUT CONVOY SAILING TOMORROW. MOTOR SKIFF HULL GREEN RUBBING STRAKE ORANGE. TANK FULL. MAN 6 FEET FAIR FRESH COMPLEXION LAST SEEN WEARING KHAKI BATTLE DRESS. NO OTHER SHIP OR ANY AIRCRAFT AVAILABLE. SEARCH FOR BOAT. REPORT WHEN YOU HAVE FOUND IT.'

I have no idea how the Admiralty got the impression that the spy was wearing battle-dress, that it was a lighthouse-keeper's boat he had stolen or that the boat in question was coloured green and orange and had a motor. In fact, according to Archie Cameron – and also to my friend Duncan Watson, then an auxiliary coastguard – he was wearing RAF uniform and the boat was an old scow, encrusted with black tar, whose only motive power consisted of oars and a home-made sail.

Captain Broome, the first lieutenant and the navigator studied the chart. After a calculation involving the estimated speed of the stolen boat and the strength of the wind and tides, they decided to follow a course almost due south. They had only forty-five minutes of daylight left to find their man. If they failed, and the spy was able to contact the German Embassy in Dublin, Captain Broome dared not think of what might happen to the convoy.

By this time the *Keppel*'s crew were on deck, eager volunteer look-outs. Captain Broome offered a free pint to the first man who spotted the boat.

In the next few minutes a number of false alarms were raised, and when finally the mast-head look-out reported an object in the water some five miles ahead, Captain Broome was guarded in his enthusiasm. If the boat possessed a motor it ought to have been much further south. But then, looking through his telescope, the chief yeoman sang out in some excitement: 'There is something there, be Jesus!'

Course was altered slightly to the bearing given, and as the destroyer closed a message from the chief yeoman came down the mast-head blow-pipe: 'It's a boat, one bloke in it, 'e's trying to row it, an' I reckon it's my pint.'

The *Keppel* got close enough for her crew to see that the boat was stopped and that the man, leaning over a heavy pair of oars, looked exhausted. 'My job is looking after fishermen, and there's a storm coming up,' Captain Broome shouted down through a loud-hailer. 'If you're in difficulties I'll hoist you inboard and take you to the Irish coast.'

The spy raised an assenting arm.

As an escort led him up to the bridge, the first thing Captain Broome noticed were his hands clutching the ladder rail. They were oily and raw.

'I've been rowing for two hours,' he explained in excellent English. 'Trying to get back.'

'Back where?'

'I'm on leave. I borrowed the boat from a friend and promised to return it before dark.'

At that moment the first lieutenant, who had been instructed to search the boat and everything in it, arrived on the bridge. Standing behind the man he held up a small book. Almost incredibly, it was *Mein Kampf*, in German.

The man looked over his shoulder and saw the book. With a shrug and a wry smile he turned back to the Captain and said: 'All right, you win.'

By this time it was almost dark. A message was sent: 'ADMIRALTY FROM KEPPEL. MOST IMMEDIATE. YOUR BOAT RECOVERED. MAN ARRESTED.'

The spy was taken to Larne and handed over to the Army. The *Keppel* resumed its passage to Londonderry, only two hours late. Next morning the convoy sailed. It never lost a ship.

Much to his indignation, Dick Gillon didn't get his boat back. Somebody in Larne, he often complained to me, must have 'nicked it'. However, months later, the new 'owner' seems to have had a pang of conscience, because Dick received an envelope through the post which contained a pound note and a written message: 'For the boat.'

Dick lived in Southend until he was ninety-two, telling the tale of the spy who stole his boat. I'm glad he never knew the contents of the Admiralty's message to *Keppel*. Like most of us, Dick was averse to sharing the limelight – especially, in his case, with an undeserving lighthouse-keeper.

Another, less obvious example of an Irish 'connection' occurred in South Kintyre more than ten years ago when Paul McCartney of the Beatles bought the small farm of High Park, a few miles north of Campbeltown. He received warm greetings from us all. One reason is that Kintyre is full of McCartneys whose ancestors crossed the North Channel from Ireland just as Paul's did on their way to Liverpool. Another reason was that St Columba left us with some good advice, which we have never forgotten: 'Always be hospitable to a stranger.'

We hoped that Paul and Jane Asher, who was his constant companion at the beginning, would not remain strangers for long. We liked the look of them both.

For a time Paul and Jane (and many of their friends) were our intermittent neighbours, welcome at local dances and cattle-sales. Even Old Sandy, a notorious 'wit', got tired of repeating his dead-pan joke: 'I tell ye, the prophecy has come true – when the moles reach the Mull of Kintyre the beetles will follow! God help my potatoes!'

Unhappily, through the years, Paul's visits to High Park have become fewer and fewer, though he and his American wife do sometimes stay there for a night or two. His conviction at Campbeltown Sheriff Court on a drugs charge has also tended to mar the picture. Perhaps Paul – like us – has been searching for a human ideal which just doesn't exist.

3

Chauffeur to a Rabbit

With its stories, its wide fresh spaces and kindly people, Southend was always full of metaphoric light as far as we in the Manse were concerned. Electric light, however, did not come to the parish until 1950.

During the Second World War, while campaigning in Italy, I was astonished to discover that all the villages we occupied – even those perched precariously on mountain tops – were efficiently linked to the public electricity supply. At home my wife and parents still struggled along with paraffin lamps and coal-fired stoves. (Some stoves in Southend, of a superior variety, were at this period fuelled by anthracite. Jean wrote to tell me how Barbara, her daily help, had arrived one morning full of enthusiasm for a friend's new 'anti-Christ' cooker.)

Once, in a village near Potenza in Southern Italy, where the 2nd Royal Scots Fusiliers happened to be 'resting', one of my sergeants, Jack Hibbett from Oakham, had a kindly inspiration to do something about my birthday. Having heard me talk of a Scottish 'clootie dumpling', he decided to make one and cook it on an electric stove 'liberated' from the local village hall. It turned out to be a beauty.

As I tucked into it that night, ravenous after a day's 'recce' in the hills, I complimented him. 'Superb! Just the right degree of toughness in the skin and of melting consistency inside. How on earth did you manage it?'

'Well, sir, I did exactly what it said in that *People's Journal* you showed me. I got most of the ingredients from the cook – flour, baking soda, sugar, suet, treacle, tinned milk watered down. In the grocer's shop along the street I managed to find some raisins and spices. I mixed the whole shooting-match in a bowl, brought a big pot of water to the boil on the electric stove and popped the dumpling in.'

'After wrapping it in a "cloot" – or cloth, as you Sassenachs would call it?'

'That's right, sir. Though actually the cloth I used was one of your vests – or semmits, as you Scots call them. There was nothing else handy.'

I still say it was one of the best 'clootie dumplings' I have ever tasted.

With the crossing from Ireland during the first few centuries AD of a tribe known as the *Scotti* – amongst whose number was St Columba – Southend experienced Christian civilization long before most other places in Scotland. Apparently, however, the ruling classes considered that moral and spiritual benefits were enough for us to be going on with. Material benefits were always tardy in reaching our 'neck of the woods'.

Old Mrs MacSporran of the plump cheeks, black-bodiced bosom and ample skirts, who lived in Keil Lodge, a quarter of a mile along the road from Achnamara, used to tell us that when she was a child her parents had lit their cottage with a 'croosie' (from the Gaelic *cruiskan*, a small dish of oil with a wick in it) and that she herself, as a housewife, had used in succession candles, plain paraffin lamps, pressure lamps (such as the Aladdin) and finally, when she was approaching ninety, 'the electrics'.

Housing conditions in Southend were also poor until the decade before the Second World War, when the Padre, along with other sympathetic county councillors, translated into action the idea of subsidized houses for farm-workers. It must be admitted that thatched roofs had almost completely disappeared; but baths and indoor toilets were available only in the 'big hooses' like Macharioch, where the Dowager Duchess lived, and Carskiey, built in the early years of the century by Mrs Boyd, a member of the Coats family, whose thread-mills had brought new work to Paisley. The occupiers of less privileged dwellings had to use, for bathing, zinc tubs filled with hot water and, for toilet purposes, either outside earthen closets or handy hedges. Windows were small and ceilings low; even in the farms chimneys smoked. Damp invaded rooms not constantly fired.

And yet, in those years before, during and immediately after the First World War, the food we ate in Southend – in respect of taste at any rate – was far superior to the processed, pre-packaged, carefully analysed diet we are offered today. Aeration and pasteurization, cans, cartons and deep freezes were all unknown. As a result, most of what appeared on our plates was natural and fresh.

Milk, straight from the cow, tasted like milk. Potatoes, unforced by artificial manures, were ambrosial compared with the watery blobs, encased in plastic, which come from the supermarkets. Bread had hard, crunchy crusts. Slices of a thickness relevant to our hunger could be cut from a loaf which smelt not of a factory but of a real bake-house. Nowadays a loaf is as neutral as cotton wool and turns green and sour if a housewife looks the other way. As far as I am concerned, the invention of sliced bread was a disaster.

I watch my neighbours' children, on a cold winter's day, daintily eating wafer-thin potato-crisps and washing them down with chilly 'coke'. What do they know of the sustaining 'jeely pieces', accompanied by a glass of milk, which always rewarded us after a day at school? (The 'jeely piece' or 'chuck' as we used to call it, consisted of a thickly cut, thickly buttered slice of bread folded over to enclose a dripping layer of, more often than not, home-made bramble jelly.)

As a family in the Manse, though poor financially, we fed like princes. The Padre's parishioners were generous. Few of them paid a social call without bearing gifts.

Potatoes. Field turnips. Pats of churn-made butter, stamped with the design traditionally favoured by the farm it came from. 'Trotters' for roasting when a pig was killed. A 'sheep's heid' from which the blacksmith would remove wool and hair by singeing so that it could be used for sumptuous broth. Healthy outdoor chickens which would boil or roast deliciously instead of turning into the tasteless bits of slimy rubber which result from the cooking of birds reared in batteries (or deep litters) and then frozen. All these, from time to time, were given us by the farmers, whose kindness was remarkable considering the poor state of agriculture at the time.

From the 'big hooses' and from the 'toffs' who crowded the Argyll Arms Hotel during the shooting season there came pheasants, grouse and woodcock, which Maimie would hang in the scullery for the requisite number of days and then pluck thoroughly, meanwhile cursing in the Gaelic at the intricacy and tediousness of the operation. The fishing tenants presented us with salmon and sea-trout clean run from the Atlantic.

(It may be mentioned here that the Padre's family, in an emergency, could also provide the occasional pheasant or salmon captured by unconventional means.)

Less exotic but no less delicious gifts of food were often left on the Manse doorstep by anonymous benefactors. These included rabbits, wood pigeons and hares. Such benefactors were always known to us, but as moral and legal complications might have arisen had the offerings been made in person, their deeds were always crowned by a halo – admittedly slightly crooked – of anonymous righteousness.

Rabbit stew, with turnips, carrots, onions and thick gravy, was a meal greatly favoured by us boys. In later years, when an increasing rabbit population threatened the corn fields, and anxious farmers introduced myxomatosis, nobody wanted to eat rabbit any more and another nourishing and tasty dish disappeared from local menus.

Recently, however, in Southend at any rate, a lusty breed of rabbit has evolved which shows signs of being immune from the disease. Sporting types from the village are often to be seen in the high fields and on the golf course, armed with ferrets, nets, guns and eager whippets. The farmers raise no objection to their hunting forays, because in a farmer's language rabbit is a distasteful word. Rabbit stew is enjoyed again by some; but Jean, implacably, refuses to let me join their number.

When myxomatosis was at its height in the parish, the roads near Achnamara crawled with blind rabbits, festering and slowly dying. They seemed to move close to human beings as if pleading for help, though no help, apart from a quick death to relieve their misery, was possible. Jean can never forget, and I don't blame her. Like Jock, our son, her attitude to all animals is affectionate and personal.

For example . . .

Last summer a young rabbit entered and took up residence in Achnamara garden. During the night watches, while I slept, it began to feed with enthusiasm on my lettuce and cabbage plants. I vowed vengeance.

Its hiding place was under a disorganized clump of heath and veronica, and it became expert at dodging my mad beatings with a spade or graip around the periphery of the bushes. Sometimes I glimpsed it far down, lurking in a tangle of twigs and leaves. I would make a quick thrust, but long before the spade or graip reached the target area it would move slinkily and silently to a safer spot. No matter how hard I tried I was unable to chase it out into the open, where the advantage would be mine. I had a feeling it was laughing at me.

Jean became schizophrenic. On the one hand she sympathized with me for having worked so hard in the garden only to find my succulent rewards being snatched away by a pirate. On the other hand she was terrified that in my rage I would kill the rabbit, which, using an epithet that didn't occur to me, she described as a 'darling'. When I made my attacks on the bushes she was always there, torn with anxiety concerning the outcome.

One morning I banged about with a graip and, no doubt in a moment of drowsy unpreparedness caused by a night's gluttony among the lettuces, the rabbit emerged. Only half grown, it looked clean and fresh and smug. I made a wild lunge in its direction but unfortunately tripped on a root of veronica and fell among the cabbages. The rabbit hopped away with contemptuous ease and took cover behind a long concrete edging tile which lay against the wall of the garage.

But that was its error. I had it now. Brushing myself down, I approached the garage and held the graip high. 'Ease that tile away from the wall,' I instructed Jean.

'No, no, please! Don't kill him!'

'Don't kill him? That rabbit is a menace! Starving us to death!'

'Poor wee thing! He's lying in there, terrified!'

'I should hope so! Ease away the tile!'

'No, no, please. You realize what you're doing, don't you? You're playing God.'

'What?'

'You're always writing about St Columba. Remember that story you often tell about when he was a little boy and he bent down to take a trout from the river and the poet Gemman said to him "How would *you* like it if God stretched down His hand and tried to kill *you*?" '

'Give me strength!' I said.

'The poor wee rabbit hasn't much strength.'

'What has that got to do with it?'

'Everything,' she said.

I lowered the graip. 'Well, if I spare its blasted life it's not going to spend the remainder of it in my garden!'

'Of course not. Wait a minute.'

She put a hand under the tile and presently withdrew it holding the rabbit. Having fondled it, uttering low-pitched words of endearment, she said to me: 'Now, take out the car. Drive me down to the graveyard and I'll pop him over the wall. He'll find the best grass in the parish there.'

It was the first time I had played chauffeur to a rabbit, and I prayed that on our journey nobody would see us. Thankfully nobody did. The pirate was left to enjoy luxury among the tombstones, a fate much better than he deserved, and for the rest of the season the garden flourished.

Except for an assault by white maggots on my onion crop.

Nature, I have learned, is relentless, infinitely resourceful in its method of attack.

No rabbits on today's menus. Nor any pigeon pie. But there was a time when Donald MacLean, the gamekeeper, made sure that we feasted regularly on both.

Donald and his wife and young family lived in a cottage by the riverside, not far from the Manse. His son Neil was one of my school buddies. From Neil, who was slightly older, I learned a lot about the birds and the bees, in more senses than one. Many a painful confrontation we had with our respective parents when we arrived home, after scrambling about on a spring afternoon among the hedges, our knees and our jerseys and our wide patched short trousers looking as if a set of harrows had been dragged over them.

From Neil I learned also the finer arts of playing 'rounders', which used to be a popular game among boys in Scottish rural schools. He taught me how to make a good 'bat' by cutting a three-foot length from an old broom handle. He taught me, too, how to wield it with a well-timed flick of the wrist. He himself, a *coiteach* (or left-hander), was the longest hitter in the school – Southend's Babe Ruth – and when he picked me for his team I basked in the reflected glory.

Has it been proved that American baseball originated in 'rounders'? It is almost exactly similar, except that in our version there was no 'pitcher' and the batsman threw up the ball himself and then hit it a 'scud'. And we called the bases 'dales'. But, as in modern baseball, our clothes and our bodies were frequently damaged when, if in danger of being run out, we threw ourselves at the 'dales'.

Neil's father, Donald MacLean, a thin, wiry man, beardless but with a ponderous moustache, resembled my own in character, being in turn kind, authoritarian, compassionate and brittle-tempered. (In those days of large and hearty families a father, in order to maintain control, was almost bound to combine several contradictory roles.) As a by-product of his trade in dealing with wild-life, he was a keen pigeon fancier and kept a loft of racing birds. I don't know exactly what happens in the pigeon-racing world nowadays, but in Donald's time, fifty years ago, the arrangements for racing appear to have been, to say the least, perfunctory.

I'm still vague about when, how and where the birds were sent for 'take-off'. All I know is that on the day they were expected back at Donald's cottage, Neil, his sister and almost everybody at the Manse were conscripted to lend a hand. As far as Archie, Willie and I were concerned – and later, Rona, Kenneth and John – we were only too happy to take part. We owed Donald plenty, on account of his generosity with rabbits and wood pigeons; and, in any case, the sense of adventure and excitement engendered on a race day was much to our liking.

The method of timing the birds was peculiar. When one landed in the loft, a ring with an identifying number had to be taken from its leg and conveyed as quickly as possible to the nearest Justice of the Peace or minister of religion, who then entered on a form the bird's number, the exact time of the ring's delivery and, finally, his own signature. When a number of birds were involved, with the chance that some of them would arrive almost together, it can be imagined that problems of logistics were liable to intrude.

But Donald had an answer to those problems. It was man-power – or, to be more accurate, child-power.

From his cottage by the riverside a steep path, more than fifty yards in length, led up to a stile on the main road. From this stile to the Manse – where the Padre carried out double duty as a Justice of the Peace and minister of religion, the way was flat and less than half a mile. On a race day Donald would take up his position on the kennel roof, in which the pigeon loft was situated. Neil and his sisters would be stationed on the ground below. At the stile, high above, three of us would watch and wait, each with a bicycle. (One bicycle was mine, the one I had bought from Bobby Kelly; the others belonged to Donald and his family.)

When the first pigeon fluttered in Donald would whip the

ring off its leg and throw it down. Neil – for example – would catch it and go panting up the steep path to the stile, where he'd hand it over, say, to Willie. Willie would immediately leap on a bicycle and, crouching over the handlebars, pedal furiously down the road. At the Manse back gate, skidding to a stop, he would be met by Maimie and Rona (the latter now outgrowing the infant stage), who would go scuttling and screaming into the Manse, past my wide-eyed mother in the kitchen and along to the study. There the Padre would be esconced, probably composing a sermon – as a rule a race reached its climax on a Saturday afternoon – but also keeping a magisterial eye on the clock. The time would be registered, the form signed and the whole business would go into reverse.

In the meantime, if another bird returned to the loft – or even another two – more teams of relay runners and cyclists were ready to go into action. Indeed, I have known collisions to occur as one cyclist arrived breathless at the Manse back gate and another, equally breathless, was riding away again.

Donald had considerable success with his racing pigeons. But one day something happened which caused anguish not only in his eager heart but also in the hearts of us all.

The great champion of his loft – a cock pigeon of impeccable breeding – was entered for a valuable money prize, and Donald reckoned that if the bird were clocked in by three o'clock in the afternoon he would have a good chance of winning it. By two o'clock Donald was on the roof, waiting beside the loft. The relay teams were at their posts. All systems were 'go'. Eyes were focussed on a patch of blue sky above the plantation which flanked the cottage. If the champion flew true to form it was in this patch that he would first appear.

At about two forty-five he did appear, like a tiny, grey-white piece of thistledown floating in the sun. A cry went up from Donald, in his lisping, burring tongue: 'Here he comes! The wee beauty! The wee beauty!' The relay teams uttered wild cheers. Individuals, eager to gain the honour of carrying the ring, began jostling for position.

Closer came the champion, swinging down. Twenty feet above the loft he ceased to descend and began, instead, to fly in circles. 'Come, my wee pet!' cooed Donald. 'Come on, now! Come on!'

The champion ignored him. He flew round and round, displaying beautiful technique but making no effort to land. Cold currents of dismay drifted among us.

'Come doon!' demanded Donald, the voice so recently filled with love and pride now changing to one of sharp authority. 'D'ye hear me – come doon!'

There was no response. Watches were consulted. It was five minutes to three.

Donald, on the roof, was hopping from foot to foot, supplicating arms held high, rage held in difficult check. 'What's the matter, boy? This is me. Come on, come tae me!'

Still no response.

Finally, inevitably, Donald's temper cracked. 'Throw me up a gun!' he shouted to Neil, below.

Fearful, but not daring to disobey, his son did so. Donald shouldered the weapon and held the barrels high. 'Come doon, ye wee bugger!' he roared with passion. 'Come doon, ye wee bugger, or I'll shoot ye doon!'

He had no intention of doing anything of the sort, of course, except in imagination; but we all held our breaths. Neil's sisters covered their eyes with their hands and began to cry. The time was three o'clock.

The champion performed another coy circle. Then, with infinite grace, he flew slowly down and settled on the stock of Donald's gun.

The brown, lean, gamekeeper's face was parchment tight. He caught the bird, oxtered the gun, slipped off the ring and threw it down to Neil. Neil dashed up the steep path, handed it to Willie at the stile. Two minutes later Maimie and Rona were invading the quiet of the Padre's study.

But the time certified was seven minutes past three. It was anti-climax. It was failure. We all sensed it.

A week later, when the results came through, Donald's champion had lost the race by two minutes.

At the time nobody derived much pleasure from the affair, with the exception, perhaps, of the Padre, who declared it had sparked off an idea for a sermon. I don't think Donald was amused when he heard the text: 'And the dove came in to him in the evening; and, lo, in her mouth was an olive leaf pluckt off: so Noah knew that the waters were abated from off the earth.' No doubt he envied Noah's possession of an amenable pigeon and brooded darkly on the recalcitrance of his own 'wee bugger'.

What amazes me, looking back, is the simple innocence – and honesty – of it all.

Fifty years ago, the system of timing a pigeon race would appear to have been open to all kinds of 'rackets'. Donald could have sent the Padre phoney rings. The Padre, as a close friend, could have 'adjusted' the time certificates. On the day of the big race, for example, he might have decided that, in justice, he ought to disregard the fraught interval before the actual landing and clock in the champion at the time it arrived above the loft. But to my father – and to Donald – such ideas simply did not occur. Standards had been set. They found no reason to question them.

In this modern, 'sophisticated' age, are standards of any kind held in such straightforward regard? It would seem not, if notice be taken of the propaganda which delights in 'interpreting' standards for political, and – sometimes – religious purposes. No wonder we are hemmed in by so many self-propagating rules and regulations, so many Royal Commissions, civil servants, local government officials and accountants. Nobody trusts anybody else any more.

If my nature weren't basically optimistic I think I would despair at all the narking and nagging that goes on. Political parties snarl at one another, forgetting that their business is to do their best for the country, not for the little kingdoms of Toryism and Socialism. The CBI and the TUC put as much trust in one another as rutting stags. Agnostics accuse Christians of providing pap for the people; Christians accuse Marxists of crimes against the individual; Marxists accuse everyone who is not a Marxist of being a Fascist pig. Youngsters denigrate 'old squares', and 'old squares', in their turn, fulminate about long hair, pop stars and scruffy denims. Television, radio and the newspapers love to stir it up – to highlight mistrust and the legacies of mistrust – because, in their pragmatic opinion, such 'scandals' help the viewing, listening and circulation figures.

I believe that politicians, aided and abetted by the news media, have gradually turned us all into a confusion of quarrelling mobs. When it suits their argument, standards are turned upside down and inside out. Political commentators have begun to regard a man's 'word of honour' as a sick joke. Cynical gossip columnists have begun to hold up as examples of probity and worth people who cheat the taxman (and, therefore, all other taxpayers), who scoff at religious observances (and, therefore, at the foundations of a caring society) and who, by public exhibitions of sexual promiscuity, cause pain and misery to their marriage partners and to their children. Is it any wonder that ordinary folk, whose instinctive desire has always been to live in amity with their neighbours, have begun to behave unethically themselves, in a pathetic effort at self-defence? Is it any wonder that the only standard which seems to be considered important today is that of material possession?

The Padre and Donald had few material possessions. They were both aware of human weakness and neither placed himself above it. But they recognized that in order to enjoy a good life standards of integrity had to be maintained. So they maintained them, without question, and never doubted that others, given the chance, would also do so.

In simple innocence? Or in wise recognition of the truth that the divinity in every man is worthy of love and respect.

4

In the Stranger's Guise

Fifty years ago in the Manse, we had no radio or television, no car, no pocket-money, no school meals, no organized games – in short, none of the advantages which children of today take for granted. And yet we had plenty 'going for us', because our parents and a few other like-minded adults helped and encouraged us to do many things for ourselves.

Such also was the situation of the tinkers and tramps who made Southend a happy hunting-ground. Though unable – or unwilling – to command official benefits of any kind, they lived comfortably enough within their own terms, because people were kind to them and offered help (remembering St Columba's *Rune of Hospitality*: 'Give to the stranger . . . because often comes the Christ in a stranger's guise') and encouraged them as well to practise the crafts and trades inherited over the centuries from their kith and kin.

The word tinker has an honourable origin. In old Scots it is 'tinkler', meaning simply a tin worker – someone who makes a tinkling sound as he applies the tools of his trade. In the past century it has acquired a nuance of derogation – like the word 'nigger' – and social workers now insist that tinkers should be called 'travelling people'.

In my childhood, the majority of tinkers slept in smokey tents. The ones we knew (we still know their descendants) were called either Townsley or Williamson. A tale is told that the Townsleys can trace descent from Huguenot refugees who, in the late seventeenth century, emigrated from the Low Countries to the East Neuk of Fife in search of tolerance. The Williamsons may constitute the remnant of a clan group rendered 'homeless and landless' after Culloden.

They moved their goods and chattels from sheltered site to sheltered site in rickety handcarts often manufactured from discarded grocery boxes and old pram and bicycle wheels. At times they earned money by thinning turnips, working in the harvest fields and digging potatoes. As a rule, however, they simply wandered from house to house in the parish begging for 'auld claes' and 'a wee puckle tea an' sugar', offering to repair pots and pans (as a gesture to their ancestral trade) and displaying for sale baskets, table-mats and clothes-pegs, all of which they had made themselves. They spoke a language of their own, which we understood derived from Romany, and never mixed with us in any social sense.

We children were scared of them. When we met on the road, and they addressed us in a gabbled mixture of Romany and English, we made polite acknowledgement but immediately scuttled past and away. On Fair Days in Campbeltown they often got drunk and quarrelled and fought amongst themselves, and when they appeared in court Sheriff MacMaster Campbell would talk to them in terms of dreadful retribution and then either admonish them or fine them half a crown. But, to my knowledge, a tinker never molested or assaulted anybody who was not a tinker.

We heard lurid tales of incest and inbreeding among their number; and, indeed, in a physical sense, they were inclined to be degenerate, many of them suffering from pulmonary diseases and spinal deformities. I retain a pathetic memory of an adolescent tinker boy, gangling, vacant-faced, six feet tall, laughing and running and dragging behind him across the shore a toy horse, belonging to Jock, which Jean had given him. Some of the braggart 'lads of the village' used to tell us gaping boys how they had been challenged by blonde tinker girls to prove their manhood; but, again to my knowledge, not even the lustiest farm-hand ever accepted such invitations. The 'tinker smell', generated by wood-smoke and unwashed bodies, was an inhibiter of normal sexual desire. In any case, the social barrier remained too wide even for casual crossings.

The tinkers were – and still are – 'a race apart'. The Padre always stopped on the road to talk to them, and frequently they brought their babies to the Manse to be christened. They did this, he suspected, in order to 'keep in' with my mother and Maimie, who had been brought up in the ancient Highland belief that when a tinker (or any stranger) comes to the door he must never be turned away empty-handed. But it was his creed that no matter what the circumstances might be, if his services as a minister were requested it was his duty not to withhold them.

He was never asked to officiate at a tinker wedding or a tinker funeral. On such occasions they followed customs and carried out rituals of their own. Each time we go to Glasgow by car Jean and I see a tinker's grave by the roadside near Lochgair. There is another on the Dunoon road, not far from the Glen Croe junction.

The sad fact is that with the coming of the Welfare State the position of tinkers has hardly changed. They are given every chance to integrate with the wider community. They are offered housing and settled education for their children. They receive social security. Well-meaning people supply them with the means to start up small businesses. But they refuse to live in houses, preferring the nomadic outdoor life of their forbears. Their children are moved from school to school, learning little. They squander their dole money on drink. The great social barrier remains almost as impregnable as before.

In our district a few young male tinkers have taken jobs on the roads and in the shipyard in Campbeltown. They have married girls who are not tinkers, live permanently in council houses and appear to be creating new lives for themselves. But in general the 'travelling people' still roam the roads with their tents and their handcarts. Their physical health has not greatly improved. Drunkenly they still quarrel and fight among themselves.

Why?

Sometimes articles appear in the press, and television programmes are broadcast, which accuse the community in general and certain councils in particular, of 'neglecting' the tinkers.

One tinker whom I know personally has told newspaper and television interviewers that 'nobody does anything for the travelling people', when in fact the local council and local individuals have done everything possible to make life easier for himself and his family. He simply gave the answer which he guessed the interviewers wanted and omitted to mention a number of factors relevant to his situation.

Twice he was placed by the authorities in a good house and in a good job but on both occasions he ultimately rejected them. A local lady, whose life is dedicated to the care of tinkers, supplied him with a caravan and the facilities to learn a country craft, but in the end he rejected her kindness, too. A local farmer offered him work at the going agricultural rate, but after a day or two he gave it up, deciding apparently that life was easier on 'the dole'.

This newspaper and television 'star' also failed to point out that he is visited regularly by Willie Webb, the tinkers' Padre employed by the Church of Scotland, who can move mountains to help those members of his scattered congregation who will accept his help. Nor did he make any reference to the care devoted to himself and his family by local doctors and nurses, who are sometimes appalled but never deterred by the insanitary conditions in which, at times, they have to tend their tinker patients.

Nobody I know turns his back on a tinker. Jean spends her life attending to their wants, as she has done since she was a girl on her father's farm half a century ago. Elderly female tinkers address her by her Christian name and wear her discarded skirts and jumpers as they travel to and from Campbeltown by bus. I wage with her a running battle to prevent male tinkers acquiring my winter golfing wear, which, though admittedly somewhat tatty, remains comfortable to use.

At every house in the parish 'auld claes' and 'a wee puckle tea an' sugar' are still supplied, even though on a basis of social security benefits the suppliers may be less well off than the recipients. There is no animus against the 'travelling people', simply a recognition that their attitude to life is different and that gratitude from them – in practical terms at any rate – is not to be expected.

For what it's worth my answer to the problem is this. The tinkers want to remain tinkers. They find houses cramping, disciplined jobs frustrating. They are glad to accept charity, but such charity must have no strings attached. Their desire is to be free, following an old way of life. The greatest kindness we can show them, in my opinion, is to take them as they are, to give reasonable help when they ask for help but at other times to leave them alone to work out their own destiny.

After all, they are not numbers on a social register, marked with an asterisk, but human beings entitled to a freedom of choice within the law.

Unlike the tinkers, who had their tents, the tramps we knew slept in barns or in caves. It was a perennial disappointment to us that they considered the Manse barn an unsuitable lodging because it contained no warm and comfortable straw. But they came regularly to our back door to canvas their 'trades' and to suggest that 'a wee cup o' tea' might be acceptable. Between tinkers and tramps, my mother and Maimie presided over a permanent running buffet.

In summer Old Fernie roamed the woods and plantations, uprooting and potting varieties of ferns and selling them from door to door. His plants were delicate and moistly fresh, ideal decorations for glass-fronted porches and 'best-room' windows. Unless carefully tended they would last only for a season; but when renewal time came round Old Fernie would be back with younger and even more exotic specimens for sale. Clearly his business philosophy resembled that of the modern car industry, which preaches that a high sales turnover depends on inbuilt obsolescence.

When we knew him, Fernie was about sixty years old, wrinkled, permanently in need of a shave. Once, when Archie quizzed him, he admitted that he had never shaved but that each day, with a rusty pair of scissors which he used for trimming fern-plants, he cut his greying beard 'to the bone', as he described it.

When he could procure them from satisfied 'customers' he favoured thick tweed trousers, tied in agricultural fashion just below the knee, and heavy boots, fastened not with the soft and poor quality laces of today but with the heavy leather thongs popular with farm-workers fifty years ago. Even in warm weather he liked to wear long coats, belted at the waist with rope or string. For one whole season he sported a khaki trench-coat which had belonged to the Padre in Salonika. With a gleam in his bright green eyes he would tell our neighbours that he was 'clothed in sanctity'. But as he appeared to sleep in his beloved coat as well as work in it during the day, by the end of that summer the odour of his sanctity was extremely pungent.

He was an introvert of sober habits. I never remember him taking a drink too many, and his only passion seemed to be for 'pan-drops', a few of which he always carried loose in his overflowing pockets. When he offered us one – sometimes he did this in lieu of discount after my mother had bought some of his ferns – we would accept it gladly, ignoring the fact that it was generally smeared with earth and fungus and covered in fragments of cigarette-ends.

We never discovered Fernie's real name nor any of his personal history. He spoke to us mainly about happenings in the parish – always in a slightly humorous way – and about his ferns. I think he loved his ferns more than he did human beings. He could tell us the Latin names of the different varieties – I wish I could remember them now – and describe the kind of soil in which each of them grew best. What intrigued us, however, was that to many of his specimens he gave personal names. For example a sonsy hart's tongue might be 'Big Sandy', a delicate maiden-hair 'Wee Jeannie'. Sitting with us in the barn, waiting like a bedraggled lord for his tea to be brought to him by Maimie, he would stroke them and speak to them and explain from which part of the woods he had taken them.

Long ago, on the braeside north of Donald MacLean's cottage, three sizeable 'craters' were excavated to provide material for bottoming the main road. Now they are filled in and camouflaged with earth, grass, trees and vegetation of all kinds; but their outlines remain clear. Old Fernie called them respectively the drawing-room, the dining-room and the kitchen. From the drawing-room came his Wee Jeannies, from the dining-room his Big Sandys. In the kitchen, he told us, he found less desirable specimens, which he dubbed 'the servants'.

Such imaginative flights appealed to us, and we would help and encourage him to spin improbable yarns about his fern people. Once, however, when I put forward the idea of a coy romance between a Wee Jeannie and a Big Sandy, he became unaccountably morose and refused to speak to us any more that day.

On the basis of the evidence available we began to create backgrounds for Old Fernie.

Archie was convinced he was a well-educated 'aristocrat' who had lost all his money. Didn't he know Latin and talk, not about parlours and 'best rooms' as did the people of Southend, but about drawing-rooms and dining-rooms – and servants? Willie, more of a realist, thought he might have been a gardener who had robbed his master and spent a long time in jail.

As a future story-teller, I was inclined to favour Archie's fancy but took pains to add a twist to it. In his youth, I suggested, he had been turned down by the girl he loved – which would account for his sudden moroseness when romance was mentioned – and thereafter had decided to spurn society and live close to nature instead.

We never did discover the truth. One autumn Old Fernie went away to wherever he used to spend the winters. He didn't come back. He passed out of our lives like a migrating swallow. Or – more truly, perhaps – like a character in a one-act play.

Another tramp about whose origins and background we had scanty knowledge was a small, wiry, cheerful, sardonic, sometimes gloriously inebriated man who, though most unlike a dignified Womble of Wimbledon, still rejoiced in the name of Tobermory – because, as we were led to believe, he had been born in Tobermory in the Isle of Mull.

His domicile in Southend, during many summers, was the big sea-smoothed cave beyond the graveyard at Keil, where Flora MacCambridge and the young James Ranald MacDonald had found refuge after the siege of Dunaverty. There, on a quiet evening, he could often be heard singing as he brewed a cup of tea on a driftwood fire. He owned two canvas bags with leather shoulder straps. The larger one contained his bedding and cooking utensils, the other the tools of his trade as an itinerant saw-sharpener.

The Padre, as has been shown, was a violent man with a saw. Tobermory, therefore, found him a regular customer. They talked about religion in a desultory way; but since Tobermory was inclined to sneer at the Kirk and deride its black-coated, 'respectable' image, their discussions seldom progressed beyond the stage of a few brittle generalities. Clearly Tobermory had a chip on his shoulder, and the Padre, though he himself had chips on both his shoulders, would stump away, muttering about people who refused to understand and make allowances. (The pot, we thought, calling the kettle black. But we remained firmly on the Padre's side.) Tobermory would glance after him, grin, spit out a stream of tobacco juice on the barn floor and resume work with his pliers on the teeth of our cross-cut.

At the appropriate time Maimie would come and tell him that his meal was ready. He would follow her into the kitchen, seat himself close to the glowing range and noisily consume large bowls of tea and, as often as not, cold chicken sandwiches. Then he would smoke a cigarette and exchange banter with Maimie in crudely mixed Gaelic and English.

Perhaps because of the Gaelic, my mother and Maimie seemed to like him well enough. Archie, Willie and I didn't.

Old Fernie conversed with us as equals. Tobermory talked down to us, making us feel uncomfortable by cracking jokes at the expense of our youthful inexperience.

Sometimes I concealed resentment and went to visit him. People who didn't know him may find it hard to believe, but during the summer a weekly newspaper was delivered to Tobermory in his cave, by bus from Campbeltown. I became very interested in that newspaper. It was called the *Worker*.

Reared on the bland Tory diet offered at that time by the *Glasgow Herald* – and without radio or television to suggest more uncomfortable points of view – I found that the articles in Tobermory's paper made me feel both excited and guilty. It was like turning over a smooth, beautifully marked stone only to discover underneath rotting vegetation and crawling creatures like worms and slaters. I thought of my father's congregation, dominated by the Dowager Duchess of Argyll and numerous 'well-bein' ' farmers and tradesmen. I thought of the tinkers and the tramps and the people of 'Teapot Lane' in the village who lived 'on the parish' and never went to church.

Tobermory would sit on his haunches, brewing up tea on his fire at the mouth of the cave and watching me read. Partially concealed by lowered lids, his eyes would be cunning. A smile would twist his narrow mouth. I never discussed the articles with him; he never tried to discuss them with me. When I put the paper down and bade him good-bye he would laugh and spit and perhaps make a sour comment about my innocence.

My mother would have been horrified had she known what I was doing. The Padre's reaction might have been less fraught, but, to be safe, I kept my knowledge of the *Worker* to myself. I hated what I read. It told me that as a privileged person (in a moral sense) I was blind and ignorant, that there was another, infinitely ugly side to the shining moon. It also posed a question: what are you going to do about it? The question caused me pain, because I felt unarmed and inadequate. It is a feeling that has never left me.

I wondered if it troubled Tobermory? I think possibly it did, because when he had accumulated sufficient money from the sharpening of saws he often went on a wild alcoholic binge which was the wonder – and, in some cases, the envy – of the people of Southend. Obviously it was his way of forgetting something.

One summer night my father was coming home after visiting a friend in the village. Dusk had fallen. As he tramped up the steep Machrimore Brae, not far from the Manse, he saw something on the summit – something silhouetted against the moonlit sky – which made him shiver. In the middle of the road was a lumpy mass which might have been a body. Round it a tattered creature leaped and swung, uttering cries. Vague intimations of black magic assailed the Padre. He moved closer, then stopped to listen, desperately trying to remember the Gaelic incantation which offered protection from the evil eye.

Gradually the cries were translated into a kind of music and the music into badly articulated words, which, nevertheless, my father could understand: 'Jean MacNeill's in love wi' me, I'm as happy as can be! How wad ye like if you were me? Fal-di-riddle-i-doh!' With some relief he recognized Tobermory, crazily drunk, dancing round his canvas bags.

Tobermory sensed his approach. As he reached the crest of the brae Tobermory stopped singing, pirouetted rapidly on one foot, then fell heavily on top of the bags and became violently sick.

Machrimore Brae was a long mile from the cave at Keil, so the Padre shouldered Tobermory's bags and, amid bouts of vomiting, helped him to reach the Manse barn and bed down for the night.

In the morning Tobermory was gone. But a few days later he was back, spry and sardonic as ever, touting for work.

As far as we were concerned, as children, Old Fernie and Tobermory emerged from limbo and eventually returned to it. Peter the Jostler was different. We knew his full name, Peter McArthur. We knew he had been nicknamed the Jostler because it was his habit, caught in a crowd, to shoulder and push a way out of it, as if his life depended on winning free. We knew that he had been a miner. We knew that his strange ways were the result of his having been involved in a pit accident and trapped underground for many hours.

Peter was not a summer visitor like other tramps. He was always with us, roaming from house to house in Kintyre, as if searching for something.

To anyone who didn't know him his appearance and behaviour were bizarre, even frightening. If presented with an old coat he usually put it on at once, on top of a grisly collection of other garments. In consequence he looked grotesque, a Michelin-man scarecrow. But what fascinated us even more – and what caused us cruel, giggling amusement – was his continual fear of being 'jammed'.

On being invited into a house, he would carefully examine the walls of the room – usually the kitchen – in which he was to be entertained. Then he would take a chair, test the strength of its legs with powerful hands and finally place it with its back to the wall, as far from the fire as possible. If his examinations and tests proved satisfactory he would sit down, still looking around him suspiciously, and await attention. If they didn't he would proceed backwards out of the room and the house, muttering through a dirty, unkempt beard that he was being 'jammed'.

Soup or tea had to be served to him in a plain white bowl. If offered a decorated bowl or a teacup with markings on it he was immediately 'jammed' and would effect a quick escape, uttering baleful sounds. My mother and Maimie, knowing him well, made few mistakes. The Manse kitchen, therefore, was one of his favourite stopping-places. Peering round a door-jamb, we often saw him sitting there after having had a good lunch, dozing in his chair while the minutes passed towards tea-time. On such occasions Maimie would go about her business quietly, and my mother would postpone an ironing session, because if Peter awoke to find a red-hot iron in his vicinity he would be grievously 'jammed' and a temporary peace would be broken.

Archie and Willie and I were never allowed to go near him.

The village children had a habit of shouting after him as he padded along the road: 'Tak' the hens oot o' yer pockets!' This oblique – and unfounded – accusation of theft infuriated him, and he would heave large stones at them in retaliation. The sight of us in the kitchen might have triggered off a similar bout of mayhem.

My father was apt to 'jam' him, too. At the beginning he had tried to speak to Peter, but nothing coherent ever issued from behind the bedraggled beard, and it seemed that the Padre's offer of spiritual comfort was either not understood or deliberately declined.

Some people were able to get through to him by means of a dram, under the influence of which he might be persuaded to sing a stave or two of a Scots song. He had a reasonable bass voice, roughened and sometimes made to waver by bronchial phlegm.

He was unpopular with the rabbit-catchers. Sometimes, during his wanderings, if he came across a rabbit in a snare, he would catch it, calm it with gentle hands, loosen the wire about its body and allow it to lope away. Hiding behind a bush or under the lip of a bunker on the golf-course, we often saw him do it. We would laugh together as he remained on his knees, staring after the released animal, a motionless heap of ragged garments black against the short green grass. We would shout insults at him, then flee with careless agility as he made stiff and ponderous efforts to rise and pursue us. Eventually, when the opportunity occurred, we would tell the tale to Dan, our favourite rabbit-catcher, who would swear and describe the Jostler as 'a bloody menace'. Our childish, undeveloped imaginations failed to glimpse the truth: to him the rabbits were 'jammed'; to him no living creature deserved such agony.

One morning he was found lying under a whin bush on a braeside not far from Campbeltown. Soaking wet, stiff as a log, he was taken to the Poor House hospital, where, without regaining consciousness, he died. They buried him at Kilkerran, in the town cemetery, in the place reserved for paupers.

Today it is likely that Peter the Jostler would be looked after by the State. Would he be any happier, confined and regimented in a geriatric hospital? Would psychiatrists discover a cure for his terrible malaise, or would their probings result in his being shut away in a mental home?

We saw him at the time as a subject for hidden laughter. Now, understanding what he must have suffered, 'jammed' in a collapsing pit-shaft, I find his memory infinitely sad. Did anybody care? My mother and Maimie did. So did many other housewives in the parish. But what about the rest of us?

5

Black Flags over Sollas

My mother was an immovable Tory.

Her childhood home was a rented farm in Kilninver, near Oban, where her family's comfort depended on the ground superior's continuing patronage. In consequence it was their creed that authority must never be questioned, that to be 'agin the government' – and therefore, by inference, 'agin the Laird' – was a mark of the scallywag.

In the years following the Second World War, when my mother made critical comments about Attlee's Labour government, I used to shake a solemn head at her: 'I'm surprised at you, Granny! Agin the government!' But my joke always misfired because she never saw the point of it. To her Tories were *always* the government, in power or out of it.

She would grieve if I expressed approval of Labour policy, not because I was opposing her but simply on account of what she considered my abnormal state of mind. She equated socialist theories with alcoholism, drug-addiction and atheism. Sometimes when I pretended to have leanings towards all such 'sins', she would smile at me: 'Angus, my dear, you shouldn't *say* things like that! I *know* you're a good Christian and a good Tory at heart. You'd never willingly do anything to put shame on your mother.'

I'm sure I did many things in her lifetime of which she might have been ashamed; but I hope she knew nothing about them. Now that she is gone and has come to know the truth – that at times I have voted Liberal and Labour, Scottish Nationalist and even Conservative – I am confident that she understands and that the love between us is stronger than ever. I can only hope that St Peter is tactful enough not to denigrate the Tories in her presence.

Politics were never a worry to my mother, because to her a change of party loyalty was inconceivable. Her Christian faith was also immutable – and immutably Protestant at that. The Padre (and I, for one, among his family) had no such reliable anchor chains.

His birthplace was a 'black house' at Claddach Kirkibost in North Uist, where smoke from a fire in the middle of an earthen floor escaped through a hole in the thatch. His father was a crofter, whose allegiance was to his fellow crofters rather than to the owner of the land.

The Padre was reared as a Tory and a Protestant, but for reasons entirely different from those in my mother's case. In the Hebrides the Roman Catholics were inclined to be Whigs. After the Disruption in 1843 some Protestants, such as the Free Presbyterians, also became Whigs – an example, perhaps, of how two extremes can sometimes meet on the rim of a circle. Therefore, as continuing members of the Established Church of Scotland, my father's parents remained Tories. Real politics didn't come into it: otherwise, on account of the long neglect and persecution of the Hebrideans by successive lairds and governments, they would have been red revolutionaries.

It was the Tories in North Uist (most of them loyal members of the old Church of Scotland) who maintained a Liberal attitude. The Wee Frees and the Free Presbyterians were the strict ones. I used to listen, fascinated, to tales my father had heard from his grandfather, another Angus MacVicar.

I wish I had known Old Angus, my great-grandfather. He seems to have been a 'character', who, though an elder of the Kirk, was not averse to enjoying a few sporting adventures on the side.

He was a crofter who also owned a small boat. As a young man he sailed this boat across the choppy Minches and down through the seven tides at the Mull of Kintyre in order to sell produce and buy goods in Glasgow. In those days such a journey must have been a sea-faring Everest. He had an eye for the girls – at any rate before he married – and though my father was inclined to gloss over this aspect of his personality I have an idea that I may have more blood relations in the islands than are recorded in the family bibles.

But it was Old Angus's attitude to the Sabbath that intrigued me most. I imagined that my ancestors had always possessed an outlook on religion that was bleak and sad, especially on Sundays. In Old Angus's young days, at the beginning of last century, this was far from being the truth. Before and after morning service he and his young friends used to enjoy such sports as the long jump and putting the stone. Business transactions were common on a Sunday afternoon, even among Kirk elders.

The services themselves were not sacrosanct. On one occasion, as the minister announced the text of his sermon, a boy came rushing into the church with the news that whales had appeared in a neighbouring bay. Shouting apologies, Old Angus and the rest of the congregation rose in a body and ran off to launch their boats. All the minister could do was to follow them and spend the rest of the afternoon watching his flock driving the whales towards the shore with sticks and stones, so that they might be left high and dry when the tide receded.

'A work of necessity and mercy,' my father would point out, unctuously. 'Tender whale meat was a change from salt beef that was always stringy and tough. Not only could the blubber be rendered down for lamp-oil, it was also a useful food. I remember a North Uist proverb which went something like this: "*Is math am biadh femanaich aran seagail agus roin.*" ("Good food it is for a seaweed worker, rye bread and blubber.")'

I suppose the truth was that if the Roman Catholics could spend their Sunday afternoons in profitable and enjoyable pursuits, some Protestants were unwilling to stand aside and let them have all the fun.

Following the Disruption, however, happy-go-lucky Sabbaths

were gradually displaced by the doom and gloom which so many Sassenachs believe, mistakenly, to be characteristic of the Church of Scotland. The pendulum swung from 'the broad way', which was how the seceders described my great-grandfather's attitude, to the 'straight and narrow'.

Indeed, the new road became so narrow as to be almost impassable. One Sunday, on his way to church, Old Angus met the Free Church minister on the road. He touched his cap: 'A fine day,' he said. The tall black figure stopped, fixed him with an eagle eye and thundered: 'This is not a day, Angus, to be speaking of days!'

When he was inducted to the parish of Southend in 1910, the Padre found that its religious history was not unlike that of his native island.

He spoke to old men whose parents had been alive at the end of the eighteenth and at the beginning of the nineteenth centuries, old men who could tell stories about Communion Sundays when tents were erected around the Kirk for the supply of food, sweetmeats and drink and in which children could be looked after while their fathers and mothers attended the long services. It was like a fair, they told him: a Holy Fair, perhaps, in the Burnsian sense. But as time went on the climate of religious opinion changed. In Southend, as in North Uist, all the joy went out of it, and I have a notion that King David, who danced before the Lord, might have thought as little of the encompassing 'blackness' as my brothers and I did.

Surely it is a good thing that happier Sundays have now, once more, become the rule rather than the exception. After all, as I understand it, Christ died to make us happy. Is the Sabbath not the most appropriate day of all to enjoy leisure and to be 'speaking of days'?

But the bitterness engendered by the Disruption in North Uist was as nothing compared with that caused by the eviction of innocent people from their crofts in order to make way for 'the great Cheviot'.

During the Clearances in the Highlands and Islands, when

absentee landlords – many of them living in England – authorized their local representatives to get rid of 'unprofitable' crofters and fill their estates with 'profitable' sheep, some of the seeds were sown of present-day Scottish Nationalism. With the thatch of their 'black houses' burning, with their wives and children blood-stained from beatings with soldiers' musket-butts and policemen's batons, with tattered plaids as their only protection from winter cold, with ranting clergymen (whose stipends were often paid by the landlords) preaching submission to God's will, with no help in sight from Government or from fat, 'I'm all right, Jack' farming neighbours in the south, the crofters of the Highlands and Islands were struck by a bitterness whose breath is still strong.

The Clearances began in the counties of Sutherland and Ross in the second half of the eighteenth century, notoriously on estates owned by the Duke of Sutherland. Their full evil came to North Uist early in the nineteenth century, when Britain was recovering from the long Napoleonic wars and the demand for meat – and especially for mutton – had become even stronger than before. Then, as on the mainland, the sad cries of the evicted people of Sollas were overcome by the bleatings of many sheep.

On the face of it, North Uist had a thriving kelp industry. The people, however, remained poor, and even before the actual physical violence of the Clearances some of them had been forced to give up the struggle and quit the island of their fathers. Crofter rents were screwed higher and higher to screaming point. Those who worked at the seaweed, collecting it, spreading it out to dry and then burning it in a kiln to make kelp, were paid thirty shillings per ton for their industry while the landlord made a profit of some £18 on the same amount. No wonder the bard Ian MacCodrum made a protest:

> Look around you and see the gentry
> With no pity for the poor creatures,
> With no kindness to their kin.

They do not think that you belong to the land,
And although they leave you empty
They do not see it as a loss.
They have lost their respect
For every law and promise
That was among the men
Who took their land from the foe.

But poetic protests fell with no more impact than confetti on leather-hard consciences. Many of my ancestors in North Uist, rack-rented into poverty, emigrated voluntarily to America and Australia. Others became vagrants, wandering southwards to Glasgow and the Lowlands, where, if they were lucky, they found menial work. Some of the young men became soldiers, fighting for officers who would later callously evict their families and for a Britain which, having used them in battle, would then cast them aside with as little concern as if they were spent matches.

Forced evictions began in North Uist in 1841, when Duncan Shaw, not only Sheriff Substitute in the Long Island but also factor for the North Uist Estates (how's that for legal impartiality?), recommended to a Select Committee appointed to inquire into the condition of the population of the Highlands and Islands that 2500 people in North Uist, out of a total of 4600, should be removed to Canada. His master, the owner of North Uist (and of other property in Skye) was Godfrey William Wentworth Macdonald, fourth Baron of the Isles, and a descendant of the Macdonald chiefs of Sleat.

According to Old Angus, Lord Macdonald was at heart a decent enough man who did his best to alleviate destitution in the island, especially during the potato famine of 1846. But it seems he was heavily in debt – some say to the tune of nearly £200000 – and the pressures on him to use 'the great Cheviot' as a means of restoring his fortunes were as great as those on less humane landowners. Finally, he, too, was petitioning for '*an armed force to enable the constituted authorities to compel the people to give obedience to the law*'.

The flash-point of the North Uist Clearances occurred in 1849, when it was decided to evict all the Sollas tenantry on the plea that they were in arrears of rent. Old Angus was a young man at the time and witnessed some of the almost incredible barbarity committed in the name of so-called law and order. As a boy, listening at the peat-fire, the Padre heard stories from the *bodach*'s own lips. He, in turn, told them to me. I will try, however, to be objective and to rely on recorded history, rather more than on legend, for the facts, though such objectivity – and such justice – was never employed by Lord Macdonald in dealing with the people of Sollas. (Nor by his ancestors in the sixteenth century, when, by offering a Judas hand of friendship, they captured and killed four MacVicar brothers in North Uist and took over their lands.)

Sollas is a square mile of flat, treeless country in the north end of the island, bounded on the west by a tidal beach of white sand and enclosed in a kind of trough between sand-blown dunes and the lower slopes of the inland hills. Though exposed to fierce Atlantic weather, the land is kind, possibly the best in the island, and in 1849 600 people lived there in the townships of Dunskellar, Malaglate, Middlequarter and Sollas itself. They were for the most part Macdonalds, with a deep love for every bare inch of their homeland.

Lord Macdonald's commissioner, Patrick Cooper, claimed that the soil was unsuited for small tenants and incapable of improvement by drainage. (Fifty years later this claim was proved to be wrong when the Congested Districts Board divided the farm of Sollas into twelve successful crofts.) On the other hand, he said, the ground provided ideal grazing for sheep. In the month of May, therefore, on behalf of Lord Macdonald, he offered to overlook the crofters' arrears of rent and to ship them all, with their families, to Canada.

Shocked and saddened by this proposal, the tenants of Sollas attempted to organize opposition. Their spokesman pointed out that the potato crop for the previous three years had failed but that they could tide over this difficult period if Lord

Macdonald would offer them employment by way of kelp-making or drainage.

But the land-owner (or his commissioner) had made up his mind. Employing what was in effect a con trick, Patrick Cooper now told the tenants that Lord Macdonald would pay all their passage money. When the offer was examined in detail, however, they found that the money was to come from the sale of their own effects, with no allowance made for their buildings.

Finally, a writ was granted for the eviction of the Sollas people.

On Saturday 14 July the first attempt to execute it was made by Sheriff Officer Roderick Macdonald and two assistants. They were driven from Malaglate by a barrage of stones.

They tried again two days later, this time accompanied by Sheriff Substitute Shaw, Patrick Cooper and twenty policemen. The same thing happened.

A third try was made on 17 July, when Cooper, sensing that he was a main source of the crofters' anger, absented himself. As the party approached Malaglate it was confronted by a crowd of 300 men, women and children. Roderick Macdonald, the Sheriff Officer, said afterwards that warning signals were flying: 'Namely a pole with some black thing on it, but I couldn't say whether it was a flag or a bonnet. The first flag was about fifty yards from the house, and three flags were on top of a hill about a mile distant. The crowd said they would not allow us to go on with the removals. They did not strike, but were speaking, and said that if we attempted the removals we should see the consequences.' Sheriff Substitute Shaw was troubled. He had no enthusiasm for his task, and when the rain came on he became even more unhappy. He ordered a retreat to Lochmaddy.

From Armadale Castle in Skye Lord Macdonald now wrote to the Home Secretary, asking for 'an armed force' to deal with his recalcitrant tenants. But his answer was a dusty one. He was told that before the military were sent the law should employ 'the county force only'.

On 1 August an all-Inverness-shire party consisting of Sheriff Substitute Shaw, Sheriff Substitute Colquhoun, Procurator Fiscal Mackay, Commissioner Patrick Cooper, Factor James Thomas Macdonald, Superintendent MacBean, and thirty-three constables advanced on Sollas. Accompanying the party were two men who might be described as neutral observers – 'Our Own Reporter' from the *Inverness Courier* and the Rev. Finlay MacRae, parish minister of North Uist. (The majority of the people of Sollas belonged to the Free Church, but at this particular time, inexplicably, their own minister seems to have been absent.) Again the crofters and their families had gathered in a tight crowd on the *machair*. Again black, defiant flags were flying. Again it was raining.

The first few hours of the confrontation were spent in argument, with the Rev. Finlay MacRae acting as mediator. On the word of the *Inverness Courier* reporter, the crofters were 'in such a state of excitement that it appeared more than questionable, should an ejectment be proceeded with, whether a promise made to Mr MacRae in the morning that no resistance would be made to the officers, would be fulfilled'.

The day went on. So did the rain. As people became wetter and colder they also became more surly and hot-tempered. Patrick Cooper shouted to the crofters, demanding that they should accept the writ and emigrate. The minister and Superintendent MacBean 'added their arguments and advices in Gaelic'. Eventually four or five families agreed to leave, but the remainder stubbornly refused. According to Old Angus's story the men were quiet and peaceable enough: the women were more militant, screaming abuse at the police in general and at Patrick Cooper in particular.

As dusk began to fall Sheriff Substitute Colquhoun and Superintendent MacBean, both mainland men without much stomach for island weather, decided to withdraw. Before doing so, however, they made a quick move to assert their authority. Policemen charged forward and, after a short, angry struggle, were able to handcuff two men and drag them out of the crowd.

The men were Roderick MacPhail and Archibald Maclean, the latter being related by blood to the MacVicars.

After the 'gentry' and the constables had left for Lochmaddy, the *Courier* reporter, like a good professional, remained behind to interview the crofters. Their argument was that there was no need for emigration: 'If Lord Macdonald would increase the crofts to double the present size for which there is sufficient improvable land, and would give leases and encouragement to improvements, we would be content to pay rents, and we would have seaware and stock sufficient.'

Next morning the authorities reached Malaglate by ten o'clock, hoping that the arrests they had made the night before would have had a salutary effect on the inhabitants. But though this time the people themselves remained indoors, black flags were again flying. The sight of them triggered off an outbreak of the violence that had been simmering evilly beneath the wind and the rain of the past twenty-four hours.

With no more discussion, no more argument, the police took up positions along the main track through Malaglate. The Sheriffs asked a question at the door of each house: 'Are you willing to emigrate on the terms offered?' If the answer was no – and almost invariably it was – then the constables proceeded with the work of demolition. Thatch was torn off the roofs; clothes, bedding, spinning-wheels, fish-barrels, tables and benches were hurled out into the open and the house-timbers stripped for burning. Patrick Cooper, surrounded by constables, himself supervised each eviction.

As the destruction went on, the neighbouring crofters of Dunskellar, Middlequarter and Sollas gathered on an adjacent knoll, underneath one of the black flags. They watched as the Malaglate folk, at first in grim silence, were subjected to indignities. Then suddenly – and this is one of Old Angus's stories – the wife of a man called John MacAskill, a weaver with nine children, emerged from her 'black house' with a child in her arms, calling out: '*Tha mo chlann air a bhi air am murt!*' ('My children are being murdered!') The watching crofters could endure it no longer. They rushed down towards the township, brandishing sticks and stones.

The police were instructed to draw truncheons. Superintendent MacBean approached the crowd. He 'explained what the men were actually doing in the house. He was listened to quietly; but as he returned a stone was thrown at him, and he had scarcely joined his men when a heavy volley of stones drove the assistant from the roof of the house, and a band of from fifty to one hundred women, with a few men and boys, came running up from the shore, shouting and armed with large stones, with which they compelled the assistants to fall back behind the police for shelter. Fresh supplies of large, sharp-pointed stones were obtained from the bed of a small stream, and several heavy volleys were discharged, most of them, however, falling short of the officers.'

The police were now formed into two divisions and ordered to attack the crowd. One division charged the women from the rear, the other on the flank. The women attempted to stand their ground, but the flailing truncheons were too much for them. They retreated first along the *machair*, then across the white shore, screaming and scratching and calling out to their less gallant men: 'Be manly and help us!' Their clothes were torn, their heads and arms bruised and bloody from the impact of truncheons and fists.

Early in the afternoon Superintendent MacBean called off the running battle. The constables returned to Malaglate. The defeated but still defiant women again gathered on the knoll to tend one another's wounds and to shout more insults. Old Angus retained a keen Gaelic memory of much of what they said. So did the reporter from the *Inverness Courier*, who later wrote that the maddened women were soon uttering 'such wishes as that their men might come down and wash their hands in their enemies' hearts-blood, and that the devil and his angels might come and sweep them out of the land'.

The men of Sollas were slow to make any heroic response, believing perhaps that their families might suffer less if they refused to meet violence with violence. Once or twice some adolescents of both sexes advanced on the police to throw stones and then run away.

Patrick Cooper found the situation difficult.

A further attempt to destroy the houses of Malaglate, he suspected, might spark off a physical battle in which the women of Sollas would at last be joined by their men-folk. If that happened, greatly outnumbered as the authorities were, death might come to the *machair* – death which would almost certainly include his own.

There was another complication. Sheriff Substitute Colquhoun had become sickened by the police brutality and, as a result, was refusing to serve any more writs, claiming that there were faults in the wording of them.

Furthermore, the Rev. Finlay MacRae was preaching less violence and more understanding of the people's plight.

Cooper decided that if they made ten token ejectments and took a few prisoners his party could then retire to Lochmaddy without losing too much face.

Two Malaglate crofters, Archibald Boyd and Roderick MacCuish (MacCuish was another relative of the MacVicars) were pursued to the shore, beaten up by the police, arrested and handcuffed. The ejectments then continued.

'The ninth ejectment was that of a family in Middlequarter, named Monk, who had taken an active part in all the previous opposition to the authorities. It was found necessary to remove the women by force. One of them threw herself on the ground, and either fell or pretended to fall into hysterics – (fortunately I have not had experience enough to know the difference) – uttering the most doleful sounds, and barking and yelping like a dog for five or ten minutes. Another, with many tears, sobs and groans, put up a petition to the Sheriffs that they would leave the roof over part of her house where she had a loom with cloth in it which she was weaving; and a third woman, the eldest, made such an attack with a stick on an officer, and missing her blow, sprung upon him and knocked off his hat.

Two stout policemen had difficulty in carrying her to the door.'

Meanwhile the Rev. Finlay MacRae talked earnestly to the crofters. His message was that if they promised to emigrate the following year they might be allowed to occupy their houses for the winter. He talked also to Patrick Cooper, finally securing from him a promise that if the crofters agreed to sign pledges to emigrate the following year he would call off the police.

Suddenly, as evening came – and the minister continued to plead passionately with both sides – the crofters' resistance came to an end, like an Atlantic gale that blows itself out into a zephyr. The confrontation was over.

Next morning the tenants put their names to a bond, promising that they would emigrate to Canada whenever and however Lord Macdonald decided. All their stock was surrendered to Cooper at his valuation, though each family was allowed to keep a cow and a pony, the cow for milk, the pony for carrying peat. The prisoners – Roderick MacPhail, Archibald Maclean, Archibald Boyd and Roderick MacCuish – were released on bail guaranteed by the Rev. Finlay MacRae and on his word that they would surrender themselves for trial when called.

But the story of the Sollas affair was not yet finished. Indeed, its futility is still being demonstrated in the crofting history of Scotland.

On 13 September 1849 the arrested men were tried before Lord Cockburn, charged with mobbing, rioting, and obstructing and deforcing officers of the law in the execution of their duties.

In the interval between the confrontation at Sollas and the trial in Inverness public opinion had taken a curious turn. Sympathy was strong, not only for the crofters but also for Lord Macdonald, who had come to be regarded as 'the victim of events rather than the creator of them'. This would seem to support Old Angus's belief that the 'Lord of the Isles' had a decent side to him. But – I wonder? In the Highlands of a century ago a person called Macdonald was liable to be more warmly regarded than somebody with a name like – for example

– Cooper. In any case, Cooper was merely an employee of the owner of the land. President Truman had a notice in the White House: 'The buck stops here.' A similar notice would have been appropriate in Armadale Castle.

Lord Cockburn concluded his summing up of the trial with these words: 'Your duty and mine is simply to uphold the majesty of the law. . . . I have no facts before me from which to applaud Lord Macdonald or the people. I do not wish to give an opinion, and so help me God I have no opinion on the subject!'

The jury, however, were untroubled by considerations of neutrality or legality. They found the accused guilty – on the evidence they could do nothing else – but recommended them 'to the utmost leniency and mercy of the Court in consideration of the cruel, though it may be legal, proceedings adopted in ejecting the whole people of Sollas'.

The spectators in the court-room rose to their feet, shouting and clapping. Lord Cockburn silenced them. Unemotionally – but betraying a personal opinion after all? – he said he found no reason to impose severe sentences. Four months in prison for each of the accused would be enough.

Before autumn was at an end Roderick MacPhail, Archibald Maclean, Archibald Boyd and Roderick MacCuish were back in North Uist, telling the tale of their adventures to Old Angus. They were full of wonder that, in spite of every indication to the contrary, justice could still be found in the hearts of powerful men.

But now comes the irony. It may be that Lord Macdonald was reluctant to flout public opinion and send his tenants away from Sollas. Or it may be that Patrick Cooper and his henchmen were less than efficient. In the event, though in January 1850 Cooper did warn the crofters that they should get ready to leave for America, in July, when they should have gone, they were still in Sollas.

Two months later, however, to the surprise and dismay of every islander, they were suddenly removed, lock, stock and barrel, to Loch Efort, in the south of the island, where each family was given twenty acres.

The land at Loch Efort was poor and some distance from the sea. The crofters, already demoralized by uncertainty, became even more confused and unhappy. Their morale reached so low an ebb that in the end they petitioned Lord Macdonald to send them to Australia. After long months of argument he agreed to help the emigration of the young and the healthy. He would do nothing for the aged and the sick.

In December 1852 the Sollas people were herded aboard the steamer *Celt*, bound for Campbeltown, here in Kintyre. At Campbeltown they were transferred with other emigrants – some from Southend – to the frigate *Hercules*. When the *Hercules* stopped for water and mails at Queenstown, in Ireland, a number of the emigrants were found to be suffering from smallpox.

How many of the victims remembered, in their suffering, the cool breezes of Sollas?

It was all a mess, a 'muck-up': an example of what can happen when respect for individual freedom becomes a matter for contempt. No wonder, in the Highlands of Scotland today, we are suspicious of absentee landlords, of cold bureaucracy, of government from a distance. No wonder the songs of North Uist are sometimes incredibly sad.

And yet it seems to me that my great-grandfather, on the evidence of some good words he had to say about Lord Macdonald – whose family the MacVicars had no reason to love – retained a sense of proportion. So did the Padre, who was always prepared to admit that a few – if only a *very* few – of the Sollas crofters were inclined to be lazy and inefficient and that Lord Macdonald, ill served by his commissioner and lacking funds, may have been weak and vacillating rather than positively villainous. But in his Hebridean heart there continued to exist sympathy for those without money or privilege. In any argument he would almost invariably take the side of the underdog.

It may have been an ancestral instinct that prompted him, in

1929, when minister of Southend, to stand for election to the Argyll County Council against the Duke of Argyll's factor, who opposed the idea of subsidized houses for agricultural workers. Most of his parishioners rented farms from the Duke, and it was a nine days' wonder, therefore, when he won by a large majority. 'That day,' commented the *Campbeltown Courier*, 'there must have been more false faces in Southend than at Hallowe'en.' I think the faces were all true – the faces of democracy upturned against those of bland, uncaring power.

I think I have the same instinct as the Padre. All my life I have been inclined to support the meek and the humble, sometimes without cause.

It has also taken me a long time to learn how to accept favours with grace and gratitude. Even yet, realizing how privileged I am to be a son of the Manse, and remembering the agony of my forbears on Sollas, I experience pangs of guilt. I try to do my best for those denied good fortune. The question is, have I tried hard enough?

In Southend, in contrast to North Uist and other parts of the Highlands, there is no history of forced Clearances. And yet, from about 1750 to the beginning of the current century, people regularly left Southend seeking a better living in Canada, Australia, New Zealand and America. Around 1750 the population of the parish was approximately 3000. When my father became minister in 1910 it had dwindled almost to its present level of about 500.

In a paper published in 1962 by the State Department of Archives and History in North Carolina, concerning men and women from Kintyre who settled there in the years 1774–5, the following reasons are given for their emigration: 'low wages, high rents, low prices of cattle, high prices of bread due to distilling, the conversion of arable lands into sheep pastures, and the exactions of landlords'.

Around the rocky shorelands of Southend there can still be seen, grass-grown and deserted, the ruins of the townships from which some of those people came. Balmagomery, Balmacvicar, Balimacmurchie, Balinamoil – the names are like an old song sighing down the wind. Today such places appear to be of interest only to local shepherds and to the Royal Commission on the Ancient and Historical Monuments of Scotland.

But when strangers from overseas come to visit us, sometimes an old song can acquire a new and vigorous tune.

In the summer of 1975 Mrs Harvey B. Hunter of Charlotte, North Carolina, unexpectedly dropped in to see us. She was accompanied by her daughter-in-law, a lecturer in history at the University of North Carolina.

Mrs Hunter is a formidable lady, eighty years of age, who, with the help of two sons, conducts the business of a large dairy farm. At the gate of her house, she told me – in an attractive Southern accent which I had imagined existed only in the movies – there stands the model of a cow, twenty feet high.

She and her daughter-in-law had less than three hours to spare. Could I, in that time, give her any information about her ancestor, Daniel Caldwell, who had emigrated from Southend in 1774? She showed me a copy of the testimonial to his good character which he had carried with him to America. It was signed by David Campbell, minister of Southend, and John Reid, elder.

We stood on Achnamara lawn, looking out over the sunlit bay at the Rock of Dunaverty and at the old jetty which lies close to it. American hustle is all very well, but this was ridiculous. Nevertheless, in courtesy to strangers, I exercised my brain – a notable effort immediately after lunch on a warm afternoon – and presently there came to me a story told by Jean's late father, old Willie McKerral: about people named Caldwell who had helped his own family in private distilling operations. 'Excuse me a minute,' I said.

I went into the house and rang up Jean's sister-in-law, Nellie McKerral. She and her husband possessed, I knew, some family papers which might indicate where the Caldwells had lived in

Southend. Sure enough, they did. In 1774, the Caldwell's had been tenants in the farm of Christlach.

I went back out on to the lawn, where the ladies were talking to Jean and admiring our roses. They reckoned they were better roses than they themselves could grow in North Carolina. Delighted by such evidence of American magnanimity, I cut two of the best blooms and presented them with one each.

I looked out over the bay again, at the jetty near Dunaverty, and another memory occurred to me.

'Do you know the month in 1774 when Daniel Caldwell left Southend?'

'August,' said Mrs Hunter.

'The ship he sailed in – was she by any chance the *Ulysses*?'

'Say, that was the very name! How did you know?'

I knew because I had heard of the *Ulysses* from many of the old story-tellers of Southend: how she had anchored in the bay while emigrants were taken out from the jetty beneath Dunaverty in a small boat and someone on the shore had played a lament on the bagpipes.

'Your ancestor,' I told Mrs Hunter, 'sailed for America from out there, less than half a mile from where you are standing now.'

She found words difficult. Her daughter-in-law made notes and worked hard with her camera.

'Now then,' I said, 'we'll use my car and have a look around.'

I stopped first at the graveyard at Keil, where I showed them the gravestone of John Reid, the elder who had signed Daniel Caldwell's testimonial. I told them that his descendants still lived in the parish and that a modern John Reid is a close friend of mine.

Mrs Hunter was all eyes, scrambling about the knolls and hollows of the ancient burying place like an adolescent. I admired her fitness and said so. 'I can still take a ladder and repair the roof of our chicken-run,' she announced, somewhat tartly. Her daughter-in-law took more photographs.

Then I drove them three miles north to Christlach Farm,

where Daniel Caldwell had tried to help the meagre family income by working – without much success, it appears – as a part-time shoe-maker. More photographs were taken. Mrs Hunter sighed. 'Just wait,' she said. 'Just wait till I tell them about this back home!'

Finally we went to the church: St Blaan's Kirk in the centre of the parish, in which the Padre had preached for forty-seven years. I told them it had been built in 1773 and opened for public worship early in 1774. I explained also that the pews of Norwegian pine were the original ones, unchanged for more than 200 years.

While her daughter-in-law used her camera and made still more notes, I led Mrs Hunter to a back pew. Sunlight fell on it from one of the small lead-paned windows. Its colour was golden brown. 'This is the Christlach seat,' I told her. 'The present owner of the farm still claims it. Your ancestor, Daniel Caldwell, was obviously a good church-goer, otherwise he wouldn't have got a testimonial signed by both the minister and an elder. In the early part of 1774, therefore, he must often have sat in this actual pew, before leaving in August. Come, Mrs Hunter, sit where he sat. Two hundred years doesn't seem such a long time now, does it?'

She sat carefully on the polished pine. For a long minute she said nothing, staring up at the empty pulpit. Then, quietly, she began to cry. 'Oh, my,' she said, 'this is the most wunnerful day of ma life!'

It was a wonderful day for me, too. It's not often one finds oneself in the privileged position of making another human being completely happy.

6

Upon a Sabbath Day it Fell

When we were boys at the Manse, the Sabbath was a day of discipline: but discipline often alleviated by private amusement.

Being the principal actor in the scene, with a service to conduct and a sermon to preach, the Padre spent the morning in a tense and anxious mood, like a champion boxer before a fight. During the time between breakfast – which almost invariably consisted of bacon and eggs, tea, my mother's soda scones and bramble jelly – and the moment of his entering the pulpit at mid-day, my mother and Maimie acted as his trainer and chief second, pandering to his needs both spiritual and physical. Archie and Willie and I were instructed to behave ourselves and to keep well out of his way.

We made certain that we kept out of his way, because Christian tolerance to his family was not one of the Padre's outstanding characteristics on a Sunday morning. None of us, for example, went near the bathroom at this time, because, in his opinion, a movement of the bowels was essential before good preaching, and the mood to achieve it might come upon him at any minute between ten o'clock and half past eleven.

Once, before experience shed light on the situation, Willie went to the bathroom at eleven o'clock, carefully shutting himself in by securing the small brass chain attached to the door. A few minutes later the Padre came quickly upstairs, intent upon action, and found his way to fulfilment blocked.

'Who's in there?' he thundered.

'It's me,' squeaked Willie.

'Come out at once and let me in!'

'But I'm just in the middle of – '

'Open this door!'

'But, Dadda – '

In a crisis the Padre was inclined to be impulsive. 'Blasted boy!' he roared and thrust so vigorous a shoulder at the door that the brass chain was torn from its screws. Next moment Willie was yanked off the lavatory seat (where he had been comfortably reading *Comic Cuts*) and hurled out, bare-bottomed, on to the landing. His trousers were thrown after him and the door slammed shut.

Even into old age – and not only on a Sunday – the Padre considered that a daily bowel movement (in the morning) was essential to good health. To make sure it came to him he cultivated two unvarying habits.

The first was a nightly glass of Eno's Fruit Salt. At about half past midnight, his regular bed-time, the peace of the Manse was shattered by a loud bang and double thud as he closed the outside front door and shot the rusty bolts. Then, at speed, he padded along the passage towards the kitchen and the scullery beyond, where the cold tap was turned on, a tumbler filled, the Eno's spooned in and loudly stirred. After only a short pause for drinking, the spoon was hurled with a crash into the empty tumbler. Thereafter the footsteps receded, a bedroom door banged and blessed silence fell upon the house.

As a small boy, my brother Kenneth slept in the bedroom above the kitchen with his youngest brother John. He remembers how, one night, disturbed by the usual post-midnight commotion, he waited breathlessly for the crash of the teaspoon in the tumbler. It didn't come. According to his own story he failed to sleep another wink, wondering what had happened. Subsequent delicate inquiries revealed that on this occasion the spoon had missed its target and landed softly and silently on a dishcloth which Maimie had left steeping in the sink.

The Padre's second habit in aid of bowel movement was smoking. At one time he had a pipe and, in memory of less inhibited Edwardian days, made good use of a spittoon. (After his retirement he discarded both pipe and spittoon and took to cigarettes. At the age of ninety-two he was a twenty-a-day man.) Immediately after breakfast he sat down purposefully by the dining-room fire, lit up and, brooking no interruption, kept on smoking and spitting until the call came.

On weekdays, though sometimes fraught, the operation was fairly leisurely. On a Sunday, because of the half-past-eleven deadline, it was much more furious and concentrated. But when my mother's prayers were answered and the bowel movement was at last successfully accomplished, he would come downstairs, slip-slopping in his slippers. 'Maimie,' he'd shout, 'bring me my boots!' (He never wore shoes, his idea being that they allowed his ankles to get cold.)

The boots would be toasting by the kitchen fire. Maimie would bring them and silently hand them over to my mother in the dining-room. She, devoted soul, would kneel down and patiently help the champ to pull them on and lace them up. Frequently, if she fumbled or her hands got in the way of his hard, darting fingers, she was rewarded by agonized groans of reproof and protest.

Then, exhausted by hard work in the bathroom and by much struggling with his boots, the Padre would lean back in his armchair. 'Mamma, my baking soda!' he'd cry.

'Yes, dear. Just a minute. I'll get it from the kitchen.'

'Look at the time! Nearly half past eleven.'

'There's no hurry. The church is only two hundred yards away.'

'I know, I know. But before you've all titivated yourselves . . . Nobody in this house has any idea of time!'

She would bring the baking soda, mixed in a glass of buttermilk. It was supposed to relieve flatulence, but the way he gulped it down usually aggravated the symptoms. 'I'm not feeling well at all,' he would inform her.

'You'll be fine once you get into the pulpit.'

'Easy to say! Go and get your hat on. And where are the boys? *Chiall beannachd mi*, why can't they be ready when they're wanted?'

But we *were* ready: paternal wrath on a Sabbath morning was even more awful than on week-days. We were lined up in the hall wearing our starched Eton collars, serge suits, knitted stockings and scuff-proof boots. So was Maimie, in frilly grey, a fugitive from cold meats already sliced, the potatoes and vegetables left simmering on the kitchen range.

Our parents led the way to the church, the Padre in black trousers, black frock coat and black, flat-topped clerical hat, my mother at times quite dashing, we thought, in a wide hat, white blouse, dark blue jacket and fashionable 'hobble' skirt. Archie and Willie and I came behind with Maimie – down the Manse drive, along the road and across the gravel towards the vestry door. We remained silent except when we met somebody and grave Sunday morning greetings had to be exchanged.

It used to puzzle us why everything was so 'black' and stern, especially when one of the hymns we were going to sing might well be 'Let all with heart and voice before His throne rejoice'. We had a vague apprehension that it had to do with mourning for the death of Christ. But in our simple minds two questions jostled for answers. Why, when we were taught in Sunday School that Christ died to make us happy, should everybody be so gloomy about it? Was it fair to Him?

Underneath the discipline we were reasonably happy ourselves. We grinned and winked at other boys in similar restraint. Once inside the church and seated in the Manse pew, we settled down contentedly, thinking our own thoughts. These might concern stamps on approval or a big salmon spotted the evening before in the Minister's Lynn or a game of football arranged for after school the following day. They beguiled the long minutes during which we waited with hope for amusing developments during the service.

We enjoyed no deep religious experience; but as we looked round at the congregation, at the sturdy pulpit bulging above the choir stalls, at the two great stained-glass windows on either side of it presented by the Dowager Duchess of Argyll – one in memory of her late husband, the eighth Duke, the other in memory of Queen Victoria – we had the comfortable feeling that God was in His heaven and that our world was all right. The faint odours coming from the water heaters, the paraffin lamps and the varnished pews, the quietness of the place suddenly enlivened by the ringing of the old cracked bell (which had been taken from a ship wrecked on the island of Sanda) – all added to our sense of security.

Then the bell stopped ringing, Mary Barbour began playing the organ, pedalling vigorously, and Old Archie the beadle stumped in with 'the Books' and placed them with professional reverence in the pulpit. Immediately afterwards the champ made his entrance, swishing down the aisle resplendent in white collar bands, black cassock, black robes and the purple hood of an arts graduate of Glasgow University. My mother, having assisted Old Archie in the proper dressing of her nerve-racked husband, slipped into the pew beside us with a shaky smile of relief.

The organ stopped. The Padre stood up in the pulpit, looked round at the congregation, raised his eyes to the dark pine beams supporting the roof and, in a loud, authoritative voice, announced: 'Let us worship God . . .' No sign of frustration or anxiety marred his holy countenance. After the service visitors to the church came to my mother and told her of the inspiration they had received from the calm dignity of his bearing, from the sincerity of his preaching (which often dealt with the patient acceptance of suffering) and from the compassionate regard for humanity evident in all his prayers. My mother would nod and smile, giving the impression that she was well aware of her privileged position as helpmeet to such a great and noble character.

The Padre was a good minister. He was also a good man. But as far as we were concerned the dog-collar that he invariably wore never camouflaged his human weaknesses. Many people in Southend recognized them, too; but I believe his influence in the parish was all the greater because of them.

There were times, during a service, when his native Gaelic tongue betrayed him.

He could never pronounce 'Egyptian'. It always came out as 'Eepgyptian', and when he began to read a biblical passage on the subject of the Exodus we were filled with happy anticipation.

Another word he mispronounced was 'bowl'. At home he handled it perfectly, as when, for example he referred to the sugar bowl – which was frequently, four spoonfuls of sugar being his normal ration in a cup of tea. But in church, reading a passage containing the same word, he always said 'bowel'. 'Or ever the silver cord be loosed, or the golden *bowel* be broken . . .' Did he consider 'bowel' a properly 'olde worlde' rendering of Holy Writ, or, in view of the alarms on a Sunday morning, was it a Freudian slip?

Another word with which he had difficulty was 'cock'. The Gaelic for a hill is *cnoc*, pronounced (with a nasal intonation) as 'chrock'. I think confusion must have occurred in his mind between 'cock' and *cnoc*, because sometimes the former would emerge in his preaching as 'crock'.

There was one splendid day – splendid, that is, for us boys and for some youthful members of the choir – when he delivered a sermon on St Peter and 'the crowing of the crock – I beg your pardon, the cock'. He repeated the mistake so often that one young bass singer in the choir contracted a wheezing cough which threatened to become infectious. Eventually the Padre was begging nobody's pardon. Above his gold-rimmed, half-moon spectacles he was glowering in terrible anger at the choir.

The crisis passed, however, and all might have been forgotten had it not been for his habit of never leaving well alone. The following Sabbath he announced his text and then, in a hearty voice, began: 'Last Sunday, my friends, I spoke to you of redemption, taking as my starting point the story of St Peter and the crowing of the crock – ' He paused. The congregation took a deep breath and held it. He flushed bright red and glared at the choir. 'The COCK!' he roared, defiantly. The young bass, with a whine of agony, slipped from his seat and hid himself beneath the book-board.

There followed a silence, broken only by sobs in various parts of the church, none of which had sad tears in them. The champ removed his spectacles and began using his eyes like those of a lion-tamer. Soon he regained control. Holiness was restored. The sermon continued.

But never again did he refer to 'the crowing of the cock' from St Blaan's pulpit.

Occasionally Archie and Willie and I were diverted by other happenings.

There was a Sunday when a sparrow appeared in the midst of the congregation, flying back and forth between two sides of the gallery with remorseless energy. Everybody did their best to ignore it – everybody, that is, except old Hugh McEachran, the Kirk Treasurer, who made two wild attempts to capture it, on his second try stumbling over the end of a pew and grabbing Mrs MacAlpine's new hat instead. The Padre stopped preaching, snatched off his spectacles, fixed his friend Hugh with hot blue eyes and ordered 'Leave the blasted thing alone!'

There was also the Sunday when a mouse caused havoc.

From time immemorial, like many another church in Scotland, St Blaan's has had a mouse. On weekdays our new organ is wrapped around in plastic because of it. Seldom, however, does it appear when the church is full of people, preferring to remain concealed and warm in the boiler-house.

But on this particular Sunday our mouse did appear, scampering purposefully along the central aisle and then turning left to dart among the choir girls' feet. A commotion began. Quick movements were punctuated by squeals and giggles. Long skirts were wrapped tightly around close-locked knees. The Padre, on the point of announcing a hymn, looked down with irritation combined with a fair amount of interest. 'What's going on?' he demanded.

Encouraged, the young bass went into action. 'It's a mouse, sir. I'll get it!'

Without delay – and obviously not unwillingly – he plunged down among the distracted legs of the choir girls, emerging a few moments later with the mouse in one hand. He held it up for inspection.

The Padre raised a pointing hand. 'Take it,' he began, then paused, searching for the right word. 'Take it hence!' he commanded finally, like a prophet.

The young bass obeyed. The mouse was put back in its proper place among the boiler pipes. There was no danger of it dying for its sins – or for the sins of others. Superstition in Scotland decrees that a church mouse is not for killing.

During the whole incident Archie and Willie and I sat silent. Our eyes were downcast but our hearts were happy. That morning, while the Padre laboured in the bathroom, we had taken some cheese from the pantry when Maimie wasn't looking and had scattered crumbs inside the church, sparsely along the central aisle, generously in the choir stalls. We had tried it once or twice before, without success; but now, at last, the ploy had worked.

This is the first time the truth has been told. I apologize to those former choir girls who are still alive and will, I hope, remain my friends.

After the morning service the Padre was a changed man. A burden had been lifted. Life was good. At lunch he was kind and considerate to us all, basking in my mother's warm praise for his sermon. After lunch he retired to his bedroom for what he called 'my snooze', which sometimes lasted until four o'clock.

When we – 'the boys' as he always called us until the day of his death, at which time I, for one, was over sixty – when we grew up and had attained what he considered to be a suitable state of maturity, he would ask for our opinions regarding his preaching.

'Well, Angus, what did you think of my sermon today? Good, wasn't it?'

Such an approach made it hard to be adversely critical. So I never was. Nor, in fact, had I ever much reason to be. The Padre could compose a first-class sermon, packed with knowledge, both worldly and mystical. As a rule it was generously illustrated by suitable stories, most of which he culled from memories of his own younger days in North Uist and from the writings of F. W. Boreham, the Australian minister whose books, countless in number, were best-sellers in the years following the First World War.

One of his illustrative stories has always been a help to me in times of trouble and confusion. It concerns a painting called *Checkmate*. The picture shows two men playing chess, one glum and despondent, the other moving his queen and triumphantly announcing 'Checkmate!' But when it was hung in the Royal Academy, a study of the pieces on the board by a chess master revealed that the man who has apparently lost can still make a move – and win.

Not long ago I wanted to tell this story on a television programme and tried to find a reproduction of the painting. Surprisingly, all my efforts failed. Everybody I asked had heard of the picture, but none had ever seen a copy or knew the name of the artist. If anyone can tell me who painted *Checkmate* and the whereabouts of the original picture, I should be grateful.

While the Padre was enjoying his 'snooze' and my mother and Maimie had a deserved rest after the events of the morning, we – 'the boys' – were free to follow our own devices, always provided that such devices were in keeping with Sabbath decorum.

If the weather was wet or stormy we stayed indoors and read books chosen from the Padre's wide-ranging library. (I remember three which gave me warm pleasure and probably fuelled my ambition to become a story-teller: *Guy Mannering*, *Lorna Doone* and *Kidnapped*. More than fifty years later I have still to find three contemporary novels with better plots.) But if the sun shone we were out and about, perhaps crawling among the whins on the hill behind the Manse looking for birds' nests, perhaps surveying the river where lurked the red-spotted salmon, perhaps clambering and scuffling along the shore on the trail of interesting flotsam, perhaps visiting Hughie Stewart in his usual 'howff' above the jetty at Dunaverty and listening eagerly to his stories of the sea.

One Sunday afternoon we discovered among the pebbles on Macharioch beach a few fragments of an amber-coloured substance, scarred and sea-washed. We brought them to Hughie.

'Bits o' resin,' he told us. 'They've been lyin' there, at Macharioch, since the wreck o' the *Argo* in 1903.'

'Tell us about the *Argo*, Hughie.'

He was happy to oblige. It is one of the stories that has become legendary in Southend. Some years ago I discovered a more detailed and accurate account of it in the records of the Royal National Life-boat Institution.

In the early morning of 27 February 1903 the *Argo* of Fredestrand in Norway, a barque of 585 tons, was making her way into the Irish Sea through the North Channel. Carrying a cargo of resin, she was coming near the end of a long journey from Wilmington, North Carolina, to London. A stiff south-east wind was blowing, and in the cold and the dark Captain Eilefson found his ship being driven ashore on the Arranman's Barrels, a dangerous reef about two miles east of Dunaverty on the Southend coast. Soon after seven o'clock, just as it was getting light, she struck.

At that time the Campbeltown life-boat was the *James Stevens II*. The coxswain was George McEachran – 'a big burly whiskery man', according to Hughie – with over a dozen rescues to his credit. The standard crew of a sailing and rowing life-boat like the *James Stevens II* numbered sixteen, double the complement of a modern boat. But that morning most of the enrolled members were absent at the herring-fishing, and when she was launched at 9.30 a.m. George McEachran had with him no less than ten volunteers out of a total of fourteen men.

By half past nine the wind changed to a whole gale from the west-nor'-west, and the life-boat, under sail, had to contend not only with heavy seas but also with hurricane squalls carrying sleet and rain. At 11.30 a.m., however, she was standing off the Arranman's Barrels, in full view of the wreck.

George McEachran now found himself with a problem experienced by all life-boat coxswains. To reach the *Argo* he had to go straight in against the gale.

Meanwhile, anticipating what might happen, the life-boat secretary at Campbeltown had asked the Clyde Shipping Company's tug, *Flying Dutchman*, to follow the *James Stevens II*. The tug had done so, and what happened then can best be told, I think, in George McEachran's own account in the official return of service filed by the RNLI:

'When we got beyond the Bastard Rocks, the wind was dead ahead so signalled the tug to take the life-boat in tow. We were towed to within half-a-mile of the wreck. Found *Argo* on a reef of rocks, hull almost under water. Her crew of nine men were in the rigging. Just as we got there her masts broke and fell overboard. The *Argo* was now on her beam ends, and the crew got outside of the hull on the port side. She was fast breaking up, seas breaking over her.

'In the life-boat we let go the anchor to windward and veered down to the wreck. Got a line made fast and hauled alongside after some bother. Got all nine men off (one man helpless through cold, etc.) and immediately picked up anchor and set sail.

'Off Ruadh Point we went alongside the tug and placed the rescued men aboard her for treatment. The tug took the life-boat in tow again and proceeded full speed to Campbeltown, reaching there at 1.45 p.m. The rescued crew were very kindly treated on the tug and supplied with food and warm drinks and dry clothes.

'Shortly after the crew were taken off, the *Argo* broke up or else sank deeper, for only her port rail could be seen above water. Great credit is due to the tug captain for so smartly coming to assist, as otherwise the life-boat might have been too late.

'Before the arrival of the life-boat, three men from the *Argo* had got ashore in the vessel's small boat. Sorry to say, two of these and a landsman had taken a shore-boat to try and rescue the others, but it was blown to sea and no word of her has been got.'

This return of service reveals a life-boat coxswain's typical modesty. George McEachran, who wrote it, remains anonymous throughout, inferring that he acted only as a member of a team, and no doubt this is exactly how he did regard himself. His warm approval of the kindness shown by the tug men to the rescued crew is evidence of a trait in every good coxswain's character – deep concern for the welfare of others. But Hughie Stewart's account was full of praise for the 'whiskery man's' seamanship and for the courage with which he tackled a difficult operation.

Hughie was also able to supply us with two additional pieces of information – one sad, one happy.

The 'landsman' who had tried to row out to the wreck, along with two of the *Argo*'s crew, was a gardener at Macharioch House, in the employ of the Dowager Duchess of Argyll. Weeks later his body and those of the two crewmen were washed ashore on the Ayrshire coast.

The last crewman to be rescued from the barque was, in Hughie's words, 'the cabin boy'. In his arms he carried a fighting black tom cat. He was scratched all over and suffered pain as the salt spray entered his wounds, but 'he hung on like a fury and the cat was saved'.

Hughie had been there that day. He had seen it all happen.

The *Argo* rescue was the first by the Campbeltown life-boat to become internationally famous, and in due course George McEachran and his men were presented with specially minted medals by King Oscar of Norway. I have seen several of these medals, proud possessions in a number of Campbeltown families.

For Hughie the story ended there. For me it didn't.

In the winter of 1951, during a violent storm, the British steamer *Solidarity* was on her beam ends, fifty miles off Romsdal on the Norwegian coast. As her captain said afterwards, 'it looked like curtains' for the twenty-four men on board. Before the radio broke down, however, they had been able to broadcast a distress call, and suddenly, just as they were giving up hope, a small boat appeared, leaping and plunging in the wild sea. She was the Norwegian life-boat *Larvick*. In the next hour, with superb skill, her crew rescued all the British seamen.

In due course the Norwegian life-boatmen received the warm thanks of the British government and were presented with specially minted medals.

When I read this story in the life-boat magazine and remembered Old Hughie's tale of the *Argo* it occurred to me that here was an instance of how the faithful carrying out of an ideal can pay dividends – dividends measured not in cash but in humanity. I suggested to the Padre that he might be able to use it in a sermon. He was immediately enthusiastic and reminded me of another example of the same kind of thing.

A voluntary life-boat service was the brainchild of Sir William Hillary, a sturdy Yorkshireman born in 1771. In the rules of the Royal National Life-boat Institution, founded in 1824, it is laid down that 'the people and vessels of every nation, whether in peace or in war' shall be 'equal objects of the Institution'.

During the Battle of Britain in the Second World War, the life-boatmen of Ramsgate rescued a British airman, whose plane had been shot down in the English Channel. To their astonishment they found he was Pilot Officer Richard Pope Hillary, author of the famous book, *The Last Enemy*. He was also Sir William Hillary's nephew in the fifth generation.

I believe – as my father did – that when properly examined the books of humanity always reveal an impeccable balance.

7

Red Flares on the Iron Rock

Southend is bounded on three of its four sides by the sea. Ever since we were children it has been in the background of our lives, lapping pale blue on summer sand, heaving sullenly against the rocks in a March sou'-easter, raging and bursting high against Dunaverty Rock when a West Indian hurricane trails a dying edge along the Hebrides.

We built Achnamara in 1936, a mile and a half south of the Manse and only a few yards above the beach. On a day of sunlight the reflection of Dunaverty shimmers towards us across Machribeg Bay. When the wind blows, and the North Channel is filled by galloping white horses, spray hurtles like sleet against our front windows, and afterwards, wielding a cleansing hose, Jean is inspired to make a few unladylike comments. During the first week in our new bungalow we went to sleep with the grumble of the waves monotonous in our ears. Since then we have become inured to the sound and are surprised when a visitor remarks on the sea noises outside his bedroom window.

I think that the mood of the sea, as I view it each day from my desk, has an influence on mine and is often the deciding factor in how and what I write. Sometimes it causes a poem to stir inside my head – a poem burgeoning out of formless ancestral memories – and I have difficulty in reminding myself that I do not possess the genius of a poet and that if I want to earn a living I must concentrate on more prosaic and more profitable ways of writing. (But when the urge to poetry is there I believe that my writing, no matter how prosaic the subject, is the better for it: simpler and less involved, because the vision is clearer.)

The sea is like life: you can never be sure of it. There is a Gaelic proverb which says this, and I believe my brothers and I have the same loving, respectful and sometimes vaguely fearful relationship with it as had the Padre and his North Uist forbears.

I think it was from them that Willie inherited his ambition to be a seaman. I remember him at the age of seven climbing a tall copper beech in the Manse garden and sitting there for hours, looking out at Sanda Sound, through which, before Board of Trade regulations were revised after the Second World War, many of the liners bound for America used to pass. The *Caledonia*, pride of the Anchor Line, was one of these. 'Some day,' he would tell us, with confidence, 'I'll be captain of the *Caledonia* and give you all a hoot on the siren when I'm passing.' Twenty-five years later he was – and did.

There was something else we inherited from seafaring ancestors. None of us has ever been troubled by seasickness. During the Second World War Archie and I spent a greal deal of time in troopships. Though in the RAF, Kenneth was also faced by long sea journeys, to America for training and to the Far East for operations. During his National Service John sailed to Singapore and back. During *his* National Service, Jock sailed to Cyprus with the Argylls and, on the way home, acted as a ship's policeman. For us all such cruises were happy holidays, our keen appetites assuaged by mounds of tasty rations spurned by less fortunate friends.

Rona had the same immunity.

In the spring of 1947 the three roads to Southend were blocked by heavy falls of snow. Telephone lines were down, drifts piled high above many of the poles; but on the morning of 15 March, for some technical reason, one local subscriber was able to get through to Campbeltown. He reported that our food and fuel supplies were running short and that an expectant mother needed medical aid.

The Campbeltown life-boat was called out, and Coxswain Duncan Newlands made a difficult journey to Dunaverty, carrying groceries, fuel oil, mail and newspapers. He also brought a doctor, a nurse and Rona, who was then a teacher in the grammar school and had been marooned in a Campbeltown hotel for almost a week. As I helped to unload the life-boat Duncan was in one of his puckish, highfalutin' moods. 'I pulled the doctor's leg,' he told me, 'saying it was a pity Rona should be so full of *joie de vivre* while he was so full of *mal de mer*.'

The coasts of Southend are littered with the skeletons of ships. More than 1400 years ago we believe that St Columba, with his discples, made a safe landing from a coracle at Keil. Since then other seamen have not been so lucky. The racing tides at the Mull and the wind swirling and bouncing back off the cliffs at Borgadaile Point, together with the fog which often moves in quietly and quickly across the Firth of Clyde, make navigation in the North Channel difficult even for experts.

On a summer's day the sea around us may look friendly and serene; but because of the sudden changes that can affect our weather any amateur with an urge to sail in it is advised to consult the coastguards before he does so. Every year holiday-makers come with their frail sailing dinghies and fibre-glass punts powered by outboard motors. Every year the Campbeltown life-boat or the local IRB (Inshore Rescue Boat) has to render assistance to somebody whose craft has been overturned by a sudden squall or carried out into dangerous waters by the fast tides. Not long ago one of our girl visitors was rescued by a helicopter. The lilo on which she had been having a restful snooze had drifted out from Dunaverty and was heading rapidly for the Antrim coast.

Centuries ago, when human life was not so tenderly protected as it is in the second half of the twentieth century, gangs of wreckers lured many a vessel to destruction on the black rocks in front of Achnamara. On a dark and stormy night, at a time when Dunaverty Castle was unoccupied by the Clan Donald, they would climb the rock and fix a light on the battlements. Unsuspecting sailors, coming round the Mull, would take it for a light on the island of Sanda and alter course towards what they believed was Sanda Sound but which, in reality, was the jagged shoreline between Borgadaile and Dunaverty. When their vessel struck and they scrambled or swam ashore they would be met by cut-throat ruffians intent upon killing them and looting their cargoes.

Old Hughie Stewart used to tell a story about a Negro slave, the sole survivor from a Portuguese ship wrecked underneath the Borgadaile Cliff. On his back he carried a small wooden barrel containing gold and jewels belonging to his master, the captain. He was able to avoid the wreckers and began climbing the cliff.

This is a difficult and dangerous ploy even in daytime. I remember, several years ago, when a Peterhead fishing-skiff ran aground at the same place, being one of a rescue-party which, as the tide rose, was forced to use the cliff as a means of egress from the shore. Scared almost to the point of paralysis, I couldn't help imagining how the Negro must have felt in the gale-filled dark.

According to Old Hughie, however, he reached the top at last and made good his escape. But – and this is the twist to the tale – at some point in his climb he became so exhausted that he had to abandon the heavy barrel. The story goes that he buried it deep in a crevice in the cliff and that as he never returned to Southend after his ordeal, it must still be there, treasure-trove for a lucky finder.

I thought about this, too, on the day I climbed the cliff but had no desire to tarry in order to make a search.

The rocky shores of Sanda Island, which is part of the parish, are strewn with rotting wood and pieces of rusty metal from the carcases of dead ships. To the north-east of Sanda there is Paterson's Rock, a sharp-toothed islet reckoned to be the deadliest danger to shipping in the whole of the Firth of Clyde. About seventy years ago a diver named Gush was sent down to investigate a casualty on Paterson's Rock. He came up, weeping and on the point of collapse. 'The things I saw! The skeletons and the dead men waving their arms! The fish and the eels, huge and bloated, feeding on the corpses!' He gave up his job and never dived again.

When our visitor friends congregate at the inn to meet us and listen to our local yarns, that one frequently stops the show. There is a more pleasant story, however, about the ship whose long, curved keel and rib-cage can still be seen at low water on Brunerican sands, east of Dunaverty. She was the *Tantivy*, bound for the Clyde with a cargo of oranges from Spain.

It was a spring morning towards the end of last century, and Jean's father, at the time 'a big laddie' according to himself, was working in a field above the shore. Suddenly he saw the *Tantivy*, sails flapping, emerging from the fog in Sanda Sound and heading straight for the sands. He rushed to tell his father, Archie McKerral, who happened to be the Receiver of Wreck, and before the vessel struck almost all the able-bodied men in the parish had gathered and were waiting to give what help they could.

As the weather, apart from the fog, was mild and almost windless, the crewmen were rescued without much difficulty. But almost at once, owing to the ground swell, the *Tantivy* began breaking up. Oranges in their thousands floated ashore. The real job was put in hand, that of salvaging the cargo.

Over the next few days the oranges were taken away in horse-drawn carts and deposited in great yellow pyramids outside Brunerican Farm, under the eye of its tenant, the Receiver of Wreck. People from every part of Kintyre came to see the remarkable sight, some doubtless with the notion that they might be able to 'liberate' the odd orange or two. But Archie McKerral had mounted a strict guard, and soon feelings of frustration occurred, especially amongst the village boys. This, however, was temporarily relieved by the arrival on the scene of a black-bearded foreigner with a barrel-organ and a dancing bear. This man, it appears, was well known throughout Scotland at the period, attending fairs and other gatherings of country folk.

But on the night before the oranges were due to be removed by their owners, the village boys made a final effort. To their delight they were able to infiltrate the guards and get away with a whole sackful of fruit. In a dark house in Teapot Lane they gathered for the feast. Oranges were peeled. Strong white teeth sank into them. Juice squirted, appetizingly. But then the groans and the disillusion came. The oranges were for marmalade, so sour as to be inedible.

One of my father's predecessors, the Rev. Peter Thomson, whose congregation had suffered depletion on account of the dancing bear, preached a resounding sermon on the subject, drawing morals by the score. It is said, however, that during the following week he accepted gratefully the gift of a pot of marmalade from the mother of one of the boys.

In more modern times, thanks to powerful engines, a watchful coastguard service, radar and the radio-telephone, wrecks are not so common on our coasts. But gales still blow and the sea remains treacherous. In the January tempest of 1953 the *Princess Victoria* sank in the Irish Sea with the loss of 133 lives. Posted at Lloyd's as 'missing' were seven other vessels – the Swedish steamer *Aspo*, loaded with pit-props, the *Leopold Nera* from Zeebrugge, the *Salland* taking china-clay to Delfzyl and four trawlers from Grimsby, Lowestoft and Fleetwood. Power-driven, and with every available navigational aid at their disposal, they were all destroyed by the cruel sea. Life-boats and the devoted men who crew them are still an urgent necessity.

In Southend and Kintyre generally many of our sea stories concern rescues by the Campbeltown life-boat. One of the most dramatic occurred when censorship was in operation during the Second World War and it received scarcely any publicity. I think this ought to be remedied.

When my old friend Duncan Newlands retired in 1962 he had been a member of the crew of the Campbeltown life-boat for forty-one years and coxswain for eighteen. He had taken part in 100 services and helped to save more than 300 lives.

His decisions were always sharp. When still an ordinary life-boatman he saw a lug-sail boat capsizing in Campbeltown harbour and throwing its crew of two small boys into the water. He collected some of his mates at the quay-head, raced for the life-boat – which was lying handy at the pier – got the mechanic to start the motors and took command. Within minutes the boys were rescued and the life-boat was back at her moorings. Only then did Duncan realize the seriousness of his offence. He had, in effect, 'stolen' the life-boat.

Soon afterwards an inspector from the RNLI visited the town, and Duncan was worried: 'I was in a blue funk in case I'd be sacked from the service.' But the local life-boat secretary gave evidence that on the day in question no other boat had been available and that if young Newlands had not acted so promptly the boys would almost certainly have been drowned. After delivering a homily on the rules and regulations of the life-boat service, the inspector smiled, shook Duncan's hand and informed him that he had been promoted to the post of bowman.

Duncan always maintained hard discipline in the life-boat, but his brilliant seamanship and his ability to turn a dangerous situation into a kind of joke gave his crew unquestioning confidence in his leadership. For his part, he has never accepted personal credit for a daring rescue. 'The strength of the coxswain lies in the strength of the crew,' he keeps telling me. 'This is no false modesty. In the life-boat you're neither modest nor immodest: you face facts. Life-boatmen don't go for glory but to help people in distress. Sometimes we actually know the men we are trying to save; and we all have the thought at the back of our minds that it may be our turn next to pray for the help of the life-boat.'

His experience of the coastal waters of the Firth of Clyde has probably never been equalled, and I believe that the contours of the seabed in this area are as clear in his eye as the land-levels are in mine. On the night of 29 January 1945 it was fortunate that he possessed such expert knowledge.

All that day a blizzard had been howling through the streets at Campbeltown. The thermometer at naval headquarters in the requisitioned grammar school, HMS *Nimrod*, was registering a few degrees below freezing-point. A number of overhead lines had been damaged by the southerly gale; but the telephone in the life-boat secretary's home remained in working order. At 6.55 p.m. it began to ring.

The call was from the signal officer in *Nimrod*, relaying the information that red distress flares had been seen off the south end of Arran.

Earlier in the day, on account of the deteriorating weather, the naval authorities had closed the harbour. Shipping was at a standstill. Because of this A. P. (Tony) MacGrory, the honorary secretary, had now to go on foot to naval headquarters, so as to make it clear that the order could not – and would not – apply to the life-boat. After a considerable argument Tony MacGrory got his way and with the help of a messenger began calling out the life-boatmen, running from door to door in the black-out.

Coxswain Newlands was the first to be told. As he raced down to the life-boat shed on the New Quay the night was as black as a peat-bog, with the wind gusting up to force 8. Sea spray showered across tarred planking and empty bollards. In the jabbling water under the lee of the pier lay the *City of Glasgow*, a fifty-two-foot Barnett, moored close to a flight of wooden steps.

Five more members of the crew assembled in the shed – John McIntyre, second coxswain; Duncan Black, bowman; Duncan MacCallum, mechanic; and deck-hands James Lang and Archie Mackay. But two of the regular crew were missing. One, it appeared, was away from home. Another had a sprained ankle.

But now a volunteer came forward, offering to fill a place. He was young Dan Black, a son of the bowman.

Dan was only seventeen and had never been in the life-boat before, and at first Duncan did his best to dissuade him. But Dan's father said: 'If he wants to be a life-boatman, now's his chance to see what it's like.' In the end Duncan agreed to let him come, because, as he explained afterwards, the Blacks of

Campbeltown had the sea in their blood and service with the life-boat was a family tradition.

As the crew put on their oilskins, sea-boots and life-jackets and listened to the drone outside of the life-boat's motors warming up, Tony MacGrory told them briefly what he knew about the casualty. She was a naval trawler, the *Dunraven Castle*, with a complement of twenty-five officers and men.

Years later I heard the story of the service from Duncan himself. Here it is, with a few salty epithets omitted, but otherwise almost exactly as he told it to me.

'We got into the boat and set off about ten to eight. As the flares had been seen at the south end of Arran, I was pretty sure the wreck would be near the Iron Rock Ledges, so I set a course for them.

'It was wild out there in Kilbrannan Sound. Between the darkness and the clouds of spray – and the snow which stung our eyes like needles – we couldn't see much; but I calculated how long the *City of Glasgow* ought to take for the crossing – just over the hour – and let her go.

'I noticed Dan was a bit shaky. I knew he was thinking about his mother. She'd been through this kind of thing before, first with her own father, then with her husband. However, I reckoned Dan would be all right with the other lads. They'd steady him, and once we got to the wreck he wouldn't have much time to think about anything but the job.

'At nine o'clock I told Duncan MacCallum to slow the engines. Mac and I were in the boat together for a long time and worked very close. I couldn't see a thing but had a notion we weren't far from the Iron Rock Ledges. The lads used to say I smelt my way along, but the answer to that is just experience. Anyway, I told John McIntyre to put up a flare, and there we saw her, three hundred yards away on our starboard bow – the *Dunraven Castle*, fast on the ledges and listing over at forty-five degrees. Almost at once she put up a flare in answer to ours.

'It looked pretty desperate. Between us and the trawler was a scummy mass of foam, heaving about and looking like blood in the light of the flares. Through the snow and the spindrift we could see waves crashing up against her bows.

'I heard Dan saying he was scared. He wasn't the only one. As the life-boat rolled and dived, and the spray lashed into our faces, I kept wondering how the hell I was going to get close enough to do any good. But I said to myself: "Newlands, you're lucky finding her so quick. Keep the luck going, think fast."

'The obvious way in was straight ahead, through a gap in the rocks, but I had a queer feeling. Something kept telling me: "Not that way – watch your step." I'm not superstitious or anything like that. Maybe it was just instinct.

'I could see the lads were wondering what had come over me, so I made up my mind. "We'll go round and approach from the nor'ard," I said. "Then get under her lee."

'John McIntyre thought I was daft. "There's only a couple o' fathoms in the passage there. It's a risk."

' "That's what we're here for," I told him. "To take a risk. Anyway, her bottom's built to take a dunting."

'Dan didn't say anything. He was whiter than a sail, and his face was all eyes. I tried shouting a joke at him, and he did his best to smile back. Then I told Mac to give us three-quarter speed and steered for the passage.

'We went by the casualty broadside, plunging and swinging, with the spray blinding us, and got round on her lee side. We turned and got ready to go in. It was a chancy business, there's no denying it. I knew that with only a couple of fathoms below us the boat might be damaged, but I kept reminding myself that on account of her aircases and watertight compartments she'd still float us home.

'I put her at it, and in the heavy seas we went through that passage like a bucket in a burn. The hull jarred and crunched and bounced, but luckily the rocks were smooth, so we were all right.

'Then we ran into deeper water, swung in towards the *Dunraven Castle* and drove alongside. It would have been dangerous to hit her side on, so I went straight ahead, bow first. We got a bit of a bash as we struck her, but the only damage was to a fender-strap.

'I started using the loud hailer, shouting to the men aboard to catch a line. Duncan fired it, but the trawler's crew didn't seem to hear, and the rope slithered back over the side.

'Having lost way, the life-boat fell off again, so I went astern – and quick at that.

'I kept shouting, trying to tell the navymen that we intended to have another go but that if we didn't make it this time we'd have to lie off until daylight and then their chances would be poor. Whether they heard me or not I couldn't be certain.

'John McIntyre put up another flare and we drove in again. We struck the trawler's side, this time damaging the anchor-stanchion.

'Duncan Black fired a second line, and this time the men aboard must have heard me shouting, because to my relief half a dozen of them showed up at the rail. They caught the line, hauled the wire aboard and made fast.

'I shouted to them to use the wire and come down into the life-boat hand over hand, but at first they wouldn't risk it.

'Then I told John McIntyre to get a preventer out. This is a safety-device – a kind of insurance if you like – a second wire in case the first one bursts. It was a necessity that night on account of the heaving and pounding.

'When John had fixed it, two of the survivors took a chance and swung down aboard us. Just then the main wire burst, but the preventer held the life-boat till we managed to rig a double wire. Then the men began swinging and tumbling down. They were wet and freezing cold and their hands got cut on the wire.

'During one of the poundings, as a solid sea came up and struck our faces and we swallowed pints of salt water, John shouted: "Another one like that and we'll have no boat to take us home!"

' "Don't worry," I shouted back, "I'm just as anxious to get home as you are! I forgot to get insured!"

'Soon all the navymen were in the life-boat except the captain. He was having a last look round his ship, maybe sick in his heart at leaving her. But this wasn't a time for sentiment, because the life-boat was in a tight spot, so I yelled to him to hurry up, and my language wasn't too polite. He came to the rail, then hesitated, looking back over his shoulder. As he stood there another wire burst and he pulled himself together and came scrambling down.

'They were all aboard now, all twenty-five of them. I had a look at my watch and saw that the whole operation had lasted only fifteen minutes. I told Mac to hammer her astern.

'We cleared the rocks, and I set a course for Davaar Island at the mouth of Campbeltown Loch. Mac radioed the completion of the service.

'If anything, the weather was now worse, dark and squally and the snow thicker than ever. All I could see as we made our way across Kilbrannan Sound was the reflection of our green and red navigation lights swinging about on the broken water. It was so cold that I ordered a rum ration to be handed round and had a good swig of ginger-wine myself – being a teetotaller.

'Dan was more settled. He'd gone through a rough baptism all right, but from that time he never looked back. He became a regular member of the crew and one of the best men in the boat, a credit to a great seafaring family.

'We reached the pier at five past eleven and put the survivors ashore. As well as being the life-boat secretary, Tony MacGrory was the local representative of the Shipwrecked Fishermen and Mariners' Royal Benevolent Society. He had organized hot drinks, food and dry clothes, helped as usual by the ladies of the Life-boat Guild, and these were now given to the navymen in the life-boat shed.

'I remember that by then the snow had turned to pelting rain.'

When a life-boatman is persuaded to tell a story nobody can tell one better; but he always tends to make it sound far too simple and straightforward as far as his own involvement is concerned. The fact that the *City of Glasgow* went out that night in defiance of the naval authorities, who judged the weather to be too rough even for a life-boat, is mentioned by Duncan only in passing. The seamanship of the crew and his own superb skill – the result of years of experience and intelligent study – are not mentioned. He describes vividly the wild confusion of the sea on the Iron Rock Ledges; but his almost incredible feat of guiding the life-boat through those deadly rocks, in the roaring, spray-filled dark and with the boat swinging and heaving like a maddened animal, is left to the listener's imagination. And when I suggested the word bravery to him in connection with the service, I got an answer: 'Brave – me! You should see me at the dentist's!'

About twenty-five years ago I was writing a series of radio scripts for Kathleen Garscadden of Scottish Children's Hour, the general title being *I'm Proud of My Father*. In each one a child told the story of his or her father, who was, as a rule, a Scotsman of courage. We found firemen, air-line pilots, miners, members of mountain-rescue teams, all of whom were willing to take part. Then I decided that a life-boatman would be an ideal choice for the first programme, and the obvious subject was Duncan.

He is a widower. At the time his only daughter May was in the grammar school, an exceptionally bright pupil keen on the adventure of broadcasting; but she and I faced an almost insuperable difficulty when we tried to sell him the idea of the programme. The prospect of a journey to Glasgow and a long recording session at the BBC filled him with dismay. 'I'm a sailor,' he growled at me, 'no' a bloody play-actor!'

I pointed out that he was showing a selfish spirit: May would be bitterly disappointed if he didn't go, and the RNLI would lose a valuable piece of publicity. As I well knew, nobody is more unselfish than Duncan, and my argument shook him. In the end, gloomy and unwilling, but comforted by his daughter's obvious gratitude, he said: 'All right, be damned to you! But I'm no' wearin' a collar an' tie!'

On the day the three of us went in my car to Broadcasting House in Glasgow he was wearing a collar and tie and a smart blue suit: May inherits not only her father's courage but also her late mother's powerful will. Kathleen Garscadden was waiting for us. Her crisp friendliness and the fact that her father had been a sea-captain immediately appealed to Duncan, and from the beginning they got on famously together. May and I raised eyebrows to each other in relief.

But when the time came for him to start recording in the studio there was more trouble. The man who had 'stolen' a life-boat, who had faced the red turmoil of the Iron Rock Ledges with scarcely a tremor, who had received more than one decoration for conspicuous gallantry – this same man was scared stiff of the microphone. Kathleen and May and I laboured anxiously to make him go on.

Eventually, however, as Kathleen continued to wield her charm and May and I used bullying tactics, he forgot about his 'nerves'. As often happens in the case of people initially terrified of broadcasting he began to tell his stories with a modest conviction which is the mark of the real 'personality'. Only one incident marred the proceedings. At one point, while recording a thrilling piece of narrative, he shook Broadcasting House to the core by stopping abruptly, snatching off his spectacles and roaring into the microphone: 'Ach, tae hell, ma glesses is a' steamed up!'

'Oh, Mr Newlands!' exclaimed Kathleen from the production panel. Dumbfounded engineers pressed buttons. Tapes were hurriedly rewound and readjusted. May cried, 'Daddy, how could you!'

Then Kathleen began to laugh. Everybody laughed, including Duncan. The session continued, the result being a notable programme still remembered by many children who are now parents – and even grandparents – themselves.

On the long way home to Kintyre that night we ran into a blizzard in Glen Croe, north of Inverary. My windscreen wipers laboured. I dipped the headlights and my eyes found some relief from a dazzle of driving snow; but even so I had difficulty in seeing the road ahead.

Beside me Duncan said: 'Angus, heave-to!'

'Duncan,' I said, 'in the life-boat you're the coxswain – what you say goes. In the car I'm in command. Right?'

'Oh, sure, sure.'

'We're not going to heave-to. You didn't heave-to on the night you rescued the men from the *Dunraven Castle.*'

'Quite right, Angus. You've got to make up your mind. But I wasn't half as scared that night as I am this minute.'

'The trouble with you, Duncan, is that you're a back-seat driver. You've got to trust your coxswain, in a life-boat or in a car.'

'Man, Angus, you'd make a grand minister! You can argue black is white.'

By the time we got to Inverary the blizzard had thinned out. The rest of the journey to Campbeltown was uneventful as far as driving the car was concerned, and Duncan's conversation made it seem all too short. I remember in particular a story he told me that night about the *Alcyone Fortune.*

In 1947 I wrote my first Children's Hour serial for the BBC. It was called *The Crocodile Men* and both Kathleen Garscadden and I were delighted when it was broadcast – and repeated twice – through all the regions. The following year 'the book of the play' was published.

The opening instalment dealt with a shipwreck at the Mull of Kintyre and with the rescue from the sea of a young native of Madagascar called Trabonjy. After the broadcast one critic said it was most unlikely that an Arab boy would be shipwrecked in the Highlands of Scotland. But on Christmas Eve 1948 the Campbeltown life-boat was called out to the rescue of a British cargo ship, the *Alcyone Fortune*, which had gone aground on Sheep Island, near Sanda. And among the survivors rescued by Coxswain Newlands and his crew was an Arab boy of thirteen, a stowaway from Aden. A great little chap he was, according to Duncan, brave and full of fun. His big brown eyes shone like stars when he saw his first Christmas tree in the foyer of a Campbeltown hotel.

One side of the life-boat picture often left in shadow is the strain imposed on a life-boatman's family when the maroons go off and the service gets under way. But in the radio programme about her father May Newlands, though then only a school-girl, shone a clear light upon it.

'When a gale blows up and Daddy and I are sitting by the fire after supper, I keep looking at the telephone, praying it won't ring.

'Then sometimes it does.

'As long as Daddy has plenty of cigarettes he doesn't worry much. He stuffs them in his pocket, then he's off down the street, running for the life-boat shed. I always want to go with him, to see what's happening; but of course he wouldn't like any fuss like that, so I just have to stay at home and imagine everything.

'I stoke up the fire and make a cup of tea. In about fifteen minutes, when I know the life-boat will be near the mouth of the harbour, I switch on the radio and set it on the trawler-band. Daddy says I should go to bed and sleep, but that would be impossible.

'After a while it begins: "Hullo, coastguard. Life-boat calling. Are you receiving me? Over." Then: "Hullo, life-boat. Coast-guard answering. Receiving you loud and clear. Over."

'From there it goes on – the guiding voice of the coastguard and the answers from the life-boat as Daddy and his men grope for the casualty and eventually find it.

'During the actual rescue there's no transmission, no sound on the trawler-band except an occasional crackle. I sit thinking of them all out there and wishing I could do something about it. But there's nothing I can do except wait. For an hour, two hours, three hours or maybe more.

'The time goes on, and the gale whistles in the chimneys and across the house-tops and I imagine what the sea is like outside the harbour. I try to read, to swot up some history, but it's not easy. I keep telling myself that everything will be all right. It's bound to be all right, because Daddy knows his job and the crew all know theirs. They've been out on stormier nights. Remember the *Dunraven Castle*: that was the worst night of all. But they still came back, and not a single life was lost.

'There's nothing on the radio yet – not even a whisper – and it seems years since it closed down. The telephone rings when you don't want it, but the radio stays silent.

'Then suddenly there are voices, and I forget to be afraid. I seem to listen with every part of me until at last it comes through.

' "Life-boat calling coastguard. Service completed. We've taken off all survivors. No casualty or damage in life-boat. Returning to station now. Over."

' "Coastguard calling. Message received and understood. Well done, lads. Over and out."

'For the first time I feel tired, but I stoke up the fire again and put the kettle on for Daddy's hot-water bottle. I want to go down to the shed to see them coming in, but he doesn't like me to be there. I don't even need to make him a cup of tea, because the secretary and the ladies' Life-boat Guild will have a meal ready for the survivors and the crew.

'I just go on waiting, and at last Daddy comes in and takes off his sea-boots and says it wasn't too bad out there, and I tell him I wasn't a bit anxious.

'And the next day he'll be at his job and I'll be at school, both of us very tired but trying to act as if nothing had happened.'

Why do men like Duncan Newlands, pressed for time and money in the hard business of earning a living, volunteer to join the life-boat, in which they know they will face danger and discomfort for a financial return averaging about 50p per hour? Why do their families put up with it?

Duncan says: 'I get a kick out of helping other folk.'

May is now married, with a daughter of her own. She agrees with her father.

8

Ghoulies and Ghosties and Long-Leggety Beasties

We were brought up in the Manse as orthodox Christians. Nevertheless, our Celtic ancestry caused us all to retain certain pagan characteristics, mainly in the form of an unwilling belief in superstitions of all kinds.

When Archie played football for Glasgow University, earning a 'blue' on the way, he carried with him a rabbit's foot for luck.

Willie's superstition might better be described as a neurosis. Before eating anything – even a chocolate biscuit stolen from the silver barrel on the dining-room sideboard – he would carefully wash his hands, in case, as he explained, he might be poisoned. An excellent habit no doubt, in moderation, but in his case carried to such lengths that the skin on his hands sometimes became inflamed. I think he forgot his 'superstition' when he joined the merchant navy.

Rona had a special locket which she wore when taking part in competitions at the Gaelic Mod. When she sang solo her handkerchief always had a knot in it.

Kenneth and John declare that with their high academic standards they are above such weaknesses; but I have noticed that when it comes to worshipping certain football teams their high academic standards are inclined to approach remarkably human levels.

Kenneth is an ecumenical miracle, a Presbyterian minister who is also a fervid supporter of Celtic. He has been known to pass himself off as a Roman Catholic priest when attending a match at Parkhead and to keep the crowd around him in happy mood by yelling encouragement to his heroes on the field.

John has been a follower of Clyde since he was a small boy. Well I remember him with tears streaming down his cheeks and with his forehead pressed in anguish against the glass of the dining-room window as the almost inevitable defeat of his team was announced on the radio on a Saturday night. I was with him once at Shawfield when Clyde suffered a one goal defeat owing to a doubtful penalty decision against them. At the end the crowd in the stand rose as one man to boo the referee off the field, and there John was among it, a distinguished doctor and professor of midwifery, highly respected by patients and colleagues alike for his calm, commanding skill: there he was, his stout face purple with anger, his voice high above all others in the vigour of his condemnation. I moved away slightly, pretending not to know him, though in fact I was filled with fraternal admiration.

For myself, I am riddled with superstition. On the way to see an editor or to do a programme with the BBC or STV I would never risk walking underneath a ladder. Every morning for as long as I can remember I have put on my left sock first and my left shoe first. If I reversed the process I suspect that the whole rhythm of my day would be upset.

I recognize the source of this left to right fixation. It came from the Druids, who, when performing religious ceremonies, always marched around their stone cairns from left to right. This, they believed, was the only way they could secure the good will of the sun-god, who moved in the same direction. To march around a cairn from right to left ('widdershins' they called it) would, they believed, summon up the devil. According to the *Glasgow Herald*, this is how they do it in their witches' covens in Bearsden and other unlikely parts of Scotland.

Maimie was, perhaps, the most truly superstitious in our household. Born in Perthshire, the reputed heartland of the small dark men called Picts – later translated into pixies – she gathered supernatural lore about her as a warm and kindly granny gathers comforting shawls. On a midsummer night she saw ghosts on the Manse lawn and met them on the dark winter road when she went to post letters in the box at the Mill Road end. The strange thing was that she had no fear of the ghosts she saw. Her voice would be steady as she told us: 'I met him at the church corner. Huge and black he was, and his footsteps on the road made no noise. I just kept on walking with my nose in the air and pretended not to see him.' She would do just that, I have no doubt: her small, five foot nothing figure was always taut with steely courage.

When we asked her why the cuckoo should be called in Gaelic 'the lady of tears', she had a ready answer. 'Don't you know that the cuckoo was once a beautiful girl who wept so much over her sweetheart's death that in the end she was changed into a bird?'

'Who by?' inquired Archie.

'Nature,' replied Maimie, firmly and finally.

As children we were taught that Easter is a Christian festival to commemorate the death and resurrection of Christ. Only later did we realize that in fact it is a Christian graft upon pagan spring rites dating back into prehistory. We had no idea that our painted Easter eggs and the Good Friday pancakes baked by Maimie in a hot confusion of eggs, flour, milk, girdles and a roaring fire in the kitchen range were symbols of new spring life in ancient Egypt, Greece and Rome long before Christ was born. Nor did we know that the Jews still include eggs in their Passover feast in celebration of their breaking out of slavery in Egypt, as the chicken breaks out of the egg. We enjoyed eating the hard-boiled eggs and Maimie's sugared pancakes – that was all that mattered. And to anyone who believes in Christ, isn't it all that should matter? Christianity developed out of paganism, and Christianity teaches that all humanity is one.

The Padre, often accused by the Rev. Kenneth MacLeod and my mother of being partly a superstitious pagan, denied the charge only with meagre conviction. His memory was full of superstitions taken from North Uist, which, when the mood took him, he would recount to our delight. I am certain that despite genuine religious rectitude he believed in them.

The story which appealed most to my romantic spirit concerned a Spanish lady seen by a grand-uncle of his on the *machair* near Claddach Kirkibost.

He and his girl were snuggled among the bent, in the gloaming of a summer day. The light on the sea and in the sky was luminous, causing the land to appear shadowed. A movement among the dunes attracted their attention. They sat up, startled, and saw a lady in a Spanish costume gliding past, only a few yards away. There was no sound, except that of the sea caressing the shore. They held each other close, for comfort. Then the girl caught her breath as the Spanish lady stopped and held out her arms and the shadow of a man came towards her. The Padre's grand-uncle used to tell his friends that at this moment the hair at the back of his neck began to prickle. He had a premonition that something terrible was going to happen. But nothing did, except that before the Spanish lady and the ghostly man could meet they both suddenly vanished.

'My grand-uncle and his girl were not the only people who saw the Spanish lady,' my father would tell us, a youthfully gaping audience. 'Many a time, as darkness came over the land and the sky remained bright, she was seen flitting among the dunes, as if lost and looking for someone. When I grew up I made inquiries and discovered that in the seventeenth century a MacDonald, one of the Lords of the Isles, married a Spanish lady and brought her to live in North Uist. Apparently it was an unhappy marriage, because of MacDonald's rough behaviour and his long absences fighting for his clan, and the Spanish lady fell in love with the young son of a local landowner. His name was MacRurie, and in fact he was related to the MacVicars. (According to the Padre, nearly everybody who ever lived in North Uist was related to the MacVicars, and perhaps he wasn't so far wrong at that.) One version of the story – the official MacDonald version – is that the lady and MacRurie fled together from the island and went to live in Spain. Another, secretly whispered, is that MacDonald came home unexpectedly, found his wife and MacRurie together on the machair and killed them both.'

At this point my father would pause, look intensely serious and say: 'I am sure that if you dug among those dunes you would find their bones, deep down.'

When Willie and Kenneth and I returned home after the Second World War he told us that every time we had been in grave danger he had known of it. This was because of a recurring dream – the dream of a ship on a stormy sea, with one of us standing in the bow. It had come to him first when Willie went missing after the sinking of the *Britannia*, and he had been comforted when the dream ship had not gone down. The next time was after the landings in Sicily, in which Archie with the Argylls and I with the RSF were later involved. My ship had not gone down, but Archie's had, and a few days later news of his death reached the Manse. Again, while Kenneth was missing in Burma, the dream had recurred several times; but the ship with Kenneth in the bow had remained afloat.

He firmly believed in what we call in Scotland 'the second sight', and many were his tales from North Uist about ghostly funerals passing a seer's house before they actually took place. He was confident that my mother possessed it, because she always seemed able to forecast his behaviour and that of her sons. She would laugh scornfully at the idea and declare that she only exercised common sense and a woman's natural knowledge of her family's characteristics. I must admit, however, that we were all uneasy when we went 'a kennin' wrang', in case she did have a mysterious ability to find out about it. Often I saw my guilt reflected in her big green eyes.

There was a legend from her homeland in North Argyll which she often quoted as proof of her 'practical' turn of mind.

'Between Duror and Kentallen,' she would begin, 'there used to be a hillock known as *Sithean na Cailliach*, 'the knoll of the old woman'. Nobody knew the origin of its name, but it was supposed to be haunted, a place where pixies gathered. Nonsense, of course. I don't believe in hauntings or in pixies. No true Christian ever does,' she would add, with a sidelong glance at the Padre.

'When the railway was being built from Ballachulish, *Sithean na Cailliach* was excavated, and inside it was discovered a stone coffin containing bones. Archaeologists said they were those of a woman less than five feet tall, who had probably lived during the Bronze Age. Everything, you see, has a practical explanation if you take the trouble to find it.'

'But what about the ghosts and the pixies?' I asked.

'People never saw them. They imagined them, just as your father and his friends in North Uist imagined things.'

And that was that, except that when the Padre and his cronies would be telling ghost stories late at night she always refused to go to bed before he did.

The Padre often teased my mother by accusing her clan, the MacKenzies, of being on the 'wrong' side at Culloden, that is, against the Jacobites. If she ventured to suggest that the MacVicars hadn't been there at all, on any side, he would remark in a superior way that the MacVicars had been in the navy – supporting the Jacobites, of course. But if he really wanted to annoy her he would attribute what he insisted was her second sight to an ancestral gift handed down by the Brahan Seer, whose name was Kenneth MacKenzie.

'Coinneach Odhar was of a different family of MacKenzies altogether,' she would say, tartly.

'He lived in Ross-shire. So did your forbears, before they fled south to Appin.'

'They didn't flee. They came because they were put out of their crofts.'

'Yes, by the Seaforths, who hated the Brahan Seer and wanted rid of all the MacKenzies.'

'The Seaforths were MacKenzies themselves. Of the same clan as my family.'

At this point the Padre would become jauntily sarcastic. 'Boys,' he'd declaim, 'down on your knees and pay homage to the Countess of Seaforth!'

Kenneth MacKenzie – Coinneach Odhar, or 'dun-coloured

Kenneth' – was the most famous of all Highland seers. His prophecies were written about and authenticated by men of such disparate philosophies as Sir Walter Scott and Sir Humphrey Davy. Among the people of Ross-shire he remains a figure as romantically real as Bonnie Prince Charlie. And yet, strangely, though he is supposed to have lived in the seventeenth century, a well-documented period in Scottish history, there is no contemporary written evidence that he existed.

The Padre had no doubt that he was a real person. My mother suspected that his name was a collective one – like that of some Old Testament prophets – covering the forecasts of many astute and far-seeing Ross-shire men.

According to tradition he was born at Baile-na-Cille in the Ness district of the island of Lewis. It is probable that he was illegitimate, because though his mother figures in many stories there is no mention of his father. As a child he came into possession of a small round stone, coloured blue and with a hole in the middle, which gave him the power of divination. Where the stone came from is as great a mystery as the life of the Brahan Seer himself; but there is a tale that when Coinneach first looked through the hole and found that by this means supernatural powers were conferred upon him, it deprived him of the sight of his right eye and that he continued afterwards to be what is called in Gaelic *cam*, that is, blind of an eye.

Being born on lands belonging to the Seaforths in Lewis, Coinneach Odhar eventually travelled east to work for the third Earl on a farm at Loch Ussie, near the family's seat at Brahan Castle in Ross-shire. There his fame as a prophet quickly spread and he was appointed Seer to the Seaforths. In those days most 'official' seers carefully predicted great triumphs for their clan and confusion for their enemies. Coinneach never stooped to 'popular' forecasts. This was to lead to his tragic end.

A portrait of Isabella, who was Countess of Seaforth at the time, hangs in Fortrose Town Hall. Her husband went to France on business and was a long time coming back. She ordered Coinneach to tell her why. At first he refused to answer, but when she insisted he said: 'At this moment your Lord is on his knees to a French woman. His arms are about her waist and his lips pressed to her hand.'

The Countess was furious. She had Coinneach arrested and tried for witchcraft, and he was condemned to be burned alive in a spiked barrel full of tar. At Chanonry Point near Fortrose there is a memorial stone, erected by the Gaels of Ross-shire, which marks the supposed site of this atrocity.

Before Coinneach died he uttered the best known and most terrible of all his predictions:

'I see into the future, where lies the doom of the House of Seaforth. MacKenzie to MacKenzie, Kintail to Kintail, Seaforth to Seaforth, all will end in extinction and sorrow. I see a chief, the last of his house, and he is both deaf and dumb. He will be father to four fine sons but he will follow them all to the grave. He will live in sorrow and die in mourning, knowing that the honours of his line are extinguished for ever and that no future chief of MacKenzie shall ever again rule in Kintail. Lamenting the last of his sons, he shall sink in sorrow to the tomb and the last of his possessions shall be inherited by a widow from the east who will kill her own sister.

'As a sign that these things are coming to pass there will be four great lairds in the days of the last Seaforth. Gairloch shall be hare-lipped; Chisholm shall be buck-toothed; Grant shall be a stammerer and Raasay an idiot. These four chiefs shall be neighbours and allies of the last Seaforth and when he looks round him and sees them he will know that his sons are doomed to die and that his broad lands shall pass to strangers and his race come to an end.'

There is no possible chance that this prophecy was made after the event, because Sir Walter Scott knew about it – and quoted from it – while the last chief was alive and two of his sons were still in good health.

Francis Humberstone MacKenzie, Lord Seaforth and the last Baron of Kintail, appears to have been a man of character and distinction, 'a nobleman of extraordinary talents', wrote Sir

Walter, 'who must have made for himself a lasting reputation, had not his political exertions been checked by painful natural infirmity'. At the age of sixteen he had become stone deaf after an attack of scarlet fever. He was also afflicted by a serious speech impediment, which resulted in his having to do most of his communication in writing. Despite all this, however, he patronized the liberal arts, encouraged young and struggling artists like Thomas (later Sir Thomas) Lawrence, was member of Parliament for Ross-shire for a number of years, raised during the war with France a regiment of Ross-shire Highlanders (the 78th) and ultimately attained the rank of Lieutenant-General in the Army. For six years he was Governor of Barbados.

Was he aware, I wonder, as with courage he pursued his public duties, that his contemporaries, the four lairds of Gairloch, Chisholm, Grant and Raasay, were all deformed in the way foreseen by Coinneach Odhar? Old men and women among his tenantry knew the situation only too well. They shook their heads, murmured in the Gaelic – and waited.

Lord Seaforth had four sons and six daughters. The eldest son died in infancy. The second died young; the youngest died in 1813 and the third and last, 'a young man of talent and eloquence who represented Ross-shire in Parliament', during the following year.

In the meantime Lord Seaforth's property in the West Indies had been so badly mismanaged that straitened financial circumstances compelled him to dispose of part of his Kintail estates, which included the 'gift land' of his family. His tenants offered to buy the land for him so that it might not pass from the MacKenzies, but before this could happen his last son died and he himself became physically and mentally paralysed. The tenants bowed to what appeared to be the awful inevitability of Coinneach Odhar's prophecy. Their offer was withdrawn.

After the death of his last son, Lord Seaforth lingered on, his fine intellect enfeebled but, according to Sir Walter Scott, 'not so entirely obscured but that he perceived his deprivation as in a glass, darkly'. Sometimes he was anxious and fretful because he did not see his son. Sometimes he complained that his boy had been allowed to die without his seeing him. But in January 1815 the last of the Seaforths died. And then:

> Of the line of MacKenneth remained not a male
> To bear the proud name of the Chief of Kintail.

But the Brahan Seer's 'revenge' was not yet complete.

On Lord Seaforth's death his Highland estates, with all their burdens and responsibilities, devolved upon his eldest daughter, the widow of Admiral Hood. She later married James Stewart MacKenzie, member of a Galloway family. One day she was driving her pony-trap, with her sister Caroline as passenger, when the horse bolted and Caroline was killed.

Thereafter, according to Alexander MacKenzie in his book, *The Prophecies of the Brahan Seer* (first published in 1899), 'one section after another of the estates had to be sold. The remaining portion of Kintail, the sunny braes of Ross, the church lands of Chanonry, the barony of Pluscarden and the Island of Lews [Lewis] – a principality in itself – were disposed of, one after the other'.

Now, finally, the doom of the Seaforths as pronounced by Coinneach Odhar was fulfilled in every detail.

The story sends a shiver down my spine. Possibly I may and probably I may not have the blood of Kenneth MacKenzie in my veins; but if ever I find a blue stone with a hole in it on the shore near Achnamara I will throw it far out into the sea. It's one thing to peer through a glass, darkly, as most writers do; quite another to see face to face.

Many other predictions said to have been made by the Brahan Seer have come true.

The sulphur and chalybeate spring at Strathpeffer was known to him, and he foresaw its future. 'Uninviting and disagreeable as it now is with its thick crusted surface and unpleasant smell, the day will come when it shall be under lock and key and crowds of health and pleasure seekers shall be seen thronging its portals in their eagerness to drink the waters.' The spring was commercially 'discovered' in the eighteenth century. Later a pump-house was built and the town advertised as Strathpeffer Spa, 'the Harrogate of the North'. For many years it did thriving business.

Nowadays 'taking the waters' at Strathpeffer is not so popular; but sufferers from rheumatism still drink from the spring, hoping for relief. I tried it once, and the only liquid I have ever considered more revolting was a nameless green liqueur which Jock brought home after a football reporting trip to Italy. (Jock himself used it as a weedkiller.)

Beyond the towers of the Cathedral of St Andrew in Inverness there is a small hill called Tomnahurich. It is supposed to mark the burial place of the Feinn, three giants of ancient Scotland. A bugle is buried with them, and it was foretold that if the bugle were blown three times the Feinn would rise and free Scotland from her oppressors. One day, long ago, a shepherd boy found an opening in the hill and went inside. He saw the bugle and blew it, not once but twice. To his horror he saw three huge figures stirring in the dark and rising on their elbows. He dropped the bugle and fled, and no one has ever found the opening again. According to the legend, therefore, the Feinn are still there, resting on their elbows, waiting for the third bugle blast to summon them to the aid of their country. (I dedicate this story to the SNP. Does it not contain some good material for propaganda?)

With all its ghostly attributes Tomnahurich was a natural object for the Brahan Seer's interest; and, indeed, he made two prophecies about it.

The first: 'I see the Fairy Hill under lock and key, with spirits of the dead secured therein.' In 1846 an area of ground including Tomnahurich, the Fairy Hill, became a cemetery. It is surrounded by a fence, with a gate which is locked at night.

The second: 'Strange as it may seem to you, the day will come when full-rigged ships with sails unfurled will be seen sailing east and west by the back of Tomnahurich.' This foresaw the building of the Caledonian Canal by Telford in 1822. Its exit to the Pentland Firth runs past the Fairy Hill.

A prophecy by the Brahan Seer which appeared to be unlikely at the time it was made: 'A Lochalsh woman shall weep over the grave of a Frenchman at the burying-place of Lochalsh.' Centuries later a wealthy laird of the district engaged a French footman who fell in love with and married a local girl. Soon afterwards the Frenchman died, leaving the widow to mourn over his grave.

'The day will come,' declared Coinneach Odhar on another occasion, 'when two false teachers shall come from across the seas. At that time there will be nine bridges in Inverness. The streets will be full of ministers without grace and women without shame.' Some people claim that in this prophecy the Brahan Seer was referring to the evangelists Moody and Sankey, who, a hundred years ago, wrote 'pop' hymns and made an attempt to revolutionize the sombre religion of the Highlands. But I'm not so sure. The bit about 'ministers without grace' would appear to indicate a more modern trend in clerical attitudes. And could 'women without shame' be an allusion to the mini-skirt? Any day now, I think we ought to be on the look-out for those 'two false teachers'. From America?

That the following prophecy has been fulfilled there can be little doubt: 'The day is coming when there will be a ribbon on every hill and a bridge on every stream. I see a mill on every river and a white house on every hill. Dram-shops will be open at the head of every plough furrow and travelling merchants will be so plentiful that a person can scarcely walk a mile on the road without meeting one. There will be men of law at every street corner.' In Coinneach's day Ross-shire was a wilderness traversed only by footpaths, crude tracks and river fords. Long after his death meal-mills powered by water-wheels became common in the county, and many new shooting-lodges and holiday-makers' houses – most of them white-washed – were built among the rolling hills. Today the area is serviced by ribbons of tarmacadamed roads and modern bridges, used frequently by butchers and bakers and candlestick-makers going their rounds in vans and cars. 'Men of law' stand at street corners in every town, in the shape of burly policemen.

'The day is coming when fire and water will run in streams side by side through the streets of Inverness.' This prediction was proved valid when gas and electricity and a mains water-supply were installed.

'Soldiers will come from Tarradale to the Muir of Ord in fiery chariots without horses or bridle.' Trains, buses and fast cars have made this come true many times.

But now, finally, here is the most fascinating of all the Brahan Seer's prophecies. I give it in composite form, though some of the predictions were made separately, at different times. In it he foresees not only the history of the Highlands and Islands from the Clearances until the present day but also what lies ahead of us.

'The day is coming when the Big Sheep will over-run the Highlands, putting the plough into the rafters and driving cattle into the northern sea. They will become so numerous that the bleating of one shall be heard by another from Lochalsh to Kintail. Clansmen, turning effeminate, will flee the country, seeking comfort in faraway places not yet known. Clansmen who remain will become degenerate, and strange merchants will appropriate the lands of the chiefs. The sheep will be gone, and in their place deer will roam a deserted land. Then will come the time of the Black Rains. They will kill the deer and wither the grasses. After that the people will return and take possession of the land of their ancestors.'

This gives a true picture of what happened in the north and west of Scotland after Culloden. The clan chiefs and the big landowners replaced the old form of agriculture (crofting and cattle-rearing) with a new one involving sheep and shepherds from the Lowlands. Crofters were evicted with a terrible, uncaring cruelty which appears almost incredible to us, reared in a gentler and more humane society.

The best and most readable book on the subject is *The*

Highland Clearances (first published by Secker & Warburg in 1963), a carefully researched and brilliantly written documentary by John Prebble, who, for 'a man of Kent', has a remarkable insight into the Highland character and a deep compassion for the victims of the Clearances. For example, his description of the treatment of the Sollas crofters in North Uist, about which I have written in a previous chapter, carries within it the same ring of authenticity and the same feeling of sad anger evident in the stories handed down by my great-grandfather, a contemporary witness.

As far as Coinneach Odhar's prophecy is concerned, the Seer's reference to 'faraway places yet unknown' is explained by the emigration of the evicted families to America, Canada, Australia and New Zealand. By 'strange merchants' he may have meant the rich industrialists who bought estates from the impoverished chiefs during the nineteenth century and stocked them with grouse and deer for seasonal slaughter.

But what is the significance of the Black Rains? Did Coinneach see the black oil pouring in from the North Sea? Or was he trying to warn us about a nuclear catastrophe and the inevitable fall-out?

Whatever the truth, the prophet of Kintail has bequeathed to me a Hebridean legacy of uneasiness.

In Kintyre, unlike Ross-shire, we have no mysterious figure like the Brahan Seer in the background of our lives. Perhaps the mingling of Lowland elements with native Gaelic blood has caused the Kintyreans to become more hard-headed than our neighbours in the north. There is superstition, but we never take pride in being superstitious.

Beneath a crust of Christian philosophy and secular education, the Padre was highly superstitious, as might be expected in a son of North Uist. But among his parishioners he stoutly denied his birthright and publicly condemned superstition as being anti-religious.

Though accustomed as a boy to the handling of small boats,

he would never, if he could help it, take a sea-trip with Archie Cameron or any of the local fishermen. The old belief that a minister in a boat is unlucky was always at the back of his mind; he was afraid his sea-going friends might resent his company.

As proof of his good judgement in this respect he liked to tell a story about a fellow minister in Campbeltown, who persuaded his leading elder, the Provost of the burgh and owner of two fishing-skiffs, to let him take part in a night's fishing in Kilbrannan Sound. Seine-netters work in pairs. That night, though all the other boats had splendid catches, the Provost's pair, one of which the minister was helping to crew, caught scarcely any fish at all.

In the morning the fleet returned to Campbeltown, the Provost's skiffs, light from lack of herring, reluctantly bringing up the rear. The main body got safely into harbour, but when the laggards were about half a mile from the entrance to Campbeltown Loch, a bank of fog drifted across from Davaar Island. The skippers reduced speed and crawled along; but just before the Provost's skiffs emerged from the fog they collided. Severe damage occurred; and a young fisherman in the boat with the minister aboard had an arm broken.

I can vouch for the truth of this story. It happened while I was editor *cum* reporter *cum* office-boy on the *Campbeltown Courier*, and I printed it. I can also vouch for the fact that as long as he remained in Campbeltown the minister concerned never went herring fishing again.

Once, as Clerk to the Presbytery of Kintyre, my father had to attend an important meeting in Islay. Much against his will, he was persuaded by colleagues to book a seat in the service plane from Campbeltown. It meant that instead of enduring a roundabout journey by bus and steamer via Tarbert, which lasted many hours, he could reach Islay in less than twenty minutes.

'A minister in a plane,' he grumbled to my mother. 'It's unlucky.'

'Oh, nonsense! The Moderator of the Kirk flies everywhere nowadays.'

'The Moderator is different. For a year at least he's not an ordinary minister. As the boys say, he has a "hot-line". Anyway, I don't like flying.'

'How do you know? You've never flown before.'

'That's what I mean. And if God is good to me I'll never fly again.'

The day of the great adventure dawned bright. My mother got up and opened the bedroom curtains. 'Time to get up, dear. It's a beautiful morning. You'll have a perfect flight.'

'All very well for you!' came a voice from the bed. 'If you think it'll be so perfect why don't you go in my place?'

In the car he was silent and on edge, all the way to the airport at Machrihanish. He climbed aboard the seven-seater Rapide with dignified resolution, like Lord Lovat on his walk to the scaffold. The door was closed. Kenneth stood on the tarmac, waiting dutifully to wave farewell.

At first the engines wouldn't start. An agonized face above a dog-collar was pressed to a window. Kenneth made encouraging thumbs-up gestures. Then the face was hurriedly withdrawn as the engines did start. The Rapide taxied to the runway. Kenneth waved as it rose on balanced wings and circled round, heading for Islay. Next minute it was heading back.

It landed and taxied to a stop near the airport office. Two mechanics hurried aboard, and the news circulated that the trouble was superficial: a minor fault in the radio. Passengers were not allowed off.

Again the face appeared at the window, more desperate than ever. Kenneth's heart bled for his father. Somebody beside him said, with a laugh: 'So there's a minister on board. We might have known.'

After a few minutes the Rapide took off again. Kenneth watched until it was a speck in the sky, losing height for Machrie airport in Islay. He was pretty sure of one thing: its clerical passenger would return the next day by way of Tarbert.

He was right. And the Padre never flew again.

A hundred and fifty years ago, in the Highlands and even in Southend, if a farmer's cattle beast took ill, there would be murmurings that 'the evil eye was on it'. An animal so afflicted was often treated by a 'wise woman', who spoke Gaelic incantations over it and then tied a piece of red worsted around its tail as an accessory to healing. Sometimes this custom was used to advantage by 'con men' in the parish.

A story is told about one hard case – his name, it appears, was Hector Mor (Big Hector) – who planned to buy a heifer on the cheap. Before the market opened he picked out the beast he coveted and surreptitiously tied a piece of red worsted around her tail. When the bidding began, other less pragmatic farmers noted the evil sign and averted their eyes. Hector was able to buy her for a song.

In the middle of last century Southend had a 'wise one', who, according to herself, was able to banish the evil eye and effect a cure. Most people were a little afraid of her. Playing on old superstitions, she made a good living for herself.

Jean's great-grandmother, Margaret McKerral, was one of those who took the 'wise one' seriously, though her husband, Old Hugh, would have no truck with such 'pagan nonsense', as he called it. Once, when a cow on Brunerican Farm became sick and refused to give milk, Margaret called in the 'wise one'. This was in direct opposition to Old Hugh's wishes; but Margaret was sure that if she didn't ask for the woman's help the evil eye would kill the cow.

Following the ritual of the 'cure', the wise one placed a ladder against the outside roof of the byre and climbed to the eaves. First she poured water on the thatch – water into which she had dipped some silver coins given to her by Margaret. Then she began pulling at the thatch, as if she were milking a cow, and muttering an incantation: 'Come, my darling! Give good milk to slake the thirst of the Druids!'

Suddenly, in the middle of it all, the ladder slipped. Squealing with alarm, the wise one fell to the ground and injured her leg.

Margaret McKerral was a kindly woman. Her faith in the

wise one was shattered, but she took her into the house and nursed her until her leg was better.

During this time the cow recovered naturally, and Old Hugh – refraining with a struggle from saying 'I told you so' – was able to convince his wife that the wise one had very little wisdom after all and that superstition was bunk.

Some day, perhaps, the pagan fears born within us will be transmuted into something happier – an untroubled sense of wonder.

I used to write science fiction for children, telling stories about lost planets, space life-boats and other objects of my imagination. I think I did it partly as a kind of release from inherited superstition concerning the unknown. Then Neil Armstrong stepped down from his space-ship on to the surface of the moon and I decided, for a time at least, to give it up. Facts had overtaken fiction. Today the achievements and discoveries of real-life scientists are to me far more wonderful than fiction – or superstition – could ever be.

Take an example. Out there in the indigo dark of space are millions and millions of stars: so many millions, indeed, that the scientists, employing statistical methods, have come to the conclusion that somewhere there must exist other worlds like ours, with creatures similar to us living on them. (Creatures who possibly find it as difficult as we do to understand – and to solve – the problems of living.)

Faced by this astonishing idea, I ask the question: 'How was such a vast universe of stars – such an unimaginably vast universe of stars – first created?' Again the scientists provide an answer. Long ago, on the very threshold of time, a gigantic explosion occurred in space, and our whirling, expanding galaxies, receding from one another even yet at a fantastic rate, are the result of it. They call it the 'big bang' theory.

But at this stage it occurs to me to wonder who created the matter that existed *before* the big bang. Neither the scientific nor the superstitious can answer that one.

9

There is Nothing like a Dame

We found it difficult, as children, to decide who was in command – the Padre or my mother. Making loud noises, threatening and dispensing punishment with a hair-brush, issuing orders to my mother and Maimie regarding his meals, his boots and his clothes, from the pulpit uttering the word 'Almighty' with such unction that he appeared to be suggesting a close personal relationship, the Padre presented the image of a man in authority, the veritable captain of his ship. It was only when sealed lofts began to be opened, and we were able to study the situation in greater depth, that we recognized my mother's power and influence in most of the decisions he made.

She handled him like a trainer with a tiger, showing kindness and understanding and a calm disregard of temperamental outbursts, but occasionally using a whip of the tongue when such an approach seemed justified. She never quite tamed him; but on most occasions, if there occurred a clash of wills, it was my mother's which prevailed. It was she who instilled in us 'the fear of the Lord' which is 'the beginning of wisdom', the ambition to make the most of what talents we possessed and the concept that it is self-discipline and not 'doing one's own thing' that leads to the good and happy life.

Her personality was quieter and less dramatic than the Padre's; but in the end we decided that hers was the stronger. Her faith was tempered steel.

Early in life we realized that the same could be said about many of the ladies of Scotland. In those days, when grey lava from the volcano of the industrial revolution was still flowing, farmers and farm-workers, neglected and almost forgotten by governments dedicated to 'big business' and an urban way of life, lived on the edge of poverty. Their womenfolk had no advantages, except those conferred on them by fresh air and an uncomplicated way of life. They worked at the milking, morning and evening, week in week out, and at the back-breaking tasks of making butter and cheese. The 'pill' had not been invented, and they bore large families and knitted and sewed and cooked for them. But all the time they had a deciding voice in the conduct of their men, and as a result the Kirk was well attended and the parish full of good neighbours. I often heard my father say: 'If you ever want anything done in Southend, get the women on your side.'

Today, when they are 'liberated', when agricultural prosperity has taken the place of penury, when on dairy farms the milking is done mechanically and on beef farms there is no milking at all, when butter and cheese are made at the creameries, when families can be planned and there is plenty of money for the purchase of spin-driers, dish-washers, freezers and other labour-saving devices, they occupy a more influential place than ever in the life of the community.

A farmer's wife used to be old, bent and 'done' at sixty, wearing a drab high-necked blouse and a 'druggit' skirt and apron. Now at the same age she looks like a fashion picture in the *Scottish Field*, drives her own car, plays golf and goes swimming whenever the mood takes her. The men 'plough and sow and reap and mow', as a rule sitting on a tractor; they tend the cattle and sheep and go to market. Many of them allow their well-educated wives and daughters to do 'the books' and decide on domestic policy. Any sharp analysis of the situation reveals that the parish is run mainly by the ladies.

All this is probably due to our inheritance from the Celts, who were a matriarchal society. And it is significant that in our Scottish history there seem to be far more notable women than men. Those range from Malcolm Canmore's wife, Queen Margaret, who, in the eleventh century caused many churches and 'welfare houses' to be built thoughout the kingdom, from Mary Queen of Scots, whose royal good sense was betrayed by a human need of love, from Flora MacDonald, the Jacobite heroine, down to our own contemporary, Winnie Ewing, who cocked a snook at the modern Whigs and Tories and gave a refreshingly different slant to the news.

As far back as the thirteenth century, the influence of the ladies was evident in a Scottish Act of Parliament, which ordained that 'ilk maiden ladye of baith highe and lowe estait shall hae libertie to bespeak ye man she likes; albeit, gif he refuses to tak her till be his wyf, he shall be mulcted in ye sume of ane hundredth pundid or less, as his estait may be, except and alwais gif he can mak it appear that he is betrothit to ane ither woman, then he shall be free'.

Most visitors to Scotland throughout the centuries have praised the ladies. Aeneas Sylvius from Italy, who afterwards became Pope Pius II, made a Scottish pilgrimage in the fifteenth century and found them 'good looking and comely', though he does add an embarrassed footnote: 'They are lavish with their kisses, giving their lips as freely as do Italian women their hands.' I suspect that Aeneas was a considerable heart-throb himself.

At about the same time another foreigner came to Scotland. He was Don Pedro de Ayala from the Spanish court of Ferdinand and Isabella. He described the Scottish ladies as being graceful and handsome, exceedingly courteous and honest, though he, too, has a word of criticism for what he calls their 'boldness'. 'They dress much better than the English women,' he goes on, 'are so fond of foreigners that they dispute as to who shall entertain them, and are absolute mistresses of their own homes, and even of their husbands.' (I like his use of the word 'even'.)

Oddly enough, it was English visitors who often seemed to be less than complimentary.

For example, Thomas Kirke, author of a book published in 1679 called *A Modern Account of Scotland by an English*

Gentleman, had nothing good to say about the Scots at all, whatever their sex. According to him they were 'arrogant, vain-glorious, bloody, barbarous, inhuman and proud'. The women, he adds, had 'legs like strong-posted timber', a discourteous allusion, I should guess, to the thickness of their ankles. And his most terrible indictment of all: 'They dislike Englishmen!' I have a feeling that somehow Master Thomas Kirke lacked the charm and good looks of Aeneas Sylvius and that his own legs were 'gey spindley'.

Sir Anthony Weldon was another seventeenth-century visitor ungallant enough to write: 'The beasts of Scotland are generally small – the women only excepted, of which there are none greater in the world.' His prejudice against Scotland and the Scots was wide and deep. 'They christen without the cross, marry without the ring, receive the sacrament without reverence, die without repentance, and bury without divine service.' The womenfolk he describes as being mere slaves, kept by jealous husbands in a state of subjection. But this opinion is contradicted by the fact that, during the insurrection of 1678, when Monmouth invited the Scots gentry to join the King's army, many of them who failed to respond gave as their excuse that their wives would not allow them to leave home and fight.

There were two English visitors, however, who did perceive admirable qualities in the ladies of North Britain.

In his *A Tour of Scotland* (1769) Thomas Pennant expresses some dismay at the servile condition of 'the female peasantry', but he further says that the townswomen 'fully emulate the character of the good wife so admirably described by Solomon'.

Another eighteenth-century tourist, Captain Burt, writing *Letters from a Gentleman in the North of Scotland*, declares that 'among the better sort there is a full proportion of pretty women', then adds a revealing postscript: 'Women, of course, grow handsomer and handsomer the longer one stays away from home.'

I have my own favourites among the ladies of Scotland.

Many a time, when sitting before a television camera, I have wished Black Agnes of Dunbar could have been there beside me, to add some zing to the programme. Her husband was the tenth Earl of Dunbar and March. In 1334, while he was away fighting for the Regent of Scotland, his countess was left in charge of the castle. For five months she defended it against an English force under the command of Montagu, Earl of Salisbury, during which time the castle was hemmed in by a cordon of troops on land and two Genoese galleys out at sea.

With her dark complexion and long, flying hair, Agnes was a born leader, brave and full of resource.

She kept a stir in tower and trench,
That brawling, boisterous Scottish wench.
Came I early, came I late,
I found Agnes at the gate.

When huge stones from the besiegers' catapults struck the castle walls she would tell one of her women to go and wipe off the dust with a white napkin. Then she would order arrows to be sent sweeping down and the enemy would retreat, furious and frustrated.

She was only twenty-five at the time. I can picture her in a leather mini-skirt and swinging beads, striding the battlements, brushing her hair out of her eyes and screaming defiance at the English down below.

At one stage Salisbury tried to use a military engine called 'the sow'. This was a huge wooden shield, under cover of which the English planned to advance and undermine the walls of the castle. When Black Agnes saw it coming she laughed and yelled:

Beware, Montagow,
For farrow shall thy sow!

And as she uttered this masterpiece of invective, if not of poetry, her men dropped a boulder on top of the sow, and it was smashed to pieces. The men underneath crawled out and fled from the wreck. She shouted after them: 'I told you! A litter of squealing pigs, that's what you are!'

But in spite of her swash-buckling humour, she had a feminine sense of pity.

> Then to the Castle yard she sped,
> Where her worn troops in order stood.
> 'Spare all you can, my friends,' she said,
> 'Nor idly dip your dirks in blood.'

And at the end, when the castle was relieved by Sir Alexander Ramsay, her reaction was again feminine. She herself opened the gate to him. She rushed forward, flung her arms about his neck and began to cry.

Black Agnes was a real warrior. She lived to an old age, a strong supporter of the church. Her wild youth was no disadvantage.

In the seventeenth century, the ladies of the Scottish Covenant were remarkable characters. Their brave and unending faith was as inspiring as that of their menfolk: even as that of the Marquis of Argyll (a changed man after his villainous deeds at Dunaverty), who, on the night before he was executed for maintaining the Presbyterian faith, spoke quietly to a friend who had suggested suicide: 'I could die now like a Roman. But I choose rather to die tomorrow like a Christian.'

The sufferings inflicted on those women sound like African atrocities today.

Sir Robert Grierson, laird of Lagg, held burning matches between the fingers of young girls to make them betray their Covenanting fathers and brothers. General Dalziel threw women into pits containing frogs and snakes because they were loyal to their persecuted kinsmen or supplied hunted refugees with food.

The flag of Presbyterianism continued to fly, however, thanks in part to the courage and endurance of the ladies of the Covenant. A list of their names is like a roll of honour.

There was Jenny Geddes, who started the campaign against the English liturgy by hurling a stool at the Dean of Edinburgh's head. 'Wad ye say mass at my lug!' she shouted at him.

There was Lady Anne Cunningham, daughter of the seventh Earl of Glencairn and wife of the second Marquis of Hamilton, who, in 1639, personally opposed a fleet sent by King Charles I in an early effort to foist episcopacy on the Scots. She appeared on the seashore at Leith, mounted on a horse and carrying a pair of pistols loaded with bullets of gold, her idea being that leaden bullets were useless against the armour of the devil's agents.

There were Isabel Alison and Marion Harvey, who in 1681 were condemned to death in Edinburgh for attending 'field preachings' and commenting adversely on the cruelty of the soldiers. On the scaffold they joined in singing Psalm Thirteen, drowning the voice of the curate who had been ordered to preach to them. Marion Harvey was a domestic servant. She told the crowd that she was dying with a light heart. 'I am here today,' she said, 'for avowing Christ to be head of His Church. I sought Him and found Him. I found Him and will not let Him go!'

There were Margaret MacLachlan and Margaret Wilson, the Wigtown martyrs, who in 1685 were tied to stakes in the Solway and drowned as the water rose, stubbornly refusing to deny their religious beliefs. 'I am not afraid,' said Margaret Wilson. 'I am one of Christ's children.'

And there was Isobel Weir, the second wife of John Brown, a mild and harmless Ayrshireman who worked as a carter. One evening, on his way home, John was arrested by Claverhouse's dragoons. He was led into the house, where his wife and children were waiting. Claverhouse gave him a few minutes to prepare himself for death.

After saying his prayers, John turned to his wife and asked her if she were willing to part with him. 'I am willing,' she whispered.

'That is all I could wish,' he said. He gave her and the

children his blessing and told Claverhouse he was ready.

The dragoons held their fire. Perhaps John Brown's simple sincerity made them unwilling to murder him in cold blood. But Claverhouse – in the interests of military discipline, as he later explained – drew his own pistol and shot John Brown through the head.

'What do you think of your husband now?' he asked Isobel.

'I aye thocht muckle o' him,' she said. 'But never sae muckle as I do this day.'

The newspapers talk about violence – in this country and elsewhere – as if it were a modern phenomenon. In its name they create arguments which divide the people and divide the churches. But I reckon steadfast men, and perhaps more importantly, steadfast women will always have the last word.

To me, one of the most endearing of all the ladies of the Covenant was Lady Grizel Baillie, the story of whose life unfolds like a film script.

Grizel Hume was born on Christmas Day, 1665, eldest of the eighteen children of Sir Patrick and Lady Hume of Polwarth. As a girl of twelve she acted as juvenile undercover-agent, conveying secret messages between her father and Robert Baillie of Jerviswood, who, at the time, was in prison in Edinburgh. While carrying out this dangerous assignment she met George Baillie, Robert's son, and a love story began which out-Cartlands Barbara Cartland.

When Robert Baillie was executed for being implicated – allegedly – in the Rye House Plot, the Humes, as militant Covenanters, found themselves in trouble. Sir Patrick was denounced as a rebel. The Hume estates were forfeited and he went into hiding, his refuge being a vault in the parish kirk of Polwarth, a mile or so away from Redbraes Castle where the family lived. Every night Grizel faced the dark terrors of the churchyard to bring her father food, encouragement and gossip concerning happenings at home.

I can imagine some of the gossip dealt with her own difficulties in smuggling out his meals. For example, there was the time when troopers were in the castle, searching for Sir Patrick. With a view to taking it out later to give to her father, she had managed to hide the greater part of her dinner in her lap when suddenly one of her younger brothers began to draw the troopers' attention to what he imagined was his big sister's greed.

'Will you look at Grizel? While we've been supping our broth, she's eaten up a whole sheep's head!'

Fortunately the troopers were too busy to pay much attention to a small boy.

In the end, Sir Patrick and his family were forced to flee to Holland. Lady Hume was an invalid (no wonder, after having given birth to eighteen children), so Grizel made all the arrangements for the journey.

But this was not all. A week or so later she returned to Scotland to collect her little sister Gillian, who was ill and had been left behind. When the two girls landed at Brielle on the Dutch coast nobody was there to meet them. They had to walk to Rotterdam, and for most of the way Grizel carried her small sister on her back.

In Utrecht, where they finally settled, Grizel looked after the household, while her father earned a small income by practising as a doctor.

One day another Covenanting fugitive from Scotland arrived on their doorstep. He was George Baillie, who had never forgotten the 'wee Hume lassie' he'd met in Edinburgh. He stayed with the family for three and a half years, boisterous, gallant, head over heels in love with Grizel. He and Patrick, the young son of the house, enlisted together as guardsmen under the Prince of Orange.

Those years, according to Grizel, were the happiest of her life. Though the household was in poverty she sang at her work and even found time to write her own songs. Perhaps because her own love affair was happy and uncomplicated, these were often about tragic lovers:

When bonny young Johnny cam' ower the sea
He vowed he saw naething sae lovely as me.
He gi'ed me gowd rings and mony braw things –
An' werena my he'rt licht I wad dee.

But in this sad song the recurring last line does suggest something of Grizel's own patience, courage and good humour in face of all the 'slings and arrows of misfortune'.

Her story had a happy ending, which may be why it has never been made into a play for television. On the accession of William of Orange to the throne of Britain, her father's estates were returned to him. So were those of George Baillie, and in 1692 he and Grizel were married.

They had three children and lived in solid style, pillars of Kirk and State. But long afterwards, when she was a widow, still helping and looking after her numerous relatives, Lady Grizel told her daughter that she would have been quite content to live with her husband 'on bread and water on the top of a mountain'.

She was buried beside him on Christmas Day 1746.

Lady Grizel Baillie and Isobel Pagan had only one thing in common: they were both Scottish ladies.

Isobel was born in New Cumnock, Ayrshire, about 1741, and spent most of her life near Muirkirk. As a child she was deserted by her parents and brought up by 'a good religious old woman who lived a quiet, sober life'. Unfortunately, Isobel didn't follow her example.

She had a squint, went about on a crutch because of a lame leg, had several illegitimate children and drank so much that she was the envy of topers for miles around.

She lived in a kind of shelter beneath a stone archway, which had originally been a brick-store. To this 'howff' there came people from 'a' the airts' to drink illicit whisky and to hear her singing songs of her own composition. Her visitors included not only local miners and farm-workers but also many of the 'gentry' attracted by her wit – and potent liquor. In the month of August, when the grouse season began, shooting-tenants from England flocked to join the bacchanalian revels.

One sporting gentleman from across the Border persuaded her to enter a singing competition in an Ayr theatre. There, to the annoyance of the manager and the delight of her backer, she defeated the leading vocalist of a touring company which was performing in the theatre at the time. She had a lovely voice, and I have no doubt that today Hughie Green would have made her a shooting star in *Opportunity Knocks*.

She often attacked, verbally, the Church and its ministers. One day, passing the door of a tent in which an itinerant divine was preaching at length on some obscure question of theological doctrine, Isobel stopped to listen. After a while she stepped inside, nodded genially to the minister and said: 'Weel, still borin' awa', I see!' Then she departed, leaving both clergyman and congregation to regain breath.

Sometimes her attacks on people were physical. An Ayrshire laird who laughed at her squint was summarily felled by a blow from her crutch. If 'guests' appeared not to appreciate her 'hospitality' she would lay about her with the same weapon until they came to heel with apologies and gifts of money.

And yet, in spite of it all, Isobel Pagan had a genuine feeling for beauty and goodness. She knew her Bible from end to end and often quoted it to help her friends. The songs she composed and sang betray a wistful longing for what might have been, in other times and other circumstances.

Probably the best known of all her poems is 'Ca' the Yowes tae the Knowes'. Robert Burns admired it greatly and used it as the basis of a song of his own which begins, 'Hark the mavis' evening sang'. But the Pagan composition I like best is 'The Crook and Plaid', written in praise of a Lowland shepherd. Here is one of several verses:

What though in storms o' winter part o' his flock should die,
My laddie is aye cheerie and why should not I?
The prospect o' the summer can weel mak' us gled,
Contented is the laddie that wears the crook an' plaid.

Isobel Pagan died in 1821, and her funeral was attended by crowds from all over the country. When I think of her the words of a hymn come into my head: 'Say, poor sinner, lov'st thou me?'

There is one other Scottish lady for whom I have always had a great deal of sympathy and affection. For one thing, her maiden name was MacVicar, though her family and mine – as far as I know – were not connected. For another, she was a writer and published books, not because she felt inspired, with a message for the world, but because, like me, she was poor and badly needed the money. She was Mrs Grant of Laggan, whose *Letters from the Mountains* became famous in her own day.

Anne MacVicar was a soldier's daughter and spent most of her childhood in New York, where her father's regiment was stationed. As a girl her taste in reading was catholic: the Old Testament, which she read from end to end at the age of six; the rough and ready poems of Blind Harry and other bawdy Scottish minstrels; Milton's *Paradise Lost*, which she knew by heart before she was eight. I wonder what modern educationists would think of that lot.

In 1768 her father's health forced him back to Scotland, where he was appointed barrack-master at Fort Augustus. It was here that Anne met the Rev. James Grant when he became chaplain to the garrison. They fell in love at first sight. In 1779, soon after the Rev. James was inducted to the parish of Laggan, they were married.

Mrs Grant had learnt to speak Dutch in New York. Now she set about learning Gaelic, in order to help her husband in the parish. She also kept up a regular correspondence with friends across the world and wrote numerous poems and songs, perhaps the most famous of which is 'Oh where, tell me where is my Highland laddie gone?'. How she found time to do all this balks my imagination, because in the meantime she was presenting her husband with twelve children.

Then the scourge of those unhealthy days struck the family. Four of her children died of consumption; and finally her husband died, too, of the same disease. She was left a homeless and penniless widow with eight children to keep.

For a while she tried farming, living in a cottage lent to her by the Duke of Gordon. But this was a failure, and once more freezing poverty came limping round the corner.

As a last resort somebody suggested that she should publish her poems, and friends gathered round to finance the project. When the book came out the *Edinburgh Review*, seldom flattering, described her verses as having 'beauty, tenderness and delicacy', and a first edition of 3000 copies quickly sold out. Mrs Grant was back in business.

She went to live in Stirling, but her family troubles were still pressing. And tragic. One by one her children died, with the exception of her youngest son; and it was to pay doctors' bills that she collected some of her letters to her friends and made a book of them. In this she was encouraged by Wordsworth and Mrs Hemans, amongst others, and in 1806 *Letters from the Mountains* was published. It was an immediate success, in this country and in America, and other books followed.

Eventually Mrs Grant went to live in Edinburgh. As a young woman she had been tall, slender and good-looking. Now she fell downstairs and broke her leg, and as she grew older, without much exercise, she became heavy and stiff. But she made a joke of her stoutness and played hostess to many literary lions, among them Sir Walter Scott.

'I think Mr Scott's appearance very unpromising and commonplace,' she wrote, demonstrating feminine honesty of a high order. 'Yet though no gleam of genius animates his countenance, much of it appears in his conversation, which is rich, easy, various and animated.'

And what did Sir Walter think of Mrs Grant? 'She is proud as a Highlandwoman, vain as a poetess, but she merits regard by her firmness and elasticity of mind with which she has borne a succession of great domestic calamities.'

I don't suppose many people today have read *Letters from the Mountains*. I think it is a book of great charm, written by one who not only loved nature and humanity but also possessed a rare gift for portraying Scottish life and character. When its author, in her old age, applied for a pension, her friends organized a supporting petition. In this they described her writings as 'addressing themselves to the national pride of the Scottish people and breathing at once a spirit of patriotism and of that candour which renders patriotism unselfish and liberal'.

Mrs Grant lived to the age of eighty-four. She died on 7 November 1838 and was buried in St Cuthbert's churchyard in Edinburgh.

Where did she find the courage to challenge the stormy world and sail determinedly through it? 'I read a chapter of the Bible every day,' she said. 'It helps me to face sorrow and triumph with equal fortitude.'

Anne Grant, as one MacVicar to another, as one writer to another, I salute you.

St Columba preached that women should be raised high on a pedestal of reverence, reminding men of the dignity of motherhood exemplified by Mary. Today the Church of Scotland remembers his words. Prejudice against woman ministers and elders is fading. The influence of women in the church is growing stronger. This, to me, is encouraging.

In the human situation it is wives and mothers, not officials of the state, who are in a key position to influence the moral and physical health of the coming generations. I believe that the tensions and strains of modern living, including the 'frustrations' of young people reared on a glib philosophy of 'take' rather than of 'give', all stem from a lack of faith in the family unit, which, in turn, leads to a lack of faith in the community as a whole. Women, by their example, have the best opportunity to bring about a resurgence of this faith. Through discipline and love they can demonstrate – like Black Agnes of Dunbar, like Lady Grizel Baillie, like Mrs Grant of Laggan and all the rest – that the family unit is the principal source of strength and happiness in any community.

They are the dreamers of happy dreams for their children and, by the same token, better placed than anyone else to give practical expression to those dreams.

St Columba's mother was Eithne, of the ruling house of Leinster. While she was awaiting the birth of her son she dreamt that an angel came to her, bringing a filmy garment, 'in which the most beautiful colours of all the flowers seemed to be portrayed'. She held it in her hands, amazed by its beauty; but almost at once the angel took it from her and allowed the soft breeze to fill it out and carry it away. Eithne saw it expanding until 'its measurement was larger than the mountains and the forests'. She was sad at losing it, but the angel comforted her. 'You are about to become the mother of a son who shall blossom for heaven and be of so beautiful a character that he shall be reckoned among his own people as one of the prophets.'

At this point I remember something my mother used to say: 'Why emphasize the differing roles of men and women? Surely we're all simply human beings, with equal rights and privileges?'

The Padre had no ready answer. Neither have I. So, in male humility, I will abandon the subject and, as they say, 'let that flee stick tae the wa' '.

10

The Ringing Grooves of Change

The stubby mountain crests on either side are less than half a mile apart. In Southend we call it the Gap. As a stranger approaches the place, on foot or in a car, he may imagine it to be a gateway at the end of the world, with nothing beyond it but the shimmer of *Tir nan Og*, the Hebridean land of the ever young. Here the narrow road leaps out over a crag and ricochets down for a dizzy 1500 feet to the Mull of Kintyre Lighthouse and the sea.

Here also John Leitch, coastguard turned shepherd, once saw an object, glowing and hovering between the crests, which he believed to be a flying saucer.

'It was in the twilight of an autumn evening,' John told a local reporter, brought by me to meet him in the Keil Hotel bar. 'There was no wind, and as I walked along the road towards the Gap I could see the sky between the mountain crests like a greyish-blue stage backdrop. The first thing I noticed was a sound – a kind of thin, rushing sound, as if a small wind had sprung up beyond the Mull. But there was no wind, and I got a strange feeling: like being surrounded by strangers. Then I saw it, hovering about fifty feet above the road-sign in the Gap. An elliptical object, dark against the sky, but with light pouring from what seemed to me like portholes. Somehow I wasn't afraid, but there was a prickling in my body, as if the air was full of electricity. I looked round behind me to see if there was anything else in the sky. There wasn't. When I faced the Gap again the object had disappeared. The only feeling I had then was one of loneliness.'

He was a good journalist, that local reporter. His rendering in print of John's occasionally blasphemous words is almost poetic and does full justice to Southend's only story about an Unidentified Flying Object. It happened nearly twenty years ago, and today only a few of us remember. We have more practical things to worry about.

On a day in 1975 Jean and I stood in the Gap, there at the Mull. Behind us the purple heather and the dry peat hags, a protest of grouse calls and an acrid scent of autumn in the air. Before us, distantly down and making our heads swim like the heads of hovering astronauts, a crawling plain of sea, pale blue like the sky and decorated with patterns composed of tides and currents. Eleven miles away, across the Channel, a basking sea monster called Rathlin, and beyond Rathlin the cliffs of Torr Head on the coast of Antrim.

In the space above it all a golden eagle soared, attended on each majestic glide and turn by a little bird flying beneath him.

Jean handed me the binoculars. '*Could* be a wren, I suppose, as in some of the stories.'

A legend that the king of birds has a valet which accompanies him even into the eye of the sun is found in many cultures, including the Gaelic, the German and the Greek. But since that day Jean and I have never found an expert 'bird man' who can identify its species. When we describe what we saw the experts look at us in much the same way, I suppose, as we looked at John Leitch when he told his tale of the flying saucer. They shake their heads, as statesmen do at poets.

The great bird and his friend disappeared beyond the mountain crest on our left. I turned the binoculars on to the sea and saw something else to cause questions and excitement. A small grey ship, miles away under the Irish coast, stationary and sinister.

'Another one,' I said.

For the past few years we have seen them: the little survey ships, prospecting for oil. Sometimes they are visible from our dining-room window, moving slowly up and down the North Channel, which, in Gaelic is called *Struth-na-Maoile*.

According to the geologists, coal exists beneath the North Channel. A seam snakes out from Machrihanish, where there used to be a pit, across to the open-cast workings around Ballycastle. And – so runs the greedy word – where there is coal there may be oil.

Another legend relates that seven tides meet at the Mull of Kintyre. They spill east from the Atlantic, south from the Minches and north from the Irish Sea and the Firth of Clyde. From the Gap they are plainly to be seen, smooth patches of azure water fringed with ragged white lace. A dangerous place for small boats – though in kindly weather Archie Cameron lays and lifts lobster creels close in along the rock-piled shore. But to men who can establish oil-rigs in the turbulent North Sea, seven fast tides present no problem.

Jean and I stood beside the painted sign:

DANGER
This hill is dangerous
Vehicular traffic
prohibited, except on lighthouse business

But the danger of the vertiginous road was not the danger we had in mind.

We saw, in imagination, a small forest of oil-rigs sprouting around the Mull, turning *Tir nan Og* into a paradise lost. We heard a cacophony of hammers at an oil platform construction yard on the Kintyre coast, harsh sounds to frighten away for ever the eagles and the flying saucers. We smelt the stink of oil from a refinery. It irritated the lungs and overwhelmed the scents of the heather and the wild thyme.

That day, as Jean and I contemplated 'progress', our mood became sour. Was this an instinctive reaction of old squares to the intrusion of new values? Or was it the result of fear that our country way of life was coming near an end and that we might find it difficult to adjust to an urban ethos?

As we left the Gap and drove away along the mountain road, back to Achnamara, we decided that our sense of proportion might be awry. To visiting friends – and to ourselves – life at the Mull of Kintyre appears attractively quiet and uneventful; but throughout the centuries hasn't it always been disturbed by excitement and change?

In the evening, after a supper of flounders – speared that afternoon by a friendly young visitor from the caravan park and left on our doorstep – I went outside, stood in the garden and tried to think.

Thinking, for me, is not an easy process. All my life, as the creator of books, plays, films and even strip cartoons, I have had to keep flogging a lazy mind into action. When the mood takes me I would much rather climb to the Gap and watch the eagles, dig in my garden and see the turnips grow, play golf and shoot a scratch 66, make tender love and forget the place and the time – I would much rather *do* all these things than write about them. But the time comes when 'a man's gotta do what a man's gotta do'.

First, I asked myself a question. Are you and Jean afraid of change? The answer came clear enough. We are afraid of change, not so much in the environment as in the Scots people and in ourselves.

When ambition ran strong, I used to visit London twice a year, flying first over the Firth of Clyde, then down and away across the 'coloured counties' into the confusion of Heathrow. Nowadays, taking account of air fares, hotel bills and a minimum of 'extras', a trip to London lasting forty-eight hours would cost me more than £100. In the jargon of the accountants, this, for a writer, is no longer 'economically viable'.

In London I talked with editors and publishers, sometimes alone, sometimes shepherded by an axious agent. If book sales were satisfactory I was entertained in a style far above my domestic station, in expensive restaurants near Piccadilly and in temporarily fashionable ones around Soho. If business languished, and my mission was the peddling of new ideas, I did the entertaining, advised and instructed by my agent. This always caused a long-suffering banker in Campbeltown to make threatening noises on my return. But I enjoyed those visits. They were exciting therapy for a lone author with heather in his ears.

I love the people of London. Professionally and socially they have always been kind to me. I know, of course, that in the Scots idiom they can 'see me coming': in appearance, manner and dress an unsophisticated Hebridean from Kintyre is naturally different from bred-in-the-bone Londoners, and the difference becomes even more obvious when I talk.

I am sure that most of the people I used to meet were inspired by a feeling of warm protectiveness, no doubt similar to that which they might experience on encountering a lost and inarticulate native of Basutoland. Shop assistants and waitresses listened earnestly to my requests. They smiled and called me 'love', speaking slowly as if to a child; and once, when I tried to walk through a confectioner's glass door, they rushed anxiously to help, soothing my hurt in clucking Cockney. Editors and publishers called for their assistants to come and inspect me, while my agent – who, for children's books, happens to be a lady – did her best to make capital out of curiosity. But I never felt uneasy or shy. The natives were friendly and did their best to make me feel at home. I hoped that if ever I met a Londoner benumbed by bagpipes, whisky and the Gaelic at a midnight ceilidh in Argyll I would offer him the same compassionate regard.

On a human level my friends and acquaintances in London were – and still are – lovely people. Sometimes, however, I felt that they were puzzled by certain aspects of my 'Scottishness'.

One day I sat in a publisher's office in Bloomsbury. My agent was telling a tale, substantially true, concerning the success of my stories in Scotland.

Harold, the publisher, said: 'Success in Scotland means nothing here. This is where the action is. This is where you learn to command big sales. Why on earth don't you live in London?'

In Madagascar, during the Second World War, I had a friend, the chief of Ivovona village. If I asked him an embarrassing question – or one he found difficult to answer – he would spit out some ochre-tinted leaf juice, raise his eyes and murmur: 'The truth is with Zanahary!' (Which, being translated into Scots, means 'God kens!') Not being a chewer of exotic leaves, nor pious like my Malagasy friend, I merely raised my eyes and, in answer to Harold's question, gave a Heath heave of the shoulders.

'Let's face it,' he went on, 'you're out of touch up there among the seals and the seagulls. You haven't a hope of capturing the market if you don't mix with people – all kinds of people, good, bad and indifferent. Here in London you'd come alive. You'd learn what living really means.'

I am not good at providing *extempore* answers to an argument. Ideas careened about in my head like bingo numbers. I wanted to tell Harold that I did mix with people, good, bad and indifferent: perhaps not so much with sophisticated townsfolk but with people all the same. I wanted to tell him that in Scotland I felt intensely alive, with the wind and the rain and sunlit golf courses as tonic nerve restorers, while in London a certain numbness came over my spirit and it was difficult for me to distinguish the wood among so many trees. I wanted to make a humorous remark accusing Harold of being only half-alive because he was out of touch with seals and seagulls. But the ideas failed to become words and all I said was: 'I don't think I could write in London. I couldn't be myself.'

The truth is, I was afraid of change, as I knew Jean would be if a move to London were contemplated. This is why Achnamara has remained our home base since we married in 1936.

I am glad to notice that our son Jock has the same instinct. Though for the past eighteen years he has worked as a sports writer with the *Scottish Daily Express* and owns a bachelor 'pad' in Glasgow, he comes home whenever an opportunity presents itself. We will keep Achnamara warm for him. Some day, in the future, he may retire to it.

That evening, in Achnamara garden, I asked myself a second question. *Why* are we afraid of change? In a lucid moment the answer became clear. We are afraid of change because, like the crofters of Sollas, we equate it with being uprooted from the people and the physical environment we know and understand. Uprooted and replanted in a more luxurious London – or elsewhere furth of Scotland – we could never tell when our spirit might wither and finally die.

For Londoners and other urban people, dreaming of a life in the country 'away from it all', the same answer may apply in reverse.

So my thinking had led me to a fairly obvious conclusion. Jean and I were Scots of the Scots. Like most of our neighbours, we were heirs to an ancient heritage, and, without evidence of that heritage around us – the rocks in our Scotch – it was difficult to imagine us existing at all. But I saw plainly enough that, in a manner of speaking, there was no future in clinging too stubbornly to the past. Jean and I should have to face up to and, in our own way, come to terms with progress.

But as George Hutcheon used to say – he was our head teacher of mathematics at Campbeltown Grammar School – a conclusion always requires a definition. In this case my problem was the definition of 'progress'.

I believe good progress has been made in providing better food for more people, better housing for the less affluent, broader bands of education for adolescents and adults, more sophisticated medicine for the sick, more efficient safeguards against crime and corruption. Today, especially for young people and old people, life is much happier than it was, say, a hundred years ago.

But is it progress, in the sense of going forward, when crofters and farmers leave their ploughs and fishermen their nets to work instead at an assembly line? Is it progress when half a dozen employees of a car firm, in the name of egalitarianism, can go on strike and so render 100000 of their 'brothers' unemployed? Is it progress when cities are built larger and larger (and fields and forests, in consequence, become smaller and smaller) and we drive in our cars through artificial canyons, bumper to bumper, inhaling exhaust fumes which are far more dangerous to health than those of tobacco? Is it progress when new weapons are invented to kill more people at longer range, when a little man – in every sense of the word – is given the opportunity to depress a nuclear switch in America or Russia or China and bring the world to an abrupt end?

For many of us, life seems to have become so drearily complicated that it can be made bearable only by using a television set to avoid reality. Are we all so mentally tired that we must allow 'the box' to do most of our thinking for us? More and better television is equated with progress. Surely, however, the quality of man's mental processes is infinitely more important than advances in methods of communication.

And what about man's physical processes? Gaping at all the advertisements which accompany 'entertainment' on the goggle box, are we not in danger of being brain-washed into eating and drinking and smoking a lot of dangerous rubbish?

Good progress has been made in education.

Until comparatively recent times the chief source of education in Scotland was the Church, before and after the Reformation. John Knox was more than a churchman: he was also a schoolmaster, whose stated purpose was to establish 'a school in every town and a school-master in every parish', so that all children, rich or poor, might have an education 'according to their capacity'. Like many other country places, Southend benefited from an application of this philosophy. At one time – less than a hundred years ago – it had three schools. Now it has only one.

But progress in education has always been hampered by politics.

In John Knox's day the men of power were the nobility and the big landowners, who were afraid that servants and labourers might be hard to find if too many people were educated, afraid that an advance in education might bring about an erosion of their own privilege. Consequently they did their utmost to delay the full flowering of Knox's ideal.

In 1872 education became the responsibility of the State rather than of the Church, and the men of power became the politicians and the bureaucrats. At the present time the stultifying arguments concern state versus private, comprehensive versus grammar, the status and payment of teachers, the perennial challenge of youth to age and experience. And once again, it seems to me, the essence of education – the intimate dialogue between teachers and the taught, the care and nurture of young minds – is liable to be overlooked.

Enormous sums are being spent on fancy subjects – on batteries of gas and electric cookers, on tools and materials which would do credit to a shipyard, on bigger and better television sets, on special buses for pupils who must learn to swim but who have forgotten how to walk. Enormous sums are being spent on sociological investigations, the results of which could be forecast free of charge by any sensible teacher or parent.

The whole situation reminds me of the country minister who one Sunday, during a spell of dry weather, prayed for rain for the farmers. Sure enough, during the week it rained incessantly, from morning to night. The following Sunday he got up in the pulpit, and, in reproving tones, prayed again: 'O Lord, I know that last Sunday we prayed for rain, but this is ridiculous!'

In all the turmoil of innovation I think young minds are still in danger of being neglected. Subjects included in the fancy side of education are all splendid in their own way, but are they educative in the true sense? Is it progress that they should be crowded into a school curriculum at the expense of the Three Rs, of the humanities, of modern languages (including the Gaelic), of the sciences, of modern studies and, above all, of history and English (and Scottish) language and literature?

Certainly all these ancillary subjects should be dealt with in good schools, but, it seems to me, only in a minor way, to reinforce basic training in the home, by parents. Then more attention could be given to the real work of educating young minds and money saved with which to improve teachers' salaries.

Instead of our 'welfare' society being kind to its young – which in all charity, I am sure is its intention – has it not become as cruel as the noblemen and landowners of John Knox's day? Are some short-sighted parents and teachers not aiding and abetting in this cruelty, encouraging take instead of give, encouraging this disastrous, anti-social modern concept that each child should be allowed to 'do his own thing'?

Teachers who really have a care for children – they are still in the majority, though perhaps an increasingly silent majority – are those who insist on discipline and the values of authority.

'But what,' it may be said, 'can you do with the kind of children we have today?' This is a valid point, though when I hear parents griping about the lack of discipline in schools I always want to ask what they themselves are doing about it at home, where discipline should begin. But I don't think that either parents or teachers should blame the children.

'The young people of today love luxury. They have bad manners, contempt for authority and disrespect for their elders. They no longer get up when old people enter the room. They contradict their parents, wolf their food and tyrannize their teachers.'

Who said this? Malcolm Muggeridge? Robin Day? The Rector of Glasgow High School? Not so. It was Socrates, another well-known headmaster, who, incidentally, got so steamed up about his apparent lack of success with children that he took an overdose and died in 399 BC.

The nature of children doesn't change, only the philosophical and political climates in which they live. At the moment, it seems to me, we are threatened by an ice age.

A teacher's sacred duty, according to one school of sociology, is to restore youth's faith in the older generation. To this end he must be unfailingly reasonable, totally unbiased, open to cultural innovation and undismayed by personal hostility. The sociologists don't explain how this is supposed to prepare the young for a world that can be relied upon to display none of these characteristics. Nor do they explain why such a burden should be put upon teachers alone, with no mention of parents, who surely have the prime responsibility.

My own idea of a teacher's sacred duty is that he should endeavour to establish in young minds not only knowledge and how to use it but also a higher concept of living, an ideal of discipline, with love and full consideration for other human beings. And surely the best way he can do this is by personal example.

In the church today there are clergymen who go to great lengths trying to be with it, pandering to what they imagine is a modern youthful taste in music, clothes, permissiveness. The Padre had a name for them: 'blasted mountebanks'. I think there are some trendy teachers who try to do the same, who try to become popular by glorifying the idea that youth must always be allowed to do its own thing. The tragedy is that such clergymen and teachers nearly always fail, discovering, often too late, that popularity and respect can be acquired only in the long term, when their congregations and their pupils have learned to appreciate that ethics and education have unchanging standards: standards laid down long ago for the benefit of society as a whole.

I remember my sister Rona telling me how one day she met another lady teacher coming along a corridor in Campbeltown Grammar School. In one hand she carried a Bible, in the other a strap. 'There you are, Rona,' she said: 'the foundations of Scottish education!' It could be argued that the Bible and the strap are twin symbols of discipline, spiritual and physical. Has Scottish education improved so much since they went out of fashion?

Robert Louis Stevenson summed up teaching in two lines:

> Lord, thy most pointed pleasure take
> And stab my spirit broad awake.

The word 'stab' infers a measure of pain, in the sense of hard discipline, and I reckon modern society is inclined to shy away from pain as a therapeutic agent. There is pain in real education. Is it progress to shy away from that, too?

Good progress has also been made in medicine. But again, is it not progress almost entirely in a material sense?

It has been pointed out to me that the boundaries of medicine are precise, that the art of medicine is the diagnosis and treatment of diseases of the body due to physical causes. But is this not as narrow a vision of medicine as Calvinism is of Christianity, as the science of statistics is of modern philosophy? I believe that real progress in medicine must encompass not only a developing knowledge of science but also a developing knowledge of integrated humanity – of what Neil Munro used to call 'the strange cantrips of the human heart'.

When he retired during the Second World War, Dr James Niven had been practising in Southend for more than fifty years. He brought Jock into the world, charging me three guineas for a long night's work, and his proud boast was that in all his professional career he never lost a baby. Dr Jim, as we called him, was typical of the old-fashioned country doctor. 'Keep warm and take an aspirin' was his panacea for many ills.

He was frank and friendly. If Old Roderick had an ingrowing toe-nail Dr Jim cut it out, either in Old Roderick's bedroom or in his own firelit surgery. Then he advised his patient not to be a vain old so-and-so but to wear boots a size larger in future. As nature completed the cure Old Roderick had an enjoyable time informing his long-suffering family and village-corner cronies about his 'operation'.

Modern medicine tends to treat Old Roderick in an entirely different way. Every resource of science is deployed for his physical benefit, but his need for spiritual solace is apt to be ignored.

In many areas of Scotland – though not, I am thankful to say, in Southend – Dr Jim has become Dr Who, a faceless member of a group practice and a comparative stranger to Old

Roderick. He examines the suppurating toe in silence and with apparent indifference. He fills in a number of suspicious-looking forms, then summons an ambulance – in certain circumstances even an air-ambulance – and Old Roderick is lugged away from his family and cronies into a distant hospital, to him a cathedral of dreadful mysteries. Nobody tells him what's going on or even what's wrong with him. Great machines are wheeled in to probe and X-ray the offending toe, and poor Old Roderick – to the scientists a mere number on a card – spends hours of anxiety, homesick and lonely, imagining that he has gangrene or foot and mouth disease – and that in any case his leg is going to be amputated.

Eventually his toe is cured – of course it is: after all, we're in the last quarter of the twentieth century – but his nerves are shattered. He is lucky if he escapes at last without being taken into care by lurking psychiatrists.

Could all this commotion and worry for a patient not be avoided if GPs in general and hospital doctors in particular were encouraged to act like human beings, not as diagnostic rubber stamps subservient to the twin gods of group practice and specialist science?

I have a vision of what may happen in the near future, if medicine continues to progress only in scientific terms. I see a Prime Minister with Margaret Thatcher's brain, Jim Callaghan's heart, Enoch Powell's lungs and Michael Foot's liver, with rib-cage by Universal Skeletons Limited and legs and arms by Road Crashes Unlimited. In the heat of parliamentary debate this monster seethes and bubbles and finally blows up in our faces. And why? Because as yet no doctor has enough skill and understanding to help it acquire a coherent personality. Because, instead of 'Onward, Christian soldiers', the slogan now seems to be 'Onward, Christian Barnard'.

Of course, all this is exaggerated – I am not a practising journalist for nothing – and entirely unfair to the good and dedicated doctors who make up the great majority of the medical profession. But it is on the good and dedicated doctors that we must rely to guide progress in medicine along human as well as scientific channels. I am convinced that doctors should never detach themselves from humanity any more than ministers of religion should detach themselves from politics, any more than politicians should detach themselves from the spiritual as opposed to the economic needs of their constituents.

So, out there in the garden, I came to an end of my think about progress. I had found a definition – a vague definition which I realized could be satisfactory only to myself (and perhaps to Jean) a definition which depended a good deal on my belief that progress should be built upon tried and tested spiritual values, such as those of Christianity.

It had, however, cleared my mind of sourness in regard to imaginary oil-rigs at the Mull of Kintyre. It showed me plainly that our parish of Southend, being a microcosm of Scotland, is constantly liable to upheavals in thought and action, for which even the coming of the black, black oil represents only a small tremor in the graph of time.

11

What about that Parish Pump?

The Padre believed that in spite of the many wrong turnings we take at times, the spiritual and physical condition of humanity is slowly improving. During quiet intervals I think so, too. Nuclear disaster may threaten. Some groups in society may lose discipline and become softly permissive. The oil industry may have an ugly side to it. Education and medicine may take curious twists. But all the time, as we continue to emerge from temporary clouds of fog, we are getting nearer the sunlight. I disagree with an erudite friend of mine at Edinburgh University who equates human progress with the labour of Sisyphus, the King of Corinth who, for his sins, was banished to Hades, condemned for ever to push a block of marble up a hill, only for it to roll back down again each time.

Sometimes, as I contemplate the hurly-burly of clashing desires and ideologies, the situation does appear Sisyphean to me. Not long ago I read about an area of green fused sand uncovered in the Arabian desert: green fused sand which, though hundreds of thousands of years old, was exactly similar to that found in New Mexico after the explosion of the first experimental A-bomb. My flesh did a cold creep. But then it occurred to me that even though my imaginings might have validity, my mind was much too finite to grasp the whole picture. Perhaps this was a sealed loft I wasn't supposed to try and open. Better to mind my own simple business and concentrate on lofts of lesser mystery.

My publisher, guide and good friend, Gerald Austin, once said to me: 'When you reach the age of about eighty and have become a doyen of Scottish letters' – 'That would be like Willie Hamilton becoming a member of the Privy Council!' I interjected – 'when you reach that stage, Angus, then you can write a book of mystic philosophy. At present you tell stories better than you philosophize. So keep on telling stories.' Then, pursuing English logic to a canny conclusion, he added: 'They pay better.'

It sounds like something my practical mother might have said, and I am grateful for the advice and for the discipline such advice imposes. But behind the gratitude, behind the image I endeavour to present of a hard-headed professional writer, there is a Hebridean mystic – perhaps a kind of latter-day Brahan Seer – struggling to get out. The Padre would have understood. I think Jean and Jock and my brothers understand, too. And suffer with patience the moody results.

In this book I have essayed a compromise, using stories to reveal some of the background details which have shaped my Scottish way of living and thinking: some of the rocks which are ingredients in my Scotch, important to me, if perhaps to nobody else. The result may be incoherent, but in its very incoherence I believe it presents a relevant picture.

I remember once being greeted at Achnamara front door by a stranger, who said he had been watching me on television. 'My goodness,' he went on, looking me up and down, 'you're a big man. Seeing you on the goggle box I thought you were a dwarf with ulcers!' It may be that the writing in *Rocks in My Scotch* creates the same effect as a television tube. If so, I have no gripe. Truth, like beauty, is in the eye of the beholder.

There are many other rocks which to me are of importance.

I remember St Andrew, who wasn't a Scot at all but, according to some scholars, a Russian.

The legend is that St Regulus, otherwise St Rule, landed in Fife from Europe with relics of St Andrew: 'an arm-bone, three fingers, a tooth and a knee-pan'. The date of this happening is uncertain, estimates ranging from the fourth century to the eighth. But it gave Scotland a patron saint and a beautiful town:

St Andrews, a miniature of cultural Scotland with its history, religion, education – and golf.

It also gave us St Andrew's Night, on 30 November, when we eat haggis, sing 'Scots Wha Hae' with suitable fervour and raise our glasses to 'auld lang syne'. On this night we are the great folk, proud, independent, free.

But on the following day we face not only a hang-over but also reality. We go back to 'auld claes an' parritch', to competing for a living as we try to sell oil and coal and steel, ships and cars and oil-rigs to the Americans, the Germans, the Russians, the Chinese – and, of course, the English. On 30 November we are 'Jock Tamson's bairns'. Next day we realize once more that Jock Tamson's bairns are international.

On St Andrew's Night we toast the thistle and the motto that goes with it: '*Nemo me impune lacessit*', 'Nobody affronts me without getting hurt'. Perhaps this is one reason why the English call us, at times, intolerant and even arrogant. But the English – especially the southern English – should remember that our memory of oppression is much more recent than theirs.

There was Flodden, when the young Scots king and his still younger soldiers – 'the floo'ers o' the forest' – were 'a' wede awa' '. There was Glencoe, when innocent men were slain in the snow on orders from London. There were the redcoats after Culloden and the savage Clearances, when the people's homes and lives were sacrificed on the altar of higher profits for the landowners. There was the martyrdom of the unemployed on Clydeside and elsewhere between the wars, an echo of which seems to be occurring even now.

This is why some of us have a thistle complex. Flodden and Glencoe, the Clearances and the 'Hungry Twenties' are not such ancient history. They can still cause prickly reaction against any threat, real or imaginary, to our chosen way of life. The memories of injustices in the new countries of Africa will not easily be forgotten either.

We are, however, aware of our problem. If Scotland is to be worth living in and worth enjoying, like our coloured brothers we must forgive and remember only with objectivity. Instead of being inward-looking, jealously guarding our pride, we must try to give something, to share our ideals with the world.

We have plenty to give.

I remember Bannockburn.

There they stood on the morning of 24 June 1314, 7000 Scots inspired by the love of freedom against 25000 feudal mercenaries of the King of England. Behind them the dark mountains of their homeland. In front, along the banks of the burn, the glittering panoply of the English army, 'banners right fairly flaming, and pencels to the wind waving'.

Before the battle the Scots knelt on the ground while a passage from the Bible was read by the Abbot of Inchaffray. 'Comfort ye, comfort ye, my people.' Then they listened to his prayer: 'Deliver us, O Lord, from our enemies and from the hands of those that hate us.'

From the low ground Edward II saw them on their knees. He laughed. 'They are afraid! Will such men fight?' But his adherent, the Earl of Angus, who knew his countrymen, shook his head gravely and answered: 'Your Majesty, they will fight. Those men are not afraid.'

Suddenly the Scots attacked: the men of Strathclyde and the Borders under Sir James Douglas; the men of Ross and Inverness under Thomas Randolph, Earl of Moray; the men of Buchan and Mar and Lennox under the King's brother, Edward. Bruce himself commanded the reserve, his own tenantry from Carrick and the clansmen from Argyle and the Isles.

The English were trapped between the rising waters of the Forth and the Bannock burn, so that their superior strength could not be deployed; and the battle swung decisively when Bruce called upon Aonghas Og, MacDonald of the Isles, to rally his men and charge the English flank. 'My hope is constant in thee,' he said, words that can still be found on the Clanranald coat of arms. Finally the *coup de grâce* was delivered by the 'small folk', the farmers, the fishermen, the clerks and the weavers, the ordinary people for whose liberties Bruce was fighting.

I am proud not so much concerning the outcome of the battle but that before it the Scots were not ashamed to pray. (It is sad to record that like Cromwell's troops in England 300 years later, who were also not afraid to pray, they went on to fight and kill and maim with savage enthusiasm. Why? What lies behind this particular sealed door?)

I am proud to remember, too, that only seven years after Bannockburn, in 1320, the clergymen and people of Scotland sent a remarkable letter to the Pope. It is now called the Arbroath Declaration.

For centuries any reference to this document was suppressed. Some years ago, in London, I spoke about it to a gathering of English writers. Few of them had ever heard of it. The passage from it most often quoted runs as follows: 'While there exist a hundred of us we will never submit to England. We fight not for glory, wealth or honour but for that liberty without which no virtuous man shall survive.'

But there is another passage which for me is equally magnificent: 'Should he [Bruce] abandon our cause or aim at reducing us or our kingdom, we will instantly expel him as a common enemy, and, under God, choose another King.'

It is hard to believe that such words were written while Robert the Bruce was at the height of his power and popularity. I look upon them as a trumpet call by Christians, echoing down the years: a trumpet call for democracy.

Frequently I have been told by my English friends that I am a typical Scot. I try to explain that there is no such animal.

To begin with, a typical Scottish accent doesn't exist. Some Highlanders have a musical lilt. Some Lowlanders are broad and deliberate. Glasgow has an accent which is often as difficult to understand as London's Cockney. My own is unique, a weird mixture of Highland, Lowland and Irish.

And what about the Scottish character? Highlanders are supposed to be either carefree and energetic or sad and lazy, according to their mood. Lowlanders and East Coasters are supposed to be dour and hard-working, tight-fisted and lacking in humour. Like all generalizations this is entirely misleading. Highlanders can be dour and Lowlanders carefree, and East Coasters can be full of fun. (In the Hebrides, where there are no trains to catch, I must admit that nobody pays much attention to the clock.)

The legend of Scottish meanness, including corny jokes about the streets of Aberdeen being deserted on a flag-day, is also misleading. In general we are a thrifty race, the result of nagging poverty in the past. But I think we can claim to be reasonably hospitable, to our neighbours and to strangers. We give foreigners a genuine if sometimes cautious welcome, and I have never encountered in Scotland anything like a colour bar.

Kushi Mohammed, born in Pakistan, comes into our homes to sell his drapery and have a cup of tea, and we return the visit to sample his curry and chapattis. There is not the slightest embarrassment on either side. Kushi is a Scot now, like the rest of us.

It may be said, however, that our hospitality is not always purely altruistic. Some of us make a handsome living looking after strangers, encouraged by the Tourist Board.

There was an old lady in Kintyre who gave board and lodging to a famous artist. Before he left he showed her a painting he had made of her cottage and the glen behind it. 'This will be hung in a London gallery,' he said. 'Thousands of people will see it. You've been so good to me that now I'd like to return the compliment. Is there anything special you'd like me to add to the picture – a tree or a bush, your favourite flowers, for example?' 'Oh, *chiall*,' she said, 'I'm not sure if there's anything really. But since you're kind enough to ask – and since it will be seen by so many people – maybe you could be putting a wee notice in the window of the cottage there: "To let for August"?'

I don't believe that as Scots we are particularly mean, though, of course, we have no monopoly of hospitality. London has the reputation of being cold and aloof, but my personal experience is that Londoners are as kind and generous to a stranger as any people in the world.

In Scotland, however, we have an advantage. We have a heritage from St Columba, who, while in Iona, wrote this poem:

> I saw a stranger yestreen:
> I put food in the eating-place,
> Music in the listening-place;
> And in the sacred name of the Trinity,
> He blessed myself and my house,
> My cattle and my dear ones,
> And the lark said in her song,
> Often, often, often goes the Christ
> In the stranger's guise.

Another legend is that we are a parochial lot in Scotland, thirled to the parish pump, for ever bolstering up our ego with songs like 'Hail, Caledonia!' and 'Scotland the Brave'. There may be some truth in it, but I believe that everybody is touched with tar from the same brush. What could be more parochial than 'Maybe it's because I'm a Londoner?' What more perfervidly nationalistic than 'Land of Hope and Glory'?

I think there is a question here as to whether pride in one's own parish is such a bad thing after all.

At the present time we are constantly being brain-washed with the idea that no one is important except as a citizen of the country as a whole, except as a member of a union or of the CBI. Statistics and balance sheets are being offered in place of character. Big Brother is doing his best to smother individuals under great blankets of bureaucracy. Resting on our shoulders in Scotland are community councils, district councils, regional councils, a Scottish Assembly, a Parliament in London and yet another Parliament in Brussels. The mind even of a spiritual Atlas would boggle at the concept. Is it not time to argue that no individual can ever be a good citizen of the country as a whole – or, indeed, of the world – without first being a good citizen of his own parish?

When the Royal Scots Fusiliers stormed ashore in Sicily, officers and men fought and died for their regiment, only incidentally for the British Army. We were the 'Fusil Jocks', Marlborough's Own, not an obscure unit in the 5th Division of the 13th Corps. People like St Columba and St Margaret, Wallace and Bruce and the ladies of the Covenant, Robert Burns, Sir Walter Scott, David Livingstone: all those have left behind examples of nobility to the world, not because they were neatly docketed citizens of the world but because they were independent individuals, ready to sacrifice wealth and comfort, even their very lives, to uphold the values of freedom and the freedom of thought so dear to them as Scots.

A Water Board office shines with chromium. Splendid. But don't let us forget that Water Board machinery is merely the extension of a basic principle. Why allow the parish pump to lie rusty and neglected?

In forty-five years as a free-lance writer in Scotland I have had good times and bad, like any other man. But fortune was with me at the beginning in that it was much easier for an apprentice author to get a book published in 1932 than it is in 1977, when financial considerations inhibit a publisher from taking too many risks. During the middle years it was again fortune – and a kindly BBC – which enabled me to earn what for Jean and me was a satisfactory income. Now, in the old age pension period, fortune still has a smile for me: my books sell in respectable numbers; I am happy with Jean and Jock and friendly with all the other members of the family; I live in the bright open spaces of Southend among kind neighbours who, on the whole, are interested in human rather than material values; I have time to write, to attend church and do my duty as an elder, to play golf, work in the garden and take part in amateur drama.

Being a member of a vital community is one privilege I would never barter, even for a block-busting bestseller. Within the past three years two things have happened to illustrate what I mean.

The first occurred on Sunday 9 June 1974 when, with the co-operation of almost everybody in the parish, including our go-getting young minister, John Russell, and his wife Sheila, and with the technical assistance of Parkin Raine from Barnard Castle and Les Hutchines from London – two BBC engineers who have become adopted Southenders – the *Pageant of St Columba* was presented at the Footsteps at Keil. I had written and produced it, at rehearsals shouting through a megaphone at a cast of over sixty like a Scottish Cecil B. de Mille.

That Sunday morning the weather was bad. Hail showers blew in from the west. But at two o'clock, when the pageant was due to begin, the sun shone on a thousand spectators marshalled on the rock-strewn turf of 'the shoulder of the congregation' by my farming neighbours, Archie Barbour and Robert Ferguson.

Recorded bells rang out, disturbing the gulls on the high cliffs. Manned by Archie Cameron and coastguards Peter Webb and Donald Toon, the coracle appeared in the bay and approached the dark rocks and undulating seaweed on the shore. Meanwhile a pagan procession led by a Druid – retired tailor's assistant Ian Carruthers – began moving towards the Footsteps. There was no more I could do, so I sat there on the edge of the crowd and watched, worrying at first that hitches might rear up like spitting snakes but, when none appeared, becoming more and more conscious of my good luck in being one of such a dedicated and competent team.

I heard Jean's nephew, school-master John McKerral, reading the narration. I watched the players: Andy Dunn, also a school-master, as Briochan, the Archdruid; my golfing 'buddy' Allan Lamont, a retired headmaster, as Gabran, Chief Elect of the Epidii; Agnes McIntyre, the local school-mistress, as his wife and young Robert Ferguson as his infant son. They gathered on the grassy knoll accompanied by male and female servants and by the children of the tribe.

The children played and moved like experienced actors, their faces wrapt and angelic. None of the admiring spectators realized that at one stage during rehearsals, when their behaviour had been less than pacific, I had threatened to throw every scoundrelly one of them over the edge of the cliffs.

I heard the sound of a bugle – a medieval bugle brought all the way from Yorkshire by Harry Hodgson, another adopted Southender. Pert and pretty school-girl Anne McSporran, aged ten, called out that strangers were coming.

Up from the beach strode the singing disciples, at their head Columba, played by Alastair Cousin, the handsome local vet. Two pagan guards armed with spears – burly farmers Donald MacCallum and Ralph Davidson – stopped them at the foot of the knoll, then, reassured, allowed them to pass. I watched the confrontation of the pagan chief and the Christian chief and, later, the baptism of Gabran's son at St Columba's Well.

During it all I listened to the singing organized by Cissie MacConnachie, a farmer's wife, and Hamish Buchanan of the Muneroy Stores. I saw the colourful costumes made by Jan Carruthers and her three assistants and the shepherds' crooks and soldiers' spears whittled into shape by George Cammish and his coastguards. It was team-work by amateurs in the original sense of the word.

At the end Columba and his disciples said farewell to Gabran and moved away along the rocky path. The coracle became a motor-boat again, speeding back towards the jetty at Dunaverty. The whole congregation stood up, and together we sang 'Amazing Grace'.

I was glad that neither film nor television cameras were there and that no professional recording was made for radio. This was a show for Southend by Southenders. It was done in the way we wanted to do it, without interference from audience researchers or chartered accountants. I believe it gave us all a sense of fulfilment.

I remember with pleasure the willingness of everybody to take part.

Alec Harvey is big and hefty, with a ruddy complexion and black curling hair, who works by day as a tractor-man and on clear summer evenings as a casual fencer, painter and chimney-sweep. Sometimes he cuts Jean's drying-green with his rotary mower, and it was on one of these occasions that I approached him to play a disciple. Alec isn't a particularly enthusiastic churchman, but, being part Irish, he looked the part, and I was sure he would be a conscientious attender of rehearsals.

At first he demurred. 'Me, a disciple? The biggest heathen in Soothen'! It's no' possible!'

But when he had finished cutting the grass I put the idea to him again. This time, to my delight, he agreed. 'Great, Alec,' I said. 'I know you're going to enjoy it.'

He looked at me in silence, then shook his head. 'Man, Angus,' he replied, in a lugubrious tone which failed to camouflage a twinkle in his bright eyes, 'ye'll ha'e me walkin' on the watter next!'

During rehearsals, one of the disciples took sick and I asked Alastair Maiden, my friend, near neighbour and the Southend doctor, if he would take his place. At once he, too, agreed to help, though he was anxious about the short time available to practise some movement and mime. 'Follow Alec,' I told him. 'Do as he does and you won't go far wrong.'

When apprised of the situation, Alec was 'fair chuffed'. 'Imagine me tellin' the doctor whit tae dae! I'll get the sack frae ma union if they fin' oot. Demarcation o' areas, ye ken!'

In the outcome they both made outstanding disciples. Alec chose to be bright and breezy, smiling and waving to the 'gallery' as he passed by. Alastair was staid and 'holy', head bent as if in prayer, folded hands hidden in the voluminous sleeves of his habit. Columba himself would have been proud of them.

In the course of the pageant Columba and his disciples were due to walk in procession from the shore to the knoll of the Footsteps. Of necessity, part of this walk had to be along the main road, and I asked the police in Campbeltown for assistance and advice.

'Can the road be closed for half an hour or so?'

My friend Sergeant Hector McKinnon, a native of Tiree, slowly shook his head. 'I'm afraid not. Closing a public highway is just not on, except, of course, if there's an accident or anything like that. And I'm sure you'll not be wanting any accident on Sunday.'

'It's going to be a bit awkward if cars or buses come barging into the procession. For one thing it could be dangerous. For another it would spoil the illusion that the whole thing is taking place fourteen hundred years ago.'

He smiled with Hebridean wisdom. 'Don't worry. I'll put men on the road on either side of the Footsteps. If anybody is bad mannered enough to want to go through, we'll tell them there's a wee hold-up on ahead and ask if they'll please have patience for a minute or two. They'll start watching the pageant and before they realize what's happening it will all be over.'

Hector was as good as his word. Not a single vehicle was seen on the road during the whole of the pageant. The tact and discretion of Scottish policemen – especially if they have Highland connections, as so many of them do – are of a high standard.

Almost as soon as the pageant was finished, the rain and the hail came down again. As we cleared away the fences and the brushwood from around the main stage we all got soaked to the skin. But that didn't worry us. I remember thinking what remarkable progress had occurred in human relationships in Southend during the 300 years since the blood-stained siege of Dunaverty.

The other great moment of my life in a civilized community took place in Campbeltown on Saturday 26 April 1975.

Since 1952 our amateur drama team in Southend, now called the Dunaverty Players, has been competing annually in the SCDA's One Act Play Festival, with varying fortunes. Along the road we have met with happy success and unhappy failure. Up till 1975 we had won the local preliminary festival in Kintyre many times. Only once, however, in 1967, had we reached the Scottish final. That year it was held in the Queen's

Hall, Dunoon, and our intimate little play was lost on the huge stage. But we had kept on trying, because we believed that competitive festivals provided the flow of adrenalin necessary for good performance.

Amateur drama is like war. There are the long periods of training during rehearsals, the sudden bursts of action at festivals, the spit and polish before local shows, the wonderful sensation, at the season's end, of going on leave. I have had more than a quarter of a century of it now, and not one moment would I have missed, even though, like other people involved, it has cost me plenty in time and money.

Why do we do it?

One reason, I think, is that amateur drama provides a means of self-expression – and thus of communicating with other people – denied to football fans and watchers of the telly. Football fans can throw bottles or go 'streaking' across pitches, telly-watchers can blaspheme and kick in their sets when a programme displeases them; but policemen and hire-purchase agents are inclined to frown on such ego-trips. It is safer and more satisfying to take part, to get rid of inhibitions and simmering moral messages by acting them out on the stage for the benefit of audiences.

Another reason is that members of a drama club, working together, can acquire a knowledge of human nature far more extensive than that of people less involved in the social situation. They acquire it in the study of plays, in the discipline necessary to understand and portray the characters in these plays, in the tolerance necessary when a discovery is made (sometimes happy, sometimes sad) of one another. In drama, as in war, team-work is a prerequisite of success. Without discipline, without tolerance there is no team-work. But with discipline and tolerance there is not only team-work but also an end-product of lasting comradeship.

On account of our geographical situation we in Southend have seldom the opportunity of measuring our productions against those in the professional theatre. (There is television theatre, of course; but though valuable as a guide to characterization this has little to offer the stage as far as plot, movement and projection are concerned.) As far as possible, however, we have tried to maintain high standards, and through the SCDA's advisers, travelling the countryside in wind, rain and snow (like our own club members), we have learned, slowly but surely, what these standards are. Occasionally we have approached attainment. More often we fail, but this is our fault, not that of the advisers.

Through the years we have also learned that amateur drama is not designed for our pleasure alone. We have recognized that the theatre was invented for the benefit of the populace, not for self-indulgent actors and producers, and that artistic achievement depends on the willing co-operation of an audience. There is nothing sadder, for me, than the yawning apathy from 'front of house' when certain 'experimental' plays are being dragged out on stage, but nothing more wonderful than the response of an audience which gives utter silence during a moment of tension then laughs uproariously when the playwright and his actors change the mood.

At the beginning of the 1974–5 season, therefore, we in the Dunaverty Players had considerable knowledge behind us, even though we do live at the Mull of Kintyre and the population of Southend is only 500. A play was chosen called *Rise and Shine*, by a Canadian writer, Elda Cadogan. Set in a graveyard, like many good plays it didn't look particularly promising at first; but the comedy was sharp and the plot appealed to our Scottish sense of humour, which can discover fun even in funerals.

Alastair Maiden, fresh from his stint as a disciple, took over production. He recruited Hamish Buchanan as stage manager; Margaret Cameron, assistant in a local shop, as prompter; Jan Carruthers as wardrobe mistress and Parkin Raine as effects man. (One of the effects was the Last Trump, so a BBC engineer was needed to cope with that one.) Jim Johnstone, manager of an ink factory, was made leading man and Jennifer, John McKerral's American wife, leading lady. Mabel Maiden,

Alastair's wife, and John McKerral himself, our most experienced actor, were given the two supporting parts.

Rehearsals were occasionally fraught, as the cast struggled with Canadian accents. The stage crew, which included Jim Johnstone's wife Maureen, farmer's daughter Janet Ferguson and Jan Carruthers' husband Ian, laboured to produce polystyrene tombstones and to paint them in mouldering shades of green and grey. But at the preliminary SCDA festival in Campbeltown *Rise and Shine* was a clear winner with both the adjudicator and the audience. (Strange as it may seem, this happy conjunction doesn't always occur.)

Our next move was to the SCDA Western Divisional Final in Castle Douglas. As we were due to perform on a Saturday evening we hired a bus and, after our work, began the journey late on the Friday afternoon. The bus-driver was young Jim Cameron, who understands about temperamental 'dramatists' and who, during our long-distance forays, regards himself as one of the team. Unfortunately, when we reached a certain roundabout near Ayr, Jim received bad advice from somebody and took the wrong road. As midnight approached we found ourselves near Sanquhar, lost in a country of heather and streaming rain and apparently as far away from Castle Douglas as we had been hours before.

The trouble was, nobody had remembered to bring a map. A committee formed itself to decide on a valid route. But as so often happens with committees its members could find no point of agreement. Through the darkness – 'through the night of doubt and sorrow' – we thundered on, following tracks which plunged down into glens and reared up across bare hills, arguments raging in the committee as we came to unidentified road-forks and junctions.

That night, in many a remote hamlet in Dumfries-shire and Kirkcudbrightshire, I am sure legends were born of a ghost bus passing through on its way to the afterworld; and if the uneasy inhabitants had chanced to glimpse the pile of tombstones and other graveyard props at the back of Jim's bus, their supernatural fears would have been confirmed. (There was one small village which, inadvertently, we encountered twice, another which heard the swishing and squelching of our tyres three times.)

At last, however, somewhere near New Galloway, we came upon a sign: 'Castle Douglas – 8 miles'. We were saved.

It was after one o'clock in the morning when we reached our hotel. Having arrived hours before by car, Jock and Parkin Raine were there to welcome us and prescribe soothing 'medicine'. Our ordeal was soon forgotten.

And forgotten so thoroughly that on the following evening *Rise and Shine* won the Divisional Cup, and we found ourselves – incredibly – moving forward to the Scottish final, with teams from Paisley, Greenock and Glasgow floundering in our wake.

While the adjudicator was making his final remarks I sat with Jim Johnstone, who had wiped off his greasepaint and made a hurried change from costume into conventional garb. As the result was announced we sprang to our feet, embraced each other and let out a simultaneous roar, like the roar of steam escaping from over-stressed boilers. All the hard work, all the frustrations and anxieties were forgotten in a moment of sheer delight. People around us laughed. What did we care?

Producer Alastair came on stage to receive the trophy. I could see that he was in a daze of glory, hardly conscious of what was happening. Tomorrow he would realize that in less than a month he would be faced with the problem of whipping his team back into action for the Scottish Final at Campbeltown. As for me, I was beginning to believe that a vision which had inspired the Dunaverty Players for almost twenty-five years might be verging on reality.

Campbeltown's Victoria Hall being our home ground, it was like Rangers playing the final of the SFA Cup at Ibrox or Celtic playing it at Parkhead. There are advantages in such a situation: the home team has no long-distance travelling to do and the 'ground staff' are sympathetic. There is also one disadvantage:

the home team becomes so anxious to do well before a local audience that pressure builds up to a dangerous level.

During that beautiful April evening, as we prepared to stage the most important performance in our history, temperaments bubbled. I dared not approach members of the team even to wish them well. Alastair, usually so kind and gentle, growled like a cornered bear. Hamish Buchanan lost his 'behind the counter' charm and snapped angrily at anybody who went near his precious tombstones. Jim Johnstone could not eat, drink or speak. Jennifer McKerral threw tantrums at Jan Carruthers about her stage 'goonie'. Mabel Maiden looked as grim as the black, Presbyterian character she was about to portray. John McKerral, old trouper though he was, kept repeating his lines and declaring that he was about to forget them all.

When the curtain went up on *Rise and Shine* I found myself sitting among the audience in a state of tension equalled only twice before in my life: first, when Jock was born, and second, when I faced a television camera for the first time. Jean was so tense herself that she had no comfort to spare. Jock, beside us, tried hard to achieve a sports reporter's blasé objectivity, but his silence betrayed him. Around us, all the Dunaverty Players not taking part were biting finger-nails and composing silent, incoherent prayers.

Soon after the performance began, I sensed that a terrible thing was happening. At the preliminary festival in the same hall, the Kintyre audience had laughed without inhibitions; now it was afraid to laugh, in case laughter might upset the players. When an audience responds actors blossom like flowers in June sunlight. When it is restrained, worrying more about the performance than the play, actors feel it and tend to strain for effect. But as *Rise and Shine* went on I began to see the value of persistent rehearsals. The players were living on the substance of what they had learned and practised. In spite of their nerves they were doing well. Not so well as at Castle Douglas, where laughter and applause had lifted their spirits, but well enough.

Afterwards, Alastair and his actors were despondent. They felt they had done badly and could not be persuaded that instinctive skill had brought success.

At the end of the festival, when the adjudicator came on stage to announce the final placings, I knew from 'a gut reaction' (to flourish a fashionable phrase) that the winner must be either Paisley Old Grammarians with *Plaza Suite, Act III* or Dunaverty Players with *Rise and Shine*. And when first place was given to Dunaverty Players – and second to Paisley Old Grammarians – with 600 others in the Victoria Hall I rose to my feet and gave a long shout of triumph. It was hard to believe. We were Scottish champions.

I went on stage to congratulate Alastair. He was clutching the cup in the zombiefied way a pools winner clutches a six-figure cheque. I put out my hand. He saw it and put out his. But he walked past me, his hand still outstretched, and became tangled with the stage drapes. At that moment he was the leading amateur producer in Scotland. No wonder he had contracted what he himself might have diagnosed as 'euphoric trauma'.

That was a night, that was. Mary Taylor, the club president, decreed that joy should be 'unconfined'. At one stage I sang a song in praise of the producer. I called it 'The Gentle Maiden', but the words bore no resemblance to those of the original. I felt like a Sisyphus, who, miraculously, has at last got his block of marble to the top of the hill.

Perhaps it wouldn't stay up there for long. In that case there would be no regrets.

After all, hill-tops are draughty places.

Index

SILVER IN MY SPORRAN

Angus MacVicar

SILVER IN MY SPORRAN

Confessions of a writing man

To encourage (and entertain)
Rona Munro
and other beginning writers

Contents

1. The Rudiments of Criticism

When we were boys at the Manse the path from our back gate to Kilblaan was a complicated one.

At first it followed a tree-screened cart-track, rutted by rain water, which curved like a boomerang down to the glebe. Then, approaching the river-bank, it darted off sideways to make use of the 'shooters' ' bridge over the Con. On the opposite bank it plunged improbably into a bramble thicket frilled by primroses, emerging at last beside a hill-burn spanned by a 'shoogly' plank. Farther on it climbed a short, steep brae, where purple irises spilled out above a disused lime-kiln. Finally, it made contact with another cart-track leading straight to the farmhouse.

The bridge, hand-railed on one side only, and the plank, less than two feet wide, were always described to us as potential hazards by our anxious mother. But we traversed the path almost daily, because at the end of our journey was Hugh McEachran, our father's kirk treasurer: bachelor Hugh, with his bushy red beard, his carpenter's shop littered with tools and aromatic wood shavings, his heavy Clydesdale horses and sharp-horned Ayrshire cattle and, above all, his enthralling, oath-encrusted stories.

Hugh was an old man when we knew him, with an old man's privileged position as 'the gaffer'. The hard work on the farm was done by his sister Flora and middle-aged bachelor nephew, Archie, while he himself pottered about the steading repairing harness, manufacturing new spokes for damaged cart-wheels, sharpening knives and adzes on a whirling, foot-powered grindstone and, most of all to his taste, attending to and conversing with visitors like us.

At least once a week we were accompanied on our journey to Kilblaan by our father, the Padre, who was not only minister of the parish of Southend at the Mull of Kintyre, but also Hugh's dearest friend.

Hugh's behaviour and attitude to life interested and puzzled us.

He was an elder, a regular churchgoer and a meticulous curator of the pennies and ha'pennies that went into the plate each Sunday, a man whose word was reputed never to have been broken and who did nobody a bad turn if he could help it. His instinct was always to succour people in distress, though he found it difficult to express deep emotion: the only way he could do this was to make himself available at the threshold of a crisis.

During World War II my brother Archie died of wounds following the battle of Gerbini in Sicily. After the Anchor Line's *Britannia* was sunk by an enemy raider, my brother Willie's life-boat remained missing in the South Atlantic for twenty-one days. My brother Kenneth, his reconnaissance Hurricane shot down by the Japanese, was 'lost' for a week in the jungle beyond the Chindwin. On each occasion, while the Padre and my mother – with sister Rona, youngest brother John and Maimie the maid – suffered the deadly news, Hugh was constantly in or around the Manse. When Archie's death was officially announced in a War Office telegram, brought to the Manse by a weeping, trembling postmistress, Hugh was there and remained by my father's side for a long time, holding his hand. When Willie and Kenneth were finally reported safe he rejoiced with my parents, broad 'hechs-hechs' issuing from his beard as preface to the words: 'I tellt ye! I tellt ye they'd be a' richt!'

Hugh was known as a deeply religious man, and he himself would have been surprised if anyone had thought of him as less than Christian. And yet it occurred to us many a time that the flow of his compassion was sometimes interruped when he dealt with people and animals he considered recalcitrant or sinful.

One day my father brought him the news that a member of a well-known local family, for centuries at odds with the McEachrans, had died of influenza. Hugh's reaction astonished us: 'Ach, him! I never kent any o' that lot tae be killed in battle or droont at sea!'

Another day I became distressed by the sorry condition of one of his heifers, which for some time had been refusing to eat and was now slumped disconsolately in its stall. Hugh came down the byre carrying a basket filled with turnips. He emptied them into a trough in front of the sick beast and, in an entirely unsympathetic voice, addressed it thus: 'Bloody wee rascal! Ye'll eat them afore they'll eat ye!' Strangely enough the heifer did eat the turnips and eventually recovered.

Sometimes his horses and cattle sustained open wounds. This was generally the result of their brushing against barbed wire fences or, at a time before the de-horning of Ayrshire cattle became fashionable, of encounters with other head-slashing beasts. Hugh's remedy was always a gout of hot Archangel tar, slapped on with a flat stick apparently without regard to the pain caused to the animal. But we noticed it nearly always brought about a cure.

Fifty years ago long-horned Ayrshire bulls were dangerous animals, especially when they grew older and more short-tempered. (Years later Hugh's nephew was gored to death by one of them.) In their second or third year of duty rings were put in their noses, so that a chain could be attached: a heavy chain which, trailing on the ground, not only hampered their movements in the open fields but could also be secured with a long-handled hay-fork when it became necessary to bring them into the byre.

Archie, Willie and I once witnessed Hugh's method of ringing a bull. First of all he put a long, slim poker into the kitchen fire, so that gradually it would become red hot. Next, with his nephew's help, he turned the bull in its stall and, with ropes, secured it to ring-bolts on either side so that its head hung stiffly over the grip. Then he sent his nephew for a pot of Archangel tar, while he himself went to the kitchen for the poker. As he advanced down the byre, poker stem glowing and sparking, I suddenly realized what was going to happen. Swiftly and without hesitation he plunged the poker through the cartilege inside the bull's nose. His nephew splashed the smoking hole with tar. Hugh himself, discarding the poker, drew the ring from his pocket, opened it, thrust one end through the hole made by the poker and finally snapped it shut.

To this day I can see and hear and smell the operation. I can still feel sick – almost as sick as I felt when the poker burned through flesh and the bull sagged and staggered in its ropes.

But there was another less traumatic day when something happened to Hugh himself which caused us joyful giggles.

As was not unusual on farms in Kintyre, fifty or sixty years ago, the threshing mill, the turnip slicer and various other machines in the barn were driven by water power. Behind Kilblaan was a small dam constantly replenished by a burn which tumbled and twisted down from the hills. When Hugh decided on threshing or slicing he stood on a wooden plank above the dam's outlet to the water-wheel and opened the sluice by means of a rusty crank-handle.

On this warm and sunny afternoon he climbed on to the plank and, puffing and blowing through his beard, began tugging at the crank. Suddenly his foot slipped. He teetered, puffing more than ever, before plunging bodily into the brown water. We rushed to the dam-side, thoughts swirling in our minds concerning a rescue by heroic schoolboys. But the dam was only a few feet deep, and in a moment Hugh emerged unscathed, spouting water like a whale, his scanty hair dripping with slime and water-lily leaves.

His immediate reaction was unexpected. In his waistcoat pocket, secured by a chain with a fob to it, he kept a silver watch that had belonged to his father, a fat hunter-type at least three inches in diameter. It was his dearest possession. Now, as he erupted from the deep, like Poseidon, he took no thought of his own condition. He whipped out the watch, surveyed it, held it against his ear and then announced to us with a triumphant smile: 'She's gaun, boys! She's still gaun!'

In spite of all the contradictions in his character, in spite of an Old Testament severity in some areas of conduct, Hugh had a faith which was the envy of us all. As he lay on his death-bed my father sat by him.

'I can see, Hugh,' said the Padre, 'that you're not afraid to die.'

'Feart, minister?' said Hugh, whispering his surprise. 'Why should I be feart?'

The McEachrans are of old Kintyre stock. Their name comes from the Gaelic, meaning 'sons of the horsemen'. It keeps recurring in old deeds and titles dating back to the sixteenth century; it is probable that the family is descended from the *Epidii*, the Celtic tribe which prompted Ptolemy, in the second century AD, to call Kintyre *Epidion Akron*, the land of the horsemen.

Cnoc Araich, a green hill beetle-browed with whins, is situated immediately behind the Manse on High Machrimore Farm, confronting Kilblaan across the valley of the Con. On its flat summit, covering about six acres, there can be seen the remains of a settlement dating from about 600 BC to 400 AD. With the Royal Commission on the Ancient and Historical Monuments of Scotland I share a theory about this *dun*. On account of its size, may it not have been the headquarters (or principal village) of the *Epidii*?

Listening, as a boy, to the Padre and Hugh discussing Cnoc Araich, I had an impression of Southend as a place in which roots go very deep; even then I think my ambition was to continue nurturing my roots in the same warm and fertile soil.

But the stories about old Southend which Hugh used to tell – stories to which we listened with the quiet concentration gifted only to children – were not only concerned with the question of family roots; they were also powerfully stimulating to the imagination. It may be that as I listened to them the idea was born that one day I, too, would become a storyteller. And possibly it was Hugh's own character, so difficult to analyse, that caused me to become permanently interested in people, the raw material out of which a storyteller constructs his products.

Later on I found that my father and mother – and Maimie, the maid – were equally fascinating characters; but at the age of nine or ten I viewed my parents and Maimie not as ordinary human beings but simply as rock-like symbols of security and authority, untrammelled by weakness, like the Holy Trinity.

Hugh's stories were much to our taste. Concerning wreckers, smugglers, poachers and other enemies of an organized society, they provided source material for many plays enacted by my brothers and myself in the Manse back yard.

The main character in one of Hugh's most acceptable stories was Black Angus MacNacht. It is said that he lived in the late sixteenth century in Gartvaigh, a farm which lies over the hill immediately behind Achnamara. According to Hugh he was a powerful man with long black hair and whiskers and a voice that could be heard 'a bloody mile away'. ('Bloody' was Hugh's favourite adjective. We were assured by the Padre that, unlike us young sophisticates, he had no idea it was a swear word.)

In his public image Black Angus was a diligent farmer, a responsible member of the community, regular in his attendance at religious services. But behind this appearance of respectability there lurked a secret: a secret making nonsense of the name MacNacht, which comes from a Pictish word meaning 'pure'. He was the leader of a wrecking gang.

Across the bay from my study window I can see the Rock of Dunaverty, a turf-coated lump of Old Red Sandstone thirty metres tall. On its northern flank there used to stand a Clan Donald Castle, the meagre ruins of which can still be discovered among the grass and the nettles. In the sixteenth century, when Black Angus prowled in the night, it must have been an imposing fortress, though in winter, when bad weather dampened the ardour of the battling clans and fighting MacDonalds went home to their wives and children in Antrim and Islay, it was often left untenanted. At such times its empty western battlements provided the ideal site for a peat-fired brazier.

As Hugh carefully explained to us, a beacon often burned on the island of Sanda, two miles south-east of Dunaverty across the Sound, dutifully lit by the member of Clan Donald currently holding the island in feu. Vessels entering the North Channel from the north or west, rounding the Mull of

Kintyre on their way into the Clyde, kept this light on their starboard bow and found a safe passage between Sanda and the mainland. But on a dark night, with showers of hail sweeping down from the hills, the master of a small ship hugging the sheltered coast of the Mull might become confused and, seeing a light on Dunaverty, believe it to be the one on Sanda. Too late he would discover he was heading not for the Sound but for the black rocks of the Gearraidh Dubh. (They thrust long, ugly fingers into the sea less than fifty metres from our front door.)

And on the Gearraidh Dubh Black Angus and his gang would be waiting. When survivors struggled ashore throats would be slit and bodies hurled back into the sea. The vessel would be boarded and the cargoes of cloth and rum and timber carried stealthily away to secluded barns and caves.

The people of the parish knew the truth but were afraid to reveal it to the representatives of law and order, in those days the local chieftains of Clan Donald. Black Angus and his henchmen had spread the word that informers would be dealt with, by maiming or even death.

At this point in the story Hugh would pause, half-hidden eyes glinting at us from behind stiff red lashes. 'But bad men,' he would tell us, while the Padre nodded grave confirmation, 'bad men aye come tae a bad end.'

We waited. We needed proof. We wanted proof.

'One wild nicht,' said Hugh, at last, 'the wreckers put a licht on Dunaverty. After a while they saw a boat makin' for the Gearraidh Dubh. She was high at prow an' stern, no' like the ordinary cargo vessels sailin' between Antrim and the Clyde. But they werena worried aboot that. They'd never yet seen a boat that hadna somethin' valuable in her. So they rushed doon tae the shore, ready for action.

'The boat cam' closer, veered a bit tae the eastward, then struck – no' on the black rocks but on the soft sand o' Dunaverty Bay. This wasna what usually happened, but still the wreckers had nae inklin' o' danger. They dashed intae the surf, wi' their clubs an' knives, an' climbed aboard.

'At first they could see naebody. Then oot o' the hatches cam' a hale airmy o' men, armed wi' swords an' shields.

Black Angus an' his gang were cut doon an' killed an' fed tae the fishes.'

Archie and Willie and I let out breaths of excitement and satisfaction. 'But who were the armed men in the boat?' I asked.

'A Clan Donald chieftain an' his sodgers. Frae Islay. Comin' tae garrison Dunaverty Castle. Roondin' the Mull they were deceived by the licht on Dunaverty, but then, as they neared the shore, they jaloused what was gaun on an' steered for the sand. Their galley was refloated next day, at high tide. But' – and here Hugh chuckled – 'Black Angus didna float again.'

Is this a true story? I believe it may contain some truth. In the parish records I find there were MacNachts in Gartvaigh from 1505 until early in the seventeenth century and that the common family name was Angus. But I imagine that in the telling, over the centuries, it has acquired dramatic and moralistic qualities geared more to fiction than to fact.

The violence in it, and the apparent callousness of the narrator, may be compared with some offerings by today's cinema and television. Had it a bad effect on our tender minds? I shivered when I heard it, but at the same time a thought was planted in my ethical garden. 'Bad men aye come tae a bad end.' In modern films and plays this proposition is sometimes overlooked and violence presented simply for the sake of violence, with evil remaining unpunished. Is this the inartistic factor which renders the portrayal of violence dangerous to young viewers? Maybe so. In real life violence is always punished, either physically or spiritually. Has there ever existed an evil man who was happy?

Archie, Willie and I found ourselves in a privileged position.

We listened to Hugh's horrific stories and witnessed the life on his farm, where procreation, birth, savagery and death were regarded in a realistic and unsensational way. We grew up with few illusions about the natural world, thus avoiding the traumatic experiences of some adolescents brought up to believe in fairies and happy endings and animals acting and talking like human beings.

We were supplied with no pocket money. The Padre, living in a Manse with eleven rooms on an annual stipend of about £300, had none to offer. And Hugh, in those days of neglected agriculture, had no surplus cash to waste on children. For the odd half-crown to buy ice-cream and Sharpe's 'Super Kreme Toffee' we had to depend on our own wits: for example, on the sale to a scrap merchant of lead bullets surreptitiously dug out of the sand behind the Territorial Army target on Brunerican shore and to a dealer in Campbeltown of stamps collected from people in the parish with relatives abroad. This, I believe was good for us. When, later on, we had to fend for ourselves in a society with about 2 500 000 unemployed (and no 'social security') we were well equipped to endure and eventually overcome bouts of poverty. And when the Welfare State did come – blessed though it was – we had enough independence of spirit to avoid its enervating influence. Though Hugh and the Padre had no money to give they presented us with something far more valuable: the idea that the source of real happiness is obedience to the ten commandments and the giving of love and consideration to other people.

I, for one, have broken many commandments. Hate has burgeoned in my heart for a few of my neighbours. The desire to commit crude violence has often invaded me like a sickness. Each time the experience has made me miserable; and my conviction has grown stronger that to follow the realistic Christianity advocated by Hugh and the Padre is the only way to a good life.

Sometimes, as I grow older, I imagine I have found this good life. More often I recognize how sadly I have missed the way.

While ethical principles were being received and vaguely understood by my brothers and myself, other influences were at work. I was listening to Hugh's stories about Southend, to my father's about his native North Uist, to my mother's about her younger days in Appin and to Maimie's renderings of old-fashioned narrative poetry (like *Horatius* and *Barbara Freitchie*) and her whispered ghost tales of

Perthshire. An excitement occurred inside me, focusing into an ambition to tell stories of my own, in words of my own choosing. Even then the vanity of a writer was apparent: I dreamt of the day when my name would appear in a magazine or – joy of joys – on the cover of a book.

But I acknowledged to myself a lack of confidence in my tools. It was hard to find words and phrases that would, without ambiguity, convey my meaning. When I wrote something down it appeared childish to me. I failed to understand that I *was* a child.

My mother kept a copy of my first 'poem'. When she died in 1963 a small cardboard box was found in the drawer of her dressing-table. It contained her few private treasures, and the 'poem' was one of them.

Willie MacVicar, the boy of the day,
Has dogs and dollies and teddy-bears.
He has a sad and unfortunate habit
Of kicking them when he is crabbit.

I remember being ashamed of having to use the word 'crabbit', which is Scots for 'bad-tempered'; but there was no other way – or so it seemed to me – that I could procure a rhyme for 'habit'. (I wasn't completely satisfied with 'bears' as a proper rhyme for 'day', but with a writer's unflinching optimism I hoped it might get by.) In those days Scots (or Gaelic) words were considered crude, the Stone Age tools of the uneducated. Magisterial influence directed my sights on the 'correct' English of the school 'readers'. *Chambers's Radical Reading*, for example, contained excerpts from the works of H. B. Stowe, H. S. Pemberton, Christina Rosetti and others.

Today the scene in Scotland has changed. When I was young only roadmen, farm-labourers and elderly waitresses were called Jamie and Jock and Maggie. Now it is the height of fashion to own such names, and the Cyrils, the Georges and the Daphnes are reserved for another stratum of 'society'. Sir Walter Scott was then the exemplar of good writing. When we went to Campbeltown Grammar School from Southend in 1920, one of the first books we were told to buy was *Scott's Narrative Poetry* published by Nelson. At that time Burns's Tam O'Shanter was ignored and its author described condescendingly as 'the ploughboy poet'. Now poor old Sir Walter is no longer considered a genius in the use of English (though even the BBC admits that his plots are still the greatest) and Burns, in spite of using the word 'crabbit' many times, is universally admired. Indeed, the Edinburgh 'literati' would claim that the late C. M. Grieve is the proper example for a young writer, even though as Hugh McDiarmid, Grieve often wrote in Lallans, an invented Scots language which might be described as dead had it ever been alive.

For the most part, fashion in writing is created by the political and economic climate of the age, and, to a large extent by the critics. It is something which must be taken into account if a writer wishes to sell his work and thus communicate with as many of his fellow human beings as possible, but any author or poet worth his salt will ignore fashion if he believes it to be an inhibiting factor. On mature consideration I'm glad I called Willie 'crabbit'.

But at the age of twelve, brain-washed by an 'English' orientated education, I knew little about Scottish history or culture. (Indeed, my ignorance in this area remained almost total until after I went to grammar school and my father advised me to read *Tales of a Grandfather*.) I had a vague notion that I wanted to write about the people of Southend and their situation, but immediately after World War I nobody seemed to be interested in the ordinary folk of Southend. I felt I ought to be aiming higher – at, for example, the exciting and, at the time, highly popular stories about Bulldog Drummond. The fact that I knew nothing about the English society in which Bulldog Drummond moved and had his Fascist being worried me a lot less than it should have.

My only available target, therefore, seemed to be the enormous market for short stories which existed in the 1920s. In London, that is.

A beginning writer today, desperately seeking a home for his work, may well gasp with envy when confronted by the following (alphabetical) list of magazines willing and eager to buy short stories in 1923: *The Blue Magazine, Cassell's Magazine, Corner Magazine, The Happy Mag, The Home Magazine, Hutchinson's Magazine, Hutchinson's Adventure Story Magazine, London Magazine, Mystery Story Magazine, Nash's Magazine, New Magazine, The Novel Magazine, Pan, Pearson's Magazine, Premier Magazine, The Red Magazine, Romance, The Smart Set, Sovereign Magazine, The Story-teller, The Strand Magazine, Twenty Story Magazine, Violet Magazine, The Windsor Magazine, The Yellow Magazine.*

On being approached by a youth with Kintyre heather in his ears, the editor of *The Green Magazine* – a rose in the flourishing chaplet of the Amalgamated Press – detailed his requirements thus: '(a) strong adventure stories, with clearly drawn characters; (b) light, humorous stories, ingenious but not too involved, with witty dialogue; (c) well-constructed "crook" stories, with novel but not sensational situations; (d) sporting stories if off conventional lines and with human interest; (e) a few nature stories by authors who know their subject, preferably of such animals as lions, bears, etc., and stories of any type that will appeal to men and women alike. Length, about five thousand words.'

My knowledge of adventure was limited to poaching salmon in the burn which meandered through the Manse glebe-land and to launching homemade rafts in the shallow rapids below the Minister's Lynn. I suspected that a London editor might scoff at such tame pursuits. English humour and dialogue considered witty by an Englishman was, I feared, beyond my capability. I knew nothing about 'crooks' – that is, about the jewel thieves, con men and train robbers so often described in the magazine stories I so avidly read. I had never encountered a lion or a bear – or even, let it be said, a fox – except in print. On the other hand, I felt that I might be able to write a sporting story, 'off conventional lines and with human interest'. After all, I played football, cricket and golf and had won a few junior races at the Highland Games.

The editor of *London Magazine* was more intimidating. 'The short story that counts,' he wrote, 'is that which deals with life *as it is*: the characters should not be merely creatures of the author's imagination, but living, breathing actors in the story he has to tell. The soul-storms arising from love, jealousy, passion – all these things make stories if logically and not too theatrically treated. They may be placed in Mayfair or Bermondsey, but if the psychology be true they are certain of their following. Either a story is written because it *had* to be written, or it is merely part of the day's work of the author.'

Today, contemplating this vision of splendour, I take a deep breath – and then do a double take. As a twelve-year-old I was discouraged. I reckoned I had not yet experienced a 'soul-storm'. And 'life *as it is*', apparently to be found only in Mayfair or Bermondsey, was a far cry from the hills and salt-sprayed beaches of Southend.

But it occurred to me that if I failed to reach those high sierras of the fictional art I might still have a chance with the hundreds of weekly and juvenile publications which also bought short stories – publications ranging from *Answers, Tit-bits, John o'London's Weekly, Home Chat* and *Woman's Pictorial* to *The Boy's Own Paper, Captain* and *Chums*.

In Scotland I could discover only two magazines which published short stories: *Blackwood's* and *Chambers's Journal*. By the high-powered and somewhat patronising market guides they were described as 'literary', for no other reason, it seemed to me, than that they paid only a guinea a thousand words, whereas London editors offered two guineas a thousand even to unknown writers.

So there I was, a country boy seduced by artificiality, with an urge to write. Though I discussed the subject with no one – especially not with my parents, who were eager that I should become a minister of the Kirk – I felt that I *could* write. The trouble was that I had no confidence that what I wrote could be exchanged for editorial money. Already what has been described as 'author's schizophrenia' was beginning to haunt me. I wanted to be a good writer. I also wanted to be rich.

Today, more than fifty years on, I am bothered with the same affliction.

One evening my brothers and I visited Kilblaan and found that a stranger – a distant relative of the McEachrans – had come to recuperate there after an illness. He was a young man, in his twenties, the son of a former schoolmaster in Southend. As a child of ten, on the Hebridean island of Coll, he had been watching builders at work, when a granite 'skelf', one of a shower sent up by a careless stone-mason's hammer and chisel, had lodged in one eye. Soon afterwards he had become totally blind.

It was our first encounter with a blind person. We were disturbed by the pale, thin face into which suffering had been cut as if by a knife, and by the dark glasses which did not completely hide wrinkled and empty eye-sockets. We felt fear and resentment: fear of the unknown, resentment of an ugliness which had invaded our comfortable small paradise.

His name was James MacTaggart. With astonishment we discovered he was not only an accomplished musician but also, through the medium of Braille, a student of English literature. From the Manse piano and the church organ he produced thrilling sounds; he sang Scots and Irish songs in a lusty baritone at odds with his fragile looks. He composed music of his own and married it to verses he himself had written. In addition he played chess on a special board constructed by a friend. The pieces were pegged into small holes, and as the game went on his fingers kept passing over the chessmen so that their relative positions might remain in his mind's eye.

At first we were shy of him, but as the months – and years – of his convalescence went by, and he became an accepted member of the community, I, for one, found his company fascinating. He was an artist, I was a lumpish schoolboy, tutored to some extent in the physical and religious aspects of life but eager to learn about literature and music and what Neil Munro used to call 'the strange cantrips of the human heart'. James was willing to teach me all he knew.

He taught me chess, demonstrating on his board some classic openings used by the masters. I enjoyed the game well enough but was never able to beat him, except when he arranged that I should. I think his blindness gave him a power of concentration beyond my scope.

He presented me with a book called *The Rudiments of Criticism*, which dealt with a concept new to me: the power of words to create music when read aloud. I began to be aware of clashing consonents and the ugly effect of too many similar vowel sounds crowded together. It also indicated how word sounds could evoke a scene, a situation, an emotion. James and I talked about *A Musical Instrument*, by Elizabeth Barrett Browning, and agreed that it illustrated both ideas.

What was he doing, the great god Pan
  Down in the reeds by the river?
Spreading ruin and scattering ban,
Splashing and paddling with hoofs of a goat,
And breaking the golden lilies afloat
  With the dragon-fly on the river.

Yet half a beast is the great god Pan,
  To laugh as he sits by the river,
Making a poet out of a man:
The true gods sigh for the cost and pain, –
For the reed which grows nevermore again
  As a reed with the reeds in the river.

Many years later, when I began to write for radio, this lesson remained with me; and Scots actors like the late Bryden Murdoch, Jameson Clark and Madeleine Christie have told me they usually found my writing easy to speak. My slightly sardonic friend, Archie P. Lee, a BBC producer now retired, once paid me a back-handed compliment: 'Your scripts, Angus, often sound a lot better than they read.'

As we talked about writing, James surprised me by his ability to 'see' words on the printed page. 'Grey', he said, 'always suggests to me something dark and sinister. "Gray" is light coloured, almost sparkling.' Ever since then I have used the different spellings according to James's ideas.

But James had more wisdom to impart.

His own stories and verses, generally based on the folk lore of Kintyre, had a vigorous life which, though it might not find favour in a sophisticated London market, I admired and resolved to cultivate, if I could. His thin, strong fingers danced across the keys of a piano with the same vigour; and in those days, when the 'wireless' was only an intriguing toy, when television was unknown and few people had cars to convey them the ten miles to a cinema in Campbeltown, he was much in demand at ceilidhs in the Manse and at the local farms.

Towards the end of his stay in Southend, when I was about sixteen, he instituted a singing class in the church hall, which was attended by almost every young person in the parish. He conducted it for love, not for money. In those post-war days of agricultural hardship, before marketing-boards were created and when the idea of subsidies was a mere twinkle in the eye of an astute Farmers' Union secretary, the spending of money on an artistic pursuit would have been considered 'daft' by country folk. Not only 'daft' but criminal. But – 'There's nobody who can't sing,' James told us with gusto. 'When you feel happy you want to sing. I'll teach you how.'

So we all sang, in our various fashions, and though it soon became apparent that in certain individual cases our teacher's optimism outpaced reality, it was arranged that before dispersing for the summer the class should give a 'grand' concert in the Territorial Hall, a more commodious and important venue than the church hall.

Parents, aunts, uncles and cousins were thrilled to anticipate the appearance of relatives on the platform. The show, therefore, was a 'sell out'. Under hissing pressure lamps and surrounded by an aroma of paraffin from heaters placed in handy corners, the audience settled back on wooden benches to enjoy it.

A young piper opened the programme. He was Ronald MacCallum, one of a family of dancers and musicians famous in Kintyre and, indeed, throughout Scotland and the Commonwealth. In later years he became a Scottish champion and piper in residence to the Duke of Argyll at Inveraray Castle.

Then, one after another, in various states of alarm and euphoria, we trooped on stage to 'do our thing'. Some of us were good singers: for example the McKerral boys from Brunerican and their small sister, Jean. They were the show-stoppers – and continued to be show-stoppers at many a festival and concert in years to come. The rest of us filled in as best as we could.

One tall, usually happy girl gave a rendering of *Whistle and I'll come tae ye, my lad*. Swaying nervously from side to side, her note rising ever higher to the edge of hysteria, she had all the young blades in the audience loudly obeying her instructions before she was done.

Another girl, who had a lovely alto voice, took stage fright halfway through her piece and ran, weeping, from the platform.

I sang a ballad called *The Wee Toon Clerk* which, to everyone's dismay, I still sing when fortified by a dram or two. As I began the second verse I caught the eye of Mrs Morton, my former teacher in Southend Public School. She was shaking with suppressed laughter, not at the words of the song but at me. In a blur of embarrassment I, too, started to laugh and retired from the scene pursued by cat-calls from unsympathetic school friends.

James also was unsympathetic. 'Why should you be embarrassed? Singing is as natural as breathing. Express yourself. Enjoy yourself. And if people scoff and won't listen, why worry! You're growing up within yourself.'

At the time I understood only vaguely what he meant.

About James there was a lust for living that was contagious. But, unlike that of the great god Pan, it was a lust tempered by gentleness and romance. On winter evenings at Brunerican he and Jean McKerral took turns to play accompaniments on the piano, while the McKerral brothers sang and their father and I listened. The little girl who had been my partner at a dancing class years before was now fifteen, and as James sang his songs of love I would catch her eye and find that she was aware of me, too.

There was stirrings in my blood. I was being offered fabulous delights, both spiritual and physical. Had I the courage to accept them?

One night I was at Kilblaan, listening to James, with old Hugh and his nephew Archie, talking about the thatchers and potato gatherers who used to cross the North Channel from Ireland to work on the Southend farms, bringing their songs and stories with them. Near midnight I said goodnight to the McEachrans and went out through the front porch into a wall of darkness. I had no torch, and the thought of the complicated path to the Manse gave me a moment of uneasiness.

'I'll see you across the bridge,' said James, behind me.

'I wish you would,' I said. Then, with sudden anxiety: 'But it's so dark! Will you manage back on your own?'

James laughed, and as he laughed I remembered. 'Sorry,' I said.

'I'm not sorry,' he told me, 'so why should you be. Come on.'

2. Ink in My Veins

When James MacTaggart left Kilblaan, for me a mite of magic was withdrawn. The ideal of writing for the sake of good writing began to blur. Being without material capital of any kind, I was being pressed towards the conclusion that writing for money rather than for artistic reasons should be my aim. I had little of the true poet's disregard for moral and physical comfort. In a situation of low wages and high unemployment I wanted to achieve financial independence.

It may seem ironical that after half a century of writing for a living, putting by each year a little silver in my sporran, I have not as yet achieved this independence. But I have achieved something else: I can live with my writing and not be ashamed of it.

James himself had to face hard facts. He married his Maid Marian and took a job in Helensburgh as a music teacher. He also became a church organist, training his choir with the same optimism and enthusiasm he had shown in Southend. And there was no namby-pampy holiness about his organ playing. When the mood of the music demanded it, the stone pillars and the stained-glass windows reverberated, echoing its power.

James and his wife now live in retirement in Campbeltown. In his mid-seventies, he still strides through the streets, fearing nothing, occasionally coming to grief against an unexpected pile of pavement rubble, but in the main giving the impression that his blindness is only a minor inconvenience. When someone greets him he recognizes the voice at once.

For more than twenty years – during World War II and for a time afterwards, while he worked in Helensburgh – I lost touch with him. One day, by a thousand to one chance, I encountered him in a Glasgow street.

'Hullo, James. How's the health?'

The reply came without the slightest hesitation. 'Angus! Great to see you again – in Glasgow of all places!'

(He always 'sees' old friends and acquaintances.)

His daughter is a doctor. His elder son, after a spell as editor of the *Campbeltown Courier*, now works with the Canadian government. His second son is a pilot instructor with the RAF. James's bravery – and that of his Maid Marian in becoming the wife of a blind man – were transmitted to them all.

For a time Dr Mary practised medicine in Ghana, though her fair skin and auburn hair made it fairly certain that the hot climate would prove a continual burden. While editor of the *Courier* Victor's outspoken reporting delighted the local community. Like his father, recovering quickly after stumbling over an unaccustomed obstacle, he would attack snobbery in one issue and then, with undiminished enthusiasm, tilt against ignorance in the next. Ian flies with nervous and unskilled pilots and thinks nothing of the danger.

My admiration for James is based partly on his artistic accomplishments but mainly, I think, on his courage. It has nothing bombastic about it and produces no specific incidents which a public relations officer could work up into newspaper headlines. It is natural, continuing and enduring, woven into the fabric of his life.

James has been a constant inspiration as far as I, an ordinary person and an ordinary writer, am concerned. He and people like him are seldom identified by the media. Newspapers, television and radio prefer to deal with characters whose lives exemplify extreme righteousness or extreme sinfulness. For them, stories concerning the discipline and courage shown day after day and year after year by ordinary folk are not dramatic enough. To use a journalistic phrase, they have 'less impact'. But such stories – and James's story in particular – appeal to me. They comfort me when I take a sour view of humanity, and strengthen me when I despair of my own courage and endurance.

It is said that God – whosoever or whatsoever He may be – rejoices in great saints and also in great sinners who come to repentance. But few of us are saints, either great or small, and fewer still are flagrant sinners who repent. Does God not also rejoice over his numerous 'middlemen', unnoticed and unsung though they appear to be? I must say I wouldn't have much faith in Him if He didn't.

I had – and still have – a stammer, a minor infirmity compared with James's blindness. But at times it can be traumatic, especially for a writer, who is occasionally compelled in the course of business to communicate with his fellows by word of mouth. Quite often, while waiting in sweaty anxiety for a television camera to blink red, or a desk-bulb in a radio studio to flash me cruelly into action, or for a chairman to end an apparently endless speech of introduction, I have thought of James, in darkness and doubt, striding with relentless courage into danger. And the thought has always helped me.

When publishers and editors regret and reject, when critics dismiss months of hard work in two or three careless lines, when bankers print DR against a monthly statement, at such times I also think of James. He has to bear similar human disappointments. But he is blind, and I am not. And, forgetting my stammer, I thank God for the mercy of sight and get on with the business of restoring my material situation.

I spent six years as a pupil at Campbeltown Grammar School. During this time, from 1920 until 1926, my stammer was no great inconvenience – to me, at any rate. Obviously it had an effect on some teachers, because, usually after a few short, shattering experiments, they were inclined to dispense with my contributions during question and answer sessions. This suited me admirably and caused me to become an envied personality among my classmates. It also resulted in careless home-work and an increasing indulgence in the idleness which lies at the root of my nature.

On the whole my schooldays in Campbeltown were happy.

Living in 'digs' from Monday to Friday, ten miles out of

range of parental eyes (and of Maimie's hard knuckles) and supervised only by a kind and indulgent landlady, I enjoyed considerable freedom. On clear nights in spring and autumn my mates and I would play football or cricket on a weird pitch halfway up a mountain, or fish from the pier or swan around the harbour in a rowing boat belonging to Big Allan MacDougall's father. On winter nights we would roam the streets in gangs, sometimes enacting cowboy and Indian dramas, howling and cat-calling up and down dark closes, sometimes chasing willing girls, only to discover when we caught them that we had no precise idea what to do with them. (Lambs leaping and running in the fields in spring have the same problem.)

Away from the influence of the Manse, I am afraid that for me ethical questions tended to receive hazy answers. At one stage, in our first year, Davie Watson and I carried out a scheme which may rank in iniquity, if not in scope, with some of the big business operations which have caused scandals in modern times.

One of our teachers – for history and geography – was Kate Stalker, an elderly maiden lady of forthright speech and manner, with piled-up grey hair and heavy spectacles. Boys and girls who came from junior schools in the country were popular with her, because, as she kept on declaring, they were better educated and more polite than the children of the town. As Watson's home was twelve miles north of Campbeltown and mine was in Southend we were among her favourites.

At the beginning of the year, as she noted our names, I remember how one town girl revealed, timidly, that her name was Valerie Joy. An insulting sound came from Kate's hooked nose. 'Valerie Joy?' she exclaimed. 'I know your mother and your granny, Mary and Jeannie. Less would do you!'

One day she lectured us about poor children of the past, children forced to work in the pits, on the farms, as chimney-sweepers' assistants. A harrowing recital which caused Valerie Joy to burst into tears. 'Huh!' said Kate. 'Tears are no good. The reformers may have cried a little, but they were also practical, and so must you be! There are still many poor and neglected children in the big cities, and it is up to you, pampered and privileged creatures that you are, to do something for them. I want some volunteers to go around the town and collect money for the National Society for the Prevention of Cruelty to Children.'

A wary hush fell upon the class. Young as we were, experience had taught us that volunteering for anything was liable to be a mug's game, a waste of time that could be spent in more pleasurable pursuits. In any case, volunteering at the behest of a teacher was a sure way to earn the title of 'sook'. ('Sucking up' was an expression which, I believe, originated in World War I and may have come, like many another linguistic gem, from America. Until World War II it applied to other ranks and employees who toadied to officers and employers. Nowadays officers and employers 'suck up' to other ranks and employees.)

In the end, faced by continuing silence, Kate had to use conscription. She pointed to and named two 'townies' and, with a sniff of disgust for our lack of social conscience, handed them collecting tins and a bundle of NSPCC literature.

Later in the day, however, when we found time to discuss it, Watson and I came to the conclusion that there might, after all, be some fun in a collecting round. I don't think the idea of financial profit had yet occurred to us. We looked forward to spending happy hours importuning the parents of some of our classmates and being rewarded with the occasional apple or slice of tasty cake. It would also provide a noble excuse if critical comments were made about our homework. Privately, therefore, and letting nobody else know, we spoke to Kate and told her we wished to help her with the collecting job.

She was delighted. We couldn't have collecting tins, she explained, because she'd been allocated only two, and these had been given to the conscripts. But would we take some leaflets to show possible subscribers?

'Yes, ma'am,' we said, with self-righteous smirks.

During the next two evenings we enjoyed ourselves. It was

January. The weather was cold and wet and we took pride in looking bedraggled as we stood on doorsteps and proferred leaflets. We collected sweets in satisfying quantities – also, to our surprise, what seemed to us enormous sums of money for the NSPCC. A ten-shilling note offered by a solicitor's wife made us blink with astonishment.

The principal reason for our success may have been that our respective parents, though living in the country, were well known and respected in the town. It is possible, too, that our soaked and shivering appearance, part natural, part assumed, may have touched the hearts of kindly folk.

At the end of the second night we discovered that in the tea-caddy provided by Watson's landlady we had just over £12. In 1921 this was sensational, the equivalent of about £100 today. As we counted it up at my digs we looked into each other's eyes and saw there the dawn of corruption.

We argued it out in what we both considered was a sensible and logical way. Kate would be glad to get as much as £10. So would the children who suffered cruelty. If we kept a pound each for ourselves it would only be just reward for the hard work we had done in adverse weather conditions.

'Our expenses,' said Watson.

'That's it,' I agreed. 'And anyway, people are cruel to *us* at times. We're entitled to something.'

Kate was overjoyed when we handed her the £10, along with a few extra coppers to demonstrate our supreme honesty. The conscripts with the collecting tins had got only about a pound between them. They were dismissed by her as 'useless', while Watson and I were lauded in public as boys of initiative and solid worth.

We kept our secret to ourselves, and everybody – everybody, that is, except perhaps the two conscripts, whose collecting tins were sealed and the contents, therefore, inviolable – appeared to be happy. But ever since then my conscience has troubled me. The pound in my pocket represented a hundred and twenty ice-cream 'sliders', riches beyond dreams. But I felt guilty – and still do, in spite of the widespread modern tolerance of inflated expense accounts.

I don't know about Watson. He became a highly successful chartered accountant.

As we laboured towards our fifth year we found most of our fun in the Latin class.

Our Latin class would have provided an interesting case-history for modern educationists, sociologists and psychiatrists.

The master was thin and pale, aged about thirty. It was rumoured that during World War I he had suffered shell-shock; but his war experiences could have been scarcely more disturbing than those he endured as a teacher. A strange smell emanated from his person – or it could have been from his clothes, which, as a rule, consisted of a folded cloth muffler instead of a collar and a threadbare grey suit. It was an acrid smell, the cause of which I have never been able to diagnose. He appeared to exist in a continual state of secret anger and frustration. Sometimes, for no apparent reason, beads of sweat would stand out on his forehead while he thrust forward a doubled-up tongue and chewed on it with savage jaws.

This unfortunate man was given the task of dealing with a mob of children who, given the slightest chance, would behave like hooligans. He gave us that chance and, being cruel and sadistic, we considered it sport to make his life even more of a misery than it already was.

He kept a Lochgelly strap, folded over once, continually in his right hand. When we boys made rude noises or gestured defiance he would leap at us, strap flailing, and deliver blow after blow on the backs of our necks. When the girls misbehaved he would control himself with a visibly hurtful effort, essay a deathshead smile and plead for obedience in a voice strained almost to breaking-point. If his control slipped, and he did flick the strap at a girl's arm or hand, we would stamp our feet and set up a growling chant: 'Ah-h-h, bully! Leave the girls alone!' At which he would stride away from the class, lean awkwardly against his desk with his thin, stooped back towards us, and bite the forefinger of the hand which held the strap. The chant would swell: 'Bully! Bully!' And at last, like a desperate animal, he would swing round and throw himself among us, lashing out in all directions.

The blows from his strap didn't worry us. Over the years the skin on the backs of our necks became as tough and insensitive as leather. We also perfected a technique of hunching. This ensured that most of the blows fell upon our shoulders, which, with intelligent forethought, we padded with newspapers.

At the beginning, so indiscriminate were his lashings, that the strap sometimes struck against our heads and ears. This was definitely painful and had to be stopped. We staged a salutary happening, therefore, with Alastair MacMillan in the principal role.

'*Soporiferumque papaver*,' intoned Alastair and continued, with error aforethought, to translate: 'And the blessed poppy went to sleep.'

'Stop, you fool!' cried the master, employing his customary epithet. '*Soporiferumque papaver* means "And the sleep-bringing poppy"!'

'Excuse me, sir,' said Alastair, who was tall, elegant and well-spoken, the son of an exciseman, 'are you not forgetting the words in the Bible: "Whosoever shall say, Thou fool, shall be in danger of hell's fire"?' (As a son of the Manse I had forearmed Alastair with the exact quotation.)

The master's body became taut. He began to chew upon his tongue. His eyes glazed. Then he bared his teeth and lunged savagely at Alastair, who by this time had sat down. Blow succeeded blow until at last, with a hoarse scream, Alastair reared up, staggered forward and finally fell prone against the master's desk.

The girls set up a moaning. Big Allan and Davie Watson and I sprang forward to kneel beside the casualty. The master's face was yellow-white. He stood over us, small strangled sounds bubbling in his throat.

Big Allan said: 'You struck him on the head, sir.'

'A wild blow,' said Davie Watson.

I put an ear to Alastair's chest. I said: 'Is he dead, sir?'

The moaning of the girls became a Hebridean coronach.

The master looked terrified. He wrung his hands, which

became entangled with the strap. He turned pitifully to May Ollar, a blonde tomboy who sat in front. 'Get water! Get brandy!' he whispered between dry lips.

'Wait!' I said. 'His heart's beating again!'

Following the script, Alastair began to stir. 'My head! My head!' he groaned. (Looking back on it, after a lifetime's experience of writing documentaries for TV and radio, I must admit the script wasn't all that bad, based as it was on an intimate knowledge of the character.)

The girls ceased their moaning, uttering instead glad and hopeful cries.

'It's a miracle!' said Big Allan. 'He's coming round!'

Davie Watson's strong hands helped Alastair to his feet. Ineffectually dabbing, alternately smiling with inane relief and chewing on his tongue, the master attempted to dust his clothes.

Alastair said: 'I want to see the headmaster.'

The master grew even pastier. 'Please, MacMillan, is there any need – '

Watson and I said: 'You nearly killed him, sir!'

'I – I'm sorry. It was an accident.'

'Well,' said Alastair, 'if you'll promise not to hit any of us on the head again. I mean, it's all right on the shoulders, but – '

'Certainly, certainly! I'll put the strap away for good. If there's anything else I can do . . .'

Looking back, I realize what sickening, hypocritical, violent creatures we were. The Latin class had the attraction for us of an unusual adventure, spiced with danger. We gave no consideration to the fact that for the master, probably ill, both physically and mentally, it must have been slow agony. I suppose that nowadays we should have been ideal recruitment fodder for the National Front, which plays upon and encourages the normal sadistic instincts of youth.

After the MacMillan 'happening' the master did not, of course, put his strap away. He continued to deliver blows, though not so often against our heads and ears. We continued to bait him, much to our enjoyment.

One of our classmates was Davie McArthur, who in childhood had contracted polio and, as a result, wore a caliper on one wasted leg. In spite of his infirmity, Davie had a wicked imagination and an IQ higher than the average. Years later, it was no surprise to me when, as headmaster of a junior school, he had several ingenious Scottish plays broadcast on BBC radio. His youthful torture of the Latin master took the form of an intellectual rather than a physical exercise.

In the top of his desk was a small knot-hole, which had been enlarged by some boy's busy penknife. One day, with Watson's help, he manoeuvred his calipered leg on to the desk. The leg being without muscular stiffening, the manoeuvre caused him neither pain nor inconvenience. Then, through his pebble spectacles, he began peering down at the hole.

'Please, sir,' said Watson, with an uncharacteristic show of solicitude, 'I'm afraid there's something far wrong with McArthur!'

The master came bustling and chewing from his desk. 'What do you mean, something far wrong?' Then he saw the complicated position into which his star pupil had got himself. 'Good heavens, boy, get that leg down!'

McArthur gave no sign that he had heard. Watson said: 'He's stuck like that, sir. I think he's in a trance.'

By this time the whole class was moving and murmuring with excitement. That our parents were paying large sums in rates and taxes in order to provide us with a sound education – and that the time we spent in the Latin class was a complete waste of their money – did not occur to us. We were having a ball, free of care. A chorus swelled: 'Ah-h-h, bully! The poor maimed boy, don't touch him!'

It was what Mr Banks, the English master, would have called an impasse.

The Latin master chewed and muttered: 'MacVicar, you are his friend. Can you communicate with him?'

I could. I did, trying hard to simulate my father's sick-bed manner. 'Tell me what's the matter, David.'

He made guttural sounds.

'Please, sir,' I said, 'he's scared.'

'Scared? Of what?'

'He's got a phobia.' (This was another word we'd learnt from Mr Banks.)

'Oh, dear!'

'He's scared he's going to fall through that knot-hole. Putting his leg on the desk is a kind of defensive mechanism.'

Noises came from the class. They were compounded of stifled giggles from the girls and groans of satisfaction from the boys. Sweat began to gather on the master's forehead.

'It's incredible,' he said. 'Is there no way – '

'Let me deal with him, sir,' I said and went on: 'Tell me, David, what do you see down the hole?'

McArthur stirred. His voice came clear and powerful: 'I see the dark depths of Hades. I see great fires. I see people dancing round the fires. I'm scared! I'm scared!'

'Good gracious!' exclaimed the master. He may have suspected he was being codded; but in that age of amateur psychiatry, after Wold War I, he couldn't be sure. His body was tense, shaking.

'Don't be scared, David.' I spoke with emotion, because this was the part of the script that everybody was going to enjoy. 'You are safe in the Latin class. Your good and kind master is by your side.'

'Master, master!' breathed McArthur.

'I'm here.' The master caught the pupil's groping hand.

'Ah! The fires are dying. The people are no longer there. It's getting darker.'

'He's coming round,' I said.

We meant the coming round bit to be as protracted and enjoyable as that which had gone before. Unfortunately, at that moment, the bell rang for the end of the period.

'He's okay now,' I said, quickly, while Big Allan and Davie Watson, assisted by McArthur himself, got the leg down from the desk.

McArthur smiled up at the master and disengaged his hand. 'Thank you, sir,' he said.

'If you agree, sir,' I suggested, 'we'll bring something from the woodwork class and plug up that hole. We'll do it tomorrow in the Latin period.'

Tomorrow was another sunshine day.

The Latin classroom was next to that occupied by the English master, the redoubtable Alexander Banks, known otherwise (to us) as Kubla. ('In Xanadu did Kubla Khan a stately pleasure-dome decree . . .') The partition between them was of flimsy wood and glass, and at one stage a regular ploy of ours, when we became bored in the Latin class, was to strike our elbows against this partition, causing minor thunder-rolls. Big Allan, at one end of the row of desks running close to and parallel with the partition, would begin the operation. As the master leapt towards him, wielding the strap, the next boy would repeat the performance. And so it went, along the line, until the master pounced, breathing fast but still flailing, on Davie Watson at the other end.

This caper continued for several weeks until one day, during a particularly happy session of partition-bashing, a knock fell upon the door of the room. We stopped bashing. The master stopped flailing. He went slowly to the door, opened it and revealed Kubla standing there in awesome majesty.

'What is going on?' he inquired, making the sibilant lip sounds which always betrayed a high charge in his temper.

'Nothing, Mr Banks.' The Latin master was sycophantic. 'The desks are so close to the partition. Bound to be accidents . . .'

'May I come in?'

'Of course, of course!'

Kubla came in, adjusting his pince-nez. His glance travelled across the back row of desks. 'MacDougall, MacVicar, Watson,' he murmured. 'I might have known.'

A chill entered our bones. In the Latin class we were heroes. In the face of real authority we were cringing cowards.

Kubla said nothing more. He left the room with a curt nod for the Latin master. We became suddenly, painfully aware that we were due to spend the next period in the English classroom.

Immediately upon entering Kubla's domain, Big Allan, Davie Watson and I were told to stand by his desk.

He took out his strap – a beautifully clean-cut model,

seldom used. When everybody was seated, he said: 'I am going to punish you three boys as an example to the others. Your conduct in the Latin classroom is a scandal. It has now begun to spread, via the partition, to the English classroom. That I cannot – and will not – allow. Roll up your sleeves.'

With cold and clinical skill, and without the slightest evidence of passion, he gave us six belts each. As honour dictated, we did not flinch as the strap came down. We shut our eyes and endured. Afterwards, when red weals appeared on our wrists, we made sure they remained hidden. We were aware that our punishment was deserved, that there was no point in trying to behave like martyrs. Had other masters – or our parents – discovered the truth about the Latin classroom there was no saying what further disciplinary action might have overtaken us.

Having completed the execution, Kubla said: 'You will remain behind after school. I will see you here, in the English classroom.'

The day dragged by: a day sad, stale and unprofitable. At ten minutes past four in the afternoon we stood before Mr Banks, who addressed us. 'I am greatly disappointed in you – three boys from good homes, three healthy boys of intelligence and resource. Yet you act like louts, like hooligans from a mediaeval slum! You pander to your own pleasure, completely ignoring the rights – and even the very existence – of other human beings. Your understanding of a fellow mortal in distress is nil. Your compassion is nil. Your social conscience simply does not exist. Let me warn you that if this state of affairs continues you will find that when you leave school and have to face the hard realities of an unprotected life your chances of survival, in both a physical and a moral sense, will be poor indeed. Others will treat you as you treat them – and in this direction lie anarchy, destruction and the death of the soul.'

Kubla was not religious. His approach to the ethical problems of life was different from my father's, but it seemed to me then – as it seems to me now – that his basic philosophy was the same. And his words that day made us feel colder and more desolate than any fire and brimstone sermon had ever done.

For days afterwards the Latin class was fairly quiet, and I think we intended to show some compassion for the master. But before our goodwill could flourish he was removed from the school. This happened only a few weeks before we were due to sit our Highers. We passed English and Maths – 'nae bother', as we told one another – but as far as I can remember, only three out of a class of about twenty passed their Latin exam. One of them was McArthur.

In years to come the happenings in the Latin class made us all feel ashamed. Our behaviour was thoughtless, inhuman, on a par with that of the morons – amongst both players and spectators – who have devalued the good name of football around the world. We played a game which gave us selfish pleasure. That other people might be hurt and humiliated did not worry us – that is, until Kubla delivered his homily.

I have not mentioned the Latin master's name. He may still be alive, and to identify him would be cruel. But though McArthur is now dead, Big Allan in Campbeltown and Davie Watson in Perth will vouch for the truth – the conservative truth – of my stories about him.

They are proof, if proof is needed, that without discipline even 'respectable' children can menace society. Children are natural sadists. It is only by example – and, perhaps, under a threat of retribution – that they learn to become sympathetic human beings, with a reverence for the divinity in all other human beings, no matter how much that divinity may be camouflaged.

From our parents – and Maimie – Rona, my brothers and I learnt that love for our neighbours and respect for their dignity help to support a caring society and make us feel good within ourselves. From Kubla we learnt that punishment of one sort or another is inevitable if cruelty, hate and arrogance are allowed to take over.

From Kubla I learnt something else: that good writing requires not only integrity but also a great deal of disciplined work. Most week-ends he gave us an essay to write. At first I regarded this as an enjoyable chore. Ideas, and words with which to clothe them, came easily as far as I was concerned. (On many a Friday night I wrote two essays, my own and one for Watson, while he in turn did homework in maths for me.) But Kubla was not impressed by my facile imaginings, as a rule awarding me fewer marks than those he gave to other pupils whose writing I classed privately as stodgy.

I was annoyed with him. My scribblings became more and more florid in style and content. I searched *Chambers's Twentieth Century Dictionary* for bigger and, as I thought, better words. Fanciful theories were deployed at the expense of sober reason.

One day he returned my essay. It was marked 5 out of 10. On the margin, in his scrawling handwriting, he gave a verdict: 'The idea is good, but the writing is WOOLLY. The words, instead of being simple and straightforward, are too big for their boots. The composition is careless, the product of a mind too idle to think things through. You have potential as a writer. Why waste it in a cloud of vanity?'

To begin with, I was angry. Then I was depressed. Then I remembered the sentence: 'You have potential as a writer.' It was a flickering light on a winter sea.

Fortunately I understood what Kubla meant, though it was hard to admit the propriety of his judgement against my own. (Even yet, in mature age, I find that an honest valuation of adverse criticism is a difficult, even painful exercise.) The next week-end I laboured long and hard by the light of a paraffin lamp on the Manse kitchen table, choosing simple words for my essay and a simple argument which I did my best to bring to a conclusion. As he handed this one back Kubla gave me a fleeting smile and said: 'Better.'

Praise from Kubla, however curt and ambiguous, was praise indeed. I glowed. I wrote voluntary essays. I tried my hand at short stories, most of which I burned, because as yet I hadn't the nerve to offer them to the magazines and newspapers whose siren calls beckoned me from beyond a far horizon.

Eventually Kubla was marking my essays at 8. And then,

on one glad day, he gave me 9.

He said: 'I will read this essay to the class. Listen carefully and tell me, at the end, why it doesn't quite get full marks.'

My pleasure was drowned in a flood of embarrassment. It was gratifying that my work should have Kubla's approval. That my essay should be read out as an example to my mates was a disaster. Big Allan and Watson and Tom Wylie would make my life a misery. I should be called 'Kubla's pet'. I should be accused of 'sooking up' to a teacher, the most unpardonable of schoolboy sins. The girls might decide I was a cissy – or even worse, a 'swot' – and the glowing halo of heroism which their eyes accorded me in the Latin class might suddenly dim.

I sat and blushed and sweated, while Watson, beside me, dug an elbow into my ribs and Big Allan and Tom Wylie, seated at the desk behind, bent forward and surreptitiously tried to pluck hairs from the back of my knees. (In those days, more than fifty years ago, boys at school wore short trousers until they were seventeen.)

My essay was about a ploughing match: about the heaving, brightly harnessed Clydesdale horses and the glint of the brown earth as they pulled the sharp plough through and turned it over; about a grey January sky tinged with sunset pink and the horses and the ploughmen silhouetted against it; about the wisdom and the drams exchanged by ancient, retired ploughmen under rattling hawthorn hedges.

I heard only snatches as Kubla read it, being too busy fending off – and camouflaging – the painful attacks on my hairy legs.

Finally the ordeal ended. 'Well,' said Kubla, 'why did I deduct one mark?'

'Because it's a load of rubbish!' giggled Big Allan behind me, for my ears alone.

Renée Smith, who was kind and friendly, put up a hand. 'I think it's a great essay. But maybe there are too many adjectives.'

'You have a point there,' said Kubla. 'But you should have read some of MacVicar's previous essays. Every second word was an adjective!'

The class laughed. This was better. I was being brought back to a mundane average, where I wanted to be. The physical attacks ceased.

'In fact,' Kubla continued, 'this time he has his adjectives fairly well under control, a sign of some newly acquired discipline. No, I took the mark off for a sin of omission rather than of commission. Can nobody spot it?'

As a farmer's son Watson had attended the ploughing match in question. He ventured a cynical suggestion. 'He doesn't say anything about the dirt at the heid-rigs. I got my boots covered in glaur that day.'

'Good, Watson, good!' said Kubla, much to Watson's surprise. 'You're getting warm. There is certainly a touch of romanticism about MacVicar's work, though I don't necessarily condemn him for that. Realism can often be overdone. But in good descriptive writing there are, in my opinion, three main elements – sight, sound and smell. MacVicar deals with sights and sounds particularly well – the silhouettes against the coloured sky, the rattling of the hawthorn hedges in the wind. But he has omitted to mention the smells of the ploughing match: the smell of the damp earth – of the 'glaur' which you mention, Watson – the smell of the sweating horses and of their dung, the smell of the whisky in the cold air. That's why I deducted a mark from what was otherwise an extremely good essay.'

I soon forgot my embarrassment – and the prickling pains at the backs of my knees – but I never forgot Kubla's lesson. (Fifteen years later, when I had been taken under the wing of a literary agent, Patience Ross of A. M. Heath & Co., Ltd., she gave me advice on similar lines. As an example of how evidence of the three senses could be woven into prose she recommended me to read the *Natural History of Selbourne* by the Rev. Gilbert White. I discovered for myself that Lewis Grassic Gibbon was good at such weaving, too.)

And Kubla had done something else. He had confirmed my own suspicion that there was ink in my veins. I was still interested in athletics, football and cricket. I could still enjoy adventure in the Latin class. My ethical standards may have been improving, but, to borrow a word from Kubla, they still remained 'woolly'. Now, however, my main (if secret) ambition was to write something that would appear in print.

3. The Extra Dimension

I suppose the desire to write burgeoned inside me in parallel with the desire to make love to girls and to worship a caring God.

Psychologists have devoted libraries of books to analyses of the creative instincts, but I don't think there is anything complicated about them. They are born in every human being, implanted by a mysterious power as yet undefined in material terms. The sexual instinct – the instinct to create and nourish sons and daughters – and the religious instinct – the instinct to show gratitude to whoever or whatever has donated such gifts as we have – are common to everybody in greater or lesser degree. But alongside them each individual has other creative instincts.

The character of a person and a person's role in society depend a great deal on whether he or she is allowed to develop the more dominant of such instincts. Some are workaday, unspectacular. Others are of incalculable value to the human race. A few are dangerous. Knitting a jumper is creative. So is cooking a tasty meal. So is building a house, a motor-car or Rapides and Concordes. So is farming and gardening, painting pictures, composing music, writing books. So is the raising of business empires. But so, it must be admitted, is the construction of an A-bomb.

Those who find their freedom to develop dominant instincts – apart from sex and religion – are the lucky ones. They are the happy people, the fulfilled and, therefore, the contented people. The sad and frustrated are those who because of accident or inhibiting circumstances are unable to nurture their inborn gift and are condemned to labour at tasks which by no stretch of the imagination can be described as creative.

The Padre was lucky. His dominant instinct was to preach, and he became a minister of religion. My mother was lucky. Her instinct was to create a home and family, and she did just that.

Their family was lucky. Archie wanted to teach. He became an English master at Dunoon Grammar School. Willie wanted to be a sailor. He retired recently after many years as senior skipper with the Anchor Line. Rona not only wanted to teach, she also had an urge to sing. She taught in Campbeltown Grammar School, and in 1948, at the Mod in Glasgow, won the gold medal for Gaelic singing. Kenneth, like his father, had the instinct to preach. He became minister of Kenmore in 1950 and is still there, nicknamed the 'Bishop of Tayside'. John's instinct was to study medicine. He is now Professor of Midwifery at Leicester University. I wanted to become a writer, freelance and independent, and by guess and by God I did it.

The Padre and 'Granny' are gone, after long lives of willing service to their family and to the community of Southend. Archie was killed by a German mortar-bomb. Rona died of cancer soon after her happy triumph at the Mod. But Willie and Kenneth and John and I are still around. We can all testify that to be allowed to follow our natural bent is one of the most valuable gifts that parents can bestow.

The Padre and my mother wanted me to become a minister. For many years there existed an unspoken agreement that one day I should enter the Church. The impression was supported by my parents when, in my hearing, they spoke about me to friends and neighbours: 'I think he has a notion for the Kirk.'

As for my own feelings, I did have an instinct to preach as well as an instinct to write (if the two can be separated), an interest in the *Church of Scotland Year Book*, which listed in my books. Therefore I did not argue with my parents or rebel against their wishes and, indeed, at one stage took an interest in the *Church of Scotland Year Book* which listed Presbyteries and parishes and the stipends on offer. (It still does, unchangingly.)

I have to confess it was the stipends which interested me

most – an early pointer, had I but known, to my unsuitability for a Christian calling. At that time, in the early 1920s, one of the best rewarded ministers in Scotland was the Rev. D. Gillies of Kenmore. I remember that his stipend of £600, double that of my father, made my eyes pop. This will be my parish, I thought: I will be rich and famous and, in time, Moderator of the General Assembly. In the quiet countryside of Perthshire, too, there would be plenty of time to write my books. The idea that I might prove an inefficient or unworthy pastor did not enter my head.

(By a coincidence, it was my brother Kenneth who, in the fullness of time, became minister of Kenmore. Nowadays, however, as a result of reorganization, he is by no means the best paid minister in the Kirk.)

Meanwhile, however, my parents – more especially, perhaps, my mother – were interested enough in my attempts at writing.

From Mr Banks, the English master, the Padre learned that I was winning good marks for essays. (I seldom discussed school matters at home. Had I boasted about my 9 marks out of 10 I should have had to keep a balance by admitting the six belts I had received from Kubla, and that was one disgrace on which I had clamped a personal D-notice.) The next thing I knew was that Alec MacLeod, owner and chief reporter of the *Campbeltown Courier*, had been informed of my so-called talent.

He was a stout, chunky, clean-shaven man with a drooping expression which sometimes, by sudden magic, became a wide, mischievous smile. His solid reporting of town council and Presbytery meetings fitted the drooping image. The leg-pulling laughter in the *Courier*'s most famous column, 'Sparks and Flashes', were in accord with his smile. To my father he suggested I should try reporting the Armistice service due to take place the following Sunday at the War Memorial in Campbeltown.

In the 1920s, with World War I memories still poignantly fresh, services at memorials all over the country attracted many people. Apathy had not yet begun to frost the warmth, nor had the denigrating propaganda of those who had dodged the column of active service begun to have an effect. Even in Southend (pop. 500) scores of people would gather at the cross-topped cairn at Keprigan and bow their heads in silent gratitude for sacrifice. Today, after another world war and with a second memorial tablet added to thc first, services in Southend are attended by only about a dozen folk, most of whom are close relatives of the dead.

This is not to say that on Armistice Sundays the Southend Church is empty. It is generally full and poppies glow in numerous lapels. But an effort is required of old sweats like Hamish Taylor, Archie Cameron and myself to keep the memorial from becoming isolated and neglected. Younger folk, concerned about the price of milk and cattle and the EEC agricultural policy, about striking power-workers and recalcitrant miners' leaders, about the cost and complications of modern technology, find it difficult to concede the importance of bygone wars.

Men died. So what?

But I think if we forget the men who died to preserve our liberty we will also be inclined to forget Christ, who died not only for liberty but also for love. And if Christ's message is eroded by inaction then the whole structure of our civilization will tumble back and down into pagan chaos.

The Campbeltown Memorial is tall and impressive, a tower of rough-hewn stone, situated on the Esplanade which crooks long arms around the harbour and the loch. Like the great religious edifices of the past five thousand years – the Neolithic and the Bronze Age chambered cairns, the crosses and the cathedrals, the churches and the yards about them – it faces east towards the rising sun.

On the day I carried out my first assignment as a reporter, the Esplanade was filled with people: kilted Argylls flanked by pipers and buglers; Scouts and Sea Scouts; Boys' Brigade members and Girl Guides; bemedalled ex-servicemen; crowds of doucely clad citizens wearing poppies – men, women and children. A minister read from St John, Chapter 15, verses 1 to 13, his rich voice trembling to a conclusion: 'Greater love hath no man than this, that a man lay down his life for his friends.'

In the silence the gulls wheeled and cried above the harbour. The water of the loch hissed over the pebbles on Dalintober beach. Then the exploding maroon broke the silence and the buglers sounded the Last Post, cold and clear, with its final note of heart-rending uncertainty.

The bustle began. The pipes skirled. I found myself in a maze of emotion.

I was only sixteen. So far life had been for jokes and pleasure. In spite of the fact that my father had spent a year in Salonika as a chaplain with the Lovat Scouts – thereby gaining his nickname, the Padre – the war had not interfered with my selfish interests in any serious way. Perhaps for the first time I realized that until now my research into living had barely disturbed the surface. Around me that day I felt an upsurge of love and pride and a determination to match sacrifice with sacrifice: love for the soldiers who had fought and won and for those whose names were black on the memorial; pride in Scotland for nurturing such soldiers, with their kilts and sardonic humour and 'gallus' bagpipes; determination to work and make patriotic sacrifices as some small recompense for what the dead had done for the living.

For myself, I understood at last how lucky we MacVicars were as a family to have the Padre back, safe and unscathed. Tears stung my eyes. To my neighbours in the gathering I could say nothing: my throat was dry. But words to describe it all tumbled in my head. I could see it – column after column in the *Courier*, by the up-and-coming literary star, Angus MacVicar. It spread out in my being like a tide, a masterpiece of reporting. The conception was wonderful. It shook me and left me spent as in the aftermath of an orgasm.

That evening I sat down to write. But now, with the paper before me white and blank and my new Waterman fountain pen poised above its surface, I found that only a trickle of words would come. I struggled to express the emotion I had felt during and after the service. The result was drab, inept, a pitiful garment for the original soaring idea.

I wanted to be regarded as a writer; but the conviction grew that the report on which I was working would do me no good at all in that respect. I became tense with frustration. Had I not been sixteen years old and, in my opinion, a man, I might have wept.

I worked on. My mother came into the kitchen at midnight. The paraffin in the cut-glass bowl of the table lamp was running low. She advised me to go to bed, because in the morning I had to cycle ten miles to school in Campbeltown and reveille, therefore, would be at half-past six. But I said I still hadn't finished my report and wanted to hand it in to the *Courier* office, complete, the next day.

'Poor Angus,' she said. 'Why do you get so worked up? You have plenty of time to learn to be a writer.'

The Padre came through, slippers slopping on the cement floor, on his way to his usual pre-bedtime consumption of health salts in the scullery. He gulped noisily, flung the spoon into the empty tumbler and came back to the kitchen. 'Go to bed,' he said. 'Put out the lamp before you go. Alec MacLeod doesn't want a masterpiece. Just a plain report.'

Maybe Alec MacLeod didn't want a masterpiece. But I did, though I stopped short of telling this to my father.

As the flame on the lamp-wick began to die I wrote my last sentence. I put the manuscript in an envelope and climbed the wooden stairs to the 'boys' room' above the kitchen. Archie and Willie were snoring peacefully, but I couldn't sleep. I had written about a thousand words, most of them desperate attempts to recapture the spirit of the service and in my heart I knew that where fires should have been leaping there was only smoking dross.

How badly I had failed was revealed on the following Thursday, when the *Courier* was published. My 'masterpiece' had been cut to pieces. Only about two hundred words remained out of my thousand, and these were concerned for the most part with names and organizations. And Alec MacLeod had given me no 'by-line'.

It was an ego-tearing experience – the first of many, I may say, throughout the next half-century – but then, as now, I followed an instinct to pick myself up, brush myself down and try again.

In her book about George Gissing, *The Born Exile*, Gillian Tindall describes the extra dimension given to a writer, a dimension which 'makes them what they are, subtly altering and colouring all their reactions and endowing them with a peculiar double vision. Gissing suffered as a writer, because writing is tiring, sometimes difficult, often lonely, but he would certainly have suffered many times more had he not had this extra outlet, this characteristic which all the time made him something more than just another highly strung, well meaning personality lost in an uncaring world.'

Gissing himself wrote: 'In the midst of serious complications in life I suddenly find myself possessed of calm and able to regard everything as a picture. I watch and observe myself as much as others. I can pause and make a note for future use, and the afflictions are to me materials for observation.'

As a writer I don't class myself with George Gissing; but I have come to understand exactly what he meant.

Archie and Willie and I had a friend called Tom Williamson.

Tom wasn't a tinker but, in modern statistical terms, one of the 'travelling people'. When we knew him he was about sixty, and rumour had it that he was an old soldier down on his luck. His back was certainly barrack-square straight and the look in his bright blue eyes was frank and direct. He had no beard or moustache, though the plentiful grey stubble on his face was clipped rather than shaved. He wore old tweed trousers, gathered under the knees with string, and layers of jerseys and cardigans. Out of doors his scanty grey hair was generally covered by a lady's knitted bonnet.

As far as we could tell he never touched strong liquor, though the story was that on being discharged from the army he acquired for a time 'a drinking problem'. (Then, as now, alcohol was a convenient peg on which to hang all kinds of social aberrations. That society itself – and its frequent lack of loving care – might have been to blame was a proposition gladly, even eagerly, ignored.)

Tom travelled on circuit, like a High Court judge, his territory being the whole of Argyll. Every three months or so he would spend a fortnight in Southend, making his headquarters in some friendly barn. More often than not this barn was at Brunerican, where the young daughter of the house was Jean McKerral. (Even when she was fourteen, two years my junior, I had an eye on her.) Her mother had recently died, so each morning it was Jean who cooked Tom's breakfast, after which he would sally forth with his battered tin box with its two pull-out drawers inside, to hawk around the parish packets of pins and needles, wire-rimmed spectacles, reels of highly coloured thread and cheap but, according to the girls, highly desirable brooches.

More than fifty years ago, in the country places, the 'travelling people' – including, of course, the tinkers – were given none of the social security benefits which ensure their comfort today. They were almost entirely fed, clothed and housed by kindly folk on the farms and in the 'big hooses' which they visited on a carefully planned rota. The money they earned from the repair of pots and pans and from the sale of trinkets, spectacles, bootlaces, needles and thread – and, in one case I knew, of potted ferns – was spent upon tobacco, drink and, sometimes, peppermints.

It was taken for granted, therefore, that at whichever house Tom happened to be around mid-day he would get a free dinner. The same thing held good at tea-time. For supper he returned to base at Brunerican, where, with the farm workers, he shared a great bowl of porridge, followed by piles of homemade soda scones plastered with butter and bramble jelly. He preferred milk to tea, so he got milk.

Jean remembers that on saying goodbye at the end of a fortnight's stay he would sometimes present her with a brooch, valued at about a shilling, in payment for his keep. She has a small collection of Tom's brooches still, and I have an idea they may be worth much more now than they were then.

Tom's dinner hour often coincided with a visit to the Manse. He would eat his meal in the kitchen, carefully handling a knife and fork under Maimie's critical eye. Then he would move out to the barn, where he would sit among the logs which awaited the Padre's devastating hatchet, fill and light a short clay pipe and exchange relaxed conversation with my brothers and myself.

I was particularly interested in Tom, because local talk insisted that he was 'weel educated'. He spent much of his time reading and always carried about with him a canvas bag full of books and magazines. Many of those were given him by wealthier 'clients' such as the Campbeltown distillery owners whose mansions provided a rich icing around the stodgy cake of the town.

One day my brothers and I, prospecting for fish in the river below the glebe, found Tom sitting on the wooden bridge which served the 'shooters', the smart businessmen from the south who, each autumn, rented the shooting and fishing rights from the Duke of Argyll. He dangled his legs from the tarry planks, contemplating the clear brown water below him. As usual he was smoking a clay pipe, the stem of which had broken off less than two inches from the bowl.

We sat on the bridge beside him. There was quietness, except for the occasional swirl of water on a partly submerged boulder or the distant cackle of a grouse on the higher ground above Kilblaan. Around us was an autumn scent created by decaying leaves and fallen crab-apples on the river bank and by late-flowering whins and brambles, yellow and white, on the path down from the Manse. The air was mild, containing only a hint of late-year chill.

'Looking for fish, Tom?'

'No. Just thinking.' His voice was deep, with gravel in it, his mode of speech deliberate. In contrast with our Kintyre brogue, his accent was almost artificially 'correct'.

That he should be thinking about anything other than fish in his present situation sounded incredible to us. Already we could see a salmon lying beside a green-slimed rock, speckled and sleek and lazy, facing upstream. Legally, of course, it belonged to the 'shooters', but had Tom not been there Archie and Willie and I might have attempted a take-over bid.

'What are you thinking about, Tom?'

'Did you ever hear of a poet called Swinburne?'

I said yes, having listened to Kubla lecturing about him.

'He wrote well for an Englishman,' said Tom. 'There must have been a bit of the Celt in him.'

Then he recited the verse which has triggered off so many sermons, both Christian and agnostic, that it has become almost a cliché:

From too much love of living,
  From hope and fear set free,
We thank with brief thanksgiving
  Whatever gods may be
That no man lives forever,
  That dead men rise up never;
That even the weariest river
  Winds somewhere safe to sea.

Was Tom letting Swinburne speak his own thoughts? At the time my brothers and I missed the implication, because an old sad man's philosophy was beyond our comprehension. We were, all three of us, in love with life; we were buoyed up by hope though, admittedly, sometimes beset by small fears; we were in no hurry to reach the safety – and dark oblivion – of the sea. It was true that a happy life depended on looking forward: our parents had taught us that much. But for us it was more adventure, more excitement, more loving that we looked forward to, not a blank 'nothingness'.

Perhaps Tom, studying our faces, realized that we were on different wavelengths. He took the broken pipe from his mouth, spat into the river twenty feet below and smiled across at us.

'When you get old,' he said, 'you'll experience sadness, as Swinburne did. As I do, too. But you recover from it. I think life is enjoyable at times. Like now, with the weather mild and the smell of autumn in the air, and the peaceful river.'

He had a schoolmaster's grip on us. We murmured responses and let him speak.

'In the winter, when it's cold, I look forward to days like this. But that's not much to keep a man going, is it? If I had my life to live over again I would be a farmer or an inventor or maybe a writer. The farmer has to plan his crops years ahead, and so the future for him is always interesting. Same with the inventor. Will he be able to patent his invention and make a fortune? While a writer works on a book he can dream about it being published and having an influence on other people. A farmer, an inventor or a writer, if they fail at times they don't see it as the end of the road. They have the next crop, the next invention, the next book to look forward to.'

'For them no weary river?' I said, or youthful words to that effect.

'Well, let us say a river that is less weary.'

Archie said: 'The way you talk, Tom, you should have been a minister. Then you would have Heaven to look forward to.'

His wry smile vanished. He frowned. 'Aye, maybe,' he said.

He got up and hoisted the tin box to his shoulder, indicating that our audience was at an end. Something had upset him. What it was we couldn't understand.

Next time we met, however, he retained none of this mood. I gave him a *Hutchinson's Magazine* in exchange for a tattered copy of *The Strand.* I found there a Bulldog Drummond story and thought: little does H. C. MacNeile realize that hundreds of miles from London, down at the Mull of Kintyre, a young rival is flexing his muscles for a fight. Compared with that exciting idea Tom's psychological problems were, to me, of small importance.

One summer he failed to appear in Southend. We never. saw him again. Nobody in the parish could tell what had happened to him. To this day, though I have made many inquiries, I still cannot tell.

I hope his journey had a happy ending, undisturbed by the callous ignorance of youth.

For a long time Tom's magazines remained piled under my bed in the 'boys' room'. My mother and Maimie would have thrown them out, for reasons of hygiene. But I explained that I wanted to re-read them as a guide to how saleable stories ought to be written. Faced by such a professional attitude, they allowed a stay of execution.

The Padre classed most of the magazines – with the exception of *The Strand, Blackwood's* and *Chambers's Journal* – as rubbish and advised me to select my reading from the more solid books in his library.

Fifty or sixty years ago, in Southend, books were hard to come by. There was no lumbering pantechnicon packed by the District Council with up-to-date literature and labelled 'Mobile Library'. Campbeltown had one or two small shops which depended for their profits mainly upon newspapers, stationery and cigarettes but which also sold books – that is, if paperback 'love romances' and adventure stories featuring Dixon Hawke and Sexton Blake could be described as such. In the country, if anyone ever bought a book, it was usually from a travelling salesman touting 'bargains' like *Chambers's Encyclopaedia* and *The Illustrated History of the Great War* in twelve volumes (two years to pay) or from a colporteur (we pronounced it 'colprature'), whose stock consisted generally of religious tracts but who, if requested, would take orders for secular books.

One of these colporteurs was called Ambrose. My brothers and I were mildly curious as to whether this was his Christian name or surname, but we never found out.

He would be about fifty, we imagined. Clad as a rule in a threadbare, tightly buttoned brown suit, he was flabbily built, with a broad, pale clean-shaven face. It appeared that he suffered from asthma, and we felt sorry that in order to earn a living he should have to pedal such a heavy bicycle – and an even heavier caseful of books – all round weather-beaten Argyll.

Ambrose's main port of call in Southend was the Manse, which he often visited just about tea-time. Unlike the tinkers and the peddlars who ate in the kitchen, he joined the family at the tea-table and rewarded us with erudite conversation regarding his trade.

(Another regular visitor accorded similar status was Campbell, the piano tuner, a round, ruddy-faced bespectacled Pickwick of a man, who, on finishing his job, always delighted my mother with a spirited recital of Highland airs, for her a more than adequate recompense for his meal.)

After tea, Ambrose and my father would discuss books.

Archie and Willie, younger than I and less interested, would adjourn to ploys of their own in the 'boys' room' or in the barn; but I always sat in to listen as the two bibliophiles talked by the dining-room fire.

It seemed to me that their main enthusiasms were for Sir Walter Scott and Charles Dickens. Jane Austen, William Makepeace Thackeray and Thomas Hardy were also mentioned in reverent terms, as was George Eliot, who, they revealed to me, was actually a woman, a Mary Ann Evans who later became Mrs J. W. Cross.

As far as I remember, the only contemporary author who found some favour in their eyes was A. S. M. Hutchinson, whose novel, *If Winter Comes,* was among the first of the modern 'best-sellers'; Once I heard my mother say that she liked stories written by Berta Ruck, but they scoffed her into smiling silence.

The Padre's library contained well-bound copies of the works of Scott and Dickens, two separate gifts from the Dowager Duchess of Argyll, who happened to be a member of his congregation. It also included *The Pilgrim's Progress*, *Pride and Prejudice*, George Borrow's *Lavengro* and James Boswell's *Life* of Dr Samuel Johnson. I tried to read them all but could discover in myself no spark of the enthusiasm displayed by my father and Ambrose. With the exception of Scott's *Tales of a Grandfather*, which includes a stirring description of the fight between Clan Chattan and Clan Kay on the Inches of Perth (enough to satisfy any boy's natural lust for violence), and of Dickens's *Christmas Carol*, mercifully short, I found them difficult, to say the least.

I had – and still have – a lazy mind, and this may have caused in me a blindness for genius. But the long descriptive passages and involved philosophical arguments with which most of them are upholstered seemed to me superfluous, a handicap to the flow of action. If ever I write a novel, I thought – and even then I was certain that one day I should – it will contain no such padding. The characters and their actions will speak for themselves; the main consideration will be the narrative.

In a more modern age, films, radio and television have

demonstrated that behind all the verbiage Scott was a magnificent storyteller, with a deep insight into the Scottish character, though it may be argued that his portraits of English men and women are sometimes dim and cardboardy. They have also demonstrated that when stripped for continuous action Dickens's characters are the very stuff of drama and that he, too, was no slouch where plots are concerned. I only wish that the publishers of Scott and Dickens had stipulated in their contracts that each of their novels should consist of, say, 60 000 words instead of the hundreds of thousands which straggle endlessly across pages and cause most young people to stop reading before the narrative takes hold of them.

I feel warm sympathy for those writers who have adapted Scott and Dickens for the media. Their dedication and hard work – and their ability to remain clear-headed while plodding through wordy morasses – make me ashamed of my own inadequacy.

A recent number of the Winchester College magazine has confirmed a suspicion that my youthful allergy to certain 'classical' authors is by no means unique. It published a census of home reading by fifth-formers who not only named their unfavourite authors in order of precedence but also listed the most boring books imposed upon them by well-meaning masters.

Dickens topped the poll of unfavourite authors, followed by Jane Austen, George Eliot, John Bunyan, Thomas Hardy, Joseph Conrad, James Boswell and Tolkien. (In my youth Tolkien's fantasies hadn't emerged upon the literary scene like a religion; but, having read him in mature years, I must agree with the Wykehamists that he is worthy of his place.)

In that list there is only one author whose inclusion I would question, personally. He is Joseph Conrad. I reckon that any boy with a proper mixture of salt in his veins will find Conrad's *Typhoon* anything but boring. Girls may not be so enthusiastic, because of its strong masculine qualities; but they ought to discover merit in the characterization of the old Scots engineer, McWhirr.

The Wykehamist list of boring books runs from *Pride and Prejudice* through *Pilgrim's Progress* and *The Mill on the Floss* to *Great Expectations;* and again I have to admit that my prejudices are generally in tune. Indeed, while at school – and at Kubla's insistence – I started to read *The Mill on the Floss* on at least three occasions and got hopelessly bogged down each time. Twice since then, as a responsible adult, I have tried reading it again, only to find that after the first chapter other interests have invariably called me away – lively interests such as amateur drama or a game of golf.

I am surprised that the Winchester fifth-formers omit Scott from their lists. Perhaps they do not know about him, their education being somewhat thirled to the English ethos. In that case, they have been spared, unwittingly, more mental weariness – though to be fair, I did dredge up some boyish pleasure from *Guy Mannering*, a story about the Solway smugglers. And I repeat that *Tales of a Grandfather*, if persevered with, yields a satisfactory crop of mayhem.

'I doubt,' said Bruce, 'that I have slain the Red Comyn.'

'Do you leave such a matter in doubt?' said Kirkpatrick. 'I will mak siccar!'

In fact, though in the Waverley Novels Scott did write great hunks of boring prose – and which of us hasn't, in our time, pressed and depressed by looming overdrafts? – I still have a warm regard for him, both as a writer and a man. His poetry combines robust narrative with lyrical passages of haunting, delicate beauty, and there is nothing boring about the bustling rhythms of his writing in *The Lay of the Last Minstrel*, *Marmion* and *The Lady of the Lake*.

After Scott's death, Lord Cockburn, the great Scottish judge, wrote vividly and movingly of his personality: 'Dear Scott! . . . It is a pleasure, which the next generation may envy, that I can still hear his voice and see his form. I see him in the Court, and on the street, in company and by the Tweed. The plain dress, the guttural, blurred voice, the lame walk, the thoughtful heavy face, with its mantling smile, the honest, hearty manner, the joyous laugh, the sing-song feeling recitation, the graphic story – they are all before me a hundred times a day.'

Born in 1771, one of a family of nine (of whom only four survived infancy), Scott had poliomyelitis as a baby, which left him with a limp. But in spite of this handicap he loved the country and its athletic pleasures. At Abbotsford he 'could ride and walk longer distances than most of his friends'. He called himself a 'rattle-skulled half-lawyer, half-sportsman' and was at pains to acquire the image of a country laird rather than that of a professional writer. To this end he often toiled in his study from about five o'clock in the morning until after breakfast-time, after which he mingled with his guests in the role of a carefree aristocrat with no need to engage in vulgar work.

There was another unusual – and, to me, engagingly human – side to his nature.

He was a regular reviewer of books for *The Scots Magazine*, and it has been discovered that he himself was the anonymous critic of *Ivanhoe*, analysing, quoting and interpreting the novel in an article stretching, characteristically, to several thousand words. He had no inhibitions about describing the story as 'masterly' and the author as 'the enchanter who peoples every region of fiction with the delightful creations of his unwearied and exhaustless (*sic*) fancy'.

A year later he published *Kenilworth* and readers of *The Scots Magazine* were advised by the same anonymous critic to regard Scott as 'the greatest genius of the age . . .who has already paid to the full all the debt to his country which her most devoted children would require'.

I have a fellow-feeling with Scott. When my first book, *The Purple Rock*, was published by Stanley Paul in 1933 I was asked – as is usual in the trade – to supply a draft blurb for the jacket. Without hesitation I did so, in the following terms: 'For sheer excitement and dramatic tension there are chapters in this novel which have seldom been surpassed in modern fiction. *The Purple Rock*, however, is not a "thriller" of the conventional type. Shrewd yet kindly humour, the competent portrayal of a group of highly original characters, and descriptive passages having a real literary value help to make it one of the most readable and entertaining books ever written by a Scottish author . . . The plot is worked up to a tremendous climax.' Probably in a daze of astonishment, my publisher, Frank Cowling, decided to use my 'blurb' without the change of even a comma.

Reading it over today, forty-five years on, I shiver with embarrassment; and perhaps it was lucky for me that in 1933 there was no Trade Descriptions Act. But in a way I can excuse myself, as I can excuse Scott for similar behaviour. A writer needs encouragement. For the sake not only of his self-esteem but also of his self-image he requires regular recognition that he *is* a writer. If nobody else seems willing to offer such inspiration then he is impelled by his own burning ambition to do it for himself.

But such lightsome aspects of Scott's character were more than balanced by his capacity for hard work and by his strong sense of pride and responsibility. His poetry having brought him fame and a flirtation with wealth, he began to live in the lairdly style which he enjoyed. Then, without warning, disaster came. His partner and publisher went bankrupt, leaving Scott penniless and in debt. But he wasted no time in self-pity. Refusing to take refuge in a bankruptcy of his own, he settled down to work as he had never worked before; and during the next few years, while producing many of the Waverley Novels, he paid off all his debts and became solvent – and independent – once again.

Though from 1821 until his death in 1832 he held literary and social court at Abbotsford, his country house in Roxburghshire, he did not die a rich man. But I reckon that in the end he achieved his ambition, living the kind of life he wanted, in gracious surroundings, owing nobody.

I suspect it was this aspect of his character, even more than his writing, which appealed to my father and Ambrose. They were both men of independence, who, like the majority of Scots, considered independence a main ingredient in the good life. (Though he lived long enough to contemplate its benefits, the Padre was always suspicious about the Welfare State. 'Makes people stop trying,' he used to say.)

In spite of his enthusiasm for the so-called 'classics', however, Ambrose took my side when I suggested that a few modern books might enhance the value of the Manse library. To my delight the Padre, albeit somewhat reluctantly, agreed.

Between us, from a small, grimy catalogue which Ambrose produced from his case, we chose a list of about a dozen books, all well bound hardbacks at half a crown apiece. The total cost was approximately thirty shillings; and if that seems a tiny amount, it has to be remembered that in the 1920s my father's annual stipend was only £300, less than a twelfth of what the minister of Southend earned in 1979. For the same number of cheap books today the Padre's successor would be faced with a bill for £17, no small sacrifice for a man responsible for the care of a large family and an eleven-roomed Manse.

But as one whose birthplace was a smokey 'black house' in North Uist, where the only light in winter was a *cruiskean* (a small dish of oil with a wick in it) and where the only reading matter comprised the Holy Bible, the Shorter Catechism and an occasional Gaelic number of the Church of Scotland magazine, *Life and Work*, the Padre always possessed great love and respect for books and was determined that his children should benefit from a catholic choice of reading, something denied to himself when young. Just before he died in 1970, aged ninety-two, he presented each of his surviving sons with a copy of the Oxford *Dictionary of Quotations*. 'It contains the wisdom of the ages,' he told us. 'You'll all find it useful when I'm gone.' (Of course, he regarded himself as our oracle so long as he remained alive; and I think my brothers will agree with me that he had sound reasons for doing so.)

The authors whose works I chose from Ambrose's catalogue were, however, comparatively unknown to him. From my point of view this may have been fortunate. But when the books arrived about a fortnight after Ambrose's visit I was glad to notice that the Padre, though inclined to mutter 'More rubbish!' on opening each one, read them all as avidly as I did.

Topping the list was Rafael Sabatini's *Captain Blood*; and I can remember the thrill of satisfaction and admiration that ran through me as I read the passage in which Peter Blood delivers his Parthian shot to Judge George Jeffreys of Wem. There were books also by Stanley Weyman, S. Walkey and Talbot Mundy. Later, when *King of the Khyber Rifles* was made into a film, the Padre admitted to me that he had enjoyed this particular book most of all. *Bones of the River*, by Edgar Wallace, was another of my choices ultimately approved by him, though today it would almost certainly be proscribed by the Race Relations Board.

That Owen Wister's *The Virginian* should have been included in the list was, I suspect, the result of the Padre (and perhaps Ambrose, too) confusing it with Thackeray's *Virginians.* But there was no confusion about Jeffrey Farnol's *Black Bartlemey's Treasure*. When my father read it he summoned me to his study and lectured me on the danger of reading 'such romantic tosh'. But I revelled in Farnol's lusty 'love stuff'. It produced a thrilling response in my adolescent body and made me dream excitedly of what I might presently do to some nubile and willing girl. It was the nearest I got to pornography.

Not long after providing us with the sensational 'new books' Ambrose ceased to visit us. There had been talk of his retirement from the road and of a journey to visit a daughter in Fife.

I wish I had discovered more about him. He had been well schooled. He was of a gentle, studious disposition. He had a weak chest and was inclined to stoutness. In spite of all this, how did he become a colporteur, roughing it in all weathers on a ramshackle bicycle and living, to some extent, on the charity of his 'clients'? Was he, by any chance, a 'stickit minister', a man with a calling for the Church who yet had failed to pass the divinity examinations?

When in Southend he always used to visit the ruined thirteenth-century chapel in Keil graveyard. One day, curious as always, Archie and I followed him on our bicycles. From a vantage point on the hillside above the roofless building we watched him go inside. On one of the ancient, recumbent gravestones he spread his waterproof coat, knelt carefully and stiffly upon it, clasped his hands against his forehead and began muttering a prayer.

Why, as we scuttled away, did I feel so disturbed, so guilty?

4. Student Irregular

Sport has always been important to the MacVicar clan.

The Padre was the first captain of Glasgow University Shinty Club when it was founded in 1901, and he once played for Scotland against an Irish team. His skill with the *caman* (shinty-stick) was transmitted to my sister Rona, who, just before World War II, played lacrosse at the level of a Scottish International trial. It has also reappeared in two of his granchildren – Willie's youngest daughter, Susan, and John's eldest daughter, Marsali. Susan is a regular member of the Scottish Women's hockey team, while Marsali, an under-23 internationalist, has recently joined Susan in the seniors.

As yet, the male members of the clan have never reached such dizzy heights of sporting accomplishment; but Archie, as well as being a good left-handed golfer, was a soccer blue at Glasgow University, and Willie, Kenneth, John and I are all happy and reasonably successful golfers. (Five years ago I had a handicap of 5. This year, to my chagrin, they have hoisted me to 12. But on my home course at Southend – the famous Links of Dunaverty – which has a standard scratch of 63, I have recently acquired a new ambition – to do a medal round equal to or less than my age. It can be done. I have done it more than once in a friendly game.)

In our day, my brothers and I were all keen athletes. Our interest in running and jumping and throwing weights was first kindled, I think, at the Southend Sports, which, when we were children, took place annually on New Year's Day.

The New Year holiday, a blessed relief from laborious work on the farms, was always celebrated in Southend with feasting, drinking and jousting. Back in the nineteenth century the jousting took the form of a shinty match between teams of about twenty or thirty men from two rival areas in the parish – Machrimore and Glenbreckrie. In the end, however, this degenerated into violence and fighting, until on one sad day a young man died on the shinty field, head broken by a blow from a homemade *caman*. After that the shinty was no longer played; and many years later, in its place, the New Year Sports were begun.

To us, as children, they afforded great excitement and amusement; and, as I think back, it seems to me that the weather was always sunny and dry, with perhaps a small hint of frost.

No singlets, pants or spikes in those carefree days. For the crack performers in the long-distance races the fashionable outfit comprised a newly laundered woollen vest and long drawers, vulnerable points secured with safety pins. The feet were left bare and usually suffered no damage on the crisp turf of the 18th fairway on the golf course, where the furlong track was delineated by a circle of snare-pegs. Some of the jumpers – and all the stone putters and hammer throwers – wore tackety boots, in order to ensure a firm footing, and, as a rule, they performed in shirt sleeves and 'gallowses' (braces).

The great sprinters and jumpers were Willie McKerral, Jean's second eldest brother, and Johnny Hunter. Stars in the mile were Willie Balloch and Jim Russell, superb figures in their off-white vests and long johns. The 'heavyweights' included the Cameron brothers, John and Archie, men of gigantic proportions to our youthful eyes and accoutred strangely not only with fancy 'gallowses' but also with wide, silvery buckled belts.

Shouts of appreciative laughter always greeted the maverick competitors. Those were usually former athletes, now in their middle years, who had started to toast the New Year early in the day and were now stricken by genial and adventurous drunkenness. When the Mile Race began they would gallop ahead of the rest, shouting and waving to the spectators, heavy boots thundering, only to collapse in heaps before the end of the first lap. Nimbly Willie Balloch and Jim

Russell would leap over them, causing fresh outbursts of applause. The mavericks would then be hauled to safety by their friends and comforted by deep draughts from flasks or half bottles of whisky.

The Padre pretended not to notice. He was no spoil-sport on a holiday.

For us youngsters there was a sack race, for which each competitor had to provide his or her own sack. The great champion in this event was Davie McKerral, Jean's youngest brother, who sometimes arranged that small tears should occur in the bottom corners of his sack, so that his feet could move more freely. None of the rest of us had the brains even to consider such an idea.

By the time my brothers and I had reached the stage of becoming senior competitors, the New Year's Day Sports had been transferred to the summer. They are now called the Southend Highland Games.

The harvest of 1926 was late, delayed by rain and stook-tumbling equinoctial gales.

Having left school in June, I had spent the summer competing at all the local Highland Games – which included those at Southend, Tayinloan, Lochgilphead, Inveraray and Oban – along with my brother Archie, Hamish Taylor ('Boskers'), Lachie Young and Neil John MacCallum, who was the second son of the local blacksmith.

In the dressing-tents, in an atmosphere of embrocation and strange oaths, we rubbed shoulders with such great men as R. Starkey, the brothers Anderson from Dundee and J. McGregor from Spean Bridge. The only real professional among us was Neil John, who eventually won the mile at Powderhall and made a fortune for a few wise backers in the know. Archie, Hamish, Lachie and I were like small birds cleaning up after the vultures. In spite of all this, however, I had been able to collect about £20 in prizes, which I proposed to use as pocket-money at the university.

The Padre had also been busy on my behalf, acquiring for me a county council bursary of £30 and a Dundonald bursary, for prospective divines, of £40. Both would run for three years and allow me to complete a degree in Arts, *provided I passed all the exams.*

But here was the rub. It was the beginning of the examination trauma which has caused me nightmares ever since – a dream set in the Bute Hall of Glasgow University where I suddenly discover that the paper before me is covered with mathematical symbols, about which I know nothing, instead of the one in French which I have been expecting.

In addition to those bursaries I was also guaranteed, like every other student, an annual grant of £10 from the Carnegie Trust. I calculated, therefore, that my annual income for the next three years would be about £100 – that is, if I managed to win £20 each summer at the Highland Games. This seemed to me an excellent prospect; and indeed it was, being equivalent to something like £800 today. But, as will be shown, the whole financial edifice was as precariously balanced as that erected by any slick and daring City tycoon.

Euphoria, however, has always been a weakness of mine – though, paradoxically, in a writer it sometimes affords strength – and I faced the future with careless courage. And that autumn, as the harvest dragged on and the date in early October of my departure for the university made its relentless approach, I took another step which required even more brave optimism. I kissed Jean for the first time – on the dark side of a moonlit corn-stack at Brunerican.

I had been helping Jean's father and brothers with the harvest, not for money – at that time farmers had little to offer – but in order to be in Jean's company as much as possible. She was only sixteen, but her mother had died two years before and she was now mistress of the farm. I enjoyed coming in at night, after the day's work was done and the cart-horses had been 'lowsed', and sitting down to a meal of ham and eggs, followed by huge wedges of sponge-cake filled with whipped cream. The sponge-cake was – and is – Jean's speciality and my joy. I tried to imagine that occasionally she baked it especially for my benefit.

On the other hand, old Willie McKerral, Jean's father, and her brothers, James, Archie and Davie, seemed to consider my presence in the family circle as natural and unworthy of special note. Nor did they try to prevent me escorting Jean to certain dances and concerts in the Territorial Hall in the village.

I am afraid that as a dancing partner she found me as unsatisfactory as she had done six years before, when together we attended Mr McLeish's dancing class and the height of my achievement was to act as an immobile statue in the statue dance. I had many pangs of jealousy as she enjoyed military two-steps, Eva three-steps, hesitation and veleta waltzes, quadrilles and the lancers in the arms of more expert practitioners. But she was always willing to let me have the last waltz, a sign in rural circles that I had been chosen to 'see her home' afterwards and that eager rivals who might try to thwart me did so at their peril.

For helping Jean with the milking, morning and evening, old Barbara MacCallum was paid half a crown a week. She also had a cot-house free of rent and as much milk, butter and buttermilk as she needed for herself, her husband and a few adopted nieces and nephews. Barbara had a sharp eye. One night I waited for Jean at the top of the byre. Milk pail slopping, Barbara nudged me and whispered: 'She kens naethin' aboot it. But keep at it. She'll learn!' Her lewd expression made me feel embarrassed and even ashamed. I 'kent naethin' aboot it' either. All I knew was that I wanted to do more with Jean than just walk and talk and be kind. What that something was remained dark and nebulous.

The night before I was due to leave for the university there was no dance or concert, no obvious excuse to be with Jean. Then *she* had an idea.

A year before, Jean's brother John had married Cecilia, the youngest daughter of the Rev. George Walter Strang, minister of the Castlehill Church in Campbeltown. Together they had set up house at Dalbhraddan Farm, about a mile from the Manse. The marriage was full of singing and laughter. But then, at the beginning of summer, John's hand was caught in the gears of a turnip-slicer and he had died, within a week, of blood poisoning. Today, with the aid of penicillin and improved methods of medical care, such a tragedy would be unlikely to happen. But Cecilia had to face it, knowing that she was pregnant.

Young John McKerral was born in August. We didn't know that fifty years later he would be in charge of Modern Studies at Campbeltown Grammar School and a leading actor with the Dunaverty Players: all that occupied our thoughts at the time was that he and his mother should be given love and help by the family and the community at large.

That October night, therefore, Jean arranged to bring gifts of a chicken and some baby clothes to Dalbhraddan; and before any of her brothers could do so, I volunteered to carry her basket.

With a harvest moon shining down on us like a spotlight we trudged the three miles from Brunerican to Dalbhraddan. Jean went in, offered her gifts and saw the baby.

I waited for her at the bottom of the farm road. It was cold and clear. Silent, too, except for a tinkle of water in the roadside ditch and the occasional complaint of an owl in the fir 'plantin'' half a mile away. Under the heedless stars, Southend lay rolling and dark against the moon sky. I was leaving it tomorrow, leaving Jean and my family and all the boys and girls who were my friends. Tomorrow night I should be among clustering buildings in Glasgow, for the first time alone against life. Why hadn't I been born a farmer's son, thirled to the earth of my native parish, able to earn a living in the kind community which was my birthright? Sadness flooded through me. A Hebridean sadness inherited from ancestors in North Uist who wept for lost homelands.

I fought against it, swallowing to ease the quiver in my throat. I would come back. I would write and make money to come back. There, in the whin-bush, the idea of becoming a minister was stripped of some glamour and impoverished.

An hour later Jean and I were trudging back to Brunerican, first along the main road and then by the side road which followed the burn. The cold sadness in the pit of my stomach had been replaced by another kind of primeval excitement.

'Trudging' is not, of course, the right word. I didn't even realize that I was walking. And though sometimes we staggered about on cart-tracks and loose rubble I kept my arm firmly about Jean's waist. She leant against me to keep her balance, and I acted the strong protector.

We scarcely talked at all, except about the baby.

'He's not very good looking,' Jean said.

'I don't suppose any of us was very good looking at two months.'

'I hope he doesn't grow up to be ugly.'

She need not have worried. As a juvenile lead in the Dunaverty Players, John became a notable heart-throb.

As we approached Brunerican I guided Jean away from the front door. She gave no sign of surprise. In the farmyard it was quiet, with the black moon shadows of the stacks like incongruities in a surrealist painting. In one of the shadows a pile of sheaves lay against the bottom of a stack. I put the basket away and put my arms about her.

She lay back among the straw and I kissed her. I must have made a poor job of it, because her response, from my point of view, was unsatisfactory. I felt her trembling, even crying a little.

'You're going away tomorrow.'

Characteristically, I refused to face reality and kissed her again.

Our trouble was the prickly corn-straws. Burns may have found no impediments 'amang the rigs o' barley', but I reckon that where non-poets are concerned passion is inhibited when sharp straws invade ears and eyes and noses.

But that night, without words, Jean and I knew that we wanted to be together for the rest of our lives. We promised to write to each other twice a week while I was away. And during the next four years we kept our promises.

As we parted she gave me a small silk handkerchief. Its colour, she told me, was heliotrope, and there was a touch of perfume on it. For the next ten years I kept that handkerchief in my pocket, below my own, and gave it back to her on the day we were married.

It was in a maze of half-understood love and home-sickness that I enrolled as a student at Glasgow University. An irregular student, as it happened.

In 1926 entrance to a Scottish University could be gained with three Highers and one Lower. Today candidates have to show a whole quiverful of A levels as well as numerous O levels; and even then, in order to 'mak' siccar', the pass 'bands' have to be well above fifty per cent. No wonder that in the past few years Glasgow University, for example, is facing a serious decline in its student population. The competence – even brilliance – of contemporary scholars fills me with admiration. Not long ago a young niece of mine who aimed not only to become a doctor but also to play hockey for Scotland carried off six A levels and three O levels, a feat far beyond my capacity.

All I was able to show after six years of happy education at Campbeltown Grammar School were two Highers, in English and maths, and two Lowers, in French and Latin. This was not enough for a regular enrolment at a university; but the director of studies at Glasgow was kind enough to suggest that I might enter as an irregular student for a year, taking degree classes in English and maths and studying French privately at the same time. If I passed the Prelims in French the following summer, along with the university exams in English and maths, then everything would be regularized and I could start my second year as a normal student.

I accepted his suggestion and spent the following winter and spring commuting between the University at Gilmorehill, Skerry's Commercial College in Bath Street and the University sports ground at Westerlands.

At Gilmorehill I sat under Professor McNeile Dixon in English and learned to appreciate a new world of literature and poetry, in which fiction writers – including Scott, Dickens and the inevitable George Eliot – were overshadowed by such as Beowolf, Henryson, Dunbar, Chaucer, Shakespeare, Milton, Burns and Keats. I felt the same thrill of excitement as had come to me while reading *The Rudiments of Criticism* and listening to the words of James MacTaggart.

All the time, however, another part of my brain kept insisting that a writer who wanted to make money – as I did – must not become too thirled to the higher flights of art. Only a genius, I argued, should indulge himself in such a way; and I was unsure as to the extent of my genius. I liked the world and its material comforts too much, along with the social and sporting side of life, to contemplate the ivory tower into which, it seemed to me, real genius must inevitably retire.

I considered the tall and lanky McNeile Dixon as a genius. Had I but known it, he was able to mix literature and the social and sporting life in an engagingly skilful manner. He was a golfer, who loved his weekly games at Glasgow Gailes and Killermont. The odd dram was another of his pleasures. But as he stood on his rostrum, lecturing to us on the subject of puritanism in literature, his sleepy eyes fixed on a point high above our heads, I had no suspicion that his own puritanism was liable, at times, to become diluted. To me, his utterances were god-like, and in my notebook I underlined with heavy pen-strokes his dictum that 'the touch of puritanism in the Scottish character is what has made Scotland a great nation, with a literature as strong and disciplined as any in the world'. At the back of my mind was the youthful hope that one day I might make a contribution to that literature.

McNeile Dixon's senior assistant was Dr Bickersteth, who specialized in Shakespeare. He was a small, round and untidy man, given to unexpected bursts of laughter. Male members of the class appreciated his bawdy jokes, which seemed to stem naturally from his absorption in the Elizabethan scene. But some of the girls declared themselves shocked by his 'coarse humour'.

One day three or four of them walked out in the middle of a lecture. As they hesitated at the door, his crumpled face, decorated with horn-rimmed spectacles, creased sideways into a smile. ' "Stand not upon the order of your going," ' he quoted at them, ' "but go at once." ' As they departed he turned to us with an impish look. Confidingly, and still lingering with *Macbeth*, he quoted again: ' "Away, and mock the time with fairest show: false face must hide what the false heart doth know." ' With deep laughter we young and sophisticated males registered immediate understanding of what the words implied; and our laughter swelled as he whispered to a few of us behind his hand: 'Let me offer a lesson of experience. The puritanical ones are always the best in bed!'

Dr Bickersteth's own private life was extremely orthodox, not to say puritanical, which could not quite be said about Professor McNeile Dixon's. It was odd, we thought, that the philosophies they preached should have been so contradictory.

I confess that as I look back over my own life I find in it echoes of McNeile Dixon's. I only wish I could have written a book like his principal work on literature, *The Human Situation*.

The English class was for me delightful. My essays, still written under the influence of Kubla Khan, nearly always got a beta plus. McNeile Dixon himself once gave me an alpha minus for a critical study of *Paradise Regained*, in which I disagreed with Milton's implication that God created Adam for God only and Eve for the lowlier function of serving God through him. This encouraged me to write an even more violent criticism of *The Pilgrim's Progress*. I described Bunyan's book as a crude fairy tale, unworthy of more than passing notice by powerful intellects. Did I convey the impression of some intellectual arrogance within myself? In any case, the essay earned me only a beta minus. Its marking taught me a lesson which emphasised not only the need for continual discipline but also the subtle dangers of swollen head. Sad to say, many editors and publishers can testify that I still have not fully learned it.

In general, however, there was no doubt in my mind that when the time came I could pass the degree exam in English. The class in mathematics was different.

At school, under the threat of George Hutcheon's baleful eye – and well-honed Lochgelly strap – I had worked hard and found the exams easy. Now, dependent on self-discipline, I became careless. The calculus was something that my woolly mind failed to grasp, and I had a feeling within myself that even though I did make a sacrificial effort and succeed in understanding it, the knowledge would be of no good to me as a writer.

It still hadn't dawned on me that a sound training in mathematics is of immense value to a writer – especially to a journalist. A mathematical theorem is set out on the lines of 'Given, To Prove, Proof, Conclusion'. What better structure for a story or newspaper article could possibly be devised?

I struggled with the calculus, but nearly always the struggle ended with my putting it aside and becoming happily absorbed in a book. One, for preference, by John Buchan, my new exemplar and hero. Towards the beginning of May 1927, it suddenly occurred to me that I faced disaster, because if I didn't pass in both English *and* maths, my university career would come to a summary end.

Meanwhile, in the afternoons, I attended the French class at Skerry's College.

Skerry's was a private institution, family owned. The place looked seedy, its dusty corridors covered with worn linoleum. Rickety wooden partitions, some with frosted windows set well above eye-level, created a maze of tiny classrooms. The atmosphere was drab, and it seemed to me that most of the teachers and students I met wore furtive expressions, as if all were intent upon covering up – and only possibly retrieving – past failures. Or was this idea merely a reflection of my own psychological condition?

And yet, in spite of appearances, Skerry's had a notable record of successful tuition. Budding secretaries and clerks and copy boys aiming for the higher flights of journalism were coached with great thoroughness in typing and shorthand. Young businessmen were groomed in the latest methods and procedures. And many, like myself, who had failed their Highers, were gently but firmly conducted towards 'Prelim' passes in several European languages. As the spring sunshine of 1927 percolated into the dull corridors I had begun to find a new interest in French, and *Pecheur d'Island* no longer proved a bore to translate.

At Skerry's I made no friends. People there were watch-watchers, counting the minutes as they hurried either to a job or from one. Time was precious to fugitives from failure. For myself, after the French class had 'skailed' I always rushed to board the blue tram-car for the Botanic Gardens. A penny-ha'penny ticket brought me into Great Western Road, across Kelvin Bridge and to the stop near Hubbard's, opposite Cooper's Clock. In the upstairs room at Hubbard's I would find my university cronies – Kenneth Tyson, James Davidson, Archie Robertson, Colin Mitchell – and there, as a reward for my labour at Skerry's, enjoy coffee and a chocolate biscuit (total cost, fourpence) and some happy argument untrammelled by time.

On winter and spring afternoons, when there was no French class, I often took a green tram to Westerlands, where Charlie Durning was in charge of training. Charlie wanted me to play rugby in the winter and start concentrating on athletics at the end of the season. 'You're big and strong and fast,' he told me. 'And a bit bull-headed. You'd make a grand three-quarter.' But I preferred soccer and spent my Saturdays playing for minor university elevens.

Donald McDiarmid, a farmer's son from Kintyre, was a senior law student at the time and also a leading figure in the soccer club. Even though my football skill was questionable, to say the least, he saw to it, being clannish, that I got plenty of games. He picked me once to play left back for the second eleven against a team from Aberdeen University. In the course of the game I scored against my own side, deflecting the ball away from the goalkeeper; I gave away a penalty by bringing down the opposing centre-forward with a scything kick and was eventually warned by the referee that if I used any more bad language I might be sent off. It was all disaster. I was immediately relegated to the fourth eleven, whose fixtures included games against precocious schoolboys and the inmates and staff of several lunatic asylums.

'I told you,' Charlie Durning said. 'You'd get on far better at rugby.'

But I never did like rugby. I dreamt Walter Mitty dreams of becoming a soccer star and being chosen for my country. The dream is still with me, and when Ally MacLeod's anti-heroes played in the World Cup I was with them on the fields of the Argentine, sweating and shouting and developing a stomach ulcer in front of the television set.

My ignominy as a footballer was thankfully forgotten when Archie, my brother, came to the university and retrieved the family honour by gaining a soccer blue. His 'blue' blazer now hangs in my wardrobe.

Donald McDiarmid played for the first university eleven, too, and won a Scottish Amateur Cup medal. Years later, when he became Sheriff Substitute in Argyll, he and I got together again, this time on the golf course. As a golfer I am less of a disappointment to him, except perhaps when, as sometimes happens, I beat him 'out in the country'.

It was as an athlete that I earned some approval from Charlie Durning. In my first year I ran in the two novice races at the university sports, coming in third in the 100 yards and second in the 600 yards. Charlie massaged my legs and in a haze of optimism and embrocation forecast that one day I should run in the 220 yards Scottish Championship.

This never happened, for a simple reason. Charlie and I suddenly realized that I was running at the university under false pretences. Because I had accepted money prizes at the Highland Games I was, in legal terms, a professional. If I wanted to run as an amateur at the university or at any other sports meeting arranged under the auspices of the Scottish Amateur Athletic Association I should have to apply for reinstatement. But I needed the money more than I needed medals. It was goodbye, therefore, to yet another dream.

I still have the medals I won for those two novice races at Westerlands, though I suppose that in strict legal terms I ought to have returned them. Should the SAAA or the university authorities now kick up a fuss I may surprise them by applying for reinstatement as an amateur even at this late date. And retrospectively at that.

I find that the word 'irregular' describes perfectly my first year at the university. And even after the summer exams it remained apposite.

I passed the degree exam in English and the 'Prelim' in

French. But in maths I failed, bemused by the calculus. It looked like checkmate.

At this juncture I remembered an article I had once read in an old *Strand Magazine*. It contained a story which the Padre often used as an 'illustration' in a sermon. The picture shows two men playing chess, one glum and despondent, the other moving his queen and triumphantly announcing 'Checkmate!' According to the writer of the article in the *Strand*, however, an expert study of the board reveals that the man who has apparently lost can still make a move and win.

Not for the first time nor for the last I found encouragement in this story. I went to see the director of studies, and sure enough, to my overwhelming relief, he indicated that a winning move on my part was still possible. I could re-sit the degree exam in maths in September. If I passed, then all would still be well.

That summer was a busy one.

The Padre growled and made frequent references to the fate of 'stickit ministers'. My mother kept telling him in Gaelic to 'let the boy alone'. Maimie, my brothers and Rona carefully avoided any mention of exams. Jean took the view that I must surely pass and was apparently unworried.

Peggy Taylor, 'Boskers' ' eldest sister, was a young maths teacher. During her summer holidays she gallantly volunteered to coach me in the calculus, and I worked hard to please her.

When I wasn't engaged in doing maths exercises for Peggy, or visiting Brunerican to see Jean, I trained regularly in the glebe (following a programme detailed in *Athletics*, the book written by Harold Abrahams after winning the Olympic 100 metres in 1924) and travelled with my mates to the usual round of Highland Games. All the time ideas for articles and short stories were turning and clicking in my head like computer wheels, but I tried to discipline myself not to think about them too much until I had 'regularized' my university year.

Thanks to Peggy, I am sure, the gamble paid off. I passed the September exam in maths, and a week before I was due to return to Glasgow I found myself at last a 'regular' student. It had been what John Buchan might have called 'a close-run thing'.

Entering my second year at the university I was in a happy mood. By a whisker I had avoided the full fury of the Padre's wrath. I had left maths behind me – for ever, I hoped. I had my bursaries and a sufficiency of money from the Highland Games. And in my pocket I had Jean's handkerchief.

This time I took classes in higher English, French and political economy. A cake-walk, I reckoned. And so it proved to be – at any rate in higher English and French. The Anglo-Saxon content of the higher English course caused me trouble; but Ritchie Girvan, who lectured in the subject, was a Campbeltown man, and this, for me, may have been fortunate. In the degree exam I translated *aetbrede* as 'wheaten loaf': it means 'nevertheless'. *Aetbrede*, I passed without further apparent difficulty. Inspired by Skerry's recent teaching, I made light of the French exam, too. But political economy was a fish of a different colour.

Anything to do with money and trade has always been beyond my comprehension. Sometimes I think it is beyond the comprehension of the so-called 'economic experts' as well.

Within recent years I have tried to follow their arguments in the public prints only to find that time and time again they contradict one another and, on occasions, even themselves. They prophesy a 'slump'. Out of the blue there comes an upsurge in trade, and from their published articles pessimism disappears like mist from a brae. They forecast great glory in oil. Then a 'slump' does come and they return to pessimism, reminding us with sadistic glee of their original prophecy. Oil, they inform us, has only about a decade to live. What happens then? Have they forgotten that in the 1960s they were saying exactly the same thing about coal? Now they tell us there is enough coal in our island to last for hundreds of years.

I voted for the Common Market, not for economic reasons but because I reckoned that any scheme designed to bring together people of different nationalities was a good thing. Some of the 'economic experts' who voted with me now bewail their 'mistake', because few advantages, money-wise, have occurred for Britain. In 1990 they may be singing yet another tune, though I am certain that money will still be their principal concern, not the moral well-being of ordinary folk.

I think it was the study of political economy at the university that made me sour and suspicious about economists. Laws such as those proposed by Malthus and Adam Smith appear to me still as depressing and unrealistic. Sounding infinitely wise in theory, in terms of human application they are as irrelevant as *The Naked Ape* to a young couple in love. I believe that any culture based on greed and a consequent manoeuvring for gain – as ours appears to be – contains a cancer which, in the end, will disfigure and destroy it.

Not surprisingly, I failed the degree exam in political economy. In September I failed the re-sit, too. The following year my subjects were moral philosophy and history. And political economy again.

Moral philosophy was a subject more to my taste. It seemed to me that it dealt with the problems of humanity as a whole rather than with the problems of a few wealthy people with money to manipulate. As an uncertain young man, uneasy and lacking in confidence, searching for solid belief, I found those parts of the course I could fully understand to be warm and comforting. I was fortunate in being able to sit under Professor A. A. Bowman, whose lectures, when read over and digested, tended to draw back dark curtains from my eyes.

I was lucky, too, in having a gentle, painstaking tutor in W. D. (Bill) Lamont. Only a few years older than I, Bill kept my spirits up with his impish humour and brought quick understanding of some – to me – obscure aspects of moral philosophy.

He and I had several common denominators. His father was a minister in Islay, mine a minister across the water in Kintyre. We would both rather talk and argue than concentrate upon making money. We both had a taste for canny Hebridean humour.

To illustrate a point I had missed in a moral philosophy essay, he told me the Gaelic legend of the Happy Man.

The King of Gaeldom, it seemed, was attacked by 'the black melancholy'. Court medicine men were baffled. None could effect or suggest a cure. In despair he consulted his chief druid, who, after a long and impressive silence, delivered an answer. 'Find a completely happy man, your majesty. Take the shirt from his back and wear it. Then you will find the melancholy lifting from your spirit like mist, and the blackness will become light.'

To every part of his kingdom the king sent messengers. Their orders were simple: 'Find a happy man and bring me his shirt.'

At first the messengers approached the wealthy people. But the wealthy people, though possessing many beautiful shirts, were all so worried in case they might lose their money, and so unhealthy in consequence of continually remaining indoors counting it, that none of them was happy.

Then they approached the wise and learned people, who also wore good quality shirts. But the wise and learned people were all so worried about their salaries and so frustrated by their failure to discover the ultimate secrets of life, that none of them was happy.

Then they approached the workmen and the labourers. But the workmen and the labourers, even though they all had shirts well designed to keep out the cold, were all so jealous of their wealthy employers and so upset because their dreams of living in a palace had failed to come true that none of them was happy.

Finally, however, a whisper was heard that in the farthest corner of the kingdom, on a little island off the beetling Mull, there lived a truly happy man. He greeted them with courtesy and pleasure, interrupting his fishing to invite them into his humble hut. (Today, after drawing his old-age pension, I reckon he might have been playing golf.)

'Are you a happy man?' they asked.

'I am, indeed. Completely happy. I live by hunting and

fishing. I am in debt to nobody, and nobody is in debt to me. I envy none. I love my fellow man and wish him well.'

The messengers were overjoyed. 'Then,' they said, 'in order to save the king from the black melancholy you will surely be willing to provide him with your shirt?'

The man wrinkled his sun-tanned forehead. 'I am sorry,' he said. 'You see me here naked as I was born. I am so poor in material things that I don't even have a shirt to put on my back!'

I enjoyed and admired Bill's story.

The following year, 1929, the new *Scottish Daily Express* erupted in Albion Street in Glasgow, in a dazzle of plate glass, cream-coloured cement and soaring sales. The editor was A. C. (Sandy) Trotter, then and for many years afterwards a good friend to young (and old) Scottish writers.

One of the first exciting features in the new paper was a short story competition, in response to which I composed a 'literary' version of *The Happy Man* and sent it in. To my joy it won first prize and was published in full. For many a night afterwards I took the paper to bed with me, to thrill at the sight of my name in prominent type, to re-read the story and, finally and happily, to say a prayer of thankfulness.

The prize was a beautiful grey and dark green rug decorated with the Celtic design of the endless snake. It had been woven in Lewis by unemployed fisher-girls, on whose behalf the *Scottish Daily Express* was running a campaign. I have it yet, the colours still bright under the tramp of countless feet in Achnamara's front hallway.

But the important thing was that Sandy Trotter had got to know about me. During the following ten years (happy, uninhibited years for non-staff journalists), which ended with World War II, I worked for him regularly as a freelance. He published my third novel, *The Screaming Gull*, as a serial and encouraged me to try short stories in addition to the usual bread-and-butter articles with titles like 'Has Highland Hospitality Grown Cold?', 'Stone Age Smokers' and 'Sour Milk for Sweet Old Age'. (This last one may have helped in a tiny way to make yoghurt popular.)

The *Express* Saturday supplement was my favourite hunting ground.

At eleven o'clock one Friday morning, not long after Jean and I got married in 1936, the phone rang in Achnamara. Sandy's voice came through. 'I want a twelve hundred word short story for tomorrow. Can you make it?'

'Sure,' I said, without hesitation, and put down the receiver.

Then I began to consider the snags. First, a new story had to be written, and I hadn't an idea in my head. Second, I had to get the typescript to Glasgow not later than 7 o'clock that same evening, and by road Glasgow is 140 miles from Southend. (At that time, for some reason, the phoning in of lengthy feature copy was discouraged. Nowadays I do it regularly, with a cheerful copy-taker egging me on.)

The answer to the second problem became clear at once. A morning and evening air service had recently started between Renfrew and Campbeltown, seven-seater de Haviland Rapides landing on and taking off from a field which bordered the road to Machrihanish. Sheep and cattle were herded away at the appropriate times, and passengers were weighed in at a little hut not much larger than a phone booth. On this particular day I remembered that the evening plane to Renfrew was due to take off at four o'clock in the afternoon. If I left Achnamara in my bull-nose Morris at half-past three I could reach the 'airfield' in time to hand my typescript to the pilot before he took off. He lived in Glasgow and would be able to deliver it at Albion Street before 7 o'clock.

The answer to my first problem depended upon another question. Could I conceive and write a 1200 word short story, correct it thoroughly and type out a 'fair copy' in the four and a half hours which remained before half-past three?

I told Jean about it. 'No lunch for me today,' I said. 'Just keep bringing me cups of tea. And let nobody near me. For the next four and a half hours you're the only one to know that I even exist.'

She sighed. She was finding it hard to sustain romance amid the realities of married life. I could see, however, that gradually she was coming to terms with the habits of a desperate writer. 'All right, dear,' she said and without further comment left me to my travail.

For the first half-hour I sat in an armchair by the fire, working out a plot. One came to me fairly quickly, because an urgent deadline is a stimulant even more powerful than whisky. (All my life I have favoured the idea that specific deadlines should be written into contracts, especially for books and radio and television work. Otherwise, as in my case, inherent laziness could take over and the project might never even get started.)

My plot concerned the adventure of a climber in Glen Croe, near Arrochar. He became lost in a blizzard but eventually, as darkness fell, found his way to a lonely cottage. Somebody – something – took him in. No lamp was lit; words spoken by the inhabitant of the cottage were slurred and indistinct, almost inhuman. Food and drink were given to the climber, but they did not comfort him. He shivered in the warmth of a peat fire, in the glow of which the other took care never to be seen.

I know. The plot is as old as the most ancient Highland *sennachie*. It resembles, too, as I later discovered, W. W. Jacob's story of 'The Monkey's Paw'. It revealed, finally, that the 'creature' in the cottage was a scientist recuperating after an accident in a chemical works. His face had been terribly scarred, so terribly that he could not bear to let anyone see it. And, of course, the climber turned out to be a plastic surgeon.

At the time I thought the whole idea inspired. In two hours I had written the story, in longhand in an exercise book. In another hour I had revised and corrected it. Half-an-hour's typing, followed by another half-hour's check on spelling and punctuation, and the job was done.

Jean came with me to the 'airfield' for the run, and thankfully the old Morris had no breakdowns on the way. I handed the typescript to an obliging pilot.

Next day, under generous headlines, the story appeared in the Saturday supplement. Sandy Trotter made no comment concerning it; but he sent me a cheque for £6 – in those days high payment for 1200 words – and that was comment enough for me.

I go into detail about all this because I believe it illustrates how much a writer's career depends on chance.

Had I not won their competition, the *Express* might never have heard of me and, in all probability, Sandy Trotter would not have helped to build my confidence and reputation by publishing so many of my articles, short stories and serials. And had I not heard the story of 'The Happy Man' from Bill Lamont in the moral philosophy class I would not have won the *Express* competition. A degree in maths enables me to add, *quod erat demonstrandum*.

Bill had an adventurous career. He left Glasgow to become professor of philosophy at the University of Cairo and for a time was principal of Makerere College in Uganda. But all the time the flame of his love for Scotland – and for Islay in particular – remained constant. Now, in his retirement, he lives in Glasgow, from where he and his wife Ann make regular forays into the West, pursuing their hobby of archaeology.

They often come to see us at Achnamara, to discuss the archaeological riches of Southend. I wonder if they know that my eagerness to help in their research is partly because of the debt I owe Bill for telling me about the Happy Man.

The story brought me material benefit. It brought me spiritual benefit, too. As did Professor Bowman's lectures, with their clear and unequivocal conclusion: 'There is a divinity within every man. Respect and reverence for this divinity is the foundation of civilized behaviour.'

When politicians denigrate one another, when demonstrators make violence, when the media resort to character assault – and even character assassination – in order to further the aims of the right or the left, I remember Professor Bowman's wise words and await, with some confidence, the ultimate triumph of the human spirit.

5. Divine Discontent

At the end of my third year at the university I passed in history and moral philosophy. With pale excitement I awaited the list of passes in political economy due to be published in the *Glasgow Herald*. If my name appeared I should have completed a degree as Master of Arts.

My name did not appear. For the third time I had failed in that dry, uninteresting, inhuman subject. My hopes of being capped at the graduation ceremony in June lay about me like melting splinters of ice.

That summer in the Manse was not happy. I felt that I had let everybody down: the family, Jean, the whole parish. The Padre seemed to agree with me. He had sympathy for failure when it stemmed from unlucky circumstances, but not for failure which he considered to be the result of idleness and a lack of application. My mother and Maimie were less critical, though the disappointment in my mother's big green eyes was a punishment even sorer than the Padre's frowns. My brothers and Rona avoided all mention of exams. So did Jean. But I heard whispers in the parish: 'If he canna pass his exams why does he no' go an' get a job in an office or something?'

An office?

Hopelessness gathered round me like a damp cloud. I wanted to write. I wanted to marry Jean and make a home for her in the country place and among the country people we both loved. But I had no money; I seemed to have very few brains, and the world gaped at me with neither encouragement nor compassion.

And I had developed acne. Shaving meant painful minutes each morning with a cut-throat razor – safety-razors were only coming into fashion at the time – while blood slid over my jaws and chin, staining the soap. This was followed by a squeezing out of pimply puss and an application of the zinc ointment recommended by my mother. I looked horrible, like a picture I had seen in a medical encyclopaedia of a youth recovering from smallpox.

I was afraid Jean might become disgusted with my appearance and begin to think about some of the clean-jawed young farmers who still, according to reports, crowded round her at the dances while I was away. I was depressed and only marginally comforted when my mother said: 'You'll grow out of it, Angus. And remember, if somebody loves you, the way you look makes no difference.'

One day, on the hillside behind the Manse, I lay alone in the summer sunshine, with the acrid, lusty scent of the whins around me, and watched a field-mouse emerge cannily from a tuft of grass. I contemplated my acne, my stammer and the turmoil of my academic career and knew how Burns had felt as he wrote the last verse of his famous poem:

Still thou art blest, compared wi' me!
The present only toucheth thee:
But och! I backward cast my e'e
    On prospects drear!
An' forward, tho' I canna see,
    I guess an' fear!

Apart from academic failure, I was now faced with the challenge of two new sprinting stars at the Highland Games. Their names were Duggie McEachran and 'Red' McGeachy. Sometimes I won – if I hadn't stayed out too late with Jean the night before. Sometimes both of them beat me; then, instead of a first prize of £1, I had to be content with a third of only five shillings. Archie and Lachie Young were beginning to beat me, too, at the high and long jumps. That summer the collection of £20 prize money was like a mirage retreating over the horizon.

'Red' McGeachy died some years ago; but Duggie McEachran still lives in Campbeltown, bright and breezy and quick. He and I like to foregather at a street corner to talk about our meetings during World War II in Palestine and Sicily, when he served with an Argyll 'beachbrick' and I with the Royal Scots Fusiliers. We also remember the old days at the Games. With ancient wisdom we discuss modern athletes and agree that they couldn't have lived with us. 'Result of the Welfare State,' opines Duggie. 'They're not hungry enough.'

But life went on. While studying spasmodically for yet another re-sit in political economy I also wrote articles and short stories. Most of them came back to me in the stamped addressed envelopes I was advised to provide. But some didn't, especially those I directed towards the St Vincent Street office of the old independent *Evening Citizen*, with its unusual pale green newsprint. I had discovered that the editor liked articles about the country, and I was only too willing to accommodate him. I sent him pieces of about 500 words dealing, for example, with the tinkers who helped with turnip-thinning, with the clipping and dipping of sheep on the upland farms, with the 'harvest home' and the custom of 'putting by' the last sheaf for the oldest mare's New Year's Day breakfast. He published most of them at half a guinea a time, which made up, to some extent, for prizes lost at the Highland Games.

Another of my markets was the *Scots Observer*, a weekly paper which had become popular under the editorship of the Rev. J. W. Stevenson, who later edited the Church of Scotland monthly magazine, *Life and Work*. Here again I had been introduced to an editor through the medium of a short story competition, in which my entry had been placed second to one by the distinguished writer D. K. Broster, author of *The Flight of the Heron*.

My story, 'The Keeper of Blaan', was the description of a poaching affair, inspired perhaps by Buchan's *John McNab*. It ran to 2500 words and was paid for at the rate of a guinea a thousand, the current rate for ordinary authors and journalists. Afterwards Jack Stevenson called on me frequently for more short stories and, eventually, for articles on current affairs in Scotland. One of those, concerning the tragic death of a Carradale man caused when a small fishing-boat was sunk by a basking shark, made a front page spread.

But then, in the early autumn of 1929, I struck what seemed to me like a 'gusher'. The editor of *Chambers's Journal* accepted a 2500 word short story which I had submitted in the normal way and offered me five guineas (i.e., two guineas a thousand) for it.

It was a 'humorous' story called *Vain Words*. The central character, the Rev. P. J. Macfarlane, an astute and rather cunning Church of Scotland clergyman, was modelled to a great extent on the Rev. D. J. Macdonald, the Pickwickian minister of Killean, a nearby parish in Kintyre. When hatching his nefarious plots, the Rev. P. J. always fingered the lobe of his left ear – a brilliant touch, I thought.

Some years previously, the Dowager Duchess of Argyll, our neighbour in Southend, had presented me with a book by Michael Joseph called *Short Story Writing for Profit*. It had become a kind of Bible for me, and had I studied my political economy text books with similar thoroughness I suspect I might have gained honours in the subject. Be that as it may, I had learnt from Michael Joseph that two guineas a thousand words was the average rate for 'professional' short story writers. The offer from *Chambers's Journal*, therefore, seemed to indicate that as a writer I might have 'arrived'.

Even in 1929 *Chambers's Journal* had an old-fashioned flavour. Compared with the bright, eye-catching covers of popular magazines like *Hutchinson's* or *Pearson's*, its printed, mustard-coloured exterior was drab. Like its contemporary, *Blackwood's Magazine*, it appeared to be aimed at oak-panelled clubs and twin-set country houses, though by the time my stories began to appear in it, I think the editor was trying to appeal to a wider, less conservative public.

Its production methods were also slow and stately, and I was disappointed when told that *Vain Words* would not be published for at least six months and that payment was due only after publication. However, all this was only a slight damper on pleasure. Six months would eventually pass. Then the story would appear and the money would come.

Something to look forward to. If I got the money now it would almost certainly be spent long before the six months had gone by.

It was my first formulation of a philosophy which I have been forced to adopt throughout my working life as a freelance writer. Most publishers make up their accounts every six months and pay their authors the royalties on books sold during this period at the end of another three months. For example, if a copy of a book is sold at any time between July and December, the author does not receive the royalty on it until the following April.

Trade unionists with the benefit of a weekly pay-packet may look upon this state of affairs with horror. But let them hear this. One publisher for whom I have written children's books has a habit of keeping me waiting for eighteen months. When I expostulate – or when my agent expostulates for me – there is always a soft answer: accountants have been changed, computers have gone awry, some important person in the organization has been sick unto death. The unfortunate fact remains, from my point of view, that in this era of inflation money which comes in today is worth a lot less than it would have done eighteen months ago.

A freelance writer can never win a financial argument, simply because he has no powerful trade union to support him. He may be a member of the Society of Authors, but this ancient foundation, while its aims are honourable and it is helpful in the maintenance of high standards among professional writers, carries no political punch. Since 1951 it has been trying to persuade the Government to pass a Public Lending Right Bill, by means of which authors whose books are lent out free by libraries may get some recompense. So far, in 1979, it has still not succeeded. I think the sooner it becomes a trade union the better, with leaders of the quality of Jack Jones or Joe Gormley who can make politicians sit up and take notice.

I often wonder what the Scargills and McGaheys of this world would say if their members were required to dig out lumps of coal for nothing so that the general public could borrow and burn them for free.

Of course, writers are on a bumpy pitch, as far as the use of industrial action is concerned.

One day, on the golf course, I was talking to a friend of mine, who is a printer. Slamming a rusty seven-iron into my bag after an indifferent shot, I said to him: 'Look at you with your £150 plus a week, paid on the nail. Look at me, with my £50 minus a week, paid sometimes eighteen months in arrears. And yet, what would you printers do if every writer in the country suddenly decided to go on strike?'

He laughed, selecting a gleaming pitching wedge from a brand-new bag. 'Don't worry, old boy. We'd still have plenty to do printing bingo tickets!'

Then he laid his approach dead and won the hole.

But in 1929, confronted with a bait of five guineas for my story, the implications for the future of payments both meagre and delayed caused me no anxiety. And presently more excitement occurred. One evening, returning to the Manse from a harvest day at Brunerican, I found that the post had delivered a bulky package from *Chambers's Journal*. The galley proofs of *Vain Words* had arrived for my urgent attention.

It was my first sight of galley proofs, but *The Writers' and Artists' Year Book* (and other published aids to journalism acquired with carefully hoarded pennies) had given me a fair idea of how to deal with them. Nowadays, beginning authors are even more fortunate. A table of symbols for authors' and printers' proof corrections, along with a guide to copy preparation, can be obtained on demand from the British Standards Institution (B.S. 1219: 1958 Recommendations).

As it happened, I found few errors or omissions in the proofs of the story. I showed the Padre my professional markings, and he seemed to be impressed. My mother made no effort to understand them. All she said was: 'I'm glad you're happy, Angus.' I returned the corrected proofs to *Chambers's* the very next day, dreaming a little of Abbotsford and a Rolls-Royce for Jean.

A few days later reality kicked me in the teeth again. Opening the *Glasgow Herald*, I found that my name still did not appear in the list of university passes in political economy.

And my acne flared up again.

The Padre made the decision.

It appeared that even without a degree I could enroll as a divinity student. While studying Hebrew, Greek and church history I could also attend – for the third time – the class in political economy. The Dundonald bursary, for budding divines, would remain with me, along with various others provided by the Church.

In my heart I was unwilling to become a minister. I felt unworthy to accept the challenge. I did want to communicate with my fellow beings, and to help them if I could, but from the pages of a book or newspaper rather than from a pulpit. If I did enter the ministry and take a stipend from the Church, the real reason would be that I wanted money to enable me to write: a mean trick for a shepherd to play upon an unsuspecting flock. But I lacked the courage to tell the Padre this. He had taken it for granted that I was eager to enter the ministry, and I baulked at the dangerous task of disillusioning him. And there was the sadness that would come to my mother if she discovered that her eldest son's principles were less holy and honourable than she had supposed. So, weakly, I let the situation drift. When the Padre laid out a scheme for a fourth university session I said I'd do my best to implement it.

That year, in the divinity hall, I rubbed shoulders with, amongst other brilliant men, Willie Barclay and Jimmy Dow, who, in the future, were both to become writers and broadcasters like myself. Even then I knew they were going places.

In later years, on a personal level, I lost touch with Willie Barclay, though, strangely enough, we both supported Motherwell Football Club. But I read all his books and listened to all his television broadcasts and, like a million others in Scotland, felt that as a result my Christian faith was strengthened. He possessed the secret of talking and writing with a simple clarity which left no doubt as to his meaning. His message was unambiguous not only to high-powered academics and practical scientists but also to cleaning ladies, farm labourers and youthful rebels. With his vast knowledge of Greek and Hebrew, he was able to give life to certain words and phrases in the Bible that had been muffed by the translators of the authorized version and by such means to bring vividly before us characters like, for example, St Paul: 'a wee man with a bad leg and a squint – and a chip on his shoulder'. No shining haloes or heroic holiness, just a 'wee man' with physical and moral weaknesses like the rest of us, who yet, in the end, gave up his life for his faith. When Willie Barclay died old Mrs Park in the village said to me: 'We'll no' get another like him.' She was right.

Jimmy Dow had the same gift of being able to communicate with people in both towers and tenements. He had a beautiful bass voice which he used to advantage in the pulpit and on TV – and also when he took the stage as an amateur actor with the Greenock Players. He translated parts of the Bible into braid Scots and by so doing brought fresh understanding to many.

His own understanding of human nature was warm and wide. He pretended to be cynical about it, but no one was fooled. He wrote a verse:

> The Church of Scotland is a place
> Fairly full of life,
> Where you'll find the Scottish working man
> Represented by his wife.

But he didn't leave it at that. In his parish of Cartsburn in Greenock he laboured, as he put it himself, to get father interested. 'There's no use mother flyting at the family on a Sunday morning to get out to Church,' he said, 'if the old man's lying in bed reading the *News of the World.*'

And by various means Jimmy Dow succeeded in his labours. He mixed with the men at the shipyards and in the pubs. Though he made no boast about it – in fact, he never mentioned it at all to me – he helped old ladies to paint and redecorate their houses and old men to dig their allotments. By exercising the humanity within himself he brought out the humanity in others.

One Hogmanay, in Achnamara, Jean and I had with us friends and members of the family, waiting to bring in the New Year. The hands of the clock eased towards midnight and I got up to pour out the celebration drinks. Jimmy Dow was speaking on the television. As I uncorked the first bottle his voice boomed out at me: 'And now, as the time approaches, and the man of the house has begun to fill the glasses . . .' He knew exactly what went on, did Jimmy Dow.

He died in harness, as the minister of Lochranza on the Isle of Arran. Like Willie Barclay he was never averse to a drink or a smoke. But his weaknesses were human. When he or Willie Barclay spoke or wrote, evil was stifled. And like St Paul and St Columba they purveyed Christianity not as a 'high-falutin' concept for saints and scholars but in terms of ordinary, everyday life. As the Padre used to say, 'There are very few saints and scholars in this world but plenty of sinners. Ministers have to tune in on their length-wave.'

(Not having learnt to speak English until the age of five, the Padre was often inclined to use the Gaelic idiom and, as he said himself, to 'put the horse before the cart'. There is no doubt, also, that his humanitarian philosophy was wonderfully broad and warm as far as his parishioners and people in general were concerned. Sometimes it came unstuck in relation to his own family!)

Willie Barclay and Jimmy Dow – and the Padre, too – were ministers who gave the lie to those clichés so often repeated in Parliament and press: 'Religion and politics don't mix. Let ministers keep their noses out of politics.'

By politics I do not mean party politics. 'Party' has now become a nasty five-letter word meaning the pursuit of personal power and financial advantage. It contains no hint of feeling for the moral welfare of the people. Politics, in my understanding, means what it infers in all the dictionaries: the study of how a nation's well-being can best be managed. One of the reasons why I hated political economy was that so many of its exponents seemed to forget that the good life has not only a material but also a spiritual side to it. The Socialists, the Tories *et al* seem to forget it, too, and almost always base their propaganda on monetary considerations. What about morality?

This is where religion has a duty to interfere in politics. It can transcend the narrow party spirit and offer judgements for the good of the people in general. Politics without a religious content leads directly to hard as iron communism or fascism, in both of which love and respect for the individual is stifled and killed.

Almost two thousand years ago something apposite to the subject was said by a man who died for love: 'He that is not with me is against me.'

'The Church should never dabble in politics.' How often do we read such a statement in a newspaper leader when the General Assembly of the Church of Scotland takes a stand on some political controversy. But, of course, this kind of talk has been going on for centuries, beginning with Pontius Pilate and going on right through the Inquisition to Hitler and Stalin.

It occurred when John Knox advocated a school in every parish, because the landowners and the rich merchants were afraid that educated servants might demand higher wages. It occurred when a few compassionate ministers dared to criticize the Highland Clearances, because this made it more difficult for the lairds to clear the land of people and make room for sheep. It occurs today when the Church stands up for the oppressed and inarticulate masses in Africa, South America, Asia and elsewhere. And for why? – as we journalists are in the habit of putting it. In most cases it is because when moral values are allowed to rear disturbing heads some profit-hungry men in some profit-hungry rackets are liable to lose money.

Four hundred years ago, before John Knox, feudalism from England was spreading into the Lowlands of Scotland. Ordinary folk were beginning to be looked upon as mere chattels, born to slave for their masters. Wasn't it a good thing, in the circumstances, that the abbey monks of the time were willing to poke their noses into politics and do their best to care for and educate the people?

Those monks suffered for their interference. Some of the

abbeys were destroyed. They themselves were sometimes banished into exile. But they thought it all worth while. They refused to compromise their moral standards by knuckling down to political pressure.

Fifty years ago, having been elected to the County Council of Argyll, the Padre advocated the building of new subsidized houses for farm-workers. This, of course, was contrary to the 'politics' of having tied cottages. As a result he had to face a barrage of opposition which might have broken the spirit of a less determined character. Nowadays, in Southend, there are scores of new 'agricultural' houses. Tied cottages, as such, no longer exist, evidence that religion and politics can – and do – mix.

At the present time, industrial chaplains visit the coalfields, the shipyards and the troubled steel-works. Parish ministers go tramping through mucky village lanes and the 'deserts with windows' of the urban housing estates. When they try to point out that those who benefit from the welfare state have a moral obligation to offer something in return and give an honest day's work for an honest day's pay, they are told to keep out of politics and mind their own business.

But life as a whole, which includes men's thoughts and aspirations as well as their moral and physical health, *is* a minister's business. It is the Church's business. An individual's life cannot be divided into compartments, the Church on Sunday, politics on Monday, business on Tuesday, sport on Wednesday. Such activities are all interrelated, one influencing the other, and the end product is the character of a man.

I am sure that religion and politics cannot possibly be kept apart. Nor can either be kept apart from business or housework or sport or music or art or any other kind of human diligence. As both Willie Barclay and Jimmy Dow were often in the habit of saying: 'For what shall it profit a man, if he shall gain the whole world, and lose his own soul.'

For me they were good ministers. In some measure, small or great, they still influence what I write.

Two of my best friends in the divinity hall were Ken Tyson

and Jimmy Davidson. Ken's tall angularity and his expression, when unsmiling, of grim righteousness concealed a warm and sensitive heart. Jimmy was a small, round man who liked to smell the flowers but was often averse to the hard work of cultivation. I liked to believe that my presence was the catalyst which brought together two such contrasting characters.

I learned to admire them both and to profit from their example of unselfishness, an unselfishness which gave them a common denominator and, at times, made me feel ashamed of my own bouts of egotism. When I committed a sin Ken would lecture me, often at great length, but he would not waver at all in friendship. Jimmy would shake his head and regard me with disappointed eyes, like my mother's; but his friendship, too, was never in question.

By a coincidence, Ken served during World War II as a chaplain with the battalion of Argylls commanded eventually by my old school mate, 'Boskers' (Lt. Col. Hamish Taylor), who came to love and respect him as much as I did. Characteristically, in battle, Ken never lurked behind the troops whose spiritual welfare was his responsibility. He went forward with them, and, in the end, was wounded with them. His hurt was so severe that he never fully recovered; but physical weakness made no difference to the efforts he made to advance Christ's kingdom. First in Switzerland, then in Portugal, he ministered to congregations of Presbyterians.

When Celtic won the European Cup in 1967, Ken's manse in Lisbon was besieged after the game by supporters from Scotland who had lost their way or their money or both. That most of them were Roman Catholics mattered nothing to Ken or to his wife Renée. Their spacious grounds and most of the rooms in their manse were put at the disposal of the unexpected visitors. Fortunately it was early summer, and the Portuguese night was warm and fragrant.

Ken made and distributed scores of sandwiches and Renée made and poured out gallons of tea. Blankets were collected from members of the congregation and the stragglers made as comfortable as possible. In the morning Ken saw the British consul and, by one means or another, the Celtic supporters were sent home, subdued but still rejoicing.

And they didn't forget the kind minister and his wife in Lisbon. In due course loans were repaid in full and gifts and letters of thanks filled the manse mail-bag. 'That night,' Ken told me, 'some of the language was what you might call spicey. But I've heard worse in a board-room. As for hooliganism, not a trace of it.' But of course Ken and Renée had treated their guests like human beings, not as specimens for sociological study, and the compliment was returned.

Jimmy Davidson failed most of his divinity exams. His dreamy nature was not attuned to the idea of hard work. And he was accident prone. On one occasion I persuaded the Padre to bring him to Southend to preach. In the middle of the Lord's Prayer he developed a tickle in his throat, followed by violent spasms of coughing which caused him to bring the service to an abrupt end, lacking even a benediction. ('Poor boy!' said the Padre to me, afterwards. 'Why on earth did you bring him?') But when engaged in quiet conversation concerning history or philosophy there was never any coughing.

This friend to whom physical exercise was anathema, who would vanish from a scene of anger or mayhem like a wraith, whose pacifism remained deep and sincere, was yet a volunteer at the very beginning of World War II. He became a radio operator on a cargo ship, which, early in the war, was sunk during a German submarine attack on an Atlantic convoy. Jimmy was not listed among the survivors. His body vanished in the cold sea; but who can assert that his gentle spirit ceased to exist? In my crowded mind it still lives on, often controlling the selfish impulses invading it.

In a way, I suppose, it was selfishness which, at the end of my one and only year in divinity, prompted me to grasp the nettle and announce to all and sundry – including the Padre and my mother – that the ministry was not for me. There were other factors, of course.

There was the nagging sense that I hadn't 'received a call', that my worldly and somewhat self-seeking character was not that of a true 'Lord's servant'. There was a handicap of a stammer and the memory of an hour in a Glasgow east end church when I had stuttered and spluttered my way through a service and my friend and fellow divine, David Elder – who had arranged for me to preach there – had looked on me with pity. (I have described the horrific sequence of events in *Salt in My Porridge*. No need, therefore, to describe them again. Chills creep along my spine even now, thinking about them.)

There was also the triumph at the year's end when at last I put a metaphorical foot on the neck of political economy, passed my degree exam in the subject and, in June, 1930, was capped Master of Arts. This gave me a feeling of independence and the courage to approach the Padre with the truth.

But perhaps the most important factor behind the decision – apart from selfishness, that is – was the comparative success of my freelance writing during the year.

In January *Vain Words* had been published in *Chambers's Journal* – there it lay in the window of a stationers' shop in Great Western Road, with my name printed on the cover – and I had received the cheque for five guineas. Another short story submitted to the editor had also been accepted. The *Evening Citizen* was publishing almost everything I wrote on country matters, and the *Daily Record* was running a series of 250-word 'shorts' based on Celtic legends which, as a child, I had heard around the fireside from my parents and Maimie. And now, towards the end of my time at the university, I had won the *Daily Express* short story competition.

The cheque from Chambers's had a printed endorsement indicating that it was payment for copyright in the story. My various well-thumbed books on the writing game had all warned me that to sell copyright was the act of an idiot. The advice given was that for a normal payment – such as two guineas a thousand words – the writer of an article, short story or serial should trade to an editor only the first British serial rights – fbsr, for short. Otherwise he would be depriving himself of any claim to second British serial rights, foreign rights, broadcasting rights and all the other rights inherent in any original piece of writing. These would belong to the newspaper or magazine which had purchased the copyright in his story.

I was upset by this turn of events and, after some anxious thought, wrote a letter about it to the contemporary Scots writer whom I considered not only the best craftsman but also the most professional in the business. He was George Blake, whose popular 'Clydeside' novels I had read with admiration – and not a little envy – and who contributed regular articles and serials to the new *Scottish Daily Express.* With characteristic generosity he invited me to come and see him at a hotel. There, over his gin and tonic and my pint of draught, he dispensed wisdom, both artistic and practical, to a young writer with heather in his ears.

He described the endorsement on my cheque as an iniquitous con-trick. 'Strike it out, then put your signature on the back of the cheque in the usual way. The bank will cash it and Chambers won't argue, because in law they haven't a leg to stand on.'

I did as he advised and heard nothing more. *Vain Words* has been republished twice since then and payment for second British serial rights came to me, not to Chambers.

Later, however, there occurred an odd sequel. A subsequent story of mine published in *Chambers's Journal* before World War II was called *MacDonald's Lament*. While I was serving my king and country in various battlefields around the world – between 1940 and 1945 – *MacDonald's Lament* appeared in the *Scottish Daily Express* under another's name and without my permission. In a letter I put the facts and a strong complaint to the editor of the *Express*. Wisely, however, Sandy Trotter made no comment, and at the time I had neither the money nor the nerve to sue him (and/or Chambers) for breach of copyright.

George Blake was a short, stout man with a fighter's jaw. Physically I towered above him; but, like Brigadier Gerard facing Napoleon, I recognized my mental superior. He told me never to force my story characters into prefabricated plots. 'Let the plots develop naturally from the actions of your characters,' he said. And, always the professional, he bade me *au revoir* with this advice: 'When I write an article for a newspaper I only take a nominal fee – say, three guineas. But I claim substantial expenses, maybe as much as twenty guineas. You see, Angus, expenses are not taxable.'

Another writer who helped me was Neil Munro, whose work ranged from short stories like 'The Lost Pibroch' and novels like *The New Road* to journalism for the *Glasgow Evening News* and the brilliantly funny Para Handy books, the latter published under the pseudonym of Hugh Foulis. Like Blake, he advised me to concentrate on character. 'Study the old Highland tales told by a winter's fire,' he wrote. 'Study the flow and rhythms of our language. Study most of all the strange cantrips of the human heart.'

Both men had strong opinions on literary style.

Blake's own character was direct and down-to-earth. In his view style was an unconscious growth, created out of a writer's own personality. 'In a way,' he said, 'it's a gift. But if you keep on writing day and daily, you will find that the proper balance and rhythm of a sentence becomes instinctive. But it's the content of what you write that matters most. Why attempt to produce exquisite, polished prose if you have nothing valuable or interesting to say? Let style, my boy, take care of itself.'

Munro's 'The Lost Pibroch' is written in a distinguished style which echoes the constructions and cadences of the Gaelic language. A little to my surprise, therefore, he, also, was insistent that the matter of a story deserves more attention than the manner of its telling. He explained that in the case of 'The Lost Pibroch' he had used a particular style to harmonize with the content, which has its origins in the Gaelic character.

In youthful ignorance I voiced a fear that pressurized, written-to-a-deadline journalism might be bad for a novelist's style. Gently he demurred, though he admitted that to a great extent it depended upon the personality of the journalist. A good professional journalist, like a good professional footballer, he said, will have a style which can survive all pressures.

He himself was an example of this. His successors in Scotland today include, amongst many others, Lavinia Derwent,

Maurice Lindsay, Jack House, Alastair Phillips, Anne Simpson, Jack Webster, William Hunter, Don Whyte – and, on the sporting side, my own son Jock – all of whose work I can recognize at once, even though left unsigned. The hard work and discipline which goes to the making of a good journalist never does harm to style. The same applies to a good professional footballer, like, for example, Danny McGrain.

For my own part, I would suggest to all beginning writers that for the foundation of a literary style there is no better model than the Bible. Here the merit of simplicity in writing is revealed again and again in the stories of the Old Testament and in the Parables of the New.

The thirteenth chapter of I Corinthians (in the Authorized Version) is, for me, the ultimate example of good style. The surge and flow of its language makes a perfect vehicle for the message it contains. ('And now abideth faith, hope, charity, these three; but the greatest of these is charity.') There is a legend that the translator of this noble chapter was none other than Will Shakespeare himself. If the legend became true history, then it would not surprise me.

As for the value of simplicity in style, here is an example.

In her novel, *Barabbas*, Marie Corelli writes: 'Water having been brought, Pilate slowly lowered his hands and dipped them in the shining bowl, rinsing them over and over again in the clear, cold element, which sparkled in its polished receptacle like an opal against the fire.'

The Bible says: 'Pilate took water, and washed his hands.'

I was grateful to both George Blake and to Neil Munro for their stimulating advice. Remembering their kindness in the midst of busy lives, I try to do for beginning writers what the old professionals in my younger days did for me. Indeed, this book is being written partly for that reason, though I reckon a book by either Blake or Munro on the same subject would have been much more valuable.

I have always attempted, as they advised, to keep my style simple; but I wish I had paid more heed to their words regarding the importance of character. I was confused, however, by the insistence of some magazine editors – and of the authors of many 'practical' text-books – that the main ingredient of a good story must be the plot. I wanted so much to sell my stories – and by this means to become important in the eyes of Jean and my family and neighbours – that I concentrated on inventing ingenious plots and then making my characters conform. I was wrong, of course. Like the Padre in his form of speech, I was putting the cart before the horse. And though, through the years, my stories have been successful enough commercially, because of this many of them lack the quality I tried so hard to attain.

One of the best stories I ever wrote, in my own opinion, is *The Canisbay Conspiracy*. It came into being out of my admiration for a certain Highland lady, an aristocrat whose belief in Christian democracy and contempt for any kind of racialism were deep and strong. I let her call the tune and, in the end, found reviewers praising my 'ingenious plot'.

6. Freelance

After being capped – after putting political economy and the study of theology behind me – I returned to the Manse and announced that I was going to be a freelance writer. For my bed and board I happily contracted to pay my mother a pound a week. On my insistence, not hers.

The Padre was sceptical about my prospects. But I had shown him evidence of my industry and ability in the form of several articles and short stories which had been published, and he seemed willing enough, as he phrased it himself, to let me make 'a kirk or a mill of it'. My mother, I know, was sceptical, too, but she tried to conceal it. 'If there's a week when you can't pay – well, never mind, Angus. After all, this is your home, not a lodging house.'

But I was determined to pay and, by so doing, establish some independence.

Without the grants and bursaries I had been lucky enough to have at the university, I found, however, that to earn even a weekly pound was difficult.

That summer and autumn, when not training for or competing at the usual round of Highland Games, I laboured to produce a stream of contributions, sending them off hopefully to addresses culled from *The Writers' and Artists' Year Book*, each accompanied by the statutory stamped addressed envelope. I reckon about a quarter of them were accepted. The others came back in a tide so steady that my mother began to intercept the post and let me have my self-addressed mail only when a cheque or acceptance letter had raised my spirits. (Not until long afterwards did I learn of this, from my mother herself. 'It was the only way I thought I could help you,' she said. 'You used to look so sad when you saw your own handwriting on an envelope.')

Until now all my contributions had been handwritten. I decided that this was a possible reason why so many articles and stories came back and that, in any case, it was time that as a professional I owned a typewriter.

I went to see Angus McInnes ('Wireless and Bicycles – Repairs') in his small shop of all trades in Campbeltown. Angus was middle-aged, dark, thin as a hazel branch, with a saturnine frown which concealed a kind and utterly honest nature. A typewriter? Yes, he had a catalogue. He would send at once for the machine of my choice.

I chose a Royal Portable, price £15. Could I pay for it in instalments – instalments, say, of five shillings a week? His frown became terrible, but – yes, that could be arranged. He would let me know as soon as the typewriter arrived.

About a fortnight later Hughie Smith, the grocer from Campbeltown, made his regular weekly call at the Manse with his new motor van. He had a message for me. 'Angus McInnes wants to see you at once. You're to be prepared for bad news.'

What on earth had happened?

The next day the Padre was going to a Presbytery meeting in Campbeltown and being taken there by his elder, Jamie Hunter, one of the few people in Southend who, at the time, owned a car. I arranged to go with them. While my father and Jamie proceeded to deliberate on matters spiritual, I went to the wee shop in Longrow, troubled by matters material.

Angus saw me come in. With a look of dark evil he went to a shelf, brought down a Royal Portable in a shiny new case and laid it on the counter. 'I have played you false,' he said.

I muttered something like, 'How do you mean?'

'I told you the price was £15 and that you could pay for it at five shillings a week. I was wrong. By instalments it costs £17.' His face had become so contorted that he looked like a villain in a Pearl White film serial. 'You have every right,' he said, 'to refuse to take it.'

He meant it, too.

'Don't worry,' I said. I handed him a pound note. 'Here's

enough for the first month. I'll pay you weekly after that.'

For the first time a sort of smile softened the dark seams on his cheeks. 'I didn't want to cheat you,' he said.

Angus McInnes would have been shocked by the small print which appears in some modern contracts.

In the next ten years I rattled out an average of five thousand words a week on that typewriter, while Angus kept it in good repair. After World War II I bought another from him, and the old one went into semi-retirement. It provided amusement for Jock, when he was small, and for various inquisitive nieces and nephews. Now it has to endure assaults from the numerous grand-nieces and grand-nephews who visit us. It is badly in need of attention, I'm afraid; but Angus is no longer around to look after it, in that undeviatingly honest way of his.

To my disappointment the acquisition of a typewriter made little difference to the amount of work that was accepted, though it did, I think, help me to gain a footing with the *Bulletin*, the picture paper published by the Outram Press as companion to the *Glasgow Herald*.

The *Bulletin* was a bright publication which appealed particularly to women. Why it was killed stone dead in 1960 is a secret known only, I suppose, to the hard-faced businessmen who streamline and amalgamate. Before the war it used to run 150-words shorts called 'Little Bulletins' and a daily column under the heading of 'Pertinent and Otherwise'. The latter was composed of small items of innocuous 'society' gossip (completely unrelated to the modern William Hickey scandals in the *Daily Express*) and of 'smart' little paragraphs not unlike the 'fillers' that used to appear in *Punch*. ('A forward named Crum has been signed by lowly placed Celtic. A crumb of comfort?') For some reason I acquired the knack of writing such paragraphs and also of producing 'Little Bulletins' on subjects like ploughing matches and agricultural shows. For a 'smart' paragraph appearing in 'Pertinent and Otherwise' I was paid half a crown, by postal order; for a 'Little Bulletin' anything up to ten shillings.

But as the months slipped by into early winter and prize-money from the Highland Games was no longer available, I began to find it almost impossible to pay my mother her weekly pound and Angus McInnes his weekly five shillings. The more work I did at the typewriter the more numerous became the rejection slips. My only comfort was a statement made by Michael Joseph in *Short Story Writing for Profit* that in the first three years of his literary career, W. L. George had collected 723 of them.

I think writing is like golf. Success in both requires relaxation and a quiet mind. The harder you try to force your shots or your ideas the less worthy they turn out to be. When you are a beginning writer or a beginning golfer, however, struggling for recognition, relaxation and a quiet mind are conditions almost impossible to achieve. It is a 'Catch 22' situation.

As the winter of 1930 made a chilly passage towards spring, my acne got better; but I developed a swelling on the back of my neck, which the doctor said was an inflamed gland. If it didn't subside of its own accord, he told me, there would have to be an operation.

I wrote and typed, constantly touching and fingering the swelling to discover if it was going down. The markets I had cultivated over the past two years seemed to become less accessible, and the number of my acceptances gradually declined. I failed to understand that desperation was lowering the quality of what I wrote.

I became depressed. If it hadn't been for Jean and my mother, neither of whom ever seemed to doubt that eventually I should succeed as a writer, I think I might have joined the Foreign Legion – or done something equally eccentric – as a dramatic gesture in defiance of the world.

What made things worse was that though I often worked for twelve hours a day, some people in Southend thought I was merely being idle, dodging a proper job. Work to them meant manual labour. The idea that stringing a thousand words together to form an artistic pattern might be as tiring as ploughing a ten-acre field did not occur to them.

Along the side road to Brunerican there is a cottage called Inishrael. Today it has been made into a modern holiday home by our close friends, Roddy and Marjorie McSween. At that time it was an ordinary greystone cottage, enclosed by byres and loose-boxes, and occupied by an elderly spinster whose name was Janet McCaig. Her only companion was a collie dog, ill-tempered and slightly deranged like his mistress. I remember passing the cottage one night, on my way home from seeing Jean. There at the gate stood the collie, barking and baring his teeth at me. And there at the door stood Janet, shouting obscenities. 'Away and work, you lazy runt! Away and work!'

I tried to ignore them both. As the barking and the shouting died away behind me I thought of all the hard work I had done, with small success and much failure at the end of it. I thought of Jean, with the prospect of marriage and a home of our own like an unseen oasis across a desert of poverty. I thought of my parents and my family, all disappointed and losing respect for me. I thought of my gland, still hard and sore and cringed at the knowledge that soon I should have to spend time in the Campbeltown Cottage Hospital having it doctored. There in the dusk, along the river-side, alone except for a few cows in the Inishrael meadow, I sat down on a stone. I let a tide of Hebridean gloom and self-pity flood over me. I cried.

But life went on. The gland was operated on successfully, and during my convalescence euphoria returned. I decided I was going to write a novel.

Janet McCaig had not always been considered 'a borderline case'. For years her brother Archie had been with her, guiding her actions and imposing discipline when required. When he died, between the wars, it gradually became clear how devotedly he had looked after his sister, concealing from us the true extent of her mental imbalance.

Archie McCaig was one of my father's elders, a small, square, grey-bearded man with a stiff neck, the result of rheumatism. He had a quick sense of humour, and a gift for storytelling. When I was in my early teens I used to accompany the Padre on all his 'visitations' to Inishrael, so that I could listen to Archie's talk.

The first inkling I got that Janet might be 'peculiar' was after he had entertained the Padre and me with one of his most exciting yarns. It concerned a fishing expedition off the Mull of Kintyre arranged by himself and two members of the McEachran family, Colin and Hugh. The boat belonged to the McEachrans and, indeed, had been built by them; and it may have been fortunate that it was a stout, homemade craft, because on that particular evening, on the way home, it was overtaken by a storm before it could reach the shelter of the slip at Dunaverty.

Archie's description of the storm and of their efforts to fight it made me thrill with admiration. I was there in the boat with them, the cold sea lifting and breaking around me, the spray stinging my eyes, the sweat tangling my hair as I rowed with the burly McEachrans and Archie, at the tiller, kept his eyes on the distant slip.

'We were being tossed about something terrible. I could see Colin McEachran was getting tired – he was about fifty at the time – and though Hugh, being younger, was still pulling hard, the tide was beginning to turn against us. "What do you think, boys," I said, "a wee rest and a bit of a prayer?" The McEachrans nodded and leant forward on their oars. They were needing all their breath, so I took it on myself to say the prayer.'

My father said: 'What prayer, Archie?'

'Well, I gave them the Lord's Prayer, minister, and the storm was so loud I had to shout it. Then I got the McEachrans to sing the verse of a psalm with me. "Yea, though I walk in death's dark vale . . ." '

'What happened then?' I said.

'It was a strange thing, boy, but after the prayer and the psalm the storm seemed to go down a bit and the McEachrans found new life. Just as it was getting dark we reached the slip.' He glanced at my father. 'And you know, minister, when we climbed ashore and felt the hard stone under our feet, we knelt down there by one of the bollards and said another prayer. In thanks to God.'

I sighed with satisfaction at the conclusion of a good story skilfully told. But Janet, who had been sitting in the shadows beyond the peat fire, suddenly sat forward and addressed her brother. 'Did ye get ony fush?' she inquired.

I saw that only with difficulty did the Padre keep his face straight. I followed his example.

Archie said: 'Tut, tut, Janet! That'll do!' Then he went on to speak about something else.

Left alone in Inishrael, Janet's condition deteriorated. She began shouting at people passing on the farm road and, indeed, often went across to Brunerican to bang on doors and windows and make animal sounds at those inside. Jean became terrified of her.

At one stage Janet was treated in a mental hospital, but in the years before World War II she returned to the cottage.

I was away from Southend, in the King's employ, when the end came. By all accounts it was bizarre and cruel.

One morning Jean's brother Peter, passing the cottage on his way to an outlying field, found the doors locked and barred. He peered in at the kitchen window and saw Janet stretched on the 'set-in' bed, clad in her night-clothes, with the collie lying beside her. He opened the window and tried to climb inside, but the collie, leaping, barking and snarling, kept him at a distance. He could see no motion of breathing in Janet's chest and was convinced that she was dead.

He went back to the farm and telephoned for the doctor and the police; and presently Dr Niven arrived, along with Constable John McVicar, the local policeman, and Constable Crae McIntyre, driver of the police car. But when Constable McVicar did what Peter had done and tried to enter by the kitchen window, he, too, was attacked by the dog and had to move out again, quickly.

The collie returned to the bed and stood there, barking, suspicious slavers dripping from his mouth.

Constable McVicar said to Peter: 'Have you got a gun?'

Peter nodded.

So did Dr Niven. 'Seems it's the only way,' he said.

The spread of the pellets from a shot-gun was the problem. By some means the dog had to be lured away from the bed. Finally, Constable McIntyre stretched inside the window and threw a stick into a corner of the kitchen. As the collie leapt to attack it, Peter fired and, in spite of the tension, did not miss.

The doctor found that Janet had been dead for some time, perhaps since the previous night as she got into bed.

When I heard it, the story haunted me for weeks. I had hated old Janet on account of her obscene shouting and for her harassment of Jean and her brothers in Brunerican. But did any human being, however unprepossessing, deserve such a gruesome death-bed?

'There is a divinity within every man,' Professor Bowman had told us, his students. 'Respect and reverence for this divinity is the foundation of civilized behaviour.' I had agreed with him. 'Love your neighbour,' was the message of the New Testament. I had agreed with that, too. But as far as Janet McCaig was concerned I had failed to put such beautiful theories into practice, and now it was too late to do anything about it.

I was learning how difficult it is to live a life of high principle. And how guilt, once experienced, has a habit of clinging to the spirit like a burr.

I also began to learn the difference between stories based on ordinary life and the contrived products recommended by the editors of popular magazines between the wars. I was fool enough not to take the lesson to heart. I continued to equate money-making with ingenious plots in which stock characters lived and moved and had their ersatz being. I was prostituting any artistic talents I possessed in much the same way as soft-porn novelists do today. Like them, I was writing what editors and publishers told me the public wanted. I was doing what I often preached against in print: denying the spiritual content of life for the sake of a possible material benefit.

Part of my trouble may have been that as a Scot I was trying too hard to achieve an English ethos.

At that time the first underground rumblings of nationalism were being felt. Vaguely I welcomed them, because it seemed to me that the Scots – and Scots writers in particular – were at a disadvantage when it came to selling their products in London. Apparently our contributions had to be of the Harry Lauder variety before they were allowed to compete with sophisticated southern culture. By every inference we were made to feel inferior by smooth English operators who had never even heard of the Arbroath Declaration.

In the past fifty years the nationalistic rumblings have threatened to become an earthquake. In many ways I wish they hadn't, because my instinct is for union rather than for separation in all departments of life. I suppose, however, that Scottish 'rebellion' against English attitudes was bound to happen, not on a 'racist' basis but as a kind of protest against government from far away and the creeping bureaucracy which such government creates.

Some Englishmen still do not understand this. Not long ago, happily riding north, I met one on the Flying Scotsman. On first acquaintance he appeared to be a reasonable fellow, possibly a member of the CBI. But when, inadvertently, I mentioned the Scottish Assembly he snorted and exclaimed: 'Devolution! Why did it happen? Who the heck do you Scots think you are?'

'A good question,' I said.

In my best preaching style I went on to explain that we are small and dark, like the Stone Age men who came from Ireland 8000 years ago; lean and red-haired like the painted Picts; stout and strong like the Brythons and Anglo-Saxons who have always, through the ages, kept moving in from the south; tall and fair like the Norsemen who, a thousand years ago, temporarily imposed their will on part of Scotland; and finally, loud-voiced and burly like the Scotti, the Irish tribesmen who crossed the narrow sea in the first centuries AD and gave us not only St Columba but also an identity and a name.

'A lot of mongrels,' said my English friend.

I resisted a temptation to quote Darwin's observation that mongrels, as a rule, are highly intelligent. Instead I agreed that there is no such thing as a typical Scot. (Is there, for that matter, a typical Englishman?)

I said: 'An old-fashioned belief is that Highlanders are either happy and energetic or sad and lazy according to their mood; that Lowlanders and east-coasters are dour and hard-working, tight-fisted and lacking in humour. But Highlanders can be dour and Lowlanders happy, and east-coasters can be full of fun.

'Then there are the Jews,' I went on, indulging myself. 'And the Italians and the Cypriots and the Indians and the Pakistanis. They are Scots, too. Some of them wear the kilt, and one Indian I know has invented his own tartan. If you saw our Pakistani boys and girls from Lewis singing Gaelic songs at the Mod you would be charmed.'

He looked more dazed than charmed. 'And you have the supporters of Rangers and Celtic,' he sneered.

'Yes. We go to football matches and play golf, just as they do in England. We attend the opera and dig disco sessions. We are Protestants and Roman Catholics, dukes and lairds and miners and farmers and fishermen. We argue and fight among ourselves. We make love and do our good neighbour bit. We laugh at and with each other and occasionally get drunk. Sometimes we even talk amicably together – that is, when we're allowed to get a word in edgeways by such dreary publicists as Iain Sproat, Mike McGahey and Teddy Taylor.'

Sourly he said: 'So you admit things have changed since Bannockburn?'

'Of course. But the people of Scotland still think in the same way.'

'Now you're going to quote from that bloody Declaration of Arbroath?'

I was, but not the bit he expected.

'*Should he, the Bruce, abandon our cause or aim at reducing us or our kingdom, we will instantly expel him as a common enemy and, under God, choose another King*.'

A blank look had come into his eyes, so I continued: 'I know. It's hard to believe that such words were written in 1320, while Bruce was at the height of his power and popularity. But for me, as for most Scots, they come echoing down the years as a trumpet call for democracy.'

I had him now. Like the Ancient Mariner I pursued my advantage. 'For years we Scots have been brainwashed with the idea that no one is important except as a citizen of the country as a whole, except as a member of a union or of the CBI. Statistics and balance sheets are being offered in place of character. Big Brothers – in London and in Europe – are doing their utmost to smother individuals and communities under great blankets of bureaucracy. Now, by means of devolution, we are trying to preserve our individuality. And our small community, which, we believe, like our family life, is a main source of strength and happiness in an increasingly soul-less world.

'St Andrew and Bannockburn,' I said, 'Glencoe and the Clearances, even the "Hungry Twenties" and "the black, black oil", are only of marginal importance in our effort to slough off poverty – a poverty, I may add, which is spiritual rather than material. When the Royal Scots Fusiliers stormed ashore in Sicily, men fought and died for their regiment only incidentally for the British Army. People like St Columba and St Margaret, Wallace and Bruce, Robert Burns, Sir Walter Scott and David Livingstone have all left behind them examples of nobility, not because they were neatly documented citizens of the country as a whole but because they were independent individuals, ready to sacrifice wealth and comfort, even their very lives, to uphold the values of freedom and freedom of thought so dear to them as Scots.'

My English friend yawned. When we parted at Glasgow Central station he was shaking his head. He still didn't understand.

And while on the subject of understanding, here is something we Scots don't understand. Why is it that those Englishmen who sneer most at Scots meanness and Scots 'coarseness' and Scots poverty in thought and action – why is it that those Englishmen are the loudest in condemning devolution and separatism? If they think of us so poorly, why don't they jump at the chance of getting rid of us? Or is their thinking influenced, after all, by visionary fountains of 'the black, black oil?'

Will the English – and the quisling Scots – ever understand? Will they ever understand that, like Frank Sinatra, we want to do it our way? And make a kirk or a mill of it.

My decision to write a novel was a calculated bid for fame and fortune. I surveyed the publishing scene and came to the conclusion that the story most likely to become a best-seller was an adventure story, spiced with romance. 'Sapper' had followed the formula with success. So had Dornford Yates, E. Charles Vivian, William Le Queux, George Birmingham, Horace Hutchinson – and, of course, John Buchan.

Among them all John Buchan was my personal favourite, even though most of his Scots 'heroes' had been to English public schools and most of his 'native' Scots were underlings, quaintly lovable characters such as poachers, forelock-touching estate-workers and unlettered Labour MPs. His women, too, were disappointing as far as I was concerned: cool, supremely well-mannered maidens who gave no promise of passion among the corn-stacks and who, it seemed to me, were put into his books merely as an acknowledgment that another sex besides the male happened to exist. Despite all this, however, my admiration of the stride and impetus of his storytelling was tremendous. And still is.

On the other hand, in my novel, I proposed to make my heroes 'native' – real Scots, living in Scotland – and my heroines as sexy as my experience allowed. In my dreams I outsold Buchan by many thousands of copies.

Back in the Manse after 'my operation', and with a bandage still sticky and uncomfortable around my neck, I got down to business. In the mornings I wrote a thousand words in a thick exercise book which I had bought for ninepence in the *Courier* shop in Campbeltown. (A similar one, today, costs 75p.) In the afternoons I typed them out on the Royal Portable. For the first chapter or two I enjoyed myself, and my mother and Jean both remarked that I looked happier and healthier. But then, as I paused to count up all the words I had written and found that they numbered less than 10 000, I began to realize what a long and sustained effort was required to complete 80 000 words, which, before World War II, was the usual length for a popular novel.

At present, partly because of printing costs, comparable books contain only 50 000 words. This makes for a much more tightly written and, therefore, more readable story, especially in the case of an ordinary 'thriller'. The amount of padding that went into pre-war pot-boilers had to be read to be believed. Long descriptions of dull scenery, 'stream of consciousness' analyses of what occurred – or failed to occur – in the minds of heroes and heroines, recapitulations of the carpentered plots – all such devices held up the action and, no doubt, bored some impatient readers to the point of an immediate return of the books to the library.

For myself, I had no clear vision of what length my story ought to be. I went by what *The Writers' and Artists' Year Book* told me was the 'correct' number of words and laboured blindly towards that goal. I lashed my brain into daily action, fought hard against inherent laziness, tried to ignore my dangerously dwindling financial resources, shut out the awful prospect of the book eventually being rejected and tried to present a happy, confident face to the world.

That summer I did my usual stint at the Highland Games but without great success. So much sitting at a table, writing and typing, kept me from being fully fit, physically. In any case, my mind was elsewhere, grappling with events and characters in *The Purple Rock*.

Weeks went by. Months went by, three of them. And it was autumn. It was also nearly the end as far as my money was concerned. I could still pay the instalments on the typewriter; but my mother, during the last month, had to do without her pounds. She made no complaint.

I finished the book and counted the words. They totalled only slightly more than 60 000, still almost 20 000 less than the number advised. But I felt exhausted, incapable of starting to expand and pad. In any case, I was down to my last few shillings, and it seemed to me that the time had come to stifle feelings of pride and independence and find a job with a regular pay-packet.

Consulting my *Writers' and Artists' Year Book*, I made a short list of literary agents to whom I might entrust the selling of my book and wrote to them all, asking if they would consider handling a novel by an unknown writer. The most encouraging reply came from Miss Patience Ross of A. M.

Heath & Co., Ltd. To her I sent off the manuscript of *The Purple Rock*.

In about three weeks Miss Ross replied that she liked the book and would try to find a publisher for it. This made me jump with joy; but even so, I was too innocent and inexperienced to realize how lucky I was. Agents like Heath, with a high reputation, are often more choosey than publishers. Perhaps it was easier in those days to storm the ramparts, because the book trade was booming, even bursting at the seams. Now, in this age of inflation and high printing costs, to acquire a good agent is not easy. For the past few years, instead of expanding their lists, agents, like publishers, have been pruning them. My heart grieves for a beginning writer today. The road to publication is far steeper and more dangerous than the one, in youthful ignorance, I so blithely followed.

With the future of my book in expert hands, I went to Alec MacLeod, editor and owner of the *Campbeltown Courier*, and asked him, humbly, if by any chance he could give me a job. Here again I was lucky. 'Why not?' Alec said, shifting a peppermint from one stout cheek to another. 'I've been editor, reporter, chief sub-editor and office boy in this place far too long. I think I deserve a little peace to write things for the paper that really interest me. All right. Come as a reporter. Three pounds a week. A bonus at Christmas, and you can keep the payments for any freelance stuff you sell to outside papers.'

I was dumbfounded. I was also extremely happy. Regions of wealth were suddenly being opened up. It occurred to me, also, that many people were able to get married on £3 a week. Back at the Manse and at Brunerican, I boasted of my new status as a writer gainfully employed.

'Good!' said the Padre. 'Now you can learn your trade.'

'I always *said* you'd make a good reporter,' my mother told me.

Maimie remarked: 'Now maybe we'll get some Southend news in the *Courier*!'

Archie, at the university, Willie at sea and Rona, Kenneth and John at school were all obviously relieved that their eldest brother would no longer hang grumpily around when they were at home.

People in Southend seemed glad that, as they saw it, I had begun to work at last. I put aside the ignoble suspicion that some of those who now became ultra-friendly were hoping I might put their names in the paper. Or, perhaps, in certain circumstances, keep them out.

'Not long now,' I told Jean. 'I'll open a bank account the day I get my first pay.'

She made a fuss of me and baked a fairy-light sponge, filled with fresh whipped cream, to celebrate. We had now been 'wenching', as the neighbours called it, for more than five years. She was accustomed to my moods. This was one of triumph; but she knew there would be more of despair to come. In consequence, I don't think she shared my high optimism. She was content, however, patient creature that she was – and is – to enjoy the moment and to let the future take care of itself.

7. *Courier* Special

For almost two years I helped Alec MacLeod with the *Courier*, as I have recounted in *Salt in My Porridge*. In those two years I learned much about the writing trade and even more about human nature.

Alec also put into practice the ideas that had come to him during our interview. After a few weeks' coaching on the technical side, I was allowed to take over his former roles as reporter, sub-editor and office-boy, while he himself took life more easily and wrote a series of feature articles about local characters and customs. He took the pen-name 'Neonach', which, in the Gaelic, means 'an awkward fellow'. But there was nothing awkward about his style of writing. Like George Blake and Neil Munro, he was an advocate of simplicity. 'It's easy to use flowery language,' he often told me, echoing Sandy Banks, my old English master. 'Not so easy to be straightforward.' He agreed with J. B. Priestley that a writer ought to be able to share his thoughts and impressions with the crowd. 'Shakespeare could do it,' he would say. 'No intellectual snobbery for him.'

Another important lesson he tried to teach me was that above all else a writer must have integrity, both moral and artistic. 'Never express an opinion that you don't believe in,' he said once, smacking his lips on the peppermint that took the place of the tobacco-wad he had chewed long years before as an apprentice printer. 'You might be tempted to do so in order to please me or some other editor. I'd respect you far more if you displeased me with something I knew came from your heart. And so would any editor worth his salt. Insincerity always shows and lowers the reputation not only of the paper but also of its readers.'

To observe Alec's law, fifty years ago, was difficult. Today, it is infinitely more difficult. I know three big-name journalists in the contemporary Scottish scene who callously flout it. Two of them vote Labour but write anti-Labour articles for Tory papers. The third votes Tory but lends his name to virulent criticism of the Tories in a Labour paper. They do it for the money, which they consider more important than principle. Is there a clue here as to why so much public suspicion and lack of respect has recently been shown for the media?

Despite recurring evidence to the contrary, I believe that the great majority of our politicians, businessmen, trade unionists and writers are honourable and decent folk. The trouble is that in our day, encouraged by the media, a few mavericks in each category keep trying to hide behind the skirts of the honourable and decent by side-stepping 'integrity' and, in the process, prostituting the English language.

At one time, when a VIP was interviewed on radio or television or quoted in the press, good people were inclined to accept his or her honesty. But with the development of an amoral and even anti-Christian quality in the art of public relations, good people are becoming confused. And suspicious. One or two coins in the currency of truth have been exposed and found to be made of lead, and the genuine ones are in danger of being devalued.

After a study of the media in recent years I have compiled, for my own guidance, a small dictionary of words and phrases, the original meanings of which have become obscured.

Here are three examples from the political section, beginning with the word 'integrity' itself.

Once upon a time a noble word, '*integrity*' is now used frequently in reference to a politician who, aided by lawyers and public relations experts, has so far been able to cover his guilty tracks. (Cf. 'There will be no whitewash at the White House.')

'*I have already made it perfectly clear*.' Nearly always, in a modern context, this means 'I have already dodged the question in a bout of double-talk and intend to repeat the process.'

'*He has a brilliant intellect*.' This phrase is occasionally employed to camouflage idleness and lack of public conscience. More often, however, it is applied to a politician whose speech-writers have access to *The Oxford Dictionary of Quotations*.

From the business section:

'*I welcome the investigation*.' This can mean 'I'm afraid I have been lumbered, but with professional assistance I will do my best to fudge the issue.'

'*Resignation from the board is my only honourable course*.' A gambit used in an effort to distract attention from a course which, up to date, has been strictly dishonourable.

'*There is a lack of confidence abroad*.' In certain cases this can be translated as 'Ordinary people in our own country are receiving so large a slice of the financial cake that the enormous profits made by foreign banks and lending institutions are in danger of being eroded.'

From the trade union section:

'*I speak for the workers*.' There is a danger that this may mean, simply, 'I speak for a few communists intent upon disruption for disruption's sake.'

'*Comrades*.' Another noble word which now, in specific circumstances, implies 'Fellow Marxists – and stuff all other members of the human race.'

'*I believe in the equal distribution of wealth*.' A platitude which often boils down to 'Soak the rich – okay – but let nothing interfere with my differentials.'

From the literary section:

'*An adult play which ignores the conventions*.' Usually a play dwelling upon sex and sadism completely lacking in artistic discipline and of little interest to normal people above the age of puberty.

'*A sensitive study*.' Common description of a novel dealing with homosexuality (for sales purposes).

'*Frank, outspoken, ingenious, Scottish to the core*.' This could well be the description of a play written in an obscure Scottish dialect, interlarded with 'daring' words like 'Christ' and 'bugger' but lacking entirely in loving respect for humanity.

It seems today that a few people are more intent upon 'projecting an image' than upon being honest with themselves and their neighbours and telling the truth as they see it. Even more to blame for this than politicians, businessmen, trade unionists and writers are some of the high-powered advertising and public relations moguls, who – along with the proliferating 'financial experts' – are attempting to rule our lives.

According to certain ad-men, the sight of a new feminine 'hair-do', a manly pipe or a yachtsman's cap has more influence upon us, the so-called 'masses', than frankness and sincerity of heart. What do they take us for? Morons? I'm afraid their answer might be a cynical 'Yes'.

Standards in the use of the English language are falling. Why? It seems to me there is only one answer: 'Because moral standards are falling.' And why are moral standards falling? Because, I believe, a mob of 'clever-dicks', some seeking personal power, most of them financial profit, are working overtime, doing their utmost to undermine the value and authority of the Christian faith.

A high-water mark in this tide of exploitation was the launching some years ago of the new cult of 'punk rock'. A group of 'musicians' calling themselves the Sex Pistols, previously signed up by the recording firm of EMI for £40 000, appeared on Thames Television, in which EMI has shares. Their performance, musically, was terrible. But it was accompanied by obscene words and gestures which caused an immediate shocked reaction from viewers and sections of the press. This, of course, was what the group's management had foreseen. Free publicity burgeoned for the Sex Pistols. 'Punk rock' was on the way, its innovators intent upon the financially rewarding exercise of assaulting and raping innocent young minds.

A few wet behind the ears sociologists argued that such 'happenings' were excusable on the grounds of freedom of expression and changing standards.

Freedom of expression? Freedom cannot exist in a world of moral anarchy.

Changing standards? Nearly two thousand years ago

Christ indicated the only kind of behaviour that ensures general human happiness. He said: 'Love your neighbour.' He didn't mean – with an ad-man's snide giggle – 'Con your neighbour.' He meant, as Professor Bowman pointed out to us in the class of moral philosophy, 'Give your neighbour the reverence and respect due to him or her as another human being.'

(It seems that the 'punk rock' publicity did not build up the outstanding success anticipated by the Sex Pistols. When I spoke on the telephone to a representative of EMI, he told me that sales of their records were 'disappointing'. Perhaps we, the 'masses', are not such morons after all.)

I enjoyed my work on the *Courier*, untroubled either by PROs or by ad-men. In a small community like Kintyre everybody knows the last domestic detail about everybody else. 'Image making', therefore, has always been regarded here as a futile exercise. Untroubled also by trade union rules, I roamed the town and countryside, chatting to people and gathering 'copy', heedless of set hours. I helped Alec to read proofs and insert heads and cross heads. I helped the printers when their work-load became heavy, as it often did on a Wednesday, the day before the paper was printed. I lived in digs in Campbeltown, paying Mrs Rankin in Cross Street 22s 6d per week, and felt it no burden to rise at six in the morning to give a hand in the composing room with wedding invitations, agricultural show catalogues – and, sometimes, urgent, black-edged funeral notices – and then to work on until eight o'clock in the evening collecting copy from, for example, the Sheriff Court, the winner of a local football pool, fishermen back from a spell at the herring in Loch Fyne.

And afterwards, in a pub, perhaps to meet a character like Big Nan, sixteen burly stones of her, who drank pint for pint with the men and outdid even the quay 'lumpers' in the coarse quality of her language.

Big Nan had a boyfriend, a wee crinkled shoemaker nicknamed the Skate, who, though socially backward and silent, was yet noted for his masculine powers. (To handle Big Nan certainly required an expert.) One night, in the Diamond Vaults, the talk turned to the latest Engagements announcement in the *Courier*, that of a distillery owner's poetry writing son to a laird's daughter. Giggling gossip had it that when he proposed the young man had gone down on his knees and recited:

> 'As fair art thou, my bonnie lass,
> So deep in luve am I;
> And I will luve thee still, my dear,
> Till a' the seas gang dry.'

I turned to Big Nan. 'What would you say if the Skate got all romantic and did the same to you?'

She snorted into her tankard. 'I'd say the bugger was drunk!' she declared.

The only jobs I did not relish were interviews with relatives of people who had died and whom Alec reckoned deserved 'obits' in the paper. In a house of mourning I became awkward and uneasy, a curtain in my brain blotting out many of the questions I planned to ask. Alec knew my weakness and often wrote the obituaries himself, from personal knowledge of the deceased. 'A reporter is like a doctor,' he said to me, once. 'In the face of death he's got to harden his heart and try to think objectively.' But I noticed that, like me, he avoided as much as possible physical intrusions upon grief.

One day I went to the home of a young man in his early twenties who had been killed when his horse bolted and the cart in which he was conveying wet draff from a distillery to an outlying farm had overturned.

His older sister sat staring into the cold kitchen range. She told me her father had gone out. 'He'll get drunk. He always does.'

'May I speak to your mother?'

'She's in there. In the back room.'

I opened the door of the small bedroom. I saw the corpse on the bed. The mother lay across it, weeping. She had cancer in one breast. Her blouse was open and the bandage on her breast had slipped. I saw pale red flesh. Pus was oozing out of it on to the corpse.

I shut the door and went through the kitchen to the back yard, where I retched up my dinner.

When I told Alec, he said: 'For some folks, Angus, life is no joke.'

I wanted it to be a joke. I still feel that it ought to be a joke, though sometimes the humour may have a black edge to it.

Having to write about five thousand words every week for a small provincial paper like the *Campbeltown Courier*, I learned the basic principle of journalism: *Names make news*. A long list of prize-winners at a bird show was more viable 'copy' than a poetic piece about a sunset. A report on, for example, the annual 'Kiltie Ball' had no relevance unless it bristled with the names of the high-ranking officers and their women-folk who sat at the top table and those of the corporals and privates who manned the door and the bar.

For a reporter, such attention to detail was more important during my time on the *Courier* than it is today, when photographs can be produced straight away from a glossy print. Fifty years ago, if we wanted a picture in the paper, we had to send the print to a firm in Glasgow which specialized in block-making. The result was that news pictures were seldom available to us in time, and names which should have appeared in captions had to be included in long swatches of copy.

Another lesson I learnt was how to write at speed against a deadline.

I remember a sheep-stealing case which ended in the Sheriff Court late on a Wednesday evening. By six o'clock on a Wednesday, as a rule, almost every scrap of copy was set and ready in the flat-bed machine so that a quick start could be made the following morning. Alec was willing to print the verdict only and hold over until the next issue a detailed report of the final day's proceedings; but I insisted on remaining in the office until midnight to complete it. Then I persuaded Archie MacMillan, the linotype operator, to come in early the next morning to set it up. Archie was as keen as I to show off his professional skill, and we were both proud peacocks when, before lunch time on Thursday, the paper was on the streets, with posters announcing: '*Sheep-stealing Trial – Full Report*'.

Though always sparing of praise – a common characteristic of editors – Alec was pleased about it. For once we had 'scooped' our prestigious rival, the *Oban Times*.

Not long after I joined the paper Alec MacLeod's wife took ill and he came less eagerly to the office. I found myself more and more involved in the intricate details of producing a paper each Thursday. In my secret thoughts I fancied myself as a whizz-kid editor and specialized in what at the time – under the influence of American films – were called 'scoops': in my case stories of local interest which I reckoned had been overlooked by the *Oban Times* or by the other Campbeltown paper, the *Argyllshire Herald*. Gleefully I printed them under headings in large black type: *COURIER SPECIAL*. In this ploy I had an advantage, because the *Courier* came out a day earlier than the *Oban Times* and *Herald*.

Big Sandy McMurchy, Arthur Henderson and Archie MacMillan – the entire printing staff – were all dubious about such revolutionary antics on the part of the conservative *Courier*. 'Alec wadna like it,' I was told. But the game was exciting – and I think that in a way they enjoyed hearing the *Courier* being talked about in the town – so, as long as Alec remained absent, they played along with me.

I kept asking in the office if the sales of the *Courier* were going up; but it seemed that in spite of all my brilliant efforts they remained much the same as they had done during the past fifty years. It was disappointing news for a whizz-kid whose joy in life depended so much upon competition.

Why compete at all if no tangible prize is forthcoming at the end of the day? During my term of employment with the *Courier* I discovered a personal answer. For me, competition for its own sake is enjoyable. Prizes, in a material sense, are irrelevant. I believe all writers who aim to endure must possess this philosophy. Almost certainly they will not gain large monetary prizes. But the more valuable prizes of inner satisfaction and independence are theirs for the taking.

Alec MacLeod's wife died. A week later he came back to the office, sad and even tearful, but determined to find comfort in work. He never discussed the *COURIER SPECIALS* with me, but they quickly disappeared, and the paper settled back into its former groove of solid worth. Advertising shopkeepers no longer complained that the paper was boosting brash new rivals at their expense. Town councillors no longer invaded the office to accuse me of giving more prominence to a colleague's 'smart alec' speeches than to their own more pedestrian but more 'sensible' ones. Members of the Presbytery of Kintyre – including the Padre – were relieved that reports of their meetings no longer highlighted the social scandals to which they sometimes referred, almost apologetically, but concentrated instead on the unctious utterings of establishment divines.

But Alec allowed me still to have my way with the 'Sparks and Flashes' column. I had made a number of good friends among the agricultural community who were always willing to supply me with the latest humorous gossip at some fellow farmer's expense – that is, as long as I promised not to divulge the source of my information. Provided that the jokes were good-natured and hurtful to nobody, I embellished them and printed them in black type, much to our country readers' delight – even sometimes to the delight of the victim.

One of my most prolific informants, as I can now reveal, was Willie Smith, a bachelor farmer whose gusty laughter often used to fill the office on a Monday morning. (Monday was – and still is – market day in Campbeltown.) But Willie had a terrible come-uppance. At the autumn show of the Kintyre Agricultural Society a small sensation occurred when, competing with hordes of expert ladies, Willie carried off the first prize in the bramble jam section. This was nothing, however, to the sensation caused by a paragraph in the following week's 'Sparks and Flashes' which revealed that Willie's jam was, in fact, bramble jelly into which, at the semi-liquid stage, whole brambles had been cunningly inserted.

'Who the hell tellt ye that?' thundered Willie, when I met him on the street.

'You'd be surprised,' I said.

'It's a bloody liberty!'

'But true?'

He burst out laughing. 'Ay, it's true. But I ken bloody fine who gi'ed the show away. Here, let me tell ye somethin' aboot him . . .'

I made some good friends among the fishermen, too. In those days, the early thirties, farmers led anxious and impoverished lives, with milk selling at only 3½p per gallon. Fishermen found existence equally hard. The behaviour of the herring shoals had become less predictable; and, in any case, the herring was losing its popularity as part of a fashionable diet.

One sea-faring friend I made was Duncan Newlands, who later became coxswain of the Campbeltown life-boat. His most famous rescue was that of fifty-four passengers and crew of the American liberty ship, *Byron Darnton*, wrecked on Sanda in March 1946. He worked at various jobs – line-fishing, boat hiring, 'quay lumping'. I remember him talking to me indignantly about the slump in the herring trade. 'Why people turn up their noses at a wholesome fresh herring beats me! I expect if you put out a story that herrings were a rare delicacy – like caviare, which in some countries is as common as porridge – you'd get folk fighting to buy them!'

An old man, now retired, Duncan has seen his flight of imagination become reality. In his younger days, when herrings were sold at threepence a dozen, only the very poor were inclined to buy them. Now, when they cost about 20p each, well-heeled housewives queue up to add them to their fashionable menus.

' "*I am ruminating,*" *said Mr Pickwick,* "*on the strange mutability of human affairs.*"

' "*Oh! I see – in at the palace door one day, out at the window the next. Philosopher, sir?*"

' "*An observer of human nature, sir,*" *said Mr Pickwick.*'

Duncan did most of his fishing at night. By day he often used his boat – the *Orange Blossom* – to go out and meet the 'puffers', thus making certain that he secured a job, unloading coal.

The puffers used to come to Campbeltown bringing house and industrial coal – industrial coal mainly for the distilleries – from the Ayrshire pits. They tied up at the Old Quay and were unloaded by means of iron buckets winched up out of the holds and then emptied directly into horse-drawn carts and lorries. And into waggons belonging to the Campbeltown and Machrihanish Light Railway. Several men were always needed in the holds to fill the buckets.

This was the kind of work eagerly sought by Duncan, and it was a recognized thing that the first man to board an incoming puffer got the bucket-filling jobs. When a puffer was due in the harbour all types of craft would sail out to meet her, and often, in the end, it would develop into a race. 'I've seen me, with my mates,' Duncan once told me, 'going as far as Ayr harbour, nearly forty miles away, to contact a puffer and "put our line aboard", as we called it.'

When regattas were held in Campbeltown, between the wars, races inspired by this idea were arranged for the 'quay lumpers', the competing punts being propelled by shovels instead of oars.

In the scramble for jobs, the *Orange Blossom*, which had an engine, gave Duncan an advantage over his oar-bound rivals. At the end of it all, however, pay for filling the buckets amounted to less than 2½d per ton. But with shipbuilding no longer viable in Campbeltown, with the town's distilleries closing down one after another, with the low price of milk, butter and cheese making paupers out of farmers and with the herring disappearing not only from the usual fishing-grounds but also from the nation's frying-pans, work was tragically scarce in Kintyre. People like Duncan who could find jobs of any kind, no matter how poorly paid, were the lucky ones. Those who didn't had to beg for a pitiful dole, amounting in some cases to only a few shillings a week.

While I worked on the *Courier* the national unemployment figure was well over two million. Marketing boards and the resultant bureaucracy, militant trade unions and the resultant aggro became inevitable.

Meanwhile, on 28 October 1932, my twenty-fourth birthday, a cruising seagull dropped a slimy 'message' on my head. 'Sign o' good luck!' said Duncan, with whom I was talking at the time. How right he was. Later in the day a letter arrived from A. M. Heath & Co. Ltd. Miss Patience Ross was 'happy to tell me' that my book, *The Purple Rock*, had been accepted for publication by Stanley Paul.

8. Rocks in My Porridge

For days after the acceptance of *The Purple Rock* I was insufferable to Jean and my family. Success always goes to my head. My neighbour, Allan Lamont, once introduced me to a golfing opponent as 'the best and most graceful loser in the business but the most obnoxious winner you're ever likely to meet.' I made a lofty response: 'On the golf-course, as in my trade, I am a loser most of the time. Why should I be grudged delight in a rare triumph?'

The Padre was inclined to be euphoric, too, praising his eldest son for being 'a real MacVicar'. He now revealed that members of his family had always been good at telling stories.

My mother was happy. 'I always knew you'd be a famous writer,' she said to me. With a glance across the tea table at the Padre, she added: 'Did you know that my great-uncle on my mother's side once published a book of Gaelic poetry?'

The Padre snapped at the bait like a cruising shark. 'One of the greatest Gaelic poems ever to come out of North Uist was *Oran Chlann a Phiocair*, "Song of the Clan MacVicar", written in the sixteenth century by an ancestress of mine. And when I come to think about it, what about Sir Walter Scott's friend, Mrs Grant of Laggan, who wrote *Letters from the Mountains*, the eighteenth-century classic? She was a MacVicar.'

'But not,' remarked my mother, 'a North Uist MacVicar.' Then, inconsequently, she announced: 'I had another great-uncle who designed bridges for the Czar of Russia.'

I think it pleased them that *The Purple Rock* was dedicated 'To My Father and Mother'. Hebridean insistence upon 'honouring thy father and mother' conforms, of course, with biblical teaching; but I am sure it stems originally from ancient laws which held that reverence for parents was necessary in creating a strong sense of 'family'.

It distresses me to hear someone say about parents, 'I didn't ask to be brought into this world. They indulged themselves to get me born. Why should I show them any more consideration than anyone else?' That is a direct quote from an acquaintance of mine in a London office. Needless to say, he shows little consideration for anybody, let alone his widowed mother. I believe he has overlooked the fact that, apart from the material benefits of food, clothing and education during his helpless years, his parents were also responsible for providing him with the greatest gifts of all, those of life and love. Is a little love and respect in return too much to ask? Is a happy and united family not the very foundation of a happy and united society?

The idea so often bandied about in modern society that the state should be responsible for the upbringing of children, leaving parents to pursue their jobs as labelled state employees, brings me to the edge of horror. Do those who advocate it realize that they are marching down a narrow road straight into the arms of Big Brother?

Rona, my brothers and Maimie were all glad about *The Purple Rock* but not, I think, greatly impressed. Neither was Jean. Neither were my neighbours in Southend. It became clear that their interest in me was as a person, not as an author; and eventually, by recognizing this, I was able to plant my feet more firmly on the ground. In a vague kind of way it was revealed to me that in a small community one earned affection and respect not by being brilliant at a particular job but by one's attitude and behaviour in relation to other people.

In the contract drawn up between Stanley Paul & Co., Ltd. on the one hand and A. M. Heath & Co., Ltd. and myself on the other, it was agreed that the novel should be published in hardback within six months at 7s 6d. Royalties would be paid to me (through Heath) at the rate of ten per cent on the first 2500 copies sold, fifteen per cent on the next

2500 copies sold and twenty per cent on all copies sold above 5000. I was to receive an advance on royalties of £25, payable on the day of publication. If the book was later published in a paperback edition priced at 6d, the royalty would be 15s per thousand copies sold. Ten per cent of all monies due to me would be retained by Heath.

The contract was signed for and on behalf of Stanley Paul & Co., Ltd. by F. A. Cowling, Director. With a flourish I signed for and on behalf of 'the author'.

Twenty-five pounds didn't seem a large advance; but I calculated that once *The Purple Rock* had sold over 5000 copies – as I was certain it would – and the royalty rate had soared to twenty per cent, I would be in sight of my first Rolls-Royce. And what if somebody published it as a serial, or even made a film of it? The possibilities were as wide and uncertain as the waves breaking on the shore.

There was one snag, however, as there always is for writers bemused by pleasurable dreams. My typescript contained only 60 000 words. Frank Cowling indicated in a friendly way – betraying only that slight hint of steel which, in the future, I came to recognize as the publisher's secret weapon – that he would like me to add 'at least' 10 000 words to it, so that it might 'approximate more closely' to the 'usual length required in a novel'.

I faced the task with confidence. For the next fortnight, after my day's work with the *Courier*, I sat down each evening in Mrs Rankin's front room to write 1000 words, mostly great swatches of 'scenic description' composed, as I imagined, in a vein of poetry. I also enlarged upon the thoughts passing through the minds of my characters and succeeded, on the whole – though I didn't, of course, realize it at the time – in clogging up the action of what had been planned as a fast-moving thriller. But when I sent the revised typescript to Frank Cowling he declared himself satisfied and, joyfully, I returned untrammelled to my reporting duties and awaited with impatience the publication of 'my book'.

In the spring of 1933 the proofs came and were corrected at speed. Dust jacket designs were sent to me for approval. I chose one picturing a glamorous girl in a tartan frock perched somewhat incongruously on a seaside rock. She had blonde hair, whereas my heroine was a brunette (like Jean); but Frank Cowling explained to me that a blonde would sell the book better than a brunette and that, in any case, there were technical difficulties in reproducing brunettes in colour. I did not argue with him.

Then I was told that publication had been fixed for the last week of May. I suggested to Alec MacLeod that I might write a piece about it for 'Sparks and Flashes'. Generously he allowed me to do so but began looking at me with his head on one side, possibly in much the same way as a suspicious hedge sparrow regards a fledgling cuckoo in the nest.

Excitement grew. My work on the *Courier* did not suffer. Indeed, the reverse took place. I wrote my pieces with abounding energy and enthusiasm. Slowly recovering from the loss of his wife, Alec took more and more time off to write his 'Neonach' articles. During this period – for once – the paper was discussed favourably in Kintyre.

A month before the magic date in May, six advance copies of the book arrived, free of charge, for the author. This is normal practice, usually covered by a clause in the contract. For me it was anything but normal. When I tore open the parcel and set eyes upon my 'baby', I think I understood what a mother must feel as she looks upon her first-born. It was a beautiful book. I said so, and everybody agreed with me. Few would be able to resist buying it. I said that, too, and again everybody agreed with me. The word 'vainglorious' must have stirred in the minds of all my relatives and friends.

One jarring note was struck by Miss Annie Morgan, who kept a bookshop in Campbeltown. Straight grey hair and a thin, bespectacled face were camouflage for a generous nature. Her conversation was sharp, earning her a reputation as a female Wyatt Earp who always shot from the hip. She saw my heroine on the dust-jacket, did a double-take, then sniffed and said: 'Angus, why on earth is your girlfriend wearing a tartan goonie?' ('Goonie' is an old-fashioned

Scots word, meaning 'nightie'.) I tried to ignore a sudden conviction that the sophisticated frock which might have looked appropriate at a Caledonian Ball in London was out of place against a background of Scottish rocks and sea and sky. I was glad to discover, however, that Miss Morgan did not hold my heroine's clothes against me. She ordered two dozen copies of the book from a delighted traveller – and, in due time, two dozen more, all of which she was able to sell.

Later on she and Jean became friends. When they got together I was frequently lectured on my behaviour in dictatorial terms. Like Kubla Khan, Miss Morgan was inclined to class me as a lazy writer and hounded me on to increase both the quantity and the quality of my work. She often criticized my books to my face; but I was told that if anybody came into her shop and spoke evil words concerning them, she would react like a wild cat protecting her young.

While I was away from home during World War II she often stayed at Achnamara, keeping Jean company and writing letters filled with hard-headed advice that would have done credit to Samuel Smiles. We still have the Tusitala edition of Robert Louis Stevenson and the ancient grandfather clock which she bequeathed to us when she died.

Frank Cowling did what I know now to have been an excellent job of providing publicity for *The Purple Rock*. He had small postcards printed showing a picture of my heroine alongside a copy of the boastful 'blurb' composed by the author. A packet containing twelve dozen was sent to me, and I had a happy time posting cards to addresses picked from a telephone book. On a visit to Glasgow I left some lying on the seats of tram-cars and laid a paper-trail of them through Kelvingrove Park. I then invaded the cloisters of the university and scattered about a dozen around the door of the political economy lecture-room. 'Put that in your pipe and smoke it, Adam Smith!'

On the Sunday before publication large advertisements appeared in both the *Sunday Times* and the *Observer*. They were set in the bold, black type which, at the time, was characteristic of the Hutchinson group of companies: bold, black type entirely pleasing to authors panting for recognition.

THE PURPLE ROCK
by
ANGUS MACVICAR

> For sheer excitement and dramatic tension there are chapters in this novel which have seldom been surpassed in modern fiction. One of the most readable and entertaining books ever written by a Scottish author.
>
> Stanley Paul & Co., Ltd., price 7/6d net.

By this time I had almost forgotten that such resounding praise had been born of my own dreams. Like Dr Goebbels, I was beginning to believe in propaganda initiated by myself. This may have been one reason why publication day proved anti-climactic.

That morning I went into the *Courier* office with high expectations. What did I expect? Congratulations? A celebration cake? A guard of honour? In the outcome nothing happened. Jenny, Isa and Cathie in the shop said 'Hullo' and went on with their business of selling newspapers and pencils and exercise books and paper doylies. As I passed into the composing room Archie MacMillan, at the keyboard of the linotype, expertly spat out a stream of tobacco-juice which, as usual, landed only a few inches away from my highly polished shoes. 'Hi!' he said, amid clattering machinery and the fumes of hot lead. Big Peter and Arthur Henderson were engaged in 'dissing' type from the previous week's *Courier* and uttered only their customary grunts of welcome. Alec sent me out to interview the Provost, who was introducing a controversial piece of local legislation at that evening's Town Council meeting. Nobody mentioned *The Purple Rock*.

To some extent the day was saved by Miss Morgan. As I passed her shop in mid-morning I saw my book placed in a central position in the window. Stopping to admire it, I was summoned inside by an imperious voice. 'Come and sign some copies, Angus. Help to sell them.' With jumping pulse and no small amount of pride I did as I was told.

During this happy session I was introduced by Miss Morgan to several customers, one of whom, marvellous to relate, actually bought a copy of the book. To witness the sale of his own product is perhaps the author's greatest thrill. That day I was enchanted. Even now, forty-six years and sixty-nine books on, when, like a poor man's Edward Heath, I go around the bookshops and sign copies for queues of beautiful customers, I am still enchanted. In fact, recognizing that it gives an author pleasure to see his work being sold for hard cash, Lavinia Derwent and I attend each other's signing sessions, buy each other's books and demand each other's autograph. *A Breath of Border Air* in exchange for *Salt in My Porridge* – what could be more appropriate?

But then, as I completed my signing stint in Miss Morgan's shop, reality returned. Willie Smith, the expert on bramble jam, came bustling in. He scarcely glanced at the book I tried to show him. 'Come ootside, Angus. I've a rare tare tae tell ye aboot auld Sammy Mitchell. It's no' jeest a "spark", it's a "flash" as weel!' First things first. I got on with my job as a reporter.

A cheque for £22-10s arrived by post the next day. This represented the advance on royalties, less Heath's ten per cent. I withdrew all my savings from the post office and proceeded to open an account with the Bank of Scotland. It seemed to me appropriate that an author should deal with a dignified bank manager, who always acknowledged a customer's individuality, rather than with a brash and sometimes dictatorial post office clerk.

For forty-six years now I have been a customer at the Campbeltown branch of the Bank of Scotland. Managers like Albert Smith, Norval Charteris, Ian Rattray and Hamish McKinnon have all been friendly, in spite of the fact that frequently my current account has been overdrawn. Their help and advice – and practical encouragement in difficult times – has been invaluable to a temperamental author who can scarcely count up to ten, even on his fingers.

Not long ago I acquired a few shares in the Bank of Scotland and am intrigued to be called, after a hoary custom, a 'proprietor'. From impecunious reporter to 'proprietor' of a bank. 'Whaur's yer Andrew Carnegie noo?'

With *The Purple Rock* safely launched, albeit with a minimum of local acclaim, I decided it was time to buy a car.

Next door to the *Courier* Office was a garage owned by John Huie & Co., Ltd. I went round to see my friend, Jack Huie, who beamed at me and said: 'I have the very thing for you. A second-hand 1926 bull-nose Morris. Going at seven pounds ten.'

She looked to me like a bargain, with her touched-up green paint, canvas hood, mica screens and polished blunt nose pointing towards the garage wall. 'May I have a go in her before I decide?'

'Sure. Get in. I'll crank her up for you.' Jack went round and inserted the starting-handle.

I had only once before driven a car, a T-model Ford belonging to Hamish Taylor's father, in which Hamish and Lachie Young and Archie and I sometimes travelled to Highland Games. But I was confident I could handle a Morris equally well.

Jack got the engine started. I manipulated the choke in expert fashion.

'Reverse her a bit,' said Jack, his back to the wall. 'Then you can drive straight out.'

I juggled with the gear-lever, heard a satisfactory click and put my toe on the accelerator. In a moment the garage was filled with wild yells and imprecations. Instead of reverse I had engaged first gear. Lurching forward, the car had pinned Jack against the wall. Fortunately the mudguards had taken the main force of the impact. He was unharmed, in physical if not in spiritual terms.

I found reverse and released my friend. 'Sorry,' I said. 'I'll just have to buy her after that, won't I?'

'Take her away,' he groaned. 'And don't come back here until you learn to drive.'

That evening, the old bull-nose shuddering at her top

speed of 40 m.p.h., I drove down to Southend and took my mother and Jean out for what we called a 'spin': a 'spin' enjoyed in carefree circumstances almost unimaginable to modern motorists. Driving tests and MOT tests were unknown, mere glints in some bureaucrat's eyes. Petrol could be had for less than a shilling a gallon. As we chugged our way along the steep, unfenced road to the Mull of Kintyre, no other car moved within miles of us. Curly horned black-faced ewes scuttered away among the heather, which, at this time of early autumn, was burgeoning into great masses of purple. When we stopped at the Gap, high above the lighthouse, the sun was shining and the Irish hills were smokey blue across the North Channel. The only sounds were those that came from bleating sheep and from the larks which sang, soaring, 'in the clear air'. Life was free and exciting, and I rejoiced to be part of it.

During that summer more rejoicing occurred. Edward Shanks gave *The Purple Rock* a column review in the *Sunday Times* – a review which included my picture – while Compton Mackenzie wrote a long article about it in the *Daily Mail*. In the first chapter of my novel the hero is discovered reading a book by Compton Mackenzie; but I am certain this had nothing to do with the future literary knight's generous treatment of a young author.

Then Stanley Paul began to advertise *The Purple Rock* as being in its 'third impression'. I had no idea then what was meant by an 'impression'. Even now it remains a mystery to me, though I have an idea it can indicate anything from 500 copies to 5000, depending on the original print order. It sounded good, however, and, the wish being father to the thought, I inferred that my book had reached the best-seller class. I made up my mind that, after all, I was going to succeed in my ambition to become a freelance writer and told Alec MacLeod that later in the year I might be leaving the *Courier*. He looked glum. 'Don't make up your mind just yet,' he advised. 'See how things turn out.'

Things did not turn out as well as I imagined. In cold figures, *The Purple Rock* sold no more than 2000 copies in hardback. As I now realize, this was a fairly satisfactory result for a pre-war first novel; but it earned me less than £75, which meant that my plan to exchange the bull-nose Morris for a Rolls-Royce had to be postponed.

Later on, the book was published as a Toucan paperback at 6d (Toucans were Hutchinson's answer to Allen Lane's popular Penguins), and this brought in another £21, which wasn't at all bad, representing as it did, at 15s per thousand copies, a sale of 30 000. A literary syndicate, the name of which I can't remember, acquired the serial rights and, in abbreviated form, the story appeared in, amongst other papers, the *Daily Record* and the *Irish Free Press*. My cut from the serial sales was £15.

Total income from *The Purple Rock* amounted, therefore, to £111, which, as it contained about 70 000 words, meant that if future books sold at the same rate I could count on earning approximately thirty shillings per thousand words. Writing a thousand words each day, which already I had found to be no great hardship, I could look forward to a weekly income of at least £7, more than double what I was getting with the *Courier*.

So I calculated, putting aside all consideration of the many booby-traps that litter the road of a freelance writer – illness, lack of inspiration, fickle editorial policies, irregular times of payment and almost total lack of security, to name, as they say, but a few. But independence beckoned. With the prospect of becoming my own master dangling before me like a super carrot, there was no way that Alec MacLeod, in spite of our friendship, was going to keep me as an employee. No Rolls-Royce, as yet, but plenty of jam on my piece. And who could tell when a film offer might come?

Frank Cowling once told me that at this period, almost fifty years ago, works of fiction poured out from the presses 'like bullets from a Gatling gun', which was a favourite simile employed by contemporary 'thrill' merchants. It had something to do, he said, with keeping printers in work. The average sale of a first novel – and, indeed, of second and third novels – was around 700, a point at which the publisher only narrowly avoided a loss. Why *The Purple Rock* should have sold about three times that number is still not clear to me. I suppose, to use political language, there were various contributory factors.

Nowadays, thrillers with a Scottish background are 'thick as autumnal leaves that strow the brooks in Vallombrosa'; but in 1933 they were rarer birds. George Blake himself had written one or two under a pseudonym, while a few serial story writers got their Scottish thrillers published in book form. On the whole, however, Scotland's main exponents of the *genre* were still considered to be Robert Louis Stevenson and John Buchan. A number of reviewers compared my work, not unfavourably, with that of both those writers; and this may have helped to sell my book.

My good fortune in obtaining long and kindly reviews from Compton Mackenzie and Edward Shanks was another factor. The pundits tell me that reviews do not greatly affect the sales of books: what matters is that people should talk about them and recommend them to one another. But what starts people talking? Surely a good review, given plenty of space, can be part of the answer?

The trouble, for a beginning author, is to get his book mentioned at all. Today, about a hundred books are published every working day in Britain: books divided by the trade into forty-four separate categories, from 'aeronautics' through 'fiction' to 'wireless and television'. In *The Publishing Game* Anthony Blond calculates that one new novel is published every twenty minutes. It follows, therefore, that the literary editors of newspapers and magazines (by whom copies received for review are sent out to the reviewers) are constantly surrounded by heaving masses of books all awaiting attention, and a beginning author has to depend upon sheer luck to have his 'baby' catch their eye. In 1933 the spate of new fiction was even more swollen than it is now; and as I grow wiser in the ways of publishing, my luck in having had *The Purple Rock* featured in the *Sunday Times* and the *Daily Mail* becomes ever more astonishing.

I think Frank Cowling's advertising of *The Purple Rock* also contributed to a reasonably successful launch. The advertising of books at the present time is on nothing like the scale habitual in 1933, except perhaps in the case of new stories by such 'block-busters' as Arthur Hailey, Jack Higgins (Harry Patterson), Alistair MacLean and Harold Robbins – and even they have the benefit of the additional publicity generated by the filming of their books. But by 1933 standards, *The Purple Rock* was given unusual space in newspapers ranging from *The Sunday Times* and the *News Chronicle* to the *Glasgow Herald*, the *Scotsman* and the *Aberdeen Press and Journal*. Then there were the postcards, exhibiting my tartan-clad heroine, which I like to think sold a few hundred copies by themselves.

Publishers with whom I have discussed the subject all declare that, like reviews, advertising makes little difference to the sales figures. What I suspect they mean is that the cost of advertising has become so high that it can be viable only if a book promises to be a best-seller. After all, a four-inch double column in, for example, *The Sunday Times* or the *Observer* costs something like £400, which may be more than the publisher is paying his thriller writer as an advance on royalties. But the question remains: how can a book become widely known and, therefore, talked about, if potential readers are not even told that it exists?

Apart from reviews and advertising, in 1933 other methods of making a book known included reference to it in trade journals, gossip columns and, best of all, the news. Agents, publishers and booksellers, when they felt inclined, were often successful in getting their more important books mentioned in the trade journals and gossip columns. They found it more difficult to turn their authors into subjects for investigation by news reporters. Sometimes, however, miracles occurred.

As a teenager, I was intrigued to learn, along with millions of other newspaper readers, that Agatha Christie had gone missing. The titles of the few books she had written at the time were mentioned in every report of her disappearance. Apparently the case was a genuine one, concerned with temporary loss of memory; but I am sure no press agent could have found a better method of establishing Agatha Christie as the most successful thriller writer of the century.

The work of another writer of the period, Mary Webb, was publicly acclaimed by the then prime minister, Stanley Baldwin. From being an obscure author, whose work sold sluggishly, she became, almost overnight, a household name, and her grim tales of country life, notably *Gone to Earth*, galloped on the back of newspaper publicity into the high peaks of best-sellerdom.

I envied both those ladies their success in terms of sales and wondered if some day, by happy chance, I might get my name in the news. I never did, to any profitable extent. My life-style has seldom been newsworthy; and press agents have always been luxuries beyond my purse. But I have never been 'blate', as we say in Scotland, to jump at any chance of free publicity.

One day, playing golf with three friends over Dunaverty, my home course, I had a hole in one. Before the customary celebrations could blur my faculties I telephoned the story – as from the *Courier* – to several newspapers. Next morning it duly appeared, alongside advertisements (already booked) which made known that my new children's novel, *The Grey Pilot*, had just been published and that in the afternoon I should be signing copies at Lyons Bookshop in Sauchiehall Street, Glasgow. The combined operation was a success. The autographing session proceeded merrily, with children and their parents, in a queue of encouraging length, congratulating me on my prowess as a golfer.

As it happens, Lyons in Sauchiehall Street no longer exists. It was destroyed in a curious accident. A laden lorry careered down the steep hill opposite and plunged across the street, like a rogue tank, straight into the bricks and mortar of the shop.

A timely parable? Perhaps. But that is another story.

Today, the basic principles of making new books known are similar to those current in 1933, though the means employed, of course, have undergone change. Newspaper coverage has been overtaken in importance by coverage on radio and television; and there is a wild scramble by authors and publishers to have their wares – and themselves – given prominence on the 'wireless' or on the 'goggle-box'.

But luck plays a part here, too. For example, consider the good fortune of William Collins Sons & Co., Ltd., when, at the same time, they published *Doctor Zhivago* and the *Memoirs* of Field-Marshal Sir Bernard Law Montgomery. Both books became the subject of news stories, Pasternak refusing to accept the Nobel Prize and 'Monty', true to his admirably abrasive character, directing schoolboy raspberries at Eisenhower's qualities as a general. Radio and television made a hearty meal of both controversies; and I am told that, as a result, Collins enjoyed a million-pound turnover in one month.

In my own small world of book-writing, I have always had help from fellow Scottish journalists, as happened in the case of my hole in one. They are the most generous people I know. When they can, they give news of my books space in their papers and have never, in my experience, betrayed the 'I kent his faither' syndrome or the slightest hint of envy or jealousy. Not that they have anything to be envious or jealous about, as far as my material condition is concerned. Most of them, like my son Jock, earn about three times as much as I do. There must be times, however, as they slog away at their typewriters in hot and narrow offices, praising the work of some suddenly successful author – like Alistair MacLean, for example – when envy for someone who has now achieved freedom from authority and from deadlines must raise a cobra head. But I have never known them allow it to escape.

Sometimes they harbour criticisms of my work, which they express to me in private. But, like good family men and women, they are loath to denigrate a brother Scot in public. As one continuously obsessed by envious and jealous neuroses, I salute them. Britain might be a happier place if certain politicians followed their example and ceased to blackguard their countrymen in the hearing of the world at large.

Why any book sells well depends in part upon a complex mixture of good publicity and good luck. But when all is said and done (as the Padre used to say when a thundering sermon approached its climax), perhaps the most important considerations concern (a) the ability of the author to 'share his thoughts and impressions with the crowd' and (b) the ability of the publisher's rep to share his enthusiasm for the book with the booksellers.

Hutchinson's chief rep in Scotland is Bob Cowan, a happy, friendly man whose golf swing is suspect but whose professional swing is sharp, incisive and a thing of beauty to those authors whose books he works so hard and so successfully to sell. With Bob Cowan in charge, who needs a press agent? When *Rocks in My Scotch* was published in 1977, he arranged for it a programme of publicity which left me limp but which he described, snarling a little, as a run-of-the-mill operation. In the programme, which took place over two days, I submitted to five separate meetings with newspapermen and photographers, a phone-through interview with BBC Radio in London, a talk-in with Jameson Clark for Radio Scotland's 'Good Morning, Scotland', an hour-long interview broadcast later by Radio Clyde, an appearance in a film made by STV, four signing sessions in various Glasgow bookshops and several meals with influential booksellers. Jean was brought into the action, too, providing a 'Woman's Page' with candid and, to me, somewhat startling comments about my domestic behaviour.

Being shy and lazy, a lover of the quiet life, I found that the only enjoyable part of the experience was meeting my fellow workers in the various media and talking shop with them. There is no question, however, that it helped not only to sell the book in Scotland but also to reinforce my shaky self-esteem as an author. I went through it willingly, as much for Bob's sake as for my own. He is proud of his salesmanship. He ought to be. So should Hutchinson. He could sell fish to the seals which bob up and down in the sea outside my window.

In the book world confident sales projections are the cause of many an accountant's duodenal ulcer. A book of high quality produced by the most prestigious publisher, recommended to booksellers by the most skilful reps, provided with coverage in newspapers and on radio and television by the most skilful PROs, given rave reviews and expensive advertising – such a book may still fall down and break its crown.

Sphere, the paperback publishers, paid £27 000 for Len Deighton's *Only When I Larf*. They printed 300 000 copies, gave it the works as far as publicity was concerned but, in the end, sold only 100 000. In a quiet backwater of publishing the University of London Press produced a slim volume called *English in Libya*. I imagine the reps did a lot of good work here; but there were no reviews, no publicity, no advertising. It sold 230 000 copies – and still sells.

Names and Addresses, an autobiography by Tom Mathews (once editor of *Time* magazine) was the subject of wide advertising and received excellent reviews, not only in the quality Sunday papers but also – on account of some scandal-skirting stories it retailed concerning the publishing tycoon Henry Luce – in the popular tabloids. It did not sell. *The Godfather*, by Mario Puzo, was meagrely advertised and ignored by reviewers but gradually became a super blockbuster all over the world. Putnam's, New York, were the original publishers of *The Godfather*. The editor-in-chief, Bill Targ, was asked if he had anticipated such an enormous success for the book when he first published it. He said: 'I knew it was good, but I didn't believe it could be all *that* good!'

A horror story is told in *The Oxford University Press: An Informal History* which always makes me feel better when I worry about the sales of my books. In 1879, Oxford published a bulky volume, translated from the German, on passerine birds. (*Passer* in Latin means a sparrow. Passerine describes a huge order of perching birds, all sparrow-like in shape.) The trade was enthusiastic and the book warmly recommended by no less an authority than Charles Darwin. It sold seven copies in its first year, one in its second, and thirteen more in the next twenty-three years. Spare a few tears for the German author, but none for Oxford. In 1881 the firm's Revised Version of the New Testament sold a million copies on publication day.

All my writing life I have aimed at producing a best-seller. The pressures of living, the need to earn money to support a family and a comfortable home makes it almost inevitable that an author should think in this way. But it is something, I now believe, that a genuinely dedicated author should never do, and it may explain my comparative lack of credibility as an 'important' one.

In the fifties, when my stories for children about the Lost Planet were being broadcast as BBC radio and television serials and syndicated as strip cartoons before being published in book form by Burke, I almost made the grade. *The Lost Planet* and it sequel *Return to the Lost Planet* both sold around 15 000 copies in hardback – and that, as Bob Cowan might put it, ain't hay! Especially when there is evidence that in those immediate post-war days many booksellers, rendered smug by a long spell of easy selling during the black-out, were by no means as efficient and on the ball as their modern counterparts.

I remember once, in 1952, visiting a Glasgow bookshop (now under new and more lively management) and inquiring politely of a female executive why none of my books appeared to be on sale. 'Get yourself on the wireless,' she told me, pertly. 'Better still, have your books *read* on the wireless. Then we'll sell them all right.' My books weren't being *read* on the wireless, but they *were* being broadcast in the form of at least two six-part serials a year, not only in Scotland but throughout the United Kingdom and abroad. I didn't argue with the lady. What was the use? She neither knew nor cared. But Bob Cowan, I suspect, would have reacted in a more positive way.

The purpose of all this rambling, sometimes inconsequential comment is to prove that *nobody knows why any book sells well or badly*. Cunning old professionals advise that sex, money and religion, with doctors and nurses lurking in the background, are the main ingredients of a potential best-seller. This may be true, but plenty of books containing all these ingredients still moulder on remainder shelves. An author, in my opinion, may be compared to the famous submarine commander who navigated 'by guess and by God'.

Take the case of *Salt in My Porridge*.

The LOST PLANET

.... AND WHEN YOU'VE DONE THAT, SEE PROFESSOR BERGMAN — HE'S WORKING ON THE ROTARY JETS .... ASK HIM TO BRING THE BLUE PRINTS AND DISCUSS THEM WITH ME AT SIX O'CLOCK !
YES, UNCLE .... BUT ... WHAT ARE THOSE ROTARY JETS FOR ?

WHAT !! HAVEN'T YOU GRASPED THAT YET ?
52

I WILL PUT IT SIMPLY, JEREMY. AS WE JOURNEY INTO SPACE, THE PULL OF GRAVITY BECOMES LESS, AND IF SOMETHING WERE NOT DONE, WE SHOULD DRIFT ABOUT INSIDE THE SHIP ! HELPLESS !
53

IF WE SET THE SHIP SPINNING AROUND THIS CENTRAL SHAFT BY MEANS OF LOW POWER ROTARY JETS IT WILL CREATE ARTIFICIAL GRAVITATION.
54

'Picture by picture instructions for strip cartoons'. One day's newspaper ration of *The Lost Planet*

As I approached the OAP stage – and, in consequence, for the first time in my life basic financial security – I decided to write a book which would show that Jean and I were grateful to our families and friends for their kind care over the years. In addition, I wanted to demonstrate that in our case, unpopular though the idea has become in a modern permissive society, family life based on the Christian ideal is still a main source of happiness. I wrote *Salt in My Porridge* in two months, letting it come out of my heart rather than my head. I didn't think it would sell more than a few hundred copies. Nor did I care. I had written it to please myself.

Gerald Austin of Hutchinson was not, I think, too sure about its sales potential, either. The first print order was for 3000 copies.

On the date of its publication in February 1971 a post office strike blanketed all communication by mail. Here in Southend, lacking any kind of documentary evidence as to the book's reception and progress, I suspected that it had been still-born. Even my cheque for the advance on royalties, payable on publication, was lost, temporarily, in the stagnant pool of some sorting office in London.

Then one day I had a phone-call from Gerald. 'Angus, we're reprinting. From all the signs it seems we have a minor best-seller on our hands.'

When the post office strike ended, the happy fact emerged that *Salt in My Porridge* had been received with kindness by several critics and was being bought in surprising numbers not only by the libraries but also by individuals. Eventually it sold about 11 000 copies in hard covers. It is still selling, now as a Fontana paperback.

Why? A clear answer fails to present itself. But now that I pause to attempt an analysis, I have to admit that the book does have to do with sex, money and religion as well as with doctors and nurses. This was not the result of deliberate planning. It simply happened. That's life, as Esther Rantzen might say.

The first book I wrote to please myself, as an amateur rather than as a professional, became in every way my most successful. Here, it would seem, I ought to add a moral. Unfortunately I'm not quite sure what it is.

9. The Pride of the Peacock

When I told Alec MacLeod, about six months after publication of *The Purple Rock*, that I had decided to give up my job on the *Courier* and become a freelance, he shook his head: 'I'm sorry. If you'd stayed on, the *Courier* would have been yours one day.'

I had a spasm of uneasiness. Had I known about this beforehand, would it have influenced my decision? The *Courier*, with its attendant stationary business, was a small gold-mine. My amateur calculations, based upon some study of the accounts, indicated that it produced an annual profit on turnover of nearly forty per cent. Here was security and the promise of positive financial reward for hard work which would almost certainly be absent from the future of a self-employed author.

But the spasm passed. My ambition was to be my own man, with a life habit removed from dependence on orders and instructions, a life in the country with Jean, where, at our own convenience, we could take time off to smell the flowers. 'I'm sorry, too,' I told Alec. 'And I'll always be grateful for everything you taught me, not only about writing.' I meant it then. I mean it now, though Alec has been dead for more than thirty years.

I have never regretted the chance I missed of becoming a newspaper boss. I like being a boss, and I am told that this becomes only too evident when I work as a producer with the Dunaverty Players, Southend's contribution to amateur drama. I am not sure, however, that I'd like to earn money by being a boss. Why? Like Pontius Pilate, I propose to dispense with an answer.

Years later, after World War II, Jean and I were forced to

make a similar decision: whether to go and live in Glasgow or London where lucrative writing opportunities could more easily be found or to remain in Southend, far from the action, where it was certain that many chances of earning a fast buck would be missed. We stayed in Southend; and I have never regretted that decision, either. Especially, for example, on a quiet summer's evening on the golf course, with the scent of the sea and of damp, newly mown grass about us, and the larks laughing as my deadly enemy, Boskers, misses a yard putt for the match on the eighteenth green.

We do not envy the lot of those who direct cameras in a hot studio or pore over dubious headlines in a computerized composing room. They are being well paid for what they are doing. We are not being paid at all for what we are doing. But we earn enough to get by, and hard work can be done when it is raining or after darkness falls. On the face of it, the appropriateness of the following quotation from the works of P. G. Wodehouse may be questioned. But let its significance sink in. 'A good woman is a good woman, but a good drive is a slosh!'

Having said goodbye to the *Courier* – though I did occasional unpaid work for Alec during the next few years – I settled down at the Manse again to pursue my chosen profession. Two books a year was the programme and, not without toil and tears, I was able to sustain it until 1939, when the war came. Sometimes I missed a contract deadline; but Frank Cowling of Stanley Paul was understanding and continued to encourage me.

Frank was good looking – and kind with it – a publisher who took a personal interest in his authors. In his private thoughts he may have agreed with Michael Legat, who, in *Dear Author*, calls them 'fickle, temperamental, unreliable, vain and greedy'. In public he maintained patience and courtesy and never once expressed the opinion, attributed to a jocular Sir Frederick Macmillan, that 'publishing would be fun if it weren't for authors'.

Years later, Jean and I were watching *What's My Line* on BBC television, when suddenly Frank appeared in the hot seat, silver haired now but still as well groomed and charming as ever. The panel guessed he was an actor, a business tycoon, a diplomat – even an income-tax collector – but they failed to identify him as a publisher. When I used to visit him in London his daughter, Brenda, was at drama school. She is now one of the best-known character actresses in television.

I remember Frank telling me once that a publisher 'lives on great expectations of the most nebulous order'. I told him he had found the perfect phrase to describe not a publisher at all but an author. In the past fifty years, however, many of my nebulous expectations have been realized.

My adult thrillers – twenty-eight of them – have all sold fairly well in this country and in various translations abroad. I made six of them into radio plays and more than a dozen into newspaper serials. My children's books have sold well, too, almost all of them starting life as radio or television serials.

I am particularly proud of the Hebrew and Japanese editions of my science fiction stories, taking childish pleasure from explaining to my young nephews and nieces that, no matter how it may seem, they have not been placed in my bookshelves upside down. A Japanese gentleman called Toho Eizo has expressed interest in making a film of *Super Nova and the Frozen Man*; but so far nothing has come of it.

Many film companies, including Ranks, have 'shown interest' in my books and, in one or two cases, have even asked how much I'd want for the film rights. But the 'interest' has always waned. Amongst authors this is a common experience. I have learned to live with it and to look forward to success in this direction in much the same detached way as I look forward to claiming another hole in one at golf.

Sponsored by the Church of Scotland and, later, by the BBC, I have however, written a number of film scripts. The most successful, *The Old Padre*, was produced and directed by the late Ronald Falconer, head of religious broadcasting in Scotland. It pictured my father exactly as he was, kind and selfish, irascible and unselfish, a blesser of babies and chastiser of wrongdoers, a chewer of peppermints for 'the wind' who found God's love in every human thought and activity.

The Old Padre has been shown around the world. A boyhood friend of mine, Archie MacKay, who emigrated years ago to Tasmania, came in from a day's work on his farm and was shaving in the bathroom. He heard a voice on the television in the living-room and rushed through, calling out to his wife: 'That's Angus MacVicar's voice! I'd know the Southend accent anywhere!'

As the star of the film, the Padre proved slightly difficult whilst it was being made, his time-table being governed by the success or failure of his bowels after breakfast and by his habit of demanding 'a wee sleep' every afternoon. At the time he was eighty-eight years old, and it must be admitted that when he did decide to face the cameras he performed with such natural and unconscious grace that few re-takes were necessary and even the hardbitten technicians in the film-crew were astonished and delighted. Ronnie and I, therefore, remained patient and indulged the star as much as was possible within the bounds of a tight schedule.

The 'wee sleep' in the afternoons presented no real problems. After a hearty lunch at 1.30 p.m., he went to bed at two o'clock and remained there until four. This was a law as of the Medes and Persians, and we planned our shooting programme accordingly. The trouble centred upon the post-breakfast bowel movement. Sometimes this occurred after two cigarettes and the lapse of only thirty minutes. On a bad day, however, at least five cigarettes might be smoked and an hour and a half might go by before we heard the slip-slop of his slippers as he advanced purposefully upon the toilet.

Then, while we waited with our gear and our frustration on the gravel outside, he would emerge at the front door, flushed but triumphant after his exertions, waving a lordly hand. 'Good morning, boys!' he'd greet us – and it must be remembered that anyone under the age of sixty-five was a 'boy' to the Padre. 'Lovely day for the shooting work. Come on, now, better get busy while the sun shines.'

Ronnie and the cameramen, who had perhaps been waiting to do the 'shooting work' for about two hours would meekly follow him as he led the way, stumping and talking, towards the morning's location.

When the film was eventually shown on television he watched it with interest. Afterwards he said to me: 'I was very good. Fortunately I wasn't constipated at the time. You were quite good, too, though maybe a wee bit stuttery. Of course you've got to have the gift.'

How right he was.

During the past twenty years while continuing to write scripts for the BBC and ITV, I have also become a speaker on radio and on the 'box'. Now that I am seventy I may retire from doing this. Fifteen years ago it was brought to my notice that a senior programme planner had declared that at fifty-five I was far too old to be working for the BBC. (Admittedly, I couldn't, at the time, score my age on Dunaverty Golf Course. I can now.) Fortunately, I have other less unimaginative friends in the Corporation, and if I stir myself I am still allowed to compete with younger speakers and script writers. But there comes a time when the bustle and the travelling and the nervous tension before and during a broadcast lose their attraction and the sea air and a game of golf, a local church meeting or exciting drama rehearsal provide more pleasure and satisfaction.

Both Jean and I consider that my writing life, though difficult at times, has been worth while. It has given us independence and the chance to find contentment – and freedom – in a happy community. Occasionally, however, the price of independence and freedom is high.

One such price is an acceptance of the odd belief among neighbours and friends that an author has unlimited time to spare. Jobs on committees, unpaid lectures to societies and clubs of all kinds, writing previews and reports about local events for the press, negotiations with councils, researching family trees for visitors from abroad, entertaining VIPs who come to open new buildings, sales of work, drama shows, etcetera, signing unemployment cards and various other documents for beneficiaries of the state – all such time-consuming activities seem to become his responsibility in spite of every effort to avoid them.

A rubicund farmer on his way to market – and an hour or two in some congenial bar parlour – will wave a lazy hand. 'Och, I'm far too busy to do that. Give Angus the job. He has plenty of time.' When this kind of thing is said in my hearing nowadays, I never hesitate to reply: 'Plenty of time? Do you realize that every time an author stops work to oblige somebody else it costs him money and that he has no means of dunning the Government into recouping his loss? A farm-worker's wages go on, no matter how often he leans back for a chat or a smoke. A farmer's crops go on growing even while he's asleep, and if the crops fail there are subsidies and grants to make up for it.' A few of my hearers have the grace to look slightly embarrassed. The great majority laugh uproariously and slap me on the back, believing that I am making a joke.

Another price paid by a writer of books is that his money (in the form of royalties) always comes in, at the earliest, three months after he has earned it. Some publishers keep him waiting even longer.

But the heaviest burden imposed upon an author is that he is expected to work for nothing in order to benefit the customers of public libraries. Brian Aldiss, chairman of the Society of Authors, has a notable word to say about this, though he does commit the common provincial solecism of using the word 'English' when he means 'British': 'English writers are not paid for the borrowing of their books from public libraries, although the English public library system is the biggest in the western world. Writers are thus compelled to deliver their life-blood as free entertainment.'

The Society of Authors has been campaigning for a Public Lending Right Bill for almost thirty years; but Parliament, while cringing and genuflecting to miners, steel-workers, farmers, ship and car builders – not to mention printers – has continued to cold-shoulder the authors, who, of course, have only minimal voting power at General Elections.

In 1976 we thought we were winning. A PLR bill passed its First Reading and was approved by the Lords. On 14 October, after two earlier adjournments, the bill began its Second Reading in the Commons and, despite the twisting and turning and the filibustering of certain miserable MPs, was approved by a majority. At this point the authors' three main enemies were identified: Roger Moate and Iain Sproat, both Conservatives, and Michael English, Labour. They warned that in committee they would do their best to kill the bill.

They kept their promises, with spates of oratory whose sole purpose was to waste time. On one occasion Iain Sproat (who is, strange to relate, a Scot) jumped to his feet, demanding to know the number required for a quorum. Then he 'suddenly rushed from the room before ascertaining that his absence would not, in fact, hold up the committee, or prevent it from finishing its business for that session'. His tactics were to try and wreck the bill at any price.

Surprisingly, however, the bill completed it committee stage by lunch-time on 9 November, and Report and Third Reading were booked for 16 November, when all available time was to be devoted to PLR.

'Discussion,' according to *The Author*, 'started shortly before 4 pm, when filibustering began again. The three wreckers were joined by five more, so that eight MPs spoke by rota, one overlapping another repeating the same point *ad nauseum*, even if irrelevant to the amendment under discussion. Their main theme was that the bill was badly drafted, and that the 'payment for use' was invalid. Even Phillip Whitehead, a consistent supporter of PLR, spoke for many when he regretted the re-substitution of 'books' for 'works', but argued nonetheless in favour of half a bill rather than none. It was all to no purpose for, in the early hours of Wednesday, 17 November, with mountains of amendments still to discuss and barely two dozen members present, the House voted to suspend the sitting; and so the bill effectively died.'

Another attempt to introduce a PLR bill was made in 1978, but again this came to nothing. In the meantime pious noises in favour of wage rises were being made on behalf of millions of militant trade unionists (and I have no quarrel with that: good luck to all workers wise enough to organize themselves), but scarcely a whisper on behalf of a handful of humble – far too humble – authors.

Perhaps PLR *will* become law one day, though it seems that I, for one, may have been born too soon to benefit by it. In this book, whether bought or borrowed, I would appeal to all fair-minded readers to give thought to the situation. Do you support PLR, or don't you care? If you support it, please tell your MP or local authority, pointing out that if PLR becomes law, writers will be paid not from libraries but from central funds and will receive a small fee each time their work is borrowed. By doing this you will be helping to sustain literature in this country.

As may be deduced from the above, since 1936, when Jean and I built Achnamara and got married, we have spent almost as much time on amateur pursuits as on professional ones.

On the subject of getting married, I think many young people may be startled to learn that our bungalow, built on a quarter-acre site, cost only £700, the garage and a surrounding wall a further £300. Achnamara is now insured for £25 000. Our furnishings were done by the Campbeltown firm of Daniel Mathews, Cabinet Maker, Upholsterer and Removal Contractor. The other day, in a drawer of her desk, Jean came across Mathews's bill, dated 19 December, 1936. Here are some of the items from it:

1 Axminster carpet, 4 yds × 3 yds for lounge	£7-0s-0d
6 yds 72″ brown underfelt	£1-1s-0d
1 Axminster carpet, 3 yds × 3 yds for bedroom	£5-5s-0d
6 yds 54″ brown underfelt	16s-0d
7⅓ sq. yds inlaid linoleum for bathroom	£1-9s-4d
28½ sq. yds inlaid linoleum for hall and kitchenette	£4-9s-9d
Time laying carpets, lino, curtain rods, blinds, etc. (24 hours @ 1/9d, £2-2s; 7½ hours @ 2s, 15s)	£2-17s-0d
Cutting and making 7 pairs net curtains for living room and lounge	6s-6d
Cutting and making 1 pair curtains and vallance for bedroom	2s-6d

1 piano stool	£1-15s-0d
1 kitchen table	£1-15s-0d
1 umbrella stand	11s-0d
1 rose coloured wastepaper basket	5s-0d

Over the years this last item has always been well filled, mainly with copy paper ripped from my typewriter and crumpled into despairing balls. Its clear colour has been tarnished by the smoke of thousands of cigarettes. But at five shillings it has paid its way. So has Jean's piano stool, the umbrella stand and the kitchen table. Perhaps our son Jock, when he becomes an old man, will be able to sell them as antiques.

A young couple setting up home today may be inclined to envy our situation in 1936. It should be remembered, however, that my annual income at the time was only about £350. Inflation and a decimal currency tend to blur the perspective.

Just as a modern permissive society tends to blur one's perspective in regard to religion.

My father was a minister of the Church of Scotland. Jean's father came of a long line of faithful churchgoers. At the beginning there is no doubt we were both bulldozed into attending Sunday School and, later, the church.

On the principle that the son of a strict teetotaller often reacts by becoming a heavy drinker, as a minister's son I could easily have taken a 'scunner' at the Church, which sometimes echoes with negative disciplines. And I confess that when the bulldozing stopped I was often tempted to favour the easy and attractive 'worship in the green fields' policy.

Then I began to understand how much the Church had done – and is still doing – for people in all stations of life. It was a pioneer of education and the social services long before the bureaucrats took over. It still provides the love and sharing care that is sometimes lacking in Government departments. I found that I wanted to be part of it. I found I *wanted* to go to church. And, finally, I found I *liked* going to church. So did Jean. So did Jock, as he grew up.

A communist might argue that we had been 'hooked', victims of 'the opium of the people'. He would be arguing from ignorance, of course, because a communist knows nothing about the freedom of the will, and a professing Christian's condition is that he is faced constantly with having to make choices.

In simple terms, I like going to church because it makes me happy to sing and pray and to share such happiness with other people when all social defences are down and when, for an hour or so, we can all forget the world and be at peace.

When Jean persuaded Barbara, once our daily help, to attend a Christmas service, Barbara enjoyed it, with two reservations. 'Yon solo aboot Jerusalem – I'd far raither it had been *Scots Wha Ha'e*! And I could ha'e been daein' wi' a wee cup o' tea at half-time.'

I agree with Barbara. Black clothes and mournful attitudes seem to me to be out of place at a religious service. Jesus died to make us happy. If we go on moaning and groaning about it, where is the point of His sacrifice?

For me there is happiness and tranquility in a well-filled church and always a new awareness of the dignity of humanity. I am grateful that a Man died to make this possible. And I am sure He would be the last to object if Barbara and Jean and I shared 'a wee cup o' tea at half-time'.

Jean and I joined the church in order to share happiness with others. Because of this I became an elder and Jean a member of the Woman's Guild. We do not claim to be good Christians, but we get occasional glimpses of the light of love. Such glimpses, I believe, are worth working for. And the spiritual faith necessary to sustain Christianity has always been a buttress for the material faith of one author at least in his ability to live by writing.

I am grateful to my parents for many things. Most of all that by precept and example they showed me that religious roads are not haphazard but have been built in the past by men of good will reaching forward towards a satisfying life.

To me, as to many far more gifted writers they are mist shrouded ways, though sign-posts may sometimes be seen, darkly, in the course of determined reconnaissance.

Modern fashionable thought tends to dismiss religion – and the Christian religion in particular – as being a fad for the few, irrelevant to a sophisticated existence. This, I believe, is ignorant thought, uttered without a proper knowledge of the human condition. 'Man,' said Edmund Burke, reflecting on the French Revolution, 'is by his constitution a religious animal.' I think he meant that the human mind is naturally tuned to a religious wavelength, that in spite of frequent oscillations in the wavelength a man cannot escape from it, be he prophet or priest, poet, publican, politician or prole. The desk at which he reads or writes, the hod he carries on a building site, his safety equipment in a coalmine, the tractor he drives when ploughing an open field – everything he sees or touches has a religious significance.

Poets throughout the ages have all acknowledged this. St Columba wrote a *Rune of Hospitality*:

I saw a stranger yestreen:
I put food in the eating-place,
Drink in the drinking-place,
Music in the listening-place:
And, in the sacred name of the Triune,
He blessed myself and my house,
My cattle and my dear ones.
For the lark said in her song,
Often, often, often comes the Christ
in the stranger's guise.

William Blake also had a vision of how the mind of carnal man is tuned:

The pride of the peacock is the glory of God.
The lust of the goat is the beauty of God.
The wrath of the Lion is the wisdom of God.
The nakedness of woman is the work of God.

Robert Burns had a vision, too, though a more homely one:

Th' expectant wee-things, toddlin', stacher through
To meet their Dad, wi' flichterin' noise an' glee.
His wee bit ingle, blinkin' bonnilie,
His clean hearth-stane, his thriftie wifie's smile,

The lisping infant prattling on his knee,
Does a' his weary care an' kiaugh beguile,
An' makes him quite forget his labour an' his toil.

The trouble with contemporary 'fashionable' thinkers is that they perceive sentiment in religion; and in the late twentieth century sentiment has become something which must be avoided at all costs, being unproductive, materially speaking. And it tends to undermine the authority of the state. But again they are arguing from ignorance and a confusion of thought. Cardinal Newman said: 'Religion, as a mere sentiment, is to me a dream and a mockery.' Mathew Arnold gives a more positive explanation: 'The true meaning of religion is not simply morality, but morality touched with emotion.'

In *The Phenomenon of Man*, Teilhard de Chardin has his own way of supporting St Columba, Blake and Burns in their belief that religion and all ordinary things are woven together: 'Christian love is incomprehensible to those who have not experienced it. That the infinite and the intangible can be lovable, or that the human heart can beat with genuine charity for a neighbour, seems impossible to many people I know – in fact almost monstrous. But whether it be founded on an illusion or not, how can we doubt that such a sentiment exists, and even in greater intensity? . . . Is it not a fact, as I can warrant, that if the love of God were extinguished in the souls of the faithful, the enormous edifice of rites, heirarchy and doctrine that comprise the church would instantly revert to the dust from which it rose?'

I believe there is no escape from religion, even in the performance of our prosaic and apparently material daily work. But St Paul has indicated through his letter to the Philippians, how we may cope with the situation. 'Finally, brethren,' he wrote, 'whatsoever things are true, whatsoever things are honest, whatsoever things are just, whatsoever things are pure, whatsoever things are lovely, whatsoever things are of good report; if there be any virtue, and if there be any praise, think on these things.'

From all this philosophical clamjamphrie it has probably

become clear that my religious aspirations are as far from satisfactory fulfilment as the literary aspirations first fertilized by my reading of *The Rudiments of Criticism*. But in both directions I struggle on. I recognize that my best is not good enough, but still I try, panting and peching a little, to achieve it.

10. Murder in Lettermore

I expect I shall die, in the middle of a chapter.

Now that I have reached my 'three score years and ten' I write less desperately than I used to do, avoiding deadlines and ulcer-creating contracts as much as possible. I give myself more time for Jean, for the church, for golf and the drama. But I don't think I will ever retire from writing. For one thing, I'd be miserable if I denied the MacVicar birthright and ceased all attempts to preach and teach and tell stories. For another, I cannot afford to stop, with the old age pension at its present level.

So each morning, after breakfast, I have a walk along the shore, in order to plan the day ahead and to breathe in lungfuls of salty air as an insurance against the cigarette smoke which will surely follow it. Sometimes I find logs and sticks washed in by the tide. I carry them home for sawing into convenient lengths for the fire. Then I sit down and write until lunchtime: 600 words if I am lucky and nobody comes in for a 'crack'.

In the afternoon, if the weather is reasonable, I play golf. (If blizzards blow I remain inside and type out what I wrote in longhand in the morning.) I tell people that I play golf in order to keep fit. The truth is that though I have never been an expert performer I love the game. When I score in less than my age (which, I admit, is not often) it makes me feel that I still retain the vitality necessary to be a writer. When I have a bad round I share my sorrow with Jean, who comforts me into forgetting about it.

In the winter evenings there is the drama. There are church meetings, too, and for Jean the Woman's Guild and the 'Rural'. In the summer evenings there is the garden, with the problems created by onion bugs and carrot fly and the dreadful chore of trying to keep an old lawn tidy. Thankfully, my Atco motor-mower, purchased in 1954, still performs with reliability.

Such continuing amateur endeavour tends to leave me with little time for introspection. But since this book is about me as a writer, I suppose I ought to make an effort at self-analysis. I'll do it my way.

While writing for various media – book publishing, newspapers, radio, television, films, the stage – I have always wanted to tell a story. And it seems, from the evidence, that I am a better storyteller than I am a philosopher.

Before I can succeed in telling an exciting story I must be excited myself, which, I suppose, though I pretend to be a cool professional, betrays an essential amateurism. My first adult thriller, *The Purple Rock*, was born of excitement, the excitement of bringing to life on paper some characters and some places well known to me. So was *The Crocodile Men*, my first Children's Hour radio serial for Kathleen Garscadden, which had as a background Madagascar in time of war. So was *Minister's Monday*, my first film, written for the Church of Scotland about the work of a clergyman. So was *The Lost Planet*, my first television serial, directed in London by Kevin Sheldon. So was *Murder in Lettermore*, my first stage play, commissioned by Bob Christie Park (Argyll County Council's answer to Tyrone Guthrie) for a festival in Duror, the parish of my birth in North Argyll.

Murder in Lettermore is a real-life whodunnit, the most famous (or infamous) thriller in West Highland history. Robert Louis Stevenson heard its echoes and from the bare bones of fact produced *Kidnapped* and *Catriona*.

The story concerns the murder in 1752 of Colin Campbell of Glenure and the subsequent trial of James Stewart of the Glen (*Seumas a Ghlinne*). I heard it first from my mother, a native of Appin, only a few miles from Duror where the murder took place. According to her, James Stewart was falsely accused; but though she claimed to know the name of the real murderer, not even for my benefit would she put a name to him. In the end, after studying a number of relevant documents, both official and unofficial, I decided to write a play which would indicate my idea of the truth.

In 1752 James Stewart occupied the farm of Acharn in Duror. His half-brother, Ardshiel, had been exiled after the '45; and in consequence James was the recognized leader of his clansmen. He was in middle life, a practical man of affairs and a member of the Episcopal Church.

In addition to his own young family, he had reared a boy called Allan Stewart, the orphan child of a relative. Allan's by-name was 'Breck', from the Gaelic, meaning 'pock-marked'. He had taken part in the Jacobite campaign right up to Culloden and then, like his chieftain Ardshiel, had escaped to France. From there, with some courage, he returned at intervals to Duror, to collect for Ardshiel the secret gifts of his clansmen.

At thirty, Allan Breck was a wild, hard-drinking character; but he seldom missed an opportunity of denouncing the Campbells, to whose gentle mercies the Hanoverian Government in London had entrusted the West Highlands. One man in particular was an object of his tirades – Captain Colin Campbell of Glenure.

Auburn-haired Glenure was nicknamed 'the Red Fox'. He was, by all accounts, a decent enough man; but to Allan Breck – and indeed, to all the Stewarts in North Argyll – he was tainted by three deadly sins. He was a Campbell. He had fought for the Hanoverians against the Jacobites. And now, in addition to being laird of Glenure, he had undertaken the duties of factor on Ardshiel's forfeited estates.

At first, however, James Stewart found him friendly and easy to get on with. The factor was ignorant in agricultural matters and had often made use of James's better knowledge. But in the spring of 1752 Glenure was reprimanded by the Commissioners for the Forfeited Estates for being too sib with the Stewarts; and, in an unwilling attempt to restore his authority, he quarrelled openly with James. Allan Breck was in the neighbourhood at the time, and it is likely that he encouraged his foster father's resentment.

But worse was to come. A few weeks later, a number of Ardshiel's Jacobite tenants were ordered by Glenure, on behalf of the Commissioners, to quit their holdings by Whit Sunday. James immediately championed the cause of his clansmen, broke definitely with Glenure and went to Edinburgh in an effort to procure a suspension of the removing process. On 5 May, however, the Court refused the suspension and James returned to Duror, reflective and dour.

On 14 May, accompanied by his servant, John MacKenzie, and by Mungo Campbell, a lawyer from Edinburgh, and Donald Kennedy, a sheriff officer from Inveraray, Glenure set out from Fort William to carry out the evictions.

On the old road which still winds along the hillside between Ballachulish and Kentallen, the party went in Indian file. As they reached Lettermore ('the hanging coppice') the lawyer was in front on horseback, followed by the sheriff officer on foot and by Glenure and his servant, both riding. It was a beautiful summer day, with warm quiet in the glen. But suddenly, in the green stillness, shots rang out. Glenure fell from his horse with two bullets in his back; and a man with a short, dun-coloured coat was seen escaping along the hillside, carrying a gun. (It was an elaborately wrought long Spanish gun, still called by the Gaelic tale-tellers *An-t-Slinneanach*, 'the gun of the misfortune'.)

Colin Campbell died almost at once, his blood oozing out among the green shoots of bracken. Mungo Campbell remained by the body, but MacKenzie galloped off for help, reaching in a short time the farm of Acharn. There he found James Stewart working in a field and blurted out the news of the tragedy. James stood upright. 'Ah, John,' he said in the Gaelic, 'whoever is the culprit I shall be the victim.'

And so it proved. A well-known Campbell had been murdered in Stewart country. Smouldering hate engendered in the '15 and '45 had once more been fanned into flame. An example must be made. It must be shown that the King's writ could run in Argyll and that Crown factors would be protected or at any rate avenged. Suspicion naturally fell upon Allan Breck, but equally that character had fled to the hills and was on his way to safety in France.

Who next as scapegoat? James Stewart was the man – and James Stewart was arrested.

On 21 September 1752, after spending four months in a filthy jail, he was brought to trial in the old court house at Inveraray. Clad in rumpled broadcloth, he stood in the prisoner's box and watched the jury and the three red-robed judges filing in. Justice was about to be done. Justice with eleven Campbells in a jury of fifteen. Justice with a presiding judge who was none other than Archibald, third Duke of Argyll, head of Clan Campbell and arch-enemy of the Stewarts. Justice which had already allowed possible defence witnesses to be threatened and suborned and even to be held incommunicado during the trial.

'James Stewart, you are indicted at the instance of His Majesty's Advocate and also at the instance of Janet MacKay, relict of the deceased, as being guilty in art and part with Allan Breck Stewart of the murder of Colin Campbell of Glenure.'

When the clerk had finished, Argyll turned to the prisoner. 'What have you to say?'

James Stewart looked at his enemy. 'My Lord, I am not guilty and refer to my lawyers to make my defence.'

Walter Stewart, younger of South-hall, though only a junior counsel, opened for the accused; and his words shine with courage and eloquence even in the dusty records. 'I cannot help complaining of the most intolerable hardships which the panel has undergone since May last. For six weeks no mortal was allowed to see him. After that, indeed, admittance was given to his wife; but his lawyers were carefully denied him until only three days before this trial. His house at Acharn has been searched three separate times and papers carried off by military force, without a warrant. These are hardships which, thanks be to God, meet with no encouragement in this free country. . . . The panel, enjoying the privileges of every free-born Briton, expects from his judges the greatest impartiality, and the same from the gentlemen of the jury.'

In conclusion he made two submissions. First, that the prisoner, charged only as an accessary, should not be tried until the principal, Allan Breck, was apprehended and found guilty. Second, that the facts and circumstances mentioned in the libel were not sufficient to infer his being an accessory to the murder.'

The answer was given by Simon Fraser, a junior counsel for the prosecution, whose legal casuistry would have done credit to his father, the notorious Lord Lovat of the '45. Rebutting the 'plea in bar of trial', he declared: 'It signifies as little what is the law of neighbouring nations, as what was once our own law, if custom, the greatest of all legislators, has now enacted the contrary.'

He went on to give a detailed account of the murder and the causes which led up to it, making his assertions as confidently as if he had been a witness rather than a pleader.

James Stewart and Allan Breck, he said, had uttered public threats against Glenure; but in the end they had decided that the only way to stop his evicting the tenants of Ardshiel was to murder him. 'This plan having been settled, James furnished his friend with a suit of his own – a dark short-coat with white buttons – and, thus equipped, Allan went first to Fasnacloich and then to Ballachulish to await the time when Glenure would cross the ferry on his way into Duror. He questioned the ferryman about Glenure; then immediately ran up the hill, from whence he had a short passage into Lettermore. And it was some time later, my Lords, in this same glen of Lettermore, that Allan Breck Stewart seized his long wished for opportunity, and when Glenure was come within convenient distance this abandoned assassin shot him dead with two bullets from behind –'

At this point, we are told, Simon Fraser stopped abruptly as a youth, dark and wild-eyed, rose shouting from his seat in the public benches: 'It is a lie! I cannot thole it . . .'

Urgent friends silenced the interrupter, who, according to the tale-tellers, was young James Stewart of Fasnacloich. Argyll stared down his long nose. 'Mr Fraser,' he said, 'pray continue.'

Simon Fraser bowed. 'My Lords, I have described the murder. And while Allan Breck pointed the black gun of the misfortune, what of the prisoner here? James Stewart remained at Acharn – and never once offered to go near the corpse. His own preservation was so closely linked with

Allan Breck's that he immediately despatched Alexander Stewart, a kinsman of his own, with money and French clothes to assist the murderer's escape. . . . These, my Lords, are the facts and the circumstances which, I submit, are more than sufficient to infer the crime libelled.'

The court, which consisted of Lord Elchies and Lord Kilkerran in addition to Argyll, then repelled Walter Stewart's two submissions and ordered the trial to proceed.

One of the first witnesses for the prosecution was Alexander Campbell, a dour, heavily built innkeeper from Teynaluib. At the end of April, he said, the prisoner had called at his house on the way to Edinburgh and had been supplied with corn for his horse and a dram for himself. A friend of the witness's had said to James Stewart: 'Give the man of the house a dram in return.' But James Stewart had retorted: 'No, indeed. The only thing I would give a Campbell would be the gibbet!' Witness asked him if he were thinking about Glenure, and James Stewart replied that perhaps he was, and that Glenure had no right to evict tenants from the Ardshiel estates.

Leading defence counsel was George Brown of Coalston, small, pugnacious and widely respected as an advocate. He rose to cross-examine.

'Mr Campbell, you are a man of the world and used to the ways of Highlanders. Didn't it occur to you that James Stewart was joking when he mentioned the gibbet?'

'No, sir. I thought he was in earnest.'

'Come now, did you not part friends?'

'Well, ay, I suppose we did.'

'And James Stewart gave you a dram after all?'

'Ay, but only half a gill.'

Next to give evidence was Mungo Campbell, the young Edinburgh lawyer who had accompanied Glenure on his last journey through Lettermore. 'As we entered the glen,' he said, 'there was a shot. I heard Glenure cry out, "Oh, I am shot!" I dismounted and ran back –' He broke off, sweating and trembling.

The Lord Advocate, William Grant of Prestongrange, raised a sympathetic hand. 'Take it gently, Mr Campbell.'

The witness wiped his forehead. 'Glenure still sat his horse. He said to me, "Take care, he's going to shoot you!" Then I looked up towards the hillside. I saw a man, a man with a short, dark-coloured coat and a gun in his hand. He was running away from me, and though I pursued him at once, he made good his escape. When I returned, Colin Campbell was on the ground. I could see that he was dying, and I sent John MacKenzie into Duror for help. Then he died, and as darkness was coming down I sent the sheriff officer back to Ballachulish. In about an hour he returned with assistance.'

Cross-examining, George Brown underlined the fact that the witness was a nephew of the murdered man's.

He continued: 'Mr Campbell, you say you made out the clothes worn by the murderer as he escaped. Were you close enough to see his face?'

'No, sir.'

'Was he knock-kneed, with a shambling gait?'

'I didn't notice,'

Another prosecution witness was Archibald MacInnes, a big, canny ferryman from Ballachulish. He told how Allan Breck had approached him on the day of the murder, to ask when Glenure would be crossing the ferry. Allan, he said, had been wearing a 'dark-coloured coat, with white buttons', which he identified as belonging to the prisoner.

For the defence, George Brown put only two questions. 'You seem to know Allan Breck fairly well?'

'Och, I've seen him here and there.'

'In that case you can confirm that he is noticeably knock-kneed?'

'Ay, so he is. A feckless-looking cratur.'

Young Donald Stewart of Ballachulish said he had seen Allan Breck on the hillside near Ballachulish House only a few hours after the murder. Allan was wearing a dark coat. He had heard of the murder and was planning to leave the country, because he was afraid he might be accused of it. Being short of money, however, he wanted witness to tell James Stewart at Acharn to send him money and clothes to a place in Glencoe.

'And did you tell James Stewart?' asked the Lord Advocate.

'I told him.'

'And he sent the money to Allan Breck?'

'Ay. On the Sunday it was. I met Alexander Stewart in Glencoe – Alexander Stewart the packman – and he told me he was taking five guineas and some French clothes to Allan Breck.'

In the cross-examination of this witness by George Brown there may be detected odd undercurrents.

'First of all, Mr Stewart – going back to the day before the murder. Did anyone else besides Allan Breck stay at your house that night?'

'Ay. Young Stewart of Fasnacloich.'

'He was a close friend of Allan Breck's?'

Donald Stewart did not answer.

George Brown continued: 'There was a set of young men in Appin – young Fasnacloich, yourself and one or two others – who went about with Allan Breck, publicly condemning the Campbells?'

Again there was no answer, and from the records it would appear that George Brown changed abruptly to a new line of questioning. Had he received a warning glance from the prisoner?

An unwilling witness was James Stewart's servant, Katharine MacColl, who was only sixteen. Nervously she told how on the day after the murder, at Acharn, she had seen the prisoner's wife put a blue side-coat and red waistcoat into a sack.

'You took that sack out on to the moor and hid it?' prompted the Lord Advocate.

'Yes. The packman was to pick it up. But please, sir, my master had nothing to do with the murder. I swear it!'

'That question will be answered by cleverer people than you, my dear. Now, during this summer, when the murder of Mr Campbell was being investigated, did Mrs Stewart tell you not to mention what you knew about the clothes?'

Katharine sobbed. 'She said not to speak about them to strangers.'

Though many other witnesses were put into the box, that, in essence, was the case for the prosecution. A plea by the defence that in justice the case ought to be abandoned for lack of evidence was rejected out of hand by Argyll. Lord Elchies and Lord Kilkerran, cowed by their colleague's stronger personality, spinelessly concurred. In the stuffy court house the trial moved to its inevitable climax.

For the defence, witnesses were few; and it may be significant that though the name of James Stewart, younger of Fasnacloich, appears on the official list, there is no record that he was called.

John Stewart, younger of Ballachulish, said he had never heard the prisoner utter threats against Glenure. James of the Glen was angry when the Ardshiel tenants were to be evicted, but he did not blame Glenure, personally.

'You frequently saw Glenure in the panel's company?'

'Yes. They were always friendly. Only last Hogmanay they drank together at the inn, and on New Year's Day Glenure had dinner at Acharn.'

'James Stewart has a dry sense of humour?'

'Ay. He used to tease Glenure about being a Campbell, and with a long face he would say that all Campbells should be hanged on a gibbet. But Glenure was fit-sides for him. He would turn round and say that the Stewarts should be hanged even higher. Then they would laugh together.'

He added that the prisoner had often helped Allan Breck out of the country before. After the murder, James had said he would do so again, though he did not think Allan had anything to do with the crime.

Simon Fraser rose to cross-examine. 'You are, of course, a Stewart?'

'Ay, and proud of it!'

'You would never betray a member of your clan?'

'Never!'

'Quite so,' said Lord Lovat's son and sat down.

Another witness, Duncan Stewart of Glenbuckie, made the point that he had seen Allan Breck wearing the dun-coloured coat long before the murder. In April, in fact.

George Brown said: 'The prosecution allege that a day or

two before the murder James Stewart gave that coat to Allan Breck, so that he might not be too conspicuous. You are quite sure that you saw him wearing it as early as April?'

'As sure as I am standing here!'

At last it was time for the Lord Advocate to address the jury. He reiterated the case for the prosecution, stressing four major points. First, that James Stewart and Allan Breck, 'conjunct and confident persons', had uttered threats against Glenure. Second, that the murderer had worn a short, dun-coloured coat and that Allan Breck, at the time of the murder, had been wearing a similar garment. Third, that the prisoner had been apprehensive for his own safety. And fourth, that James Stewart and his wife had facilitated Allan Breck's escape by sending him money and French clothes.

But at the end, with a scrupulous fairness which must have irritated the presiding judge, he reminded the jury: 'In all circumstantial evidence there is a possibility of innocence. If you can believe that Allan Breck committed the murder purely on his own accord, then it will be your duty to acquit the panel.'

George Brown spoke for the defence. Squat and grim, aware of the hostile atmosphere in the court, he defied the brooding menace of Argyll.

'Gentlemen of the jury,' he said, 'all along the prisoner has been labouring under a disadvantage. An impression has been industriously raised that the panel, being a Stewart, *must* be guilty, and that if he is acquitted it may be a reflection on this part of the kingdom.'

He went on to state the obvious, that in general all the evidence led by the prosecution broke down at once under examination. 'Nor have they proved that Allan Breck is guilty,' he went on. 'On the contrary, Mungo Campbell admits there was nothing remarkable about the gait of the murderer as he escaped along the hillside; and Allan Breck is notoriously knock-kneed.'

At this point the foreman of the jury, Duncan Campbell of South-hall, interrupted rudely: 'Pray, sir, cut it short! The trial has lasted long enough.'

'Yes, sir,' George Brown blazed back at him, 'it has lasted

long. And if this is your attitude to a man's struggle for his life, then the memory of a great injustice will last even longer!'

In conclusion, defence counsel emphasised the point that Allan Breck was the prisoner's foster son. 'If James Stewart sent him money and clothes after the murder, it was something he had done many times before, the act of a generous and perhaps over-indulgent guardian.'

There was no summing up by Argyll, otherwise known as the Lord Justice General. He knew his men. In a short time the jury brought in a unanimous verdict of guilty. Sentence of death was intoned by the dempster.

In a speech which gives a remarkable insight into his character, Argyll addressed the prisoner: 'James Stewart, we have had a long and most impartial trial, but your guilt is plain. You ate Colin Campbell's bread, then shed his blood. You are one of those incurable enemies of our good and gracious King, stirring up disaffection with every word you speak. Had you and your Highland friends been successful in the rebellion of 1745, you would now have been trampling on the liberties of your fellow subjects. We, who this day are your judges, would have been tried before one of your mock Courts of Judicature and in all likelihood sentenced cruelly to death.'

How often similar speeches have been heard since, in Germany, Russia, Africa, the Middle East, in America, South America and the Far East. And, more's the pity, in the United Kingdom. Political scheming and private hatred are like the bishop-weed in my garden, almost impossible to eradicate.

On 8 November, before a gathering of his countrymen, James Stewart stood beneath a gibbet on *Cnap Chaolis Mhic Pharuig*, near the south end of the new Ballachulish bridge. He met his death with courage, repeating aloud the 35th Psalm, known to this day in the West Highlands as 'James of the Glen's Psalm'.

'I am not afraid to die,' he told his friends. 'But what grieves me is my character, that after ages should think me capable of such a barbarous crime. I declare my complete innocence. Nevertheless, I bear no grudge against the jury and the witnesses; and may this my hard fate put an end to all discords among you. May Stewart and Campbell be united in brotherly love and charity; and may God grant us all a joyful meeting at the Great Day of Judgment.'

Over a hundred years later, John Francis Campbell of Islay collected and wrote down several Gaelic tales relevant to the murder. These were later incorporated in a compendium of Argyll folklore known as the Dewar Manuscripts. According to the Dewar MSS (which, it must be made clear, was a Campbell enterprise), while Donald Stewart of Ballachulish and young James Stewart of Fasnacloich were watching James of the Glen being hanged in chains, Donald had to be restrained by friends from shouting a public confession.

Another of John Francis Campbell's tales provides an interesting sequel. Many years after the murder, when the Stewarts and the Campbells had become friendly again – on the surface, at any rate – Stewart of Ballachulish and Alexander, the brother of Glenure, went shooting together. With his long gun Donald Stewart brought down a stag at long range. Alexander Campbell examined the peculiar double wound in the stag and immediately identified it with the bullet holes in his late brother's back.

'The talk,' says the manuscript, 'produced a coldness between the two. They separated, and each of them chose a road for himself to go home, and they did not henceforth go to hunt together.'

Who shot 'the red fox'?

Allan Breck was charged in his absence with having fired 'the gun of the misfortune', with James of the Glen as an accessary before and after. Allan was certainly capable of such a deed; but, remembering his long experience as a hunted guerilla, I believe that had he done it he would have made a more efficient job of both the killing and the getaway.

My mother's story hinted at a conspiracy hatched by a number of young men in North Argyll, all Stewarts or sib to the Stewarts. This may come near the truth. I reckon that a secret IRA-like meeting was held at which it was decided that Colin Campbell of Glenure, representative of a suppressive and hated regime, should be murdered. Whose gun was best suited to accomplish the killing at long range? And which of the young men should fire it? The long Spanish gun belonging to Donald Stewart of Ballachulish, much superior in every way to weapons of local manufacture, was an obvious answer to the first question. The answer to the second, as I imagine it, was decided by lot. And I think, in common with many another canny storyteller in the West Highlands, that the short straw was drawn by young James Stewart of Fasnacloich.

I also think that James of the Glen knew all about the conspiracy, though he took no active part in it himself and probably disapproved of any violent reaction to Campbell enmity. Why, then, in order to save his life, did he not turn King's evidence? The answer is simple. He was the 'father' of his clan. And its protector. He gathered all the guilt into himself and allowed his young clansmen to remain alive.

Murder in Lettermore was staged in a marquee at the Duror Festival in July 1951. Outside, the rain and the wind howled insults at a Scottish summer. But inside, a local audience forgot about the weather as the story was told of events which, two hundred years before, had occurred in the surrounding green countryside.

As well as being a 'first' for me, it was also a 'first' for John Cairney, the actor. Still at drama college, he played his first big part – that of Argyll, the presiding judge at the trial – with imagination and astonishing maturity.

I have written about Colin Campbell's murder in some detail because, having been brought up with the thrill of it – at my mother's knee, so to speak – I came to recognize that a thriller with similar question marks was the kind of book I wanted to write.

I also recognize that *Murder in Lettermore* has a kind of affinity with the news stories which today come out of many countries around the world. It tells of political intrigue, of angry young men resorting to violence when tired politicians cease to talk, of authoritarianism refusing to recognize the divinity which resides in every individual. And of a man, who, even in the face of death, can still forgive his enemies and show the way to a happier future.

James Stewart of the Glen was doubtless no saint. But his final words have often helped me to recover a sense of proportion when spite and a desire to do violence (in word if not in deed) threaten to submerge more worthy instincts.

Not long ago I met James MacTaggart on the street in Campbeltown. We talked about James of the Glen and the peculiarly Highland characteristics of the story which appealed to us as Highlanders ourselves. Even as old men we were suddenly excited when the idea sparked between us that we might write a 'musical' based on the tragedy, words by MacVicar, music by MacTaggart.

Then I told James I was writing this book and reminded him of the old days at Kilblaan, when he gave me *The Rudiments of Criticism* and we had discussed poetry into 'the wee sma' 'oors'.

'I'm afraid I never reached your high ideals of writing,' I said.

He laughed. Had there been eyes behind the dark glasses they would have been twinkling. 'I'm afraid I never reached your high ideals of music. But I made my living by it, and you made yours by writing. We can't have been all that bad.'

'Thwarted amateurs?' I said.

He laughed again. He said: 'You could be right at that.'

Index

BEES IN MY BONNET

Angus MacVicar

BEES IN MY BONNET

Reminiscences of a Highland boyhood

Fifty years ago my first book, *The Purple Rock*, was accepted for publication by Hutchinson (Stanley Paul). I dedicated it to my father and mother, the Rev. Angus John and Marjorie MacVicar. This one, the thirty-third of my books accepted by Hutchinson, I dedicate to their happy and inspiring memory.

Contents

1. The Ghost in the Graveyard

On 7 May 1912, I was three and a half years old. Archie, the eldest of my four brothers, was born that day. It is the first specific date I can remember; and I remember it for two reasons, both traumatic for a small boy in a big manse.

My father had been minister of the parish of Southend, at the Mull of Kintyre, for over two years. On an annual stipend of £180 he was yet able to afford two maids. One was Maimie, from Perthshire, five feet nothing of flashing temper and Gaelic kindliness. The other was Ina, a happy, red-haired girl from Campbeltown – the 'Wee Toun' – which embraces the loch of the song eight miles north of the Manse over a metalled road.

There is no question that in the Manse of St Blaan, with six bedrooms, a drawing-room and dining-room, a large kitchen and scullery and eight outhouses – one of them an earth closet – Maimie and Ina were kept busy all day, especially at times when my mother was bearing and nursing her babies, which occurred often during the first twenty-one years of her married life. Each time, on the whispered advice of her mother and grandmother, she prepared not only baby clothes but also a shroud for herself. The 'good old days' were anything but 'good', as far as women were concerned.

Maimie and Ina had to rise early, at about half past six, in order to set and light fires in the drawing-room and in the dining-room which served, too, as my father's study. And in the kitchen, where all the cooking was done on a great iron range. The fire in the range was also supposed to heat water in the copper boiler above it; but sometimes it didn't. Then Maimie, hitching up her black druggit skirt and white apron, would stand on one of the kitchen chairs (manufactured by

Sandy MacCullum, the local joiner), strike the pipes of the boiler hard blows with a poker and swear at them in the Gaelic. As a cooking medium, however, the range was efficient enough, though, along with the other fires, it devoured a ton of coal a week. (Before the First World War coal cost about ten shillings a ton. Your Scargills and McGaheys, where were they then?)

The fires had to be primed with paper and what Maimie called 'morning sticks', dry kindlers which she and Ina used to collect nearly every day from among the whins on the hillside behind the Manse. Then the porridge oatmeal, which had been steeping in water overnight, had to be salted and put on the range to cook – and be stirred regularly to avoid lumps – for the best part of two hours. No packets of instant Porage (*sic*) in those days. Ground from oats harvested in the fields around us, the meal came straight from the water mill at Machrimore, half a mile down the road. And savoury it was, eaten with a bowl of milk into which we dipped each horn spoonful.

For the minister, when he came downstairs at about half past nine, calling for his boots (polished in the kitchen the night before by either Maimie or Ina), there was supplied also a dish of ham and eggs: this to sustain his strength as he pedalled around the parish on his bicycle, visiting the old, the infirm and the recalcitrant. For the rest of us, porridge and a cup of tea were considered sufficient.

But on the morning of 7 May 1912, I became aware that something out of the ordinary was happening. Nobody wakened me in my small bedroom at the back of the house. I came downstairs, slowly and uneasily, and found nobody in the dining-room. The breakfast table wasn't even set. Suddenly frightened, I rushed to the kitchen. Ina was boiling kettles on the range. Maimie pushed past me as if I were invisible, carrying towels and jugs of hot water and muttering fiercely to herself.

'Where's Mamma? Where's Dadda?' I demanded.

Ina said, 'Your mother's not well. Your father's gone on his bicycle for the doctor.'

'I want to see Mamma.'

'No. Stay here. She'll be better soon. Here, sit at the table.' Her voice, usually so caressing, was hard, authoritative. 'I'll make you a piece.'

The world was turning upside down. I was no longer important. Nobody cared for me. Resentful tears had to be blinked away, because, even though I cried out loud, it seemed that nobody would listen.

I gulped down a jelly sandwich and went out into the garden: a huge garden with flowers and vegetables. There were gooseberries and currants and apple trees, too; but as their fruits were only in the early stages of growth I could not plunder and eat them to find comfort. Then I saw that Geordie, the odd-job man from the village, was already at work in the sunshine, earthing up potatoes.

Geordie had a ragged beard, though he was only middle-aged, and grey eyes that were cold and unfriendly. In his snarling voice he often used to call me names. For example: 'Get oot o' there, ye wee bugger!' When I told my mother about this and asked her the meaning of the word 'bugger' there was consternation in the Manse. If I used such a word again, I was told, my mouth would have to be washed out with soap and water. The reason for this was beyond my understanding. It was many years later that the exact meaning of 'bugger' was revealed to me, by an erudite schoolmaster.

Hatred for Geordie smouldered in my heart. That morning I saw him before he saw me. I took avoiding action by crawling along behind one of the rose beds and entering the outside closet, where gardening grapes, rakes and hoes stood beside the wooden seat. I pushed my pants down and clambered onto the seat. At that time small boys were just beginning to wear pants instead of effeminate frocks. The pair I wore had been designed and made by my mother from an old red dress of her own. A quarter of a century later she made ones for my son, Jock, on the same pattern and from much the same material. Dangling my legs and feeling low and unhappy, I suffered stoically the splintery feel of earth-encrusted wood on my bare bottom.

After a time I accomplished my duty. This made me feel

less martyred. Now nobody would threaten me with a tablespoon and the castor-oil bottle.

I used the torn-off corner of an old *Glasgow Herald* – a pile of newspapers served as a toilet roll – pulled up my pants and wandered off, by way of a broken down stone wall, into the hill where the whins grew. Whin spikes scratched my bare legs; the acrid, lusty scent of young summer in the whin blooms disturbed me. I felt unhappy again, even though a few young rabbits, scuttering on a bare patch of grass, afforded me temporary amusement.

I sat down on the bare patch, but even the rabbits were not prepared to be friendly. They took sidelong looks at me, then slipped off into the whins and disappeared.

By this time somebody ought to have discovered that I was missing and begun calling out for me. But no calls came, and I decided that the disappearing game was useless, as far as drawing attention to myself was concerned. I went back to the garden and moved round to the outhouses near the road, still keeping out of Geordie's sight.

In the stable I heard the sound of mewing. I pushed open the door. The interior was shadowed and smelt strongly of horse dung, because when people visited the Manse, or members of the congregation came to church on a Sunday in their 'machines', their horses were tethered here-with bags of oats slung around their muzzles. I saw Susie, our ginger cat, crouching in a dark corner.

Surely here, at any rate, was a friend. I ran towards her, then stopped. Three small, damp, ugly kittens sprawled and squirmed beside her, and she was giving birth to yet another. It was the first time I had seen anything being born, and it made me feel scared.

But even in my ignorance I could see that Susie was discomfited. I knelt beside her and smoothed her fur, and she produced her last kitten and began to rub herself against my hand, purring. Soon, however, she withdrew her interest from me and began to lick her kittens.

I stayed with Susie and her family for a long time, marvelling at how quickly she transformed the palpitating, bedraggled blobs into the semblance of real kittens. I watched them nuzzle her stomach for milk. Eventually I forgot to be resentful and decided it was time to convey the exciting news of Susie's performance to everybody in the Manse.

I found Ina alone in the scullery, peeling potatoes.

'Susie's had kittens!' I told her.

She scarcely listened. '*Everybody's* having kittens this morning," she said. 'No!' She caught the sleeve of my jersey. 'Don't go through in there. Away you go outside again!'

This was insufferable. With deliberate intent I began to howl. I stamped one foot and would have attempted to circumvent Ina and run through the kitchen into the dining-room had not Maimie appeared in the doorway, no longer looking cross and harassed but with a dreamy smile on her face.

'It's a lovely boy,' she said to Ina. 'Everything's fine.' Then she caught my hand. 'Oh, *chiall*, they've been neglecting you, have they? Well, just you come with me and say hullo to your new wee brother.'

I became dumb. A brother? Nobody had prepared me for this. I felt lonelier and sadder than at any other time that morning. Even at this early stage the idea came to me that my best plan might be to run away. Then they would be sorry and come to look for me, and I would be important again. But a feeling of caution welled up. What if they *weren't* sorry and didn't come looking for me after all?

I followed Maimie upstairs. 'Your father and the doctor are in the dining-room having a refreshment,' she told me, adding with a chuckle, 'They need it, I'm thinking!' Why, I wondered?

My mother was propped up on pillows in the big bed. In a small cot beside it there lay an object which looked as ugly to me as the newborn kittens. I went to my mother, who looked paler than usual but very happy. She caught me to her and kissed me.

'Isn't he beautiful, Angus? He's going to be called Archibald. After my father, your grandfather in Appin. Being his big brother, you'll have to look after him and teach him how to be a good boy. I'll be depending on you.'

Well, this wasn't so bad. I was to be the boss, and Maimie was there to hear my mother say it. I looked down at the creature sleeping among the fleecy blankets, smelt the baby powder, resisted an impulse to do cruel things to the interloper and said, 'I'll look after him, Mamma.'

Having extracted this promise, my mother, like Susie, appeared to lose interest in me. She and Maimie began to croon over the baby. With sad dignity I retired and went downstairs to the dining-room where my father and the doctor were chatting together, tumblers in their hands. I smelt the aroma of what my father called 'spirits'. The golden liquid in the tumblers came from a bottle in the sideboard. I had been told that if ever I tried to drink from that bottle I should be poisoned and die in agony. Why did my father and the doctor not die in agony, too? If it came to that, why didn't Geordie get his mouth washed out with soap and water when he called me a 'wee bugger'?

My father patted my head. The doctor remarked that I was becoming a big boy.

'Susie's had kittens,' I told them.

I couldn't understand why they laughed. And I couldn't understand what my father meant when he said, 'We'll have to tell Geordie about her.' He added, 'Now off you go and play, Angus. It's a lovely day outside.'

No comfort here. Lacking desire to go outside and breathe the same air as Geordie, I trudged upstairs again and went to my bedroom, ignoring on the way the laughter and baby talk going on behind another door on the landing. I had a picture book detailing the adventures of a boy called Buster Brown. I climbed onto my bed, forgetting that my sandshoes were dirtied from the garden, and began to look through the book.

Soon, however, I tired of Buster Brown. I saw the earth from my shoes scattered on the yellow quilt. I got off the bed and, with difficulty, brushed the quilt with my hand. Some earth fell on the carpet. Eventually Maimie would chastise me for this, perhaps with a hard knuckle against my ear. But that was in the future. Just then I was so low in spirits that the prospect scarcely worried me at all.

I went to the window. Movement in the garden, beyond

the currant bushes and near the wall under the hill, attracted my attention. Geordie was digging a hole.

He paused at last, stuck his spade into the turf and spat out a stream of brown tobacco juice. He lifted a small bag from the ground. From it he brought out a kitten. Holding the kitten by the tail, he bashed its head against the wall and threw it into the hole. He did the same with the other three. Finally he filled in the hole and stamped down the earth on top of it.

I was rigid with horror and hate. I wished I were a man. Then I could have rushed out and struck him down with his own spade. Even now I can feel the nausea of frustration. Geordie was an ogre who deserved terrible punishment, but I had no means of administering it.

After a while I went to the stable. Susie was moving about, mewing. She came to me, rubbing against my legs. I took her in my arms and sat down under the manger in one of the stalls. It was dark and warm among the dung-scented straw. Susie mewed and I cried, with anger and selfpity.

Maimie found us there. She took me inside and gave me lunch in the kitchen and smacked me for not eating my mashed potatoes and leaving most of the rhubarb tart. But I didn't cry any more. Adults never changed their ways because you cried.

In time I forgot about the kittens. I became more interested in Archie and did my best – which, admittedly, sometimes fell short of perfection – to carry out my promise to look after him.

He became the strongest and best-looking male member of the family. At Glasgow University he graduated with honours in English and won a soccer blue. He played cricket right-handed and golf left-handed and showed no contempt for those of us with less athletic skill.

During the Second World War he became an officer with the 7/10th Argylls. He fought at Alamein and was wounded there. In the action for which his commanding officer won the Victoria Cross he was mentioned in dispatches.

In 1943 he fought in Sicily. During the battle for Catania in July, the 7/10th Argylls were on the left of my battalion, the

2nd Royal Scots Fusiliers. When the immediate fighting was over I took a jeep and in some excitement bucketed across the scarred countryside to greet him. I was too late. The driver of an Argylls truck told me that my brother had been mortally wounded at Gerbini the day before.

I went to see his temporary grave. Then I returned to my battalion dug in on the low, damp banks of the Semeto. That night I lay in my bivouac shivering with a minor recurrence of malaria. I remembered the day Archie had been born. I had wept then because I imagined I hated him. Now I wept again, silently and secretly, because I knew that I loved him.

Being three and a half years younger, for a considerable time Archie remained a baby in my eyes and therefore unfit to join in proper adventures. My companion and mentor in such adventures was Neil MacLean, a son of the gamekeeper who lived up the road, in a rose-covered cottage by the burnside. He was my senior by about eighteen months, wiry and strong, with a sportsman's keen eye. Wielding his broomhandle bat left-handed, he could 'scud' the ball at rounders farther than anybody else in the infant school. I accorded him the respect his prowess warranted and followed him faithfully and sometimes fearfully on bird's nesting and bathing expeditions and into dangerous places in and around the Manse.

It was Neil who made me challenge the monster who lived in the larger of our two attic rooms.

My bedroom was a floor down from the attics, but the wall against which my bed was placed extended upwards past the ceiling into the wall behind which the monster lived. On silent nights, before going to sleep, I often heard him growling and clanking; and sometimes I imagined that the wall shook as he hurled himself against it.

For a long time I kept my fears to myself. I knew that if I revealed them to my parents – or to Maimie – they would look on me with disfavour and refuse to listen. (Even now, when the idea for a book occurs to me, I try not to discuss it with anybody before submitting it to a publisher. On the few occasions I have done so, the idea had always been devalued for me, all freshness and enthusiasm gone.) But at last one day during the Christmas holidays, I spoke to Neil about the monster.

He looked at me. 'Ye're daft!' he said.

We were in the stable, sitting in one of the mangers. 'I'm not daft!' I told him. 'Come on up. Maybe you'll hear him!'

We squatted on the bed in my room, eating hazelnuts found during a furtive exploration of the pantry downstairs. Neil and I had not yet been introduced to chewing gum. Our chewing of the nuts served the same nerve-calming purpose.

All was quiet, for a time. I made known to Neil my theory that the monster was a dry-land octopus.

'There's nae monster!' he said.

'There is so. I hear him often, moving and growling.'

He shook his head amused. But when there occurred a sudden clank and grumble above us, followed by what sounded like a long-drawn sigh, he was startled enough to swallow a mouthful of half-chewed nuts and jump off the bed.

I, too, slid to the floor. 'That's him,' I said, my voice a whisper.

We both wore short trousers, the cloth of which came from garments discarded by our parents. From one pocket Neil took a catapult fashioned from a Y-shaped hazel twig, elastic secretly removed from one of his sisters' knickers and a small square of leather (with a hole in the centre) cut from the tongue of an old boot. From another he took a handful of marbles, some jarries, some glessies. Jarries were dull, buff-coloured and lacking in liveliness, available in Mrs Galbraith's shop in the village at three for a penny. They were the kind with which, as a rule, poor marble players like myself had to operate, because the odd glessie we did happen to come by – multicoloured and expensive, costing a whole penny – was always won off us by the experts like Neil.

'Come on,' he said. 'We'll see what that is.'

'No. I'm scared.'

'There's nae monster in a manse. God wouldna allow it.'

The thought was comforting. 'What is it, then?'

'We'll find oot.' He was brave, compared with me a hero. 'Face up tae it!' he said.

Was it the first time I ever faced up to anything? The exercise was hard then; it remains hard now, more than sixty years later. Sometimes I slither out of it, by means of self-administered doubletalk. But the result is always discontent, a condition even less supportable than moral or physical fear. The awkward human factor called conscience – unknown in the world of animals, however wise they may seem – must surely come into it somewhere. And that day, along with Neil, I discovered that 'facing up to it' can bring a spiritual reward which is entirely human.

We emerged from my bedroom and began to climb the attic stairs. On this winter afternoon they were unlit and dark-shadowed. Neil went first, his catapult at the ready, charged with a glessie. I followed close, in case I might become detached from him and have to face the shadows alone. We heard Maimie running water in the sink in the scullery. Soon afterwards the monster above us clanked and gurgled.

'Ach, I ken what it is!' shouted Neil, a burden lifted from his tone. He put his catapult and its ammunition back in his pocket.

His confidence fed mine. Quickly we climbed to the attic landing and went into the room on the left. I was no longer behind him. Bravely I had taken up position shoulder to shoulder.

The sounds were coming from a small grey door in the wall of the attic. Neil pushed it open, and there, in the darkness, stood my monster; the main watertank, with tentacles of dust-covered copper pipes jointed in bulbous lead. It was bubbling and groaning as water flowed down the ancient plumbing to the kitchen and scullery.

We laughed in wild relief. My own courage astonished me. I climbed on to the tank top and with light-hearted enthusiasm began to pull and push a metal lever. A ritual slaying of the monster in my mind?

One clanking pull dislodged part of the tank top and brought into view an enormous, dripping copper ball. Water swirled and leaped and began to splash everywhere. With a yelp of fear I jumped away and scrambled out into the attic. Neil tried to thrust the copper ball back into the tank. He failed and followed me out. Water pursued us. We ran for our lives, downstairs, passing Maimie on the landing, demanding to know what was going on.

'The tank's burst!' shouted Neil, without pausing in his flight.

'There's a flood!' I contributed, not pausing either.

'*Chiall beannachd mi!*' screeched Maimie. 'Get Geordie! Get Geordie!'

Geordie was in the old barn, splitting logs with iron wedges and a heavy mell.

'You tell him!' I entreated Neil. My hatred for Geordie was constant.

He put his head round the barn door. He shouted, 'The tank in the attic's burst, Geordie!' Then he turned and we ran fast from the yard on to the cart track leading down to the burnside.

The afternoon was darkening. We crawled into damp whin bushes above the water. A smell of raw earth came from a landslide scar beneath the whins. Wild geese flew over, honking. In Kilblaan farmyard, half a mile away across the river, a dog was barking. Probably chasing hens for sport, Neil thought.

We had some nuts left. Cracking them open with our teeth, we chewed without pleasure. Our thin jerseys were poor protection against the cold.

The truth came to me that sooner or later, if I were to escape death by exposure, I should have to return to the Manse and face the consequences of our visit to the attic. Neil was luckier. He could go home and, by keeping quiet, escape retribution.

Imagination leaped higher and a terrible picture occurred to me of great waves of water pouring down from the attic, flooding the Manse and engulfing my parents, Archie and baby Willie – and Maimie. What if even now they all lay drowned in dark corners? The thought that Geordie, heedless of our warning and continuing to work in the barn, might have escaped only increased the misery which overwhelmed me.

As imagination continued to coruscate, I saw myself left alone in the world, perhaps at the mercy of Geordie. Panic seized me. I rushed out of the whins, leaving Neil gaping after me, and ran, panting, up and along the cart track to the Manse.

It was still there, in the dusk. Lights shone in the kitchen and dining-room and an upstairs bedroom. There was no water to be seen. Geordie had left the barn. I ran in by the back door.

In the kitchen the range was glowing. A paraffin lamp with a spherical glass oil-holder and a tall white globe spread a soft light from the dresser. Behind it, on the wall, a row of pewter ashet covers (hung in order of size) reflected its gleam. Maimie, now in sole charge because Ina had left to be married, was having a cup of tea at the wooden table, like the dresser another of Sandy MacCallum's products. She wasn't smiling.

'Where,' she demanded, 'have you been?' Adding, sinisterly, 'Your father's back from visiting. He wants to see you in the dining-room?'

'Was there a – a big flood?' I asked.

'If it hadn't been for Geordie there might have been. You're a bad boy, Angus! And now you're going to catch it!'

Inside me relief mingled with apprehension. Physically I was getting warmer and more comfortable. The Manse, my home, was normal again, without threat of flooding. But I had to face my father, who, in spite of being a minister of the gospel, was inclined to be hard hearted when dealing with the guilty.

The dining-room cum study was lit by a squat brass paraffin lamp on the oak table. The fire was bright, fed by some logs split by Geordie. They gave out an astringent smell, like the smell in Sandy MacCallum's joiner shop. Surrounding my father's rolltop desk in the corner by the window were laden bookcases. He himself sat in a big armchair, smoking a pipe. A spitoon lay within the hearth. My mother's chair, on the opposite side of the hearth, was empty. I imagined I heard her upstairs, playing with Archie and the baby. I was alone with justice. But that day I had faced a monster and overcome it. Facing an angry father was now, surprisingly, less fearsome than it had been before.

'Where's Neil?'

'He's – he's gone home.'

'I'll speak to his father tomorrow. Which of you damaged the cock-ball?' Having known no English until he was five years old, my father was always liable to think in the Gaelic idiom, often, as he said himself, 'putting the horse before the cart'!

Though tempted I did not fall. 'I did. But – '

'No "buts"! You might have caused terrible damage. I was out. Lucky Geordie was here to put it right.'

Even had my father been in, it would have been Geordie – or perhaps my mother, who was practical and pragmatic both in deed and thought – who would have done the repair. For the son of a crofter in North Uist my father was strangely inept with his hands, except when wielding a garden spade. I said nothing.

'Why did you do it?'

I couldn't explain about the monster and the euphoria that had seized me when it had been laid low. I continued to say nothing.

'All right. Bend over.'

I bent over the arm of my mother's chair. He got up and smacked me twice on the bottom with his hard hand. At other times, for sins less heinous in my opinion, he had taken me to the piano stool in the drawing-room and used the back of a hair brush.

'Never go near that tank again!' he commanded, clearing his throat and spitting rather shakily into the spitoon.

I felt like crying, not because of a physical pain or fear but because of the apparent lack of love for me shown by my father. Here in the quiet parish on the tip of Kintyre, where most people depended for news of the world outside on secondhand copies of the *Glasgow Herald*, I was only vaguely aware that a violent war was going on. That winter afternoon in 1915 I had no idea that in a few months' time my father was due to leave us for service abroad as an army chaplain. At the age of six I had no idea that he was sad and sick at the thought of going away, and that to punish me at such a time, in order to preserve the sense of discipline that would stand me in good stead when I finally sloughed off parental care, had cost him far more in unhappiness than it had cost me. It was years later, when my son Jock was growing up, that I understood.

My father was abroad with the Lovat Scouts, mainly in Salonika, for a year. When he returned we called him the Padre. Like everybody else in Southend, we continued to call him the Padre until he died in 1970 at the age of ninety-two.

Assisted by Maimie and supported by kind neighbours, my mother looked after the three of us during his absence. I tried hard to perform my duties as senior male member of the household but seldom felt that I achieved success. For example, I would willingly have helped in the garden, but Geordie was still there and I still hated being near him. When Peter Galbraith's stirks forced a way through the garden fence and plunged with cloven hooves across the soft front lawn, I was only too happy to try and chase them out, yelling and throwing stones with sweating vigour. But the extent of my inadequacy soon became clear when one of them got stuck in the bottom fence, a leg caught between crossed wires, and appeared about to injure itself in desperate struggles to break free. I became so agitated that I rushed away and hid in the attics, allowing my mother to go by herself to the farm and bring back Peter with a wire cutter. From an attic window I saw her running, hobble skirt pulled high to her knees, and felt shame that I remember to this day.

Part of my trouble has always been that I'm afraid of being afraid. (This may be one reason why my golf handicap has never been less than 5 and why now, in my advancing years, with a handicap of 12, I am sometimes afflicted by the 'yips' on the putting green.) My imagination was – and still is – particularly fertile, leading me to discover fear in situations which Neil MacLean, for example, would approach with cool common sense. I related ordinary life to high drama and, even now, often fail to realize that on the whole life is singularly undramatic. This may have helped me as a writer but is a considerable burden in a world in which chartered accountants rather than Robin Hoods wield the power and the glory.

While my father was away I would often wander off with the other boys on a summer evening to play on the beach at Dunaverty, essaying leaps from high dunes to the sand below and bathing in the sea, 'bare scuddy', when we became tired and hot.

Real excitement would attend the bathes if, as often happened, sinister grey warships came speeding through Sanda Sound, the two-miles-wide channel between the island and the mainland of Southend, whipping huge bow waves in against the shore and smothering us enjoyably with solid water and flying spray.

After the war it was the great ships of the Anchor Line that came ploughing proudly through the Sound – the *Caledonia*, the *Circassia*, the *Britannia* – bound for America with passengers and cargo. Today the Board of Trade has banned the sound as a passage for the big ships, and, in any case, all the lovely liners have gone, rendered obsolete by blind and stuffy aircraft. From my present home, overlooking Dunaverty Bay, the only passing vessels to be seen are fishing skiffs, whisky puffers from Islay, and oil-exploration craft, all waddling through the sound like ducks, and in the distance, far out in the North Channel, long and ugly container ships apparently chopped off fore and aft by giant hatchets. When we were boys, there on the beach, we could see, beyond the ships, the blue, round hills of Antrim, seventeen miles away across the narrow sea. For us they were hills of magic and romance as we imagined leprechauns in their shadowed valleys. Now the magic has gone, buried in harsh reports of bombs and bullets.

Sometimes, after one of those expeditions to the shore, darkness would have gathered before I reached home, and my mother would chide me for being late. I had no wish to make her feel anxious; but the fun was so good that a knowledge of time deserted me. She accepted my excuses more readily than my father would have done.

One evening, at dusk, pulling on my shorts and jersey after a bathe, I looked up and saw a light in the graveyard at Keil, half a mile along the shore.

'Do you see it?' I said to Neil.

'Ay. That's funny!'

One of the boys – Jamie the Clinker – said, 'My faither says there's a ghost at Keil.'

Neil glowered. 'Whit kind o' ghost?'

'An auld tinker. They thocht he was deid, but he wasna. They buried him alive. He comes up tae haunt them.'

I had an idea – only a vague idea, it must be confessed – that this story lacked the ring of logic. 'How does anybody know they buried him alive? They didn't dig him up again, did they?'

'They ken because his ghost comes up. That light. That's him, standin' at the door o' the auld chapel, lookin' oot tae sea. So my faither says.'

Neil must have seen that I was shaken. He put an arm about my shoulders. 'Ach,' he said to Jamie, 'yer faither's only tellin' yarns. Tae frighten ye indoors when it gets dark.'

That sounded good sense and made me feel better. Many a time Maimie had called me out of the dark at the Manse with the threat: 'If you don't come in soon the *bochcans* will get you!' (*Bochcan* is the Gaelic for a spiteful gnome.)

'Come on,' said Neil, the man of action. 'We'll hae a look.' And, as I hesitated, 'Ye're a meenister's son. There's only wan ghost ye should believe in – the Holy Ghost!' He screeched with laughter at his own joke, and I joined in, without conviction.

The moon was already riding high above the sea peak of Ailsa Craig to the south-east. I wanted to go home. I was afraid of the ghost. I was also afraid that I was going to hurt my mother by staying out so late. But Neil's philosophy was always to 'face up to things'. It had resulted in making a mockery of my monster. Perhaps it would make a mockery of this ghost, too.

We kept close together as we approached the graveyard

along the narrow, metalled road. In those days, when only two motorcars existed in the parish and horse-drawn 'machines' were seldom used at night, everything was quiet except for the occasional complaint of a seagull. In the salt-laden air midges moved in small clouds. We scratched continuously, which may have helped to take our minds off that light. It grew more brilliant as we came closer.

In the moonlight we could make out, inside the graveyard, the ruined walls of St Columba's chapel and the arched doorway beside which the ghost was standing. Behind the graveyard were St Columba's footprints carved in a rock. Not far from the jagged north wall of the chapel was St Columba's Well, with whose water my father baptised the parish babies. I wondered if the ghost might not be that of a tinker at all but of a long-dead monk, perhaps even the great Columba himself. (Even then I knew a little about Columba, who came with his disciples from Ireland in the sixth century to bring Christianity to his kinsfolk, the Scotti. He was a hard man with sinners, according to my father, but with the needy and the poor in spirit kind and gentle. If only he knew how poor in spirit I felt at that moment.)

Suddenly the terror was on us. Two figures, looking huge in the dark, came leaping down from the wall by the graveyard gate. I yelled and tried to run, but Neil held on to my arm. 'It's only Big Doser and Kleek!'

I remembered having seen them on the beach, bathing some distance away from us, hulking lads of seventeen who worked as farm labourers. We always tried to give them a wide berth because of their reputation as bullies. No doubt they had noticed us making for the graveyard, guessed our purpose and hurried to be there before us, intent upon giving us a real fright. As far as I was concerned they had succeeded; but Neil and some of the others were hardier.

We outnumbered Big Doser and Kleek by four to one. 'Get at them, boys!' shouted Neil.

Our enemies were surprised. Small boys swarmed at them like bees, kicking and tripping and lashing out with fists. Presently both were down, scrabbling in the gateway, with Neil and his allies on top of them. I took my turn at striking and kicking, now that Big Doser and Kleek appeared to be helpless.

But triumph, as is the way of triumph, lasted only a few seconds. The enemy heaved themselves up, like twin Gullivers in Lilliput. We were thrown aside and came face to face with serious trouble. Big Doser's broken teeth showed in a grin of anger. His raw hands, protruding on wrist stalks from short, ragged sleeves, were curling, I imagined, towards my throat. Smaller and ratlike, Kleek was wiping blood and 'snotters' from his nose and howling intimations of vengeance.

Neil and the others ran. So did I. It was something I could do well. (I still can. Running, that is, in both its literal and metaphorical senses.) Big Doser and Kleek had no chance of overtaking us in the dark.

It was my mother, when I explained my lateness in dramatic and almost truthful fashion, who laid for me the ghost in the graveyard. The following night she took me for a walk and showed me how the moonlight fell on the granite of a polished and shining gravestone, embedded in the ancient wall of the chapel. Part of the inscription on the stone is as follows: 'Sacred to the memory of William MacMillan, died 17 October 1892, and of his wife, Margaret MacKerral, died 18 January 1892.' Years later it dawned on me that the Margaret MacKerral remembered on the ghost stone was a grand-aunt of the girl I was eventually to marry.

In a way, however, I had lost interest in the ghost. A psychic fear was supplanted by a physical one. Every time I visited the village or the shore I kept a sharp lookout for Big Doser and Kleek. But this fear was an exhilarating fear, almost enjoyable. If the worst came to the worst I knew I could outrun them both, like a gazelle which cocks a snook at lumbering rhinos.

2. Mull of Kintyre

The parish of Southend includes the Mull of Kintyre.

The Mull became famous 1800 years ago when Ptolemy, the Greek, made a map of it and named it *Epidion Akron*, 'the promontory of the horse people'. It became famous over a millenium later when Robert the Bruce took refuge with the MacDonalds in Dunaverty Castle before crossing the narrow sea to Rathlin and having his legendary encounter with a spider. It became famous yet again only a few years ago when Paul McCartney wrote 'Mull of Kintyre', the song which remained top of the pops for many week and provided newspaper men with a topical and romantic point of reference. All murders, shipwrecks and aircraft accidents occurring within fifty miles of Southend, on land or sea, are now described as having taken place on or near the Mull of Kintyre. Even the location of Paul McCartney's publicity pictures was not the actual Mull but a lonely shore at Saddell, some twenty-five miles to the north.

Paul McCartney was wise not to photograph or film the real Mull, which, if Kintyre is imagined as a giant leg, comprises only the big toe of the club foot. An enormous pile of metamorphic and volcanic rock spewed up in a series of ancient eruptions, its cruel magnificence, rising to 1404 feet at the summit of Beinn na Lice, has nothing in common with the sentimental softness of the song, which is derived from music and poetry first composed by Gaels in the sad flatness of the Hebrides.

McCartney's was not the first piece of music to be called 'Mull of Kintyre'. Some years ago a pipe tune was composed by Archie Duncan, one-time pipe corporal in the Royal Scots Fusiliers, to which he gave this name. It is well known in piping circles and has been performed on radio.

Archie still lives in Campbeltown, struck down with a rheumatic ailment caused in part by an experience in the Second World War during which he spent many hours in a lifebelt, floating helplessly in the cold sea off the Dutch coast, after the vessel in which he had been travelling was sunk by enemy gunfire. He now has four artificial joints, in his hips and in his knees.

He does not begrudge McCartney his commercial success. He is an artist, as clever at drawing and painting pictures as he is at composing tunes, and, like a true artist, derives his rewards – and his satisfaction – from the tributes he receives from all those who have enjoyed his work. Money means nothing to him. Appreciation does. As a writer myself – and, incidentally, a wartime Fusilier – I can understand this only too well.

Here in Kintyre we believe that long after the pop tune has been forgotten, Archie's pipe tune will live on.

The cliffs at the Mull, some over 500 feet high, and the boulders strewn along the tide lines below, like debris from a giant's quarry, make dubious appeal to gently nurtured visitors. Those with weak hearts or a tendency to vertigo are warned that even the road lassooing down to the lighthouse from the high moor can be a killer. And if a southerly or westerly gale is blowing, and they venture near the cliffs, they are advised to do so on hands and knees through the sopping peat hags. But at the end of this uncomfortable approach they will be rewarded – or perhaps intimidated – by a scene of splendour equalled only in parts of Sutherland, where, for example, Eas-Coul-Aulin, by far the highest waterfall in Britain and the fourteenth highest in the world, hurtles down 658 feet of sheer mountainside.

From the Mull, as the seaspray flies upward, salting lips and cheeks, there occurs, far below, the meeting of seven tides – from the Firth of Clyde to the east, from the Irish Sea to the south, from the Atlantic and the Antrim coast to the west and from the Minches to the north – a white-fringed maelstrom threatening to engulf any small craft which dares to challenge it. Out and beyond the tumult of the tides, in the near distance, lie the island of Rathlin, a lumpy boomerang, and, behind Rathlin, the beetling eminence of Fair Head and the lower lands of Ballycastle.

The eleven-miles-wide restless flow of water between the Mull and Northern Ireland is called the North Channel. During the two world wars convoys moved slowly through it, heading out into danger. In the First World War, as I remember, such convoys were escorted by cruisers and airships; in the Second World War they were festooned with anti-aircraft balloons and shepherded by darting frigates and destroyers.

Once, in the First World War, at about the age of nine, I was horribly scared by the sight of an airship, trailing some kind of rope or wire cable, as it appeared around the corner of a plantation near the Manse, heading, as I know now, for the North Channel. I was alone, searching for birds' nests on the low road to Kilblaan. It came straight for me, engines growling. I stood, shivering with fear, while it floated over, the dangling cable cutting a swathe in a nearby corn-field and snapping at least one roadside telegraph wire. As it receded in the direction of the Mull, I recovered mobility and ran, panting, to the Manse. I was gratified when my mother and Maimie came quickly outside to catch a glimpse of the disappearing monster. Having successfully given them the impression that on the Kilblaan road I had faced it alone, motionless and unafraid, I was even more gratified when Maimie remarked that I was a lot braver than she would have been. I began to persuade myself that though my father was away, in Salonika, as his stand-in at home I was playing a hero's part.

Seventy years ago, children in Southend seldom ventured to explore the Mull. The lighthouse was six miles from the village and seven from the Manse. The narrow road, though roughly metalled, climbed and swooped in hair-raising violence, making it a difficult one even for animals. In any case, parents were aware of menace in the high cliffs and promised their offspring painful punishment if ever they went near them.

I went to the Mull once, during the First World War, along

with my mother and some other youthful members of the Woman's Guild. We were taken to the high moor above the lighthouse – to Barney's Moss, a flattish green island in a rock-infested, turbulent sea of heather – in a farm cart drawn by a plodding Clydesdale mare. A farmer's daughter sat high on the front end of the cart driving, a man's cap on her head, a man's tweed jacket about her shoulders, her long, voluminous skirt tucked in close about her ankles. The rest of us crouched in the well of the cart, sheltering as best we might from a snell wind, though at one stage my mother moved forward and took the reins for a spell, reminding the driver that she, too, was a farmer's daughter. I remember feeling smugly proud of her.

The journey from the village took about two hours, because on long, steep ascents we had to lighten the horse's burden by getting out and walking behind the cart. We got out, too, during some of the descents. The weight of the cart would suddenly thrust against the harness on the old mare's hindquarters – harness called locally 'the breechins' – and it seemed possible that as she held back, slithering and sliding, the cart might overturn. It never did, slightly to my disappointment. Even then I had a nose for the truffles of sensational stories.

The purpose of our expedition was to gather sphagnum moss, which at the time, owing to a shortage of cottonwool, was in demand as a field dressing for wounded soldiers. The most plentiful supply of sphagnum in the parish, according to one knowledgeable kirk elder, was to be found in Barney's Moss. The elder was right. Scraping and pulling for hour after dreary hour, like coolies in a rice field – pictures of whom I had seen in the Church of Scotland magazine, *Life and Work* – we filled four big sacks with the stuff and hoisted them into the cart. The only relief – for me – was a picnic organized by my mother. The ladies drank tea brewed up on a fire of heather twigs augmented by small pieces of dried peat gathered from disused workings nearby. As a special treat I had a bottle of lemonade, a bottle which, to my delight, had a small glass ball for a stopper. (Neil MacLean would have to look out next time we played marbles. I now possessed a glessie.) During the day we saw buzzards flying overhead and another great bird, gliding high above the distant cliffs, which my mother said was a golden eagle.

It was almost dark when we reached home. I was tired and bored with the ladies' chatter. My only consolation was the thought that if my father, fighting in some savage Grecian glade, happened to be wounded, perhaps some of the moss we had gathered that afternoon might save his life. Telling nobody, I began to write a story along such lines. But I soon gave it up. Describing even imaginary wounds on my father's body made me feel sick. And afraid.

The road to the Mull was not contructed until 1830, though the lighthouse itself had been built in 1787–88.

The Mull of Kintyre lighthouse is often referred to in guidebooks – and by authors who should know better – as a 'Stevenson light'. This is not true, though, as they say in the panel games, there is a 'Stevenson connection'.

In 1786 a body of nineteen persons known as the Northern Lighthouse Trustees was set up by an act of parliament. It still exists under the original constitution but is now called the Northern Lighthouse Board (NLB). This body decided that four new lighthouses should be built: at Kinnaird Head near Fraserburgh, at North Ronaldshay in the Orkneys, at Eilean Glas in Scalpay, Harris, and at the Mull of Kintyre. Casting about for a good lighting engineer to do the work, they found Thomas Smith, originally a lampmaker in Edinburgh, who accepted the contract with enthusiasm, even though his promised remuneration was scant and sometimes slow in coming.

Soon he encountered daunting problems. He employed as an assistant George Sheills, 'a mason well recommended', along with two other Edinburgh tradesmen, John and William Purdie. They tackled the Mull lighthouse first, in July 1787, because bad weather was making journeys to the islands difficult and 'at least the Mull was on the mainland'.

Smith had already been warned by the Provost of Campbeltown, himself a Lighthouse Trustee, that much money and time would be required 'to contract for a building in a place so difficult of access and so remote'. He found the warning to be true. Building materials could not be landed at the Mull itself because of the violent tides and 'the steep, 250-foot cliff' on which the lighthouse was to be erected. Everything, therefore, had to be made up into 'tiny parcels' and conveyed by packhorses from Campbeltown seventeen miles away. In his reports, Smith refers to 'rough, trackless moorland and mountainous paths' so dangerous that a horse could make only one journey in a day and that with a load of less than a hundredweight.

Nevertheless, by the end of November George Sheills and the Purdies had built the keeper's house and most of the tower. (Sheills earned 4s. 2d. for 'each lawful day's work', the Purdies 3s.) Meanwhile, Smith had got the lamp and reflectors ready in Edinburgh, but 'with wintry storms now buffeting Kintyre, it was decided to defer shipping the precious light until the spring, and Sheills and the Purdies were recalled home.'

In April of the following year Thomas Smith and his masons returned to the Mull and by June, with the help of some local workers, had completed the tower and installed the light. Each of the reflectors, designed by Smith, was formed of 350 facets of mirror glass one-sixteenth of an inch thick, set in plaster on brass plates. Smith also made sure that a high wall was built between the lighthouse and the cliff edge, 'to prevent the keeper or any of his family from being blown over by the strong winds'.

It was some time, however, before a keeper could be appointed and settled in with plenty of provisions for the winter months, during which, in Smith's words, he would be 'totally removed from society and frequently employed in winning peats for fuel'. But at last, in October, the lantern was officially lit. Since then, undergoing modifications and reconstruction along the years, it has never ceased flashing a warning to ships heading into or out of the North Channel.

Soon after the building of the Mull lighthouse Thomas Smith took as an assistant Robert Stevenson, the nineteen-year-old son of a widow whose maiden name had been Jean Lillie.

Jean Lillie's first husband was a dashing young Glasgow merchant called Alan Stevenson, who, during a business expedition to the West Indies in 1774, died of a fever in St Christopher (now St Kitts), leaving her alone and almost penniless with a two-year-old son. Soon afterwards she married a certain James Hogg, a Glasgow manufacturer about whom almost nothing is known, except that in 1778, whether on account of death or divorce, Jean was no longer married to him. Jean and her son then moved to Edinburgh, where, through meetings at church, they became friends with Thomas Smith and his first wife, Elizabeth, and their two children, Jane and James. They remained friends with the Smith family during the years when Thomas's first wife died of whooping cough and his second, Mary Jack, died of tuberculosis after having given birth to a daughter, Mary Ann.

During Thomas's long absences from home, on lighthouse business, Jean Stevenson (who never referred to herself as Jean Hogg) looked after his fatherless children; and when her own son Robert began looking for employment, declining interest in Latin and Greek having caused him to give up the idea of becoming a minister of the Kirk, it was natural that he should be invited by Thomas Smith to enter his workshop as an apprentice. He became so apt and enthusiastic a pupil that in 1791 he was appointed chief assistant and partner in the business.

In the summer of 1792 he was sent to instal a reflector light at the dangerous entrance to Portpatrick harbour, the Scottish end of the postal service in Ireland. This was his first independent job and marked the beginning of the Stevenson family's long, devoted and widely known involvement with the building of lighthouses. The fact that Robert's first instinct was to be a clergyman, with a care for souls, may indicate the origin of his and his successors' deep concern for the safety of seamen.

That same year Thomas Smith and Jean Stevenson were married. At forty-one she was an ideal partner. She knew his children as well and loved them almost as much as her own son; she shared his religious beliefs and could be depended upon to care for the young folk while he travelled about the country on lighthouse business.

In 1799 a final link was forged in the close family alliance. Robert Stevenson married Jane Smith, the girl who for so many years had been his playmate. It was a happy marriage which produced a daughter, Jane, and four sons, Alan, Bob, David and Thomas. Thomas, the youngest, was the father of Robert Louis Stevenson (whose middle name, incidentally, was always pronounced 'Lewis' by the family, because in fact, long before a kind of literary snowblindness crept in, he was christened 'Lewis'.) From David are descended the contemporary generations, including the novelist, D. E. Stevenson.

Lighthouses and books. Signals flashing in the dark from a family whose loving care for others has always been well matched by their energy and skill in their chosen professions.

It all began with Thomas Smith, the pioneer of modern lighthouse building in Scotland. But in spite of the fact that he was well known to the public in his time, nobody seems to be sure what he looked like. All that R.L.S. could discover about his great-grandfather's personal appearance was contained in the words of an old lighthouse-keeper: 'A tall, stout man coming ashore with a gun over his arm.'

In 1830, when a decision was made to build a road to the Mull of Kintyre, Robert Stevenson's son, David, was put in charge of the work. He brought men and horses from Edinburgh (but also engaged some local labour), and while the road gradually took shape, in general following the direction of the old bridle paths, he lived for six weeks in one of the crofthouses which at the time lay scattered along the wild coastline. But even then the Duke of Argyll was relentlessly depopulating the crofts in order to make way for sheep. For the past hundred years the Mull has been a wilderness almost entirely empty of people: and today archaeologists study the mouldering ruins of the little crofting townships with the same passionless regard as they do the Iron Age duns and Neolithic chambered cairns which are also to be found near the lighthouse.

Before the road was finished David Stevenson had to face at least one unexpected crisis. One of his workmen died of cholera. This caused the entire labour force to down tools and flee to Campbeltown, putting the local population into a considerable state of panic. Helped by his assistant from Edinburgh, a young man called David Rome, David buried the unfortunate victim in a lonely spot at the Mull, far from human habitation. Then, showing an example by himself staying on at the work site, he spent many hours trying to persuade his men and the people of Campbeltown that no danger of infection existed. In the end he succeeded. The road building went on.

When, in 1917, I accompanied my mother and her Guild ladies to the Mull the road was in much the same rough condition as it had been when David Stevenson completed his task. For over a hundred years it had remained a private road, owned and serviced by the Northern Lighthouse Board. After the Second World War, however, all of it except the last swooping, corkscrew mile down to the station was taken over by Argyll County Council, which gave it a coat of tarmac to tempt adventurous tourists. And tempting it has proved. In the first year after the record of 'Mull of Kintyre' was released 3500 people – including Europeans, Americans, Asians and Africans – signed the visitors' book at the lighthouse.

Thomas Smith and David Stevenson would have rejoiced in the interest aroused by the lighthouse and the road. Possibly, however, it remains a matter of indifference to the cholera man who occupies a lonely grave, far from the road and difficult to find. About the place there is a kind of cosmic loneliness: a trough in a tumbling sea of heather, smooth and green like the lee side of a wave. The wind whines over it; and the peewits and the whaups (curlews) fly with the wind, calling to unseen companions. The grave is marked by a single bare stone. It is seldom visited by strangers.

But somebody cares, and the loneliness is not absolute. The last time I made a pilgrimage to this secret sepulchre a bunch of wild flowers lay fading on the stone.

*

The high aseptic savagery of the Mull gives way suddenly to low green hills and fields in the hinterland of Southend.

Today parts of the Mull and some of the uncultivated glens are covered with spruce and fir, planted there by private owners and by the Forestry Commission; but sixty years ago few trees existed in the parish. West wind constantly blustering in from the Atlantic makes it difficult to grow them and, in any case, farmers and shepherds have always regarded trees as useless encumbrances. In their opinion dry stane dykes – as mortarless stone walls are called in Scotland – provide adequate shelter for flocks and herds.

One or two clumps of ash and sycamore were – and still are – to be seen in odd corners on the arable farms; but almost all of these were planted to cover the deep graves of cattle slaughtered during outbreaks of anthrax. (Thanks to stringent regulations and inspections, anthrax is now practically unknown in Scotland, as is bovine tuberculosis.)

When Neil MacLean and I were young only two sizable plantations existed for our pleasure. They were situated on either side of the Con water near the Manse; and from Neil I learned they had been planted by the Duke of Argyll, his father's employer, as cover for the game birds – grouse pheasant, woodcock – hunted by the ducal shooting tenants.

These plantations still exist. But now they are untended, unkempt, like old rubbish dumps. The duke no longer owns the ground on which they stand. In 1955 his predecessor sold off almost all his farms and houses in Kintyre to the sitting tenants, in order to meet an accumulation of debts. The shooting and fishing rights came into the hands of farmers more concerned with the rearing of profitable cattle than with the sheltering and preserving of sometimes highly expensive game. So the plantations decay, the game birds decrease in numbers (mainly owing to disease) and rich business men, carrying double-barrelled shot-guns and wearing knickerbocker suits in startling checks, have ceased to make their autumnal visits to Southend. Were Neil's gamekeeper father alive today he would long ago have added his name to the list of the sad unemployed. (In any case, even though our plantations and moors were kept in good condition, would many business men from the south – of native British origin that is – be able to afford a shooting at £5000 a day, which is the rental for some moors for which figures are available, or handmade guns selling in London at £20,000 a pair?)

But for Neil and me – and our brothers, as they grew older – the larger of these plantations, which lay across the river, was a playground of delight, even though, strictly speaking, we committed trespass every time we entered it.

In winter and early spring the ground beneath the trees was soggy and wet, and we sank in it up to our ankles. At such times our visits were infrequent, though occasionally we found an eerie pleasure in standing silent in a woodland aisle, aware of the dank, earthy smell of winter and surrounded by tall, gaunt trees like cathedral pillars which sheltered us from the wind moaning among their tops. The experience resembled our life in the Mull of Kintyre, I think: a little frightening in its stark remoteness but not so frightening as the chill intimations of a different kind of life outside and beyond, of which we had only a vague comprehension.

In late spring and summer, however, when the ground was dry and fallen twigs cracked sharply beneath our feet, when leaves were bursting out in hanging bundles of green, this was the time for our happiest 'plantin' ploys'. There were birds' nests to find and brightly coloured eggs to blow, with pin holes pierced at either end by trembling, nervous fingers. There were rabbits and grouse and woodcock to spring unexpectedly from under our feet and cause us momentary alarm and abiding pleasure. There were swathes of primroses and wild blue hyacinths (which we called bluebells) and a certain small clearing where wild raspberries grew. The raspberries tasted dry and sour, but we ate them with relish because, on two counts, they were forbidden fruit. First, they belonged to the Duke of Argyll. Secondly, our parents had issued orders that no wild berries of any sort should pass our lips.

We regarded the clearing as our secret headquarters; and as each of our brothers joined us in the plantation he was taken to it, blindfold, and then made to promise, on pain of terrible physical punishment – even of hanging from a rafter in one of the Manse outhouses – never to betray its existence to anyone, not even to the Duke of Argyll, should he suddenly appear to accuse us of trespass and make us his prisoners.

The clearing with the wild raspberries is still there; but today the boys of Southend know nothing about it. The plantation is not approachable by car. Even for me the glamour of the place has diminished. Fallen trees, rotten with acrid-smelling fungus, lie on the turf and block the way through; and I am sad that its fresh innocence has vanished. But the sadness does not last long. Memories remain, and they are real, like small intimations of man's immortality.

If I had the courage I would collect a few of my OAP contemporaries – sadly not including Neil, who died many years ago – and spend afternoons in the plantation, crawling among the undergrowth, plaiting twigs together to make snares and manufacturing bows and arrows out of hazel branches and string, in a satisfying game of Cowboys and Red Indians.

Instead, I sometimes go alone to collect wood for our living-room fire. We have night storage heaters, that expensive brood sired by a con trick out of government ineptitude; but Jean insists she would be unhappy without a coal and log fire to sit at on winter evenings. My daily exercise, therefore, includes chopping or sawing wood found in the plantation or washed up on the seashore. I have learned to pick and hoard the right kinds of wood for a glowing fire and can vouch for the truth of the old rhyme:

> Beechwood fires are bright and clear
> If the logs are kept a year.
> Chestnut's only good, they say,
> If for long 'tis stored away.
> Birch and fir logs burn too fast
> Blaze up bright and do not last.
> It is by the Irish said
> Hawthorn makes the sweetest bread.
> Elmwood burns like churchyard mould,

E'en the very flames are cold.
Poplar gives a bitter smoke,
Fills your eyes and makes you choke.
Apple wood will scent your room
With an incense like perfume.
Oak and maple, if dry and old,
Keep away the winter cold.
But ash wood wet or ash wood dry
A king shall warm his slippers by.

So does Jean. And so do I.

Florrie Nail lived alone in a wooden hut by the riverside, a few hundred yards downstream from the plantation.

Her real name was Florence MacNeil; but in Southend, as in many another west-coast parish of mixed Highland, Lowland and Irish population, we are inclined to be lazy and drop the 'Mac'. As further examples, Archie MacInnes becomes Erchie Eenis; John MacShannon becomes Joannie Shenak; Margaret MacEachran becomes Peggy Kechran. I suppose that one reason for this habit is that the local versions glide more easily across the tongue. But, of course, 'Nail', 'Eenis', 'Shenak' and 'Kechran' are all approximate reversions, in pronunciation, to the old original Gaelic names. With a 'Mac' before each they mean respectively 'child of Neil,' 'child of Angus', 'child of the storyteller' and 'child of the horseman'. It is interesting to observe that the MacShannons, plentiful in Kintyre, are still, as a family, superb singers and storytellers and that the MacEachrans, inhabitants of the peninsula for two thousand years, are still experts in the handling of farm animals.

Florrie Nail was a good friend of us boys. She was between sixty and seventy years of age when we knew her: ancient in our eyes and indeed much older looking, on account of her dress and a stooping posture caused by hard physical labour and the onset of rheumatism, than sixty-year-old ladies are today. In Florrie's time youthful fashions for grandmothers were frowned upon as vanities of vanities, bad for the soul, and the national health service was but a gleam in Lloyd George's caring eye.

Florrie's clothes were bundled about her from chin to heavily booted feet, revealing nothing of the body beneath, unlike my mother's smart blouses and hobble skirts. They were of thick black material, so rumpled that it often occurred to Neil and me to wonder if she ever took them off. Her dark-skinned face, framed in long wisps of iron-grey hair, was broad and gaunt. Most of her teeth were missing, and she spoke in a husky voice which often became submerged in bouts of bronchial coughing. Sometimes she smoked tobacco in a broken-stemmed clay pipe, but this was only when some neighbour (like my father) presented her with an ounce of 'thick black'.

Her wooden hut, painted light grey and consisting of a single room, was raised a foot above the turf on four corner posts. Her heating came from an iron stove, its rickety tin chimney emerging from the corrugated iron roof like a drunken question mark. It burned wood and peats and sometimes coal, and on it she cooked porridge and broth and boiled water in a skillet (or shallow pan) for countless cups of strong tea. Her light was furnished during the day by two small windows (placed oddly high up under the eaves so that she couldn't see out of them) and at night time by a cruisie (a small dish of oil with a wick in it). She had two wooden chairs, one for herself and one for visitors whom she considered important. Her bed was a low bunk attached to the wall.

Neil and I usually sat on the wooden floor while she talked to us in a high-pitched voice, which often broke when she had to cough, about people and events in the parish. Sometimes she would spread butter, with a thumb, on high-edged 'dollar' biscuits and present us with one each. We enjoyed her talk and the dollar biscuits and were unaffected by the heavy smell of wood smoke and tobacco and homespun garments and bedclothes which always filled the hut. I believe now that in her turn she enjoyed our company.

She had a small garden in which she grew kale and parsley. Neighbouring farmers allowed her to collect occasional turnips and cabbages from their fields in addition to making sure that she had adequate supplies of butter and cheese. Unknown to the shooters, Neil's father left rabbits and hares on her doorstep. Her monetary income was half a crown a week, poor relief from the parish council.

In Southend today an old lady in a similar situation has a comfortable council house, an old age pension, a supplementary pension, a television set, regular visits from a doctor or a nurse and an ambulance service to convey her to a hospital in Campbeltown should she require specialized medical treatment. If she takes flu, in spite of an annual 'flu jag', or contracts any other temporary illness, a home help attends her domestic needs. Assistance in the administration of her social needs is provided by the church (often through the Woman's Guild), the Women's Rural Institute and the community council.

The minister of the parish was Florrie Nail's only regular visitor. The minister today visits her modern counterpart and is grateful that the Christian ideals of love and care have flowered to such an extent that his burden and concern is shared by many others, making it so much lighter than that of his predecessor.

In my childhood the old folk in Southend, like Florrie, inhabited huts and noisome village hovels, cast up like flotsam on the beaches of old age. But they all possessed one characteristic which continually aroused my boyish admiration. This was a tough independence of spirit, a courage in the face of want and deprivation which seemed incredible to Neil and me, happed around as we were – according to the standards of the time at any rate – with every physical and moral support. And Florrie Nail possessed another characteristic which caused us to shiver in our sandshoes.

We were prowling in the plantation one summer afternoon, pioneering a new route through heavy undergrowth to the clearing. We kept a sharp lookout for Indians, snakes and tigers and froze into immobility when any recognizable sound occurred which could be construed in imagination as threatening danger. We were confident there was no danger among the tall trees; but we could achieve full enjoyment only by creating the idea of it in our minds. Green twigs brushed our faces. Our knees were scratched by bramble thorns and smeared with damp, acrid-smelling leaf mould. Sunshine glinted through the treetops and shadows flickered with thrilling menace when the treetops moved in the wind.

Suddenly we heard a heavy sound – a sound we were unable immediately and instinctively to identify and which caused us spasms of real terror. Neil flattened himself so close to the ground that when after a moment he raised his head one cheek was covered with leaf mould, like a Hallowe'en mask.

We waited. The leaves of a rhododendron bush in front of us were trembling. What terrible creature crouched behind them, ready to spring at our throats?

Without warning a face appeared in the midst of the bush. A hawklike female face with a wide mouth – a mouth which suddenly uttered a heart-stopping screech. I had heard my father preach about the witch of Endor. Was this a witch of Southend, intent upon casting a spell on Neil and me, turning us perhaps into toadstools or even pillars of salt?

We lay there, desperately afraid but incapable of any physical action. And then the rhododendron branches parted and through them stepped Florrie Nail, cackling with laughter.

'I gi'ed ye a fricht, boys! I gi'ed ye a fricht!'

Our relief was so great that I, for one, was ready to howl and shed tears. But Neil was made of harder stuff. He scrambled to his feet.

'Ye bloody auld bitch!' he shouted at her. 'Whit are ye daein' in the plantin'?'

By the age of ten all Southend schoolboys (including the minister's sons) had acquired a substantial repertoire of swearwords. Florrie, therefore was unsurprised by Neil's outburst.

'Trackin' ye doon. Fur a tare!' she screeched, bursting again into banshee laughter. 'I used tae play here in the plantin' masel' when I was a lassie. I was gey guid at the trackin', and I jeest wunnert if I could still dae it. Ye never heard me, did ye?'

'Fur a tare', in our local dialect, means 'for a joke'. For

Neil and me, however, it was no joke. Pride in our courage and manly skills as hunters had been gravely undermined; and the knowledge that an old woman like Florrie had outmanoeuvred us and scared us almost out of our wits was hard to stomach. But Neil, as usual, was able quickly to adjust to the situation and make the best of it.

He laughed. 'Ach, we heard ye a' richt. We were jeest playin' alang wi' ye.'

I have always been able to accept with alacrity any excuses offered by friends for my mistakes and errors of judgement. Neil's brave words made me feel happier at once.

'What about another game, Florrie?' I said. 'You hide and we'll try to track *you* down.'

'Richt ye are,' she said with delight. 'Jeest gi'e me five meenits. Then ye can come efter me.'

At the end of the afternoon she took us back to the hut, where she gave us tea and dollar biscuits.

As a boy I lacked the wit to identify Florrie's reasons for coming to play with us in the plantation; but now, being even older than she was at the time, I can understand them very well.

About a year later, Florrie died of influenza. Her hut remained empty for a time, rotting and crumbling in the wind and rain. In November 1918, soon after the signing of the Armistice, there occurred a day and night of heavy rain when the river Con roared down from the hills in a brown flood. Some of the trees in the plantation were broken and swept away. Florrie's hut was lifted from its supports. At high speed it leaped and rolled downstream, eventually crashing against a stone bridge and splintering into a hundred pieces. Part of the bridge collapsed and a ten-foot gap yawned in the road.

I was seedy and swollen with mumps at the time. When Neil and I went to inspect the damage I had on a balaclava helmet which my father had worn in Salonika. Perhaps it was my debilitated condition which made me feel like crying when I thought of Florrie and her hut, both gone for ever.

Was she a spinster or a widow? Was she a native of

Southend, or a traveller who had come to visit and decided to stay? Had she relatives in Kintyre?

I knew none of the answers then. I still don't know. Nobody is old enough to remember and tell me.

3. Downstairs, Upstairs

Florrie Nail was only one of the many characters who, sixty years ago, shared in the life of Southend.

My aged contemporaries are inclined to complain that no such characters exist today. This is partly true in the sense that the welfare state has helped to do away with real poverty and also to alleviate many of the diseases, both mental and physical, which handicapped old age in the early part of the century. Better education has tended to smooth out the oddities which attracted us to people older than ourselves, and television has made less urgent the search by youth for enlightenment and amusement from their older neighbours.

But I keep reminding my friends among the OAPs that their complaints may not be entirely valid. Young people today live in a different world: a world of technological wonder gradually merging into another of the microchip. They may look upon us old squares, digging in our heels against the pull of the twenty-first century, in much the same was as Neil and I looked upon the Florrie Nails of our time. Some of *us* may be the characters about whom a budding author, now concealed in our midst, will write books in the years to come.

Not long ago this idea was strengthened in my mind when from my favourite armchair in the clubhouse I saw my son Jock and a friend of his – unaware that I was watching – doubled up with laughter on the eighteenth green while another young man, shaping up to a three-foot putt, suddenly leaped inches into the air and hysterically prodded the ball past the hole by several yards. It dawned on me that this was an exact demonstration of my method of putting (since the 'over-sixty yipps' afflicted me) and that it was being done with deliberate intent to amuse. Afterwards I said nothing to anybody, not even to Jock. But I remembered how Neil and I and the other boys had often put into mocking action the foibles of *our* characters.

The children of a Scottish manse are privileged. They are brought up in the knowledge not only of the love of God but also of the fear of God which engenders self-discipline. They learn, too, by reason of contact with visitors to the manse of every sort and condition, not to be snobs or, which is as bad, anti-snobs.

As a small boy I knew and was able to communicate with, for example, Geordie the odd-job man, Danny the Tink, and Ina, Dowager Duchess of Argyll; Hughie MacKay the drainer, and Mrs Boyd of Carskiey, who was a millionairess; Big Doser and Kleek, Mrs Galbraith in the wee shop, and Robert Ralston, the prosperous farmer who was also a ruling elder. I knew and sometimes visited Jamie Doyle who lived rough with a woman companion in a cave above Kilmashenachan shore.

My parents treated them all as equal in the sight of God and made no difference in the quality of their hospitality. When the occasion arose they all got tea from my mother and some of her own locally renowned home-baked scones. Then, again if appropriate, my father would take them into his study to discuss their business and dispense benign encouragement or forthright criticism as he saw fit. He had words as readily with the Dowager Duchess as with Danny the Tink and commanded the respect of both.

There were some who refused to enter the drawing-room and, indeed, would only come inside as far as the kitchen on a cold day. Those were the tinkers, or 'travelling people' as they are now called by sensitive social workers: the Townsleys and the Williamsons who for generations made Kintyre their happy hunting ground. (They still do, though today many of them live in council houses.) But it was the tinkers who laid down the rules, not the minister or his wife.

As a result of all this I grew up almost unaware of the class distinction which I now realize was widespread, even in the remoteness of Kintyre, before the levelling influence of the two world wars and of preaching politicians like Keir Hardie. I am thankful for it. Having to calculate the warmth – or coolness – of your approach to another human being must cause difficult mental and moral problems, and I am an advocate of the simple and uncomplicated life in which you can always be yourself and never need to act a part.

Though learning to respect him as an individual, I disliked and was scared of Geordie, our occasional gardener. I was also, in a way, scared of Danny the Tink, an old man with brown, weathered features so aquiline that his nose and chin seemed ready to touch every time he champed his toothless jaws. He looked like a cunning wizard in one of my picture books.

When I knew him, he lived alone in a two-roomed cottage in the village, though in the mirky past, on the road as a tinker, he had fathered a family. A married daughter sometimes came to do washing for him and to tidy up, as best she could, the dull, dank rooms, which, even on a summer's day, required the light of a candle or paraffin lamp.

The cottage was one of a row of broken-down buildings, like decaying teeth, which had once been thatched but were now roofed with rusty corrugated iron. The place had no official designation but was nicknamed locally Teapot Lane. This may have been because the cobbled pavement outside the front doors sloped down to an open drain into which tealeaves, fish heads and even human excreta were often thrown. The furnishings of each cottage were incomplete without a heavily sprung rat trap.

In his younger days, as well as being a tinker selling and repairing pots and pans, Danny had done a great deal of casual labour on the farms, especially during the sowing season and at harvest time. But he disliked the idea of permanent work. He was tall and strong and, with the best of them, could dig hill drains, plough straight with a 'high-cutter' and toss cornsheaves powerfully on to ladder-sided carts. While it lasted his work was regular and faithful. He had no taste for drink and never went on the spree like so many of the farm workers of his day, desperate to forget, even for an hour or two, the unrelenting dawn-to-dusk labour to which they were condemned. But Danny had his own peculiar weakness. Suddenly he would tire of effort and tell the farmer he had to go. Confiding in nobody, he would disappear for many weeks, though rumours might circulate that he'd been seen in faraway and, to us, outlandish places – such as Arrochar and Inveraray – in the company of tinkers.

Danny, however, always returned to Southend and, because he was a good worker, usually found employment on some farm and a place to sleep in an attic or an outhouse.

When he became old and the fires of travel lust began to cool, he was given the house in Teapot Lane by the parish council. Instead of labouring on the farms, he augmented his weekly half a crown poor relief as a repairer of clocks and watches.

His reputation was made by work he did on a famous old grandfather clock in Brunerican, Jean's family home. Years before it had been brought there from another farm in the parish, in an iron-shod cart drawn by a Clydesdale mare. The cabinet containing the main works and the round white face (hand-painted with scenes depicting the four seasons) had been laid carefully on a pile of straw; but the pendulum had been removed so that it could be held aloft throughout the journey by a devoted old woman sitting in the cart to ensure that at no time did it 'go off the plumb'. Despite all precautions, however, something had gone wrong, and for many years in Brunerican the clock refused to go. Then Danny came along, searched its entrails with a candle and set to work. Within a few hours, to general amazement, the clock was ticking and striking the hours with healthy emphasis. Seventy years later it is still going, worth a great deal of money, I believe, and a memorial to Danny's skill.

Small clocks and watches were taken away by Danny to work upon in his home. How his ancient eyes coped with their intricate interiors was a puzzle to Neil and me. Sometimes we sat on the wooden floor, watching. A dumpy, one-wick paraffin lamp burned by his elbow, on a table littered with tiny wheels and springs, small screwdrivers and delicate tweezers. He wore wire-rimmed spectacles and, as he worked, held the clocks and watches only an inch or two away from them. Every so often the spectacles would begin to slide down the long, pointed nose. Then he would straighten up, adjust them carefully and, with a muttered Gaelic curse, resume the operation. The whole picture comes back to me now, like a study by an old Dutch master.

Danny's last illness struck him down soon after the outbreak of the First World War. The Padre sat at one side of the straw bed, while the daughter, a widow now of almost seventy whose name was Phemie, sat on the other. A candle stood in its wax on a packing case, its flame flickering in the draught from a window stuffed with rags.

The night crept into morning, and my father shivered in his overcoat.

The slow breaths became shallower. 'It's his time,' whispered the daughter.

Danny was moving painfully, trying to speak. The Padre heard the words: 'The earth, Phemie. The earth.'

On the mantelpiece was a saucer containing a white-brown mixture. The daughter looked at the saucer, then at my father. He nodded.

She took it and laid it on her father's breast, carrying out, by means of the earth and the salt, an ancient pagan ritual for death.

And then, as the Padre prayed, the withered flesh ceased to move and the shallow breathing stopped.

The earth and the salt. The bread and the wine. Is there a difference?

Teapot Lane no longer exists. In place of the seven or eight small dark cottages there are three private houses and a modern store. Hygiene is maintained at a high standard.

But there is nobody in Southend today who can repair a watch or a grandfather clock.

With my parents I visited Danny the Tink in his unsavoury 'but and ben'. I also accompanied them when they went for lunch – as happened fairly frequently – to the mansion house of Carskiey. (In the bay below the house, some distance from the shore, there lies a half-submerged rock shaped like a bird's wing. In the Gaelic it is called Carraig Sgeith, the winged rock. Hence Carskiey.)

Mrs Boyd was an elderly widow, small and round and sombrely dressed like Queen Victoria, one of the Coats family whose fortunes derived from the thread mills of Paisley. She was a millionairess, a fact which we bandied about amongst ourselves with quiet awe. According to the stories her father was so rich that when his numerous family was young he and his wife often hired a train for the holidays, in which, with a multitude of servants, they visited not only many parts of Britain but the Continent as well.

Neil and I spent many an interesting hour in the Manse attics speculating on what we should do with a million pounds. Neil's most bizarre idea must have occurred to him soon after the outbreak of the First World War. This was to manufacture a huge gun, to be placed on top of Tapoc, the 700-feet-high volcanic rim which overlooks the village: a gun so powerful that it could hurl a shell all the way to Berlin.

'I'd aim it at the Kaiser's palace,' he said. 'If we kilt *him* the bloody Germans wad soon stop fechtin'!'

My own instant reaction to the acquisition of a million pounds would have been to purchase a brand new bicycle with a three-speed gear. I also considered buying Southend and declaring it a separate kingdom, with the Padre as king, of course, and myself as heir to the throne. And with Neil, as he grew older, as my prime minister. But when my parents once put the question to me, I was cunning enough to strike a note neither worldly nor material.

'I'd give it to the poor,' I told them, unctuously, adding as a small salve to conscience, 'Most of it, anyway.'

'Ay, you have the right way of it,' my father said, obviously gratified that his eldest son should harbour such staunch Christian ideals.

My mother, saying nothing, looked at me with the small sidelong smile which I learned later indicated scepticism. But her silence did not worry me. I knew that no matter what I said or did she would still love me.

A great oblong pile of masonry turreted with scores of chimneys, Carskiey had only recently been built (in 1905) and contained every kind of amenity described as 'modern' at the time. For example, salt water baths then being considered essential to good health, all the bathrooms were piped to receive water pumped up from the sea half a mile away and heated by coal-fired boilers. There was electricity, generated in a small building at the back of the house from which there issued hummings and whinings much to my youthful taste. (It was to be another forty years before the North of Scotland Hydro-Electric Board brought electricity to the general public in Southend.) The tall french windows at the front of the house opened on to a paved patio of enormous extent. Not long ago an architect told me that today the paving alone of such an area would cost approximately £100,000. With trees and garden bushes sheltering it on three sides I have always thought it would make a wonderful stage for an open-air presentation of *A Midsummer Night's Dream*.

My first visit to Carskiey remains clear in my memory.

Mrs Boyd sent a car to collect us: a dignified Daimler with studded tyres. Those tyres caused me some anxiety. I knew they were pneumatic. Was it not possible, therefore, that the studs, if hammered into the rubber in the same way as tackets into boots, would eventually work their way in and burst the inner tubes? Lacking, as people often remind me, a proper scientific education, I am still vague as to how those flat, highly polished metal studs were fixed in the rubber, and, indeed, as to their value in strengthening the tyres.

My father and mother sat in the rear, the Daimler's hood folded back because the day was fine, their knees covered by a tartan rug. I sat beside the chauffeur. Apart from my worry about the tyres, I enjoyed the run from the Manse to Carskiey. Though the distance was only about four miles, it took us at least twenty minutes. (After all, the days were not long past when a motorcar had to be preceded by a person waving a red flag.) We met farm carts on the way. The horse in one of them reared and plunged at the sound of the Daimler's engine and had to be taken off the road and held steady as we passed. But the main reason for my enjoyment was a conversation with the Cockney chauffeur, whose uninhibited language, when my ear became attuned to the accent, was greatly to my liking.

As we passed a cottage in which the occupants, a young man and his wife, were said to have quarrelled bitterly in public over the past few days, I ventured a phrase I had picked up from a book.

'A rift in the lute there,' I said.

He grinned. 'More like a lute in the wrong rift,' he told me in a hoarse whisper, so that my parents could not hear.

Hours later, that night as I lay in bed, the meaning of his diagnosis occurred to me. It was an important addition to my education as a man of the world.

The chauffeur stopped the car at Carskiey's main entrance. He sprang from the driving seat, polished leather leggings twinkling in the sunlight, hurried to the rear, lifted the rug from my parents' knees and handed my mother out. Then, precisely timed, the great oaken doors opened, like curtains on a stage, revealing a tall, handsome butler wearing immaculate tails. Slowly, like an actor, he descended the shallow steps and greeted us with a bow. Finally, dismissing the chauffeur and the car with a gesture, he led us into the house.

Having dealt personally with the Padre's coat and hat and my school cap, while a maid in a black dress and white apron fussed around my mother in a side room, he preceded us along wide, softly carpeted corridors to the drawing-room. Opening the door and using his voice as unctuously as any minister, he announced, 'The Reverend Angus John and Mrs MacVicar. And Master Angus.' (He was a Scot and knew, of course, that to refer to my father as the Reverend MacVicar would be to reveal social ignorance: social ignorance similar to that of the American who, in the distant future, was to address a prime minister as Sir Churchill.) I liked the 'Master Angus' bit. In an age when small boys were encouraged to be neither seen nor heard, it gave me an unusual sense of importance.

Mrs Boyd laid aside an intricate sampler on which she had been working and rose from her rocking chair. My father and mother towered above her, because she wasn't much taller than I was. 'Come, dear people. Please make yourselves comfortable by the fire.'

The fire was huge, containing coals and logs blazing in extravagant profusion. I felt hot even though I sat as far away from it as possible. The room was bright with cascading chintzes and white lace covers. It appeared to me to be chock-full of furniture, flowers and pictures. Scattered about were small tables containing books, papers and magazines. They represented for me, accustomed to comparatively bare rooms in the Manse, highlights of luxury, and I resisted a strong temptation to go and inspect them. The mantelpiece was decorated in white and gilt. Above it hung an oil painting in a gilt frame of an impressive, bearded gentleman who, I suppose, was Mrs Boyd's father.

Chattering with animation about events in the Parish, Mrs Boyd pressed a bell. A footman made an entrance carrying a silver tray of drinks: sherry for my parents, soda water for Mrs Boyd and lemonade, made from fresh lemons and sugar, for me.

For the first time in my life I found ice cubes in my lemonade. It was the most beautiful drink I had ever tasted, and when it was done, in an attempt to prolong the enjoyment, I tried to slide the melting cubes down the side of the glass into my mouth. One of them missed my mouth and, as I spluttered and choked in an effort to retrieve it, fell with a *plop* on the thick carpet.

'Angus!' My mother was mortified.

Mrs Boyd uttered a tinkling little laugh. 'Dear little boy!' she said, while the footman sidled forward with silver tongs to retrieve the ice. He also snatched away my empty glass. The confidence boost of 'Master Angus' was engulfed in a wave of embarrassment.

When the butler announced that luncheon was served, and Mrs Boyd led us into the dining-room, the table at which we sat caused me further embarrassment. It was covered, end to end, with a huge, white tablecloth, a virgin setting for gleaming arrays of cutlery, crystal jugs and glasses, silver condiment dishes and vases of flowers. Arranged before me was an assortment of spoons, knives and forks, the like of which I had never seen before. I decided to play it cool and follow my mother's example in their use, reckoning that my father, never one to show much interest in the fripperies of life, might lead me into a few false moves.

The footman brought plates of soup from the sideboard, where the butler presided over what I know now to have been a kind of electric grill on which there sat various tureens and chafing dishes. I watched my mother. She took the big spoon on her outside-right position. I took the same spoon on mine and essayed a few quiet sips in time with her. Meanwhile, the Padre, having taken a spoon from *above* his plate, was downing his soup with noisy enjoyment, carrying on, at the same time, a discourse directed at his hostess on the subject of bad housing in the village.

Then we were served with something covered in a white parsley sauce which I decided was a kind of fish. Again I watched my mother and found the appropriate knife and fork. I was tempted to use the broad flat of the knife to convey to my mouth the last of the parsley sauce, but a glance from my mother gave me a timely warning. It was a delicious sauce; but it dripped through the prongs of my fork and eventually I had to leave most of it, uneaten. How did this, I wondered, fit in with my mother's frequent injunctions to remember the poor starving boys of Africa and China and eat up every scrap on my plate? Rebellious thoughts stirred in my slightly dazed mind. Had I been eating in the house of Danny the Tink would I have been under such artificial restraint?

Soon my situation appeared to become even more confined and confused. As slices of roast mutton were offered on large warm plates, the butler poured wine into all the glasses except mine.

My father took a swig of it and smacked his lips in appreciation. 'Hock,' he said. 'Nothing like a good hock.'

'I'm so glad, minister,' smiled Mrs Boyd, looking more and more like Queen Victoria. 'I'm not a connoisseur of wine myself.'

'Neither am I, Mrs Boyd. But I like a good hock.'

In passing, I may say that we remembered his taste on

all his birthdays until he was over ninety.

But on that distant day I appeared to have been forgotten and left with nothing to drink. Presently, however, I noticed that on the table in front of me was a white porcelain bowl filled with a clear liquid in which floated small slices of lemon. Was this a new kind of lemonade concocted for my benefit? The receptacle was oddly shaped and perhaps not easy to drink from; but I was thirsty and began stretching out my hand to give it a trial.

I caught my mother's eye. My hand ceased to move. I watched, almost holding my breath, while she dipped her fingers in the bowl which fronted her and then wiped them dry on her napkin.

It was my first introduction to fingerbowls, and I was awestruck. I wondered if even King George and Queen Mary in Buckingham Palace ate their food in such style. But again I took my cue from my mother. Slowly my hand moved forward. I twiddled my fingers in the water and finally wiped them dry on my napkin in what I hoped was a natural, yet sophisticated manner.

Later on I noticed that the Padre completely ignored his fingerbowl except on one occasion when he used it as a repository for some mutton gristle which he had found difficult to chew. I must say I admired his brusque attitude to the prim rules of etiquette and his lack of embarrassment when he broke them. And I was interested to observe that Mrs Boyd appeared not to notice anything wrong and listened closely to his every word as he commented upon various religious and social topics.

In any case, soon after my narrow escape from a humiliating gaffe, the footman was reminded by Mrs Boyd that my glass was empty. He filled it with more lemonade and ice – his nose somewhat in the air, I thought, perhaps due to the memory of the mess I had made on the drawing-room carpet – and I continued to eat my lunch with enjoyment.

Before we went home that afternoon I was left to look at some picture books which Mrs Boyd – as she explained – had purchased specially for the occasion. To my disappointment they were of an improving nature, the text so profuse that it left scarcely any room for the promised pictures. And the pictures themselves, of children dying in the snow, for example, and of drunken fathers driving their offspring into despairing female arms, were so far removed from my own experience of life that, though at first a little upset, I became, after a while, extremely bored.

One particular picture, however, sticks like a burr in my memory. It was of a boy and girl in ragged clothes sprawling in the gutter of a city street. Beside them lay a broken handcart from which a few scrawny herrings had spilled out on to the pavement. Passing by was a smart horse-drawn carriage driven by a gentleman wearing a top hat, whose carelessness had been the obvious cause of the accident. To the sprawling infants and their scattered herrings he paid no attention whatsoever.

Even at the time it occurred to me to compare this cruel indifference to poverty with the concern for the needy shown by Mrs Boyd, whom, as I pretended to read, I could overhear arranging with my parents for various charitable gifts to be made on her behalf. Blankets for old Mrs MacAlpine up the glen, canisters of tea for certain families in Teapot Lane (very appropriate, I thought), parcels of food for the Doyles in Kilmashenachan Cave. But no money for anyone. Mrs Boyd was adamant about that. 'Drink is the curse of the lower classes,' I heard her say. 'We cannot encourage it.'

She used the term 'lower classes' quite naturally, and, I am sure, without derogatory intent. Her concern was always for those less well placed financially than herself, and she voted Liberal all her life. But that evening, in the Manse, before being sent to bed, I heard my father say to my mother, 'I wish Mrs Boyd would go and see those people for herself, instead of leaving everything to us. It would do her and them a lot of good.' He did not refer to 'upper' and 'lower classes' then, nor at any other time.

I suppose it was that day at Carskiey, in spite of the fact that I was less than nine years old, that the divisions in society began to worry me. They still do, sixty-five years later; but answers to the problem remain elusive.

They are elusive, I believe, because people have varying opinions upon what constitutes the good life. It would seem that in the world today, on the evidence of declarations issued by both the so-called Rightists and Leftists – higher profits for the former, higher wages for the latter – the majority of people consider that the good life depends upon the acquisition of more and more money: a situation born of need but nurtured in greed which inevitably leads to inflation and unemployment and thus defeats its own ends. There are others, including the members of various religious and philosophical bodies, who preach the benefits of higher education reinforced by an example of charitable service to others: people who find self-satisfaction not in counting their money but in counting the good deeds they are allowed to perform. But somewhere underneath the pile are those trapped by power politics, those who are both physically and spiritually impoverished, with neither money nor education, and who have no vision whatever of a good life because the clouds of their misery loom so dark.

What *is* the good life? The ancient tale of the search for a happy man, which ended on an island in a peaceful sea inhabited by a greybeard who hadn't even a shirt to put on his back, may have some relevance to the question. So, I think, may a text from the Bible, used first in the Old Testament and repeated in the New: 'Love thy neighbour.' Which does not mean 'Love thy neighbour in theory, at a comfortable distance.'

Sometimes, living in the countryside as I do, working among pleasant people, I try to persuade myself that I have found the good life. But as long as poverty and disease and misery exist in our own and distant lands can *anyone* say he is enjoying a good life?

Every few years I am offered the good life by Socialists, Liberals, Tories and Scottish Nationalists. And now by Social Democrats. I have voted for them all and been disappointed in the results, because their manifestos invariably turn out to have been conceived on a basis of materialism. I cling to an idea given to his students by Professor A. A. Bowman, my old Professor of Moral Philosophy at Glasgow University:

'There is a divinity within every man. Respect and reverence for this divinity is the foundation of civilized behaviour.' May I say that in this idea I also glimpse an answer to the question: 'Who – or what – is God?'

While I was growing up my father was often visited by Robert Ralston, the farmer at Macharioch. When he came, if I was anywhere near the Manse at the time, I made haste to sit in on their conversation. It introduced me to a fascinating subject about which I knew practically nothing.

Robert Ralston was a burly, red-faced man with a high-pitched voice which did not match his size. He liked a dram and looked as if he might be more at home in an agricultural sale ring, with its roaring cattle and dung and dirt and loud badinage between rival bidders, than in the quiet study of a manse. But I soon discovered this was not true. When he called upon the Padre it was to discuss literature: particularly the works of Burns and Shakespeare.

He was the descendant of a long line of Lowland lairds brought to Kintyre in the late seventeenth century by the Duke of Argyll, chief of Clan Campbell. In 1647 the Covenanting Protestant Campbells had seized possession of Kintyre from the Roman Catholic MacDonalds. Many of the Highlanders in the peninsula, followers of the Clan Donald, had been killed or had died of plague or had fled to Ireland, and the duke, killing two birds with one stone, decided to bring to his deserted lands good farmers who would also support his Covenanting activities. The result was that from that time the population of Kintyre became one third Highland, one third Lowland and, on account of age-long comings and goings across the narrow sea, one third Irish.

The first Ralston in Southend was also named Robert. In the graveyard at Kiel the headstones face the east and the rising sun, a custom derived from our sun-worshipping ancestors. But, alone among hundreds, old Robert Ralston's stone faces dourly north, because, according to legend, his last command was that he should be buried with his back to Rome.

His descendant, my father's friend, was more tolerant. His

interests, too, were wider. He studied English literature and discussed it regularly with my father. This often happened on a Monday morning while other farmers were attending markets in Campbeltown but when Robert Ralston knew that the minister had a day off. I made little sense of what they talked about; but something in the sound of the poetry they quoted gave me strange stirrings of excitement.

Then gently scan your brother man,
  Still gentler sister woman;
Tho' they may gang a kennin wrang,
  To step aside is human.

And again:

What is love? 'tis not hereafter;
Present mirth hath present laughter;
  What's to come is still unsure:
In delay there lies no plenty;
Then come kiss me, sweet and twenty,
  Youth's a stuff will not endure.

These verses, only two among the many tossed about between the minister and the farmer, have remained in my memory because of their lilting sound. Years later I came to understand what they meant, and it is possible their influence has caused me in the end to write this book. 'Youth's a stuff will not endure.' But may I not try to prove that youthful recollection does? With its influence on people for good or ill.

Recollection has nagging qualities. Robert Ralston's own education was important to him; but as a member of the Southend School Board had he as wide a concern for the education of others? The policy of the board, composed almost entirely of farmers, never changed. It was that children should be encouraged to leave school as early as possible so that the supply of cheap farm labour might be ensured. Top wages in those days amounted to about £10 in the half-year. And yet I still possess, in my library, a well-used copy of *Cassell's Book of Quotations* by W. Gurney Benham, which Robert Ralston presented to my father nearly seventy years ago, knowing that a minister's stipend did not make easy the purchase of expensive reference books.

In my privileged position as a minister's son I was able to study society from many angles. It wasn't – and still is not – a comfortable position.

4. Fata Morgana

As boys coming on for eleven years old, Neil and I called him Old Charlie, though at the time he must only have been in his middle forties. A casual farm worker, employed mainly as a drainer and fencer, he had just been demobbed from army service in the First World War, and his language was salty. He and his wife had a large family. One day the eldest boy was overheard by the schoolmaster uttering loud swear-words in the playground. The strap was used, and Charlie was informed officially of his son's misdemeanour. He was shocked. He told the schoolmaster, 'I'm bloody sure he never heard language like that in oor hoose!'

Charlie was rough and ready. He was related distantly to Big Doser, our enemy, but showed no favouritism on that account. One evening he stood leaning against the wall of the hotel coach house – a favourite stance of his – holding court with Neil and me, a fascinated audience. The subject of his discourse was sex.

Sixty years ago Clydesdale stallions from 'outside' travelled the district, serving local mares. Whenever we could, Neil and I were present to witness the coverings, dramatic events accompanied by much neighing and rearing and clattering of passion-powered hooves. They caused in us feelings of excitement which we made no effort to analyse. And they taught us all we needed to know about the practical side of sex.

Charlie chuckled as he told us about a stallion which that day had visited the farm he was working on – the stallion's name was Dunure Footprint – and described to us how the Footprint had refused to have anything to do with a young virgin mare but how happy he had been and how well he had performed when an old mare whom he'd often covered before had been brought out to him. 'Ay,' Charlie said, shifting the wad of tobacco in his jaw, 'stallions is like men. They ken that the aulder the fiddle the sweeter the tune!'

Neil and I were admiring this pearl of wisdom when suddenly we saw Big Doser and Kleek approaching from the direction of the village. We stopped talking and began to move away.

'Back here!' snarled Charlie.

We stopped.

'Ye've nae spunk!' he said. 'Ye're bloody feart!'

I was only too ready to agree; but Neil said, 'We're no' feart!'

'Ye're runnin' awa',' Charlie told him. 'Turnin' yer back tae the enemy.'

The big farm lads came nearer. Neil didn't move. I stayed beside him, queasy in my stomach.

Big Doser saw us. 'Ye wee cunts!' he roared; and Kleek, wiping 'snotters' from his nose, shrieked, 'Tak the balls aff them!'

They stopped, obviously surprised that we didn't turn tail, as we usually did when they appeared. I wanted to escape, while yet there was time, but Charlie said, 'Stan' yer grun'!' Something in his sergeant-major voice made me obey.

Big Doser glowered at us. He reminded me of a bad-tempered Ayrshire bull, pawing the ground while he made up his mind to charge. Kleek, sniffing and sniffling, looked vicious.

Kleek bent and picked up a stone. Big Doser charged.

We backed away. Charlie put his foot out. In full flight Big Doser tripped over it. Arms spread wide, he sprawled on the cobbles, winded. Kleek, exposed, dropped the stone.

Charlie pulled Big Doser to his feet. 'Lea' the weans alane! If ye want a fight try somebody yer ain bloody size!'

But Neil and I had taken enough. Pride was jettisoned in the interests of safety. We ran off, up the road, as fast as our legs could move.

It had been a rough evening, what with the talk of sex and

the onset of violence. For once we appreciated the peace of our respective homes.

Not long ago, over a sociable dram, I was telling this story to a retired farmer in Southend: a tall spare old man, straight-backed still as when he had served with the Argylls in the First World War, and incredibly, about twenty years older than I was.

'Dunure Footprint,' he mused. 'I remember him well. A son of the famous Baron of Buchlyvie.'

I nearly said, 'So what?' Instead I stayed silent as the warmth of reminiscence glowed in his eyes.

'The Baron travelled in Southend when I was a boy: the best breeding Clydesdale stallion that ever lived, and the most famous. Did you know that a case about him went to the House of Lords?'

'Have another dram,' I said, and soon the memories came to life.

The Baron, I learned, was bought as a two-year-old colt at the Aberdeen Highland Show in 1902. The purchaser was a hard-headed Ayrshire farmer, James Kilpatrick of Craigie Mains. The price he paid was £700, plus a gelding as a kind of 'luckspenny'.

A few months earlier Kilpatrick had sold a prize-winning stallion to his neighbour at Dunure Mains, another dour character called William Dunlop. This stallion had died of an unexpected ailment before being put to work, and to recompense Dunlop for the bad bargain Kilpatrick gave him a half share in the Baron. The deal was made with a hand slap, a custom that still lingers. Nothing was put in writing.

Soon the Baron was fertilizing mares so infallibly and so handsomely that Dunlop made up his mind to become the sole owner. At a Kilmarnock Show, again without putting pen to paper, he persuaded Kilpatrick to part with his share in the stallion for £2000. The Baron was taken at once to Dunlop's farm, Dunure Mains, and a few days later the pair foregathered in the Tam o'Shanter Inn at Ayr to conclude the financial side of the transaction.

It was then that the trouble started. Over their drams

Kilpatrick and Dunlop quarrelled furiously, and intrigued witnesses understood that in the end the deal was called off and an agreement made that the two men should continue to divide the stud fees, with the stallion remaining at Dunure Mains.

In 1904, however, Dunlop stopped paying over Kilpatrick's share and, oddly enough, nothing was said about this by his partner until 1908, when the pair met at a sheep sale. Keenly interested onlookers heard the two men arguing loudly, with Kilpatrick demanding his share of the stud fees which had accumulated over the past four years. Dunlop shouted back at him that he had no right to any share: he had sold his interest long ago.

While the Baron's production line of foals continued to increase in numbers and profitability Kilpatrick took his case to the Court of Session, where Lord Skerrington, a judge with knowledge not only of the law but also of Ayrshire farmers and Clydesdale horses, found for Kilpatrick as half-owner.

Grimly Dunlop appealed to the Inner House, where, to everybody's surprise, he won.

But Kilpatrick, determined Ayrshire man that he was, could not stomach defeat. He took the case to the House of Lords; and there, amid a conflagration of publicity which, in Scotland at any rate, equalled that which later accompanied the outbreak of the First World War, he achieved final victory.

Afterwards the fame and fruitfulness of the Baron showed no sign of decreasing. Unfortunately, the arguing and backbiting between the two farmers showed no sign of decreasing either. Bitterness became so acute that eventually some neighbouring farmers, in a bid to salve it, persuaded them to put the Baron up for sale.

But Kilpatrick still did not trust Dunlop, and Dunlop still did not trust Kilpatrick. Each reserved the right to bid; and it was a condition of the sale that the full price had to be paid over before the delivery of the purchase.

The sale turned out to be Scotland's most popular of the century. An audience of over 500 crowded the sale ring at the

Ayr mart, with Kilpatrick and Dunlop standing stiff and scowling on either side of the auctioneer.

The bidding opened at £3000. For a time it continued between Dunlop and a breeder from Paisley. When £4000 was reached, however, Dunlop retired and, to the delight of the sensation-hungry audience, Kilpatrick took over. The bidding became brisker; but when it rose to £7000 the Paisley breeder tore up his programme in despair and dropped out.

A stranger now appeared in the gallery and began bidding against Kilpatrick. The audience held its breath. Dourly and doggedly the price mounted until it seemed that the magic and almost incredible figure of £10,000 might be reached. But at £9500 Kilpatrick finally shook his head in angry despair and the Baron was knocked down to the unknown individual in the gallery.

Almost at once the denouement came, a blinding surprise to some, half expected by others. While the ring was still loud with excitement the auctioneer announced that the stranger in the gallery had been bidding on behalf of William Dunlop.

'Nine thousand five hundred pounds! Just imagine!' said the old farmer who was relating the facts for my benefit. 'In 1911. What would be the equivalent today? Something like a quarter of a million!' Then, the awe draining from his voice, he added with a smile, 'The gauge of an Ayrshireman's dourness!'

Three years later, in 1914, the Baron had to be destroyed when a recalcitrant mare lashed out and broke one of his forelegs. He was buried in the rose garden at Dunure Mains. But his breeding prowess and the epic struggle between Kilpatrick and Dunlop to possess him had aroused so much international interest that in 1924 his skeleton was dug up, reassembled and mounted in the Kelvingrove Art Galleries in Glasgow, where this model of Clydesdale perfection may still be seen.

It is pleasant to record that, in one way, the story had a happy ending. In the early thirties some neighbours conspired to bring the two old enemies together at the Scotstoun Stallion Show. By now they had mellowed: so much, indeed, that they agreed to deliver a joint lecture at a meeting of Clydesdale breeders at Milngavie. They called each other 'shrewd antagonists' and admitted that the price of the Baron, both morally and materially, had been altogether too high.

They had tears in their eyes when the Baron was described as 'that sensational and bewitching horse'.

There was nothing prim or prissy about the upbringing of a country minister's son. Frequently he had to come to terms with nature in what my mother liked to describe as its 'coarsest aspects'. But who can say this wasn't good for him? Swear words, physical fights, torture (of and by others), sex knowledge and sex jokes, all came within his experience at an early age. On the other hand he was exposed daily to the Christian teachings of his parents, so that his knowledge of good and evil was provided in balance. Whether a proper balance was acquired in my case – and in that of my four brothers – must remain a matter of opinion.

Sixty years ago a country minister's son could scarcely avoid finding out that coarseness is not necessarily evil and that fine professing Christians can be terrible hypocrites. A minister's son today is able to discover this by watching television, listening to the radio or reading the newspapers. We had neither radio nor television; and only about half a dozen copies of the *Glasgow Herald* came to the parish before and during the First World War, to be shared among the few, like my parents, who were interested in what was going on outside Southend. (And who depended upon the *Herald*'s brilliant correspondent, Philip Gibbs, to present a sane view of the international situation.) But I believe we had an advantage over our modern counterparts. We were involved not vicariously but at first hand in the rawness and nobility of life.

One piece of advice recurring in the Christian content of our upbringing was a nut we found hard to swallow: 'Love thy neighbour.' We could never summon up thoughts of love in regard to Big Doser and Kleek. And when my father roared and rampaged against members of his congregation whom he judged to be sinners we wondered if he always practised what he preached.

My brothers and I, however, genuinely loved many of our neighbours. Mrs Galbraith at the shop, for example, who had a stammer and was inclined to shower with saliva the liquorice straps we bought with our pennies.

Everything to Mrs Galbraith was 'Tarrible, tarrible!' Pessimism concerning the weather, the government, attendances at church, the behaviour of her neighbours – and, in particular, our appetite for sweeties – were all condemned. But when we were sent for the messages she had an endearing habit, as we lifted the laden basket from the counter and prepared to leave, of picking large aniseed balls out of a jar and popping them into our mouths. (Experts on hygiene had not then begun to worry us. We belaboured one another with the liquorice straps and used aniseed balls for marbles, after which we ate them with unimpaired enjoyment.)

Then there was Mr Gutcher, the big, burly, heavily moustached lighthouse-keeper from the Mull, whose voice seemed to us to be as loud and resonant as the great mechanical horn he operated when fog lay thick across the North Channel. He was married to a prim, often silent little lady, deeply religious and dressed habitually in black, who, born in North Uist, was a distant relative of the Padre's. This blood connection, so important to the Gaels, was why they often came to tea at the Manse, which they used as a kind of staging post on their arduous shopping journey by horse and trap from the Mull to Campbeltown.

What his first name was I have no idea. We knew him simply as Mr Gutcher. Sixty years ago the habit of calling even casual acquaintances by their first names did not exist. Now, mature in years and striving to be with it, I am able to meet almost everybody on first-name terms, including ministers, lawyers, doctors, peers of the realm and many other people whose work and social position might seem to merit more unctuous respect. But there remains in my conscience a doubt as to the propriety of this, a legacy from the time when, as children, we were taught that age and learning and hereditary titles should be accorded full dignity. And yet it delights me that even the youngest child in Southend now calls me Angus. I should feel deprived of human contact if anybody addressed me as Mr MacVicar.

But in those more inhibited years it was Mr Gutcher. And Mrs Gutcher, even to my father, her cousin only a few stages removed.

What impressed me about Mr Gutcher was his knowledge of the many shipwrecks that had occurred at the Mull throughout the centuries. When his garden was out of season as a source of healthful exercise, he spent a great deal of his spare time in climbing along the rocky shores north and east of the lighthouse, searching for items cast up from broken and battered ships.

One day he brought two pistols to the Manse, both rusty and obviously no longer of practical use. One had been a lethal weapon, perhaps of American origin. The other was what I now know to have been a small gun for firing distress or other signals. To my delight and excitement he asked me to choose one to keep. The signal gun looked good: bigger and much more important looking than the other. So I chose it.

Next day, unknown to anyone in the Manse, I took it to school and had a satisfying time pointing it at Neil and other friends, threatening them with sudden death. Any girls whose curiosity brought them near were also threatened and made to run, screaming, from my powerful presence. I swaggered like a cowboy whose Indian enemies were biting the dust.

At last, of course, the inevitable happened. Some of the bigger boys, jealous of my newly acquired importance, ganged up to make an attack. They cornered me in the privvy and, as I struggled with my back against the wet, iron-lined wall of the urinal, wrenched the pistol out of my hot and slippery hands. Gallantly Neil tried to protect me; but they kicked him aside and ran out into the playground, shouting and fighting amongst themselves for possession of the prize.

In the midst of the commotion a whistle was blown with

loud authority. Into the playground strode Mr James Inglis Morton, the headmaster, his blond moustache bristling with anger. The bully boys dropped the pistol. I remember it lying there on the ash and gravel surface, silvery and sinister, while we all sucked in deep breaths of apprehension.

Mr Morton pointed. 'To whom does this belong?'

My nose was bleeding and the sleeve of my jersey was torn. I wanted to run away and hide; but there was no possible escape from Mr Morton's justice. I put up my hand.

He caught me by the ear. 'You have committed a crime of the most heinous nature,' he told me. 'Bringing a weapon to this school – it has never happened before in all its history. And,' he added, with terrible emphasis, 'it will never happen again as long as I am here!'

He paused. I was conscious that most of the girls had now gathered round, giggling. Anger began to dilute selfpity. Some of the boys who had attacked me, suddenly hopeful that I might be going to receive all the blame for the disturbance, were also smirking in the background. Tears of frustration mingled with the blood on my face. The taste of the mixture was bitter.

Then Mr Morton noticed my dishevelled appearance. 'Who did this to you?' he inquired.

Honour insisted that I remain silent. To be branded a 'clipe' (the Scots word for an informer) would be far worse than any physical scar. The same code kept other boys, including Neil, from telling the truth. But the girls had no such inhibitions.

'It was them!' they shouted, pointing at my attackers. 'They gi'ed him a moolkin in the privvy!' ('Moolkin' can be roughly translated as a 'beating up'.)

'Ah!' said Mr Morton, picking up the pistol while still retaining a grip of my ear. 'Come inside, all of you!'

The four boys who had taken the pistol were lined up alongside me in the empty classroom. Mr Morton took out his strap. Quietly and methodically he administered six of the best to each of us.

'I will now confiscate this horrible weapon,' he went on. 'During the next few days I will make up my mind whether or not to report the affair to the police.'

The sting of the belt soon passed and was as nothing, in terms of mental torture, compared with the menacing cloud of police action which now hung over us. I thought with horror of the shame which would come to my parents – innocents unaware of my criminality – if I were taken from the Manse in handcuffs and sent to prison. My assailants were in a similar state of fear. We became comrades in distress and full of friendship for one another. (Two of them are still alive. We remain friends.)

Of course, Mr Morton had no intention of bringing in the police. In time the menacing cloud disappeared below a clear horizon, and we essayed other forms of wickedness.

I never saw my signal pistol again. Years later, as an adolescent, I often played golf with Mr Morton, who was treasurer of our local club, Dunaverty. But my nerve always failed when I attempted to question him about it. He died a long time ago. I wonder what happened to it.

Mr Gutcher's pistol is a vivid memory. So is the story he told us about a Negro slave, the sole survivor from a Portuguese vessel wrecked in the eighteenth century underneath Borgadaile Cliff at the Mull. On his back he carried a small wooden barrel containing gold and jewels belonging to the master of the ship. He began climbing the cliff.

This is a dangerous business even in daylight. About twenty years ago, when a Peterhead fishing trawler ran aground at the same place, I was one of the rescue party which, as the tide rose, was forced to use the cliff as a way of egress from the shore. Scared almost to the point of paralysis, I could well imagine how the Negro must have felt in the gale-filled dark.

According to Mr Gutcher, however, he reached the top at last and made good his escape. But at some point in his climb he became so exhausted that he had to abandon the barrel and bury it deep in a crevice.

'The Negro,' said Mr Gutcher, as we listened with excitement, 'never returned to Southend. The treasure must still be there, in the cliff, waiting for some lucky boy to find it.'

That day as I climbed up from the stormy shore I

remembered the legend, but no longer did I feel an urge to search. I was only too thankful to reach the top. In any case, my eyes were closed most of the time.

Another of our favourites was old Mary MacAulay, who lived alone in a tiny 'but and ben' flat in the village and was often employed by my mother as a babysitter when she went with my father to Presbytery meetings in Campbeltown or – once a year – to the General Assembly in Edinburgh.

When sent to tell Mary that she was needed at the Manse, I always entered her flat with feelings of claustrophobia. The walls of her sitting-room were covered with several layers of paper. Above the small, deep-silled window the layers had curled upwards, like the bottom pages of a well-read manuscript, revealing plaster below. The room was crammed with cheap furniture, clocks and framed photographs. Being a clumsy boy, I kept barging into chairs and tables and tipping photographs from their precarious perches. But Mary never lost her cool. She restored the furniture and pictures to their original positions, patting my head and uttering giggles as she did so.

She was a small, round spinster of about sixty, enveloped from neck to toes in bulging garments. Her face was rosy and round. So was her mouth, which had a damp pout like the undersides of the limpets we sometimes gathered from the sea rocks. (My one fear of Mary was that she might try to kiss me. She never did.) In the village she was reputed by head-tapping wiseacres to be 'slightly . . . you know!' On the other hand she loved children, calling them 'my wee dears', and her care of us at the Manse, when our parents and Mamie the maid were absent, was devoted and warm, even though her constant use of endearments was, to me at any rate, somewhat cloying.

It was her stories that I loved to hear. Sitting in the sun outside the Manse, sheltered from salty breezes by the rhododendron bushes, she would gather us round her like a hen with chickens and in her soft, slightly monotonous tone embark upon tales which were to us anything but monotonous.

A story we always asked for was about a fairy city which could sometimes be seen in the sea off the Mull of Kintyre. She made it real for us. In our imaginations we could picture without difficulty the tall buildings and the shimmering turrets that she described. On visits to the Mull we kept looking out beyond Fair Head in Ireland in case something might be visible in the great sweep of the Atlantic. We were always disappointed.

One day I asked her, 'When does this city appear?'

'Always in hot weather, dear, like the flowers in summer.'

'Have you seen it yourself, Mary?'

She looked sly. Glancing round to see if anyone but ourselves was listening, she whispered, 'Yes, I have seen it. On a day in August when I was gathering firewood on the shore. But this is a secret, mind. I don't want anyone else to know in case they think something is wrong with me.'

We wanted to believe that she had seen the fairy city. But I, for one, was content to appreciate the artistry of the story while remaining convinced that Mary was wandering and that the turrets and the sunlit streets that she described existed only in a fey corner of her mind.

Now I am not so sure.

The classical description of the Fata Morgana, the mirage of a magnificent city seen across the Straits of Messina, was published in 1773 by the Dominican friar, Antonio Minasi. (The name derives from Morgan le Fay, King Arthur's enchantress sister, whose magic could make a city appear on any shore in the world, luring seafarers to destruction and death.)

When the rising sun shines from that point whence its incident ray forms an angle of about 45 degrees on the sea of Reggio, and the bright surface of the water in the bay is not disturbed either by wind or the current, the spectator being placed on an eminence of the city, with his back to the sun and his face to the sea – on a sudden he sees appear in the water, as in a catoptric theatre, various multiple objects, such as numberless series of pilasters, arches, castles well delineated, regular columns, lofty towers, superb palaces with balconies and windows, extended alleys of trees, delightful plains with herds and flocks, armies of men on foot and horseback, and many other figures, all in their natural colours and proper action, and passing rapidly in succession along the surface of the sea, during the whole short period of time that the above-mentioned causes remain. But if, in addition to the circumstances before described, the atmosphere be highly impregnated with vapour and exhalations not dispersed by the wind nor rarefied by the sun, it then happens that in the vapour, as in a curtain extended along the channel to the height of about thirty palms and nearly down to the sea, the observer will behold the scene of the same objects not only reflected from the surface of the sea, but likewise in the air, though not in so distinct and defined a manner as in the sea. And again, if the air be slightly hazy and opaque, and at the same time dewy and adapted to form the iris, then the objects will appear only at the surface of the sea, but they will be all vividly coloured or fringed with red, green, blue and the other prismatic colours.

As I discovered during a wartime visit to the area, Minasi was born in Reggio in southern Italy. He saw the Fata Morgana three times. It is now accepted by scientists that his visions, in practical terms, were the refracted images of towns on the Sicilian coast (or, in one case, on the Calabrian coast), all remote from the place of observation. Since the time of Minasi, it seems that many people living in and around Reggio have witnessed the phenomenon.

At first, when reading about the Fata Morgana, I regarded it merely as a fable which might help me, as a writer, to illustrate how sin – and the sometimes beautiful face of sin – can lead the unwary to their souls' destruction. Because of its fabulous quality it aroused in me no memories of the tale told by Mary MacAulay about the city she had seen beyond the Mull, off the north coast of Ireland. Then, as in Reggio I encountered at first hand a popular belief in similar stories, a question stirred in my imagination.

After the Second World War, in an old copy of *Symons's Monthly Meteorological Magazine* for July 1871, I was surprised to find an anonymous article which indicated that the Fata Morgana might be pertinent to Scotland.

For some time past the atmospheric phenomena at the mouth of the Firth of Forth have been of a remarkably vivid and interesting character, and have attracted a great deal of attention. During the past week especially, scarcely a day has passed without exhibiting extraordinary optical illusions in connection with the surrounding scenery, both at sea and on shore.

As an instance of the unusual nature of these phenomena, the whole of the Broxmouth policies, mansion-house and plantation, were one day apparently removed out to sea.

One of the finest displays of mirage, however, occurred on Saturday afternoon. The early part of the day had been warm, and there was the usual dull, deceptive haze extending about half-way across the Forth, rendering the Fife coast invisible. The only object on the Fife coast, indeed, which was brought within the range of the refraction was Balconie Castle on the 'east neuk', which appeared half-way up the horizon, and in a line with the Isle of May.

The most extraordinary illusions, however, were those presented by the May island, which, from a mere speck on the water, suddenly shot up in the form of a huge perpendicular wall, apparently 800 or 900 feet high, with a smooth and unbroken front to the sea. On the east side lay a long low range of rocks, apparently detached from the island at various points, and it was on these that the most fantastic exhibitions took place.

Besides assuming the most diversified and fantastic shapes, the rocks were constantly changing their positions, now moving off, and again approaching each other. At one time a beautiful columnar circle, the column seemingly from 20 to 30 feet high, appeared on the outermost rock. Presently the figure was changed to a clump of trees, whose green umbrageous foilage had a very vivid appearance. By and by the clump of trees increased to a large plantation, which gradually approached the main portion of the island, until within 300 or 400 feet, when the intervening space was spanned by a beautiful arch. Another and another arch was afterwards formed in the same way, the spans being nearly of the same width, while the whole length of the island, from east to west, seemed as flat and smooth as the top of a table.

At a later period the phenomena, which were constantly changing, showed huge jagged rifts and ravines in the face of the high wall, through which the light came and went as they opened and shut, while trees and towers, columns and arches sprang up and disappeared as if by magic.

It is a singular fact that during the four hours the mirage lasted, the lighthouse, usually the most prominent object from the south side of the Firth, was wholly invisible.

The last appearance which the island assumed was that of a thin blue line half-way up the horizon, with the lighthouse as a small pivot in the centre; and the extraordinary phantasmagoria were brought to a close about seven o'clock by a drenching rain, which fell for two hours.

Some time later I discovered a more recent Scottish connection: an article by D. Brent in a copy of *Nature* dated 17 February 1923.

The article described how, on the morning of 5 December 1922, at about 10.30 a.m., Mr John Anderson, lighthouse-keeper at the Cape Wrath Lighthouse, Durness, observed a strange mirage. He had focused his telescope on a conical hill about a quarter of a mile away (the height of the hill was approximately 200 feet) and was watching a sheep grazing there when suddenly he noticed something unusual in the surrounding atmosphere. He swung his telescope slightly upwards and saw a stretch of land and sea in the sky, at a height of about 1000 feet and in a southerly direction. Almost at once he recognized it as the coastline from Cape Wrath to Dunnet Head, as it might be seen from a ship ten miles out at sea.

Mr Anderson said that the mirage was visible only from a restricted area. At a distance of twenty yards on either side of the original position it could not be seen, though a movement of five yards from this point made no difference to the picture.

The mirage lasted for about half an hour. Then it was blotted out by heavy black clouds rearing up from the south-west. Rain began to fall, and during that afternoon the rain gauge at the lighthouse gave a total of 1.97 inches. The picture in the sky was seen by practically all the residents at the station.

All very factual and sensible. For me the Fata Morgana had become less of a fable, more a subject for scientific inquiry.

It seems, however, that scarcely any serious investigation by scientists has been carried out. In his book, *The Unexplained*, published in 1976, William R. Corliss writes:

Mirages sometimes display highly magnified objects. Islands and sites hundreds and even thousands of miles away may appear on the horizon. Polar ice may seem to be a distant mountain range; a fact which led to the embarrassing 'discovery' of Crockerland in the Arctic a few decades ago. Stones and hillocks became buildings and great mountains. To magnify in this fashion, the atmosphere must behave like a lens. Just how magnifying air lenses are formed is not well known.'

And then, finally, I came upon something which caused me not only surprise but also considerable excitement. It was contained in the *History of the Parish of Ramoan (Ballycastle)*, by the Rev. William Connolly, published in 1812.

The Rev. William, it appears, had received 'a minute description of the Fata Morgana from several persons who saw it, on different summer evenings, along the shore of the Giant's Causeway.' Castles, ruins and tall spires had appeared on the surface of the sea, sometimes expanding to considerable heights. He had been told also that a man who lived near the causeway had seen an 'enchanted' island 'floating' along the coast of Antrim.

From Irish friends I have now discovered that stories about the Fata Morgana – such as that, for example, concerning the green island that every seventh year rises from the sea off Rathlin Island, opposite Ballycastle – are common in Ulster. In fact, specific instances have been recorded by that august body, the British Association. What appeared to be a city, with its streets, its houses and its spires, was seen in 1817 over the Ferry at Lough Foyle. A similar mirage appeared close to the Bannmouth on 14 December 1850.

The legendary references to Rathlin and the Giant's Causeway are for me particularly significant. We can see them both clearly from the Mull of Kintyre, a dozen miles away across the North Channel. And it was in this area, out at sea, that old Mary MacAulay said she had seen a 'fairy city'.

Was she so wandered after all?

Perhaps some day, if I am lucky, I will stand among the heather high above the Mull and see, on the horizon beyond the Giant's Causeway, the fantastic city that was her secret pride.

And secret fear.

I suppose that the Fata Morgana, in a metaphorical sense, occurs frequently in all our lives. Like James Kilpatrick and William Dunlop, like Mr Gutcher and old Mary MacAulay, like the Negro slave with his barrel of jewels, we catch a glimpse of beauty and romance and, when the vision fades, experience secret disappointment.

But sometimes the vision becomes real. It is then we have an intimation of the meaning of divine love. Instead of an ideal seen through a glass darkly we come, for a moment, face to face with it; and our courage is renewed.

5. A Boy in Uist

Long before I was born there had been another boy.

One day he sat cross-legged on a flat stone in a cleft of the rocks: rocks which sheltered him from a snell east wind. In his hand was a rusty, blunt knife with which he was shaping, in labour and frowning difficulty, a plank of wood he had found on the strand below him.

His hair was plentiful and Viking fair, his face, red with exertion, spotted with freckles. His feet were bare, the soles dirty and leather-hard. He wore a woollen jersey and a pair of carefully patched trousers. The jersey had been knitted by his mother with wool garnered from the family sheep and spun on her clacking wheel. She had also fashioned the trousers from sturdy cloth made with the same wool on an island loom.

The year was 1889. It was Sunday, and he was eleven years old.

Across the sound, a late spring sun was dipping above the islands which lay between the flat shore of North Uist and the Atlantic. Banks of yellow and purple faded down the sky, squeezing the sun rays into brilliant laser beams. As the beams moved they caused tiny explosions of light to occur on the sea and on the piles of wet dulse and tangle at the sea's edge. Congregations of black oystercatchers, which the boy knew as *gille bride* (the servants of St Bride), strutted on stiff red legs, sometimes on the wet sand, sometimes in the slow curl of the wavelets. They complained harshly when seagulls, careless on evening joy flights, strayed into their feeding grounds.

From the little township on the machair land above and behind the rock cleft there came an aromatic drift of peat smoke. It overwhelmed the acrid scents of young vegetation from the low hills in the island's interior and the salt scents from the shore. The boy's concentration was broken. Burgeoning peat smoke meant that his mother was cooking the daily supper of maizemeal porridge, and it came to him with a small shock that it was long past the time when he ought to have been home.

He shivered. His work with the knife was only half done, but he would have to leave it, for the time being at any rate. It would grieve his mother that he had stayed out so late, especially on a Sunday, and he had no wish to add to her grief. What excuse could he make to her? One thing was sure: he could never say that he had become so absorbed in the making of a shinty stick – he called it a *caman* – that he had forgotten the passage of time. Cutting a *caman* on a Sunday.... Dark fears invaded his brain. Precursors of the pains of Hell?

Within the cleft a narrow crevice burrowed farther into the rocks. Into this he pushed the hacked wood and the knife. He hoped nobody would look into the crevice until he could retrieve them tomorrow after school. New apprehension came to him as he remembered this was a place his grandfather often visited to say his prayers. Then apprehension faded. His grandfather was ninety-four and blind. There was no real danger.

He emerged from the cleft into the east wind, which blew cold across the flat, treeless land of North Uist from the mountains of Ross and Inverness-shire beyond the Minch. By this time dusk was falling, and he could see a blink from the Monach lighthouse, far to the west. His cousin Donald, who was five years older, had once told him that if he looked through a linen handkerchief he could see the slats in the lighthouse windows. His parents being too poor to afford linen handkerchiefs, he had never been able to make the experiment. He suspected that his cousin was making a joke at the expense of his ignorance, but he wasn't quite sure. He had been brought up to believe so many strange stories, both sacred and secular, that at the age of eleven he wasn't sure of anything. Except, perhaps, of one thing: he needed that *caman* to show the other boys – and especially his cousin Donald – that he was as strong and as good at playing shinty as they were. If not stronger and better.

He was met by his mother at the back door of the crofthouse. She spoke – and he answered – in the Gaelic.

'Where have you been, Angus John?'

'On the shore.'

'On a Sunday? Until this time of night?'

'I'm sorry, mother.'

'What were you doing?'

He said nothing. He couldn't lie to her.

'Were you with the other boys?'

'Yes. But they went home a long time ago.'

She asked no more questions.

Seventy years later Angus John was to tell us, 'While my mother washed my feet preparatory to my going to bed, she lectured me about what, according to the Book, would happen at the last to bad boys who broke the Sabbath. That night, I remember, I fell asleep with a sore heart, sobbing bitterly, not because I had possibly displeased God but because I had hurt my mother's feelings.'

And he found little comfort in the knowledge that he would have hurt them a great deal more had he confessed he'd been using a knife to make a *caman*. His father had forbidden him to carry a knife, because of the danger to himself and to other people. To use one on a Sunday was surely a terrible sin. Made even more terrible, perhaps, because he was keeping it a secret.

In the event, like all sins, it did not remain a secret for long. While his mother was washing his feet, Angus John noticed that his grandfather was absent from his usual chair in the dark, smoky kitchen. Supping porridge with a horn spoon, his father explained, 'When he heard you coming in he went out, down to the shore, to say his prayers.' Another tremor of apprehension troubled Angus John; but it was soon forgotten in his sorrow at having made his mother unhappy.

Next day, carrying his peat for the classroom fire (a daily duty for all the children), he went to the Claddach Kirkibost school, which had been built in 1883 only a few hundred yards down the road from his parents' croft. With sixty others he began the day by repeating the Lord's Prayer, in English, and answering a few questions from the Shorter Catechism. Then he settled down to the tedious and painful process of learning to read and write and do simple arithmetic. His teacher, a girl from Elgin, spoke no Gaelic. Not until he was five years old had he himself learned to speak English, and his brain still worked in the Gaelic. Frustration resulted, for both of them.

Coming home from school in the afternoon, Angus John took a roundabout route, by way of the shore. When he reached the cleft in the rocks he found, to his acute discouragement, that his grandfather was sitting on a nearby boulder. The old man's chin rested on the horn handle of his *cromack*. His blind eyes stared out towards the sea. But he heard – and recognized – the footsteps on the shingle.

'There you are, Angus John, I have been waiting for you.'

'It's getting cold, grandfather. Don't you think you ought to be going back inby?'

'In a minute, in a minute. Last night I found some interesting things in that crevice in there.'

Angus John felt as if he might choke. What awful punishment was this old man – so venerable, so severely upright in all his ways according to the stories – about to bring down on him? He swallowed a spittle and did not speak.

'A knife, Angus John, and a piece of wood.'

Would his grandfather tell his parents? Or would he, here and now, utter some curse against sinning boys: some cruel curse dredged up from the pagan lore of the island? Still he remained silent.

Then, in wheezing weakness, like a fading thunderstorm, the old man began to chuckle. 'Whoever is trying to make a *caman* out of that stick is making a terrible bad job of it!'

To share the secret, whatever the consequences might be, brought relief. And release.

'It's a terrible bad knife, grandfather. I found it on the rubbish heap.'

'A lambing knife that I once used myself, fifty years ago. I kept it in the byre. Your father threw it away when it got rusty.' He held out his hand. 'Come here, *laochain*.'

Angus John hesitated.

'Don't be afraid. I'll not be telling a soul.'

Angus John moved forward and found his hand gripped by the gnarled old one. 'You're a bad boy, of course,' said his grandfather. 'But all boys are bad. I was bad myself at your age. Do you know, Angus John, we used to *play* shinty on a Sunday!'

'On a *Sunday*, grandfather?'

'Ay. Before the morning service. And we would be running and jumping, too. And putting the stone.'

'*Chiall!* Did you not get into terrible rows?'

'Ach, we did so, especially from the minister if he caught us at it. But everybody was doing it, so we didn't mind the rows so much.' He sighed. 'Nowadays, everything is so stern and black, there's no joy in it.'

'I can see what you mean, grandfather.'

'Jesus Christ died to make us happy. If we find no joy in living, is it not unfair to Him?'

They listened to the small waves hissing on the sand. After a while the old man said, 'Are you keen on the shinty?'

Angus John's astonishment at his grandfather's revelations was replaced by enthusiasm. 'Desperate keen,' he said. 'Cousin Donald says I'm no good, but if I had a real *caman* I would show him!'

'Ay, so you would. But by the feel of it you'll never make a decent *caman* out of that old plank. Listen. Do you know Roderick MacAulay over at Claddach?'

'Ay, Gillesbuig's father. Gillesbuig and I are in the same class.'

'Well, go and see Roderick. In his day he was a great man at making *camans*, and he still has a few left. Tell him I sent you to get one.'

'Oh, grandfather . . . '

'Now I must be going back to the house. Your mother will be wondering what on earth I'm doing.'

That night Angus John went to sleep in a mood completely different from that of the night before. His thoughts were happy and excited. Liberated, too. The grandfather he had always looked upon as a kind of brooding Jehovah was, after all, a human being like himself. Perhaps the grown-up people in North Uist – like his father and mother, for example – weren't all as good and holy as they made themselves out to be. Perhaps life wouldn't prove to be the unhappy burden they so often sighed and groaned about. And now, now there would be a real shinty stick to play with.

Years later Angus John wrote about his grandfather with love and regard. But he didn't put the story I have just told into print: that was given to his sons in private when he considered them mature enough to understand. Instead, as an outwardly staid old minister, approaching the age of ninety, he published the following:

> My grandfather chose a place for private prayer between two slabs of rock on the shore below the croft house. Sometimes on a Sunday evening, and always at times of sorrow and distress, he would kneel there on a flat stone in the cleft of the rocks, facing the east with clasped hands, making his requests known to God and seeking forgiveness, mercy and help. In my memory's eye I can still see him, returning to the house from his place of prayer, bent and blind, wearing a Highland bonnet and with a staff in his hand. Was his choice of that 'Stony Bethel' something he had inherited from his ancestors, the priests?

Fine resounding stuff, appropriate to a man who had preached from the pulpit of St Blaan's at the Mull of Kintyre almost every Sunday for forty-seven years. He meant it, I believe, to be an example of holy living for the benefit of his congregation and his less than holy family.

But there was more to the Rev. Angus John MacVicar, MA, JP, than the ability to sermonize. I ought to know. He was my father.

In the summer of 1920, at the age of eleven and a bit, I went to Nortl Uist with my father. It was a long journey.

First, a horse-drawn bus conveyed us from Southend to Campbeltown, where we boarded the steamer *Kinloch* for Gourock.

As the *Kinloch* ploughed an elegant passage through Kilbrannan Sound we breakfasted on ham and eggs, warm barm biscuits and strong tea. Spreading marmalade on a third barm biscuit, I thought I had never tasted anything so good. Oily smells from the throbbing engine room mingled with a fresh saltiness gusting down the companionway from a spray-damp deck. The steamer plunged among short and shallow waves. Some passengers, cocooned in rugs, lay prone and silent on the saloon benches. My father said they were seasick. My sorrow for their condition soon faded, and I would have tackled a fourth barm biscuit had there been any left.

At Gourock we took a train to Glasgow. There, at his flat in Berkeley Street, we stayed for a night with yet another Angus MacVicar, a retired detective sergeant who was my father's second cousin.

Early the following morning we caught a train for Mallaig, and as the sun rose above the smoke-grey mountains of Argyll which came towering up on either side of us, I was filled with excitement. This was the life. Surely, around every corner of the track, there must lurk astounding adventure and romance: explosions, an attack by Red Indians, a pride of lions which had escaped from a zoo. When adventure and romance failed to materialize (though it did occur in my imagination), I was only vaguely disappointed.

During the Second World War, journeying with my battalion in varying degrees of discomfort through Madagascar, India, Persia, Palestine, Sicily, Italy, France, Belgium and Germany, I often experienced the same sense of excited anticipation. In the final count, however, it was my eventual return home to Southend which provided me with the only real and lasting satisfaction.

I think most Celts have this kind of nature: we love to travel and taste adventure; but what we love most is home and the comfort of friendly neighbours. Few of us are bred to endure the hard and lonely lives of emperors and kings. Like his forebears who saw visions and lit up our dangerous coasts, Robert Louis Stevenson was a Celt. In his *El Dorado* (a title which, in a sense, may be translated as Fata

Morgana) he wrote: 'To travel hopefully is a better thing than to arrive, and the true success is to labour.'

At Mallaig my father and I took the steamer *Sheila* for Lochmaddy. Her skipper, in the Gaelic, hailed the Padre as a long-lost friend. We were taken to his cabin, where I felt some constraint as they talked, with much laughter and a succession of drams, in a language that wasn't mine.

I didn't know it then, but this stout, benign, whiskery character was to become a legend amongst travellers to the Hebrides. Stories about him are still bandied about in the saloon bars of many little steamers plying the island seas from Ullapool and Stornoway to Port Ellen and Tarbert.

It seems that when he spoke in English he always pronounced 'th' as 's', a common habit of the Gaels. Once, in the Kyles of Lochalsh, he was hailed by the owner of a small yacht, an anxious Englishman, who, when asked if something was wrong, shouted up at him, 'I'm sinking, skipper! I'm sinking!' To which, leaning comfortably on the bridge, the skipper replied, 'Well, well, and what are you sinking about?'

Another tale told of him is worth repeating. It concerns a North Uist girl setting out for Glasgow, where she hoped to enter domestic service. Halfway across the Minch in the *Sheila* she was asked to show her ticket. As she fumbled for it in her handbag, a testimonial to her character supplied by her local minister was snatched away by the gusty wind. She began to cry, believing that she might miss the chance of securing work if she were unable to produce a reference. But the redoubtable skipper was equal to the occasion. 'Never you mind, lassie,' he said. 'I'll give you a certificate that will see you through.' And there and then he sat down and wrote it: 'This is to certify that on the night of the seventh November in the Minch, on board the SS *Sheila*, Kirsty MacLean lost her character.'

That day in the *Sheila*, however, as my father and I crossed to Lochmaddy, I was kept in ignorance of such Gaelic delights. In fact, I was bored. And even more bored, perhaps, when we left the skipper's cabin and went on deck, where my father spoke to several of the crew, again in the

Gaelic. He told me that most of them came from North Uist and were related to the MacVicars. He found pleasure in their company. I didn't. Communication between me and them appeared to be impossible.

Later on, in North Uist, while my father and I holidayed with my grandparents in their old 'black house' at Claddach Kirkibost, I began to get the proper feel of the island.

I went about barefoot. On the shore I found the two slabs of rock with the cleft between them which, according to the Padre, my great-grandfather had used as a place of prayer. (He didn't tell me then about the knife and the half-finished *caman* he himself had hidden in the cleft.)

I visited my cousins, the MacAulay boys, at their family farm of Balelone. Roderick and Angus were both slightly older than I was and, even by the standards set by Big Doser and Kleek, fairly hard men, tough and rough. They had a big *garron* (a small island-bred horse) which they said I must ride bareback. Apprehensively, I allowed them to give me a leg up. As I sat clutching the beast's mane and trying to achieve a balance on her broad but slippery back, they struck her on the rump with a stick. She took off like a demented thing, rearing and squirming, and I was flung high into the air. I landed on the ground head first. Luckily the ground consisted of peat moss covered with scraggy heather, and the only lasting injury was to my self-esteem. But it shook me a little to observe that the dent I had made in the turf was only a few inches away from a large boulder.

That evening, at dusk, Roderick and Angus played the same joke on me – so I learned years later – as my father's cousin Donald had tried to play on him. They told me to look through my linen handkerchief at the Monach light in the distance. 'Can't you see them,' they said, 'the slats in the lighthouse windows?' Still suffering both morally and physically from my fall, I was in no mood to offer a polite reply. I remembered crude words used by old Charlie in Southend and addressed them, with some vehemence, to my cousins. They laughed, but from that time they treated me more as an equal.

I loved the days with Roderick and Angus, helping to

gather sheep for clipping, working with them in the hayfields and coming home to supper at the farmhouse, at which, on one occasion, a dish of skate was served and I was astonished by the way my Uncle Roderick – big, blond and hearty – crunched through all the gristly bones and swallowed them along with the rest of the fish.

But even more I loved the summer evenings at my grandparents' 'black house', when they and my father and I would sit outside in the quiet, tangle-scented air, while neighbours (most of them close relatives and all of them male) gathered to talk.

At first I had difficulty in teasing out the relationships between all the Anguses, Donalds, Gillesbuigs and Rodericks who took part in those *ceilidhs*. There were (translated from the Gaelic) Big Anguses and Wee Anguses, Black Donalds and Fair Donalds, Frowning Gillesbuigs and Smiling Gillesbuigs, Balelone Rodericks and Claddach Rodericks, Balelone and Claddach being the names of the farms or crofts occupied by the individuals concerned. In addition, there were Donald Gillesbuigs and Gillesbuig Donalds, Roderick Anguses and Angus Rodericks. (Among my female cousins I had already found in the same family a Mary Maggie and a Maggie Mary.) After a time I began to realize that behind it all there lay a steady logic, based on custom, and soon – after about the third or fourth *ceilidh* – I was able to judge the degree of consanguinity almost at the drop of a name.

In most Hebridean families, including my own, there is an unwritten law which dictates that the eldest son should be called after his grandfather on the father's side and the eldest daughter after the grandmother on the mother's side. The second son is called after the maternal grandfather and the second daughter after the paternal grandmother. Other children inherit their names from great-uncles or great-aunts in strict order of seniority. Maggie Marys and Mary Maggies occur in the same family when the appropriate great-aunts happen to have the same name. Then *their* mothers' names are taken into account.

One boy I met in North Uist answered to the unusual

name of Nappy Neil. At one of the *ceilidhs* I learned that this was because of an unfortunate hiccup, some generations back, in the age-old custom. A young crofter and his wife had been arguing about a name for their newborn second son. The young crofter's father was Neil, so, of course, they already had a son who had been christened Neil. As misfortune would have it, the maternal grandfather was also Neil. The young crofter wanted his wife to waive her father's right and choose another name: but the mother was adamant. 'We will call him Neil, Donald. But if you like we can put another name before it, just to make a difference.' It was about this other name that the argument continued to rage.

The day came when the young father had to register the child's birth, and, as he prepared to go, no solution to the disagreement had been reached. He was about to slam his way outside when his wife, highly incensed, shouted after him, 'Och, have it your own way! Call him what you like! Call him Napoleon if it suits you!' In his highly charged state of mind Donald took her at her word. The little boy's name was registered as Napoleon Neil. And, because the old custom was never again tampered with, there are a number of boys in the Hebrides, even to this day, known as Nappy Neil.

Another story which I thought was funny – amongst others concerned with superstitions, most of them sad and inexplicable – concerned a *bodach* (elderly man) in Claddach Kirkibost who was going home one night in the dark and heard behind him the slide and slither of footsteps. He began to run. The footsteps quickened, too. Courageously he slowed down again. The footsteps slowed as well. At last, panic-stricken, he took full flight and eventually irrupted into the house, where his wife was preparing supper. 'Kirsteen, Kirsteen,' he panted, 'the hounds of hell are after me!' She looked down at his right foot. 'It's a funny kind of hound,' she said, calmly, pointing to a length of straw, caught in the heel plate of his boot, which had been trailing behind him.

Those evening *ceilidhs* at my grandfather's house were generally conducted in the Gaelic; but sometimes, for my benefit, my father or grandfather would translate the stories, especially if they concerned our ancestors in the island. Gradually, even though in a boyish blur, I became aware that I was acquiring lessons in heredity. The blood of those ancient people of North Uist ran in my veins. Their physical characteristics and modes of conduct were my heritage. Their triumphs and tragedies might well come to be echoed in my own future.

It intrigued me how all my relatives spoke about our forebears in a detached kind of way, as if they were referring to some family in which they had no personal interest. The MacVicars, they told me, while 'short in the grain' (a Scots phrase meaning quick-tempered but originally descriptive of brittle wood), had a reputation for generosity. They were also foolish so far as money was concerned. According to legend, they were deeply religious, though it appeared that some, including my great-grandfather, had eyes for the girls, and I deduced that in spite of our aspirations to holiness we had more blood relatives in the Hebrides than those born with the same name.

Each night, when the *ceilidh* was over, the four of us would go indoors, where, by the light of a paraffin lamp, my father would conduct family worship.

My grandfather was a middle-aged, round, choleric man, with the greying remnants of a blond beard. My grandmother was slim and quiet and dark, with a look in her eyes which I could not – and still cannot – explain. It might have been one of shyness. Or perhaps, more likely, of suffering. It struck me, however, as gentle, threatening nobody.

Sadness appeared to be the background to all their religious exercises. As my father prayed or read from the Bible they would groan and sigh and shake lowered heads. This was such a contrast to my grandfather's robust behaviour at other times that, even then, I was inclined to wonder if the whole performance might be tainted a little by hypocrisy. The meekness and sad resignation with which my grandfather listened to the Word were completely out of tune, in my opinion, with his voluble rage, punctuated by terrible Gaelic oaths, when I failed to do his bidding and turn a group of frisky young cattle from the roadway into a field.

I remember how bitterly I resented being made the target for his anger. I left him to deal with the cattle himself and went into the house to sit, sulking, with my grandmother. Patiently, while stirring a big iron pot hanging from a soot-encrusted chain above the fire, she posed question after question until at last I blurted out the truth of what had happened. Then she smiled and said, 'Ah, *laochain*, you're a real MacVicar!' She herself was a MacLean of Boreray (an island district in North Uist), the daughter of a family which claimed ancient kinship with the Lords of the Isles. Perhaps that was why she was able to understand and forgive the petty tantrums of the less aristocratic MacVicars.

As we sat there talking, my grandmother and I, my bruised feelings were almost forgotten; and what I now remember most vividly about that day was the evening meal she gave us. It consisted of flounders and new potatoes boiled together in sea water in the big pot, followed by a dish of *carageen* and cream. (*Carageen* is a kind of blancmange, the main ingredient of which is powdered dulse, a variety of seaweed found plentifully on Hebridean coasts.)

I have never tasted a meal more appetizing. They tell me that my enjoyment of it resulted from the fact that I was young and healthy at the time. I believe this argument to be specious. It resulted from the fact that the fish had been taken straight from the sea, that the potatoes had been grown on the croft without artificial aid, seawrack from the nearby shore being the only fertilizing agent, that the *carageen* was homemade and the cream taken from the tiny dairy at the back of the house: nothing packed in tin or plastic to make its flavour flat, nothing with all taste processed and frozen out of it. I feel sorry for most young people today, especially for those born and brought up in an urban environment. They just don't know how delicious natural food can be. Even though old, I still have a healthy appetite and can tell immediately the awful difference between a sweet and tender chicken, reared naturally out of doors, and a battery-produced monstrosity, frozen and packed in plastic and tasting like slimy rubber.

My grandfather and grandmother, though groaning and

sighing whenever the name of Christ was mentioned, still gave thanks to God continually for His material mercies. They invoked His blessing at all times – before meals, before milking the cows, before clipping the sheep, before setting out for a night's fishing. Those observances struck me as being basically different from the Sabbath-orientated religion generally practised on the mainland.

The people of North Uist acknowledged their dependence on God on all occasions, secular as well as sacred: ostensibly, at any rate. It was only long afterwards that I came to understand that they were carrying out the practices of the old Celtic Church founded in Scotland by St Columba: practices which implied that religion was bound up with everyday things and could not be divorced from 'ploughing and sowing and reaping and mowing' and which, indeed, endorsed the Druidical belief that to identify with nature was also to identify with God.

But it seemed to me, though still only a boy, that such practices, as carried out by my grandparents, had become little more than superstition: a kind of lip service to religion, which decreed groans and sighs at the thought of the death of Christ rather than shouts of joy, as was His will. St Columba and his disciples had made the original Celtic Church a happy band of brothers. This latter-day version was a pale imitation, partially drained of vitality, though still containing traces of wry humour.

An example of this humour is contained in a story I heard my grandfather tell, accompanied by quiet chuckles in his beard. It concerned a middle-aged cousin of his in North Uist who, for years, on Tuesday and Saturday nights, travelled on foot a distance of almost ten miles to see his girl. One day a friend took Donald to task. 'Donald,' he said, 'you're not getting any younger, and here you are, year after year, every Tuesday and Saturday, walking all those miles to see Morag. Why don't you make up your mind to marry her?' 'Well,' said Donald, 'it's true what you say about me getting older. But if I married her, what on earth would I do for recreation?'

But such happy stories were rare in comparison with the

sad and unhappy ones. How had all this pessimism and lack of vitality come about? The question lay in a corner of my mind for years, existing in parallel with a growing interest in the people and the environment which had produced my father. During our time in North Uist he took me to see many places and many people. About them he told me an abundance of tales and legends which I put aside in quiet storage for a time when I might be faced with trying to explain, in part at any rate, the kind of man he was.

This time has now come. And it occurs to me that if by engaging in such an exercise I can find clues to his character, then, by the laws of heredity, I may find some to my own.

When I stayed in it on holiday in 1920, my grandparents' 'black house', thatched with heather, had few comforts. It had still fewer, about a hundred years ago, when the Padre was a boy.

At that time it was like every other crofter's house in North Uist, a long narrow building with the kitchen and bedroom at one end and the barn and the byre at the other. The windows were glazed slits in the stone walls. The kitchen had an earthen floor, and the smoke's main exit was a hole in the roof. Under the kitchen window a wooden bench flanked a box for the peat. Along the opposite wall there stood a dresser and a row of chests containing the family's Sunday clothes. In the other room – the only other room – were two wooden beds. The bedding consisted of clean straw or dried bent grass, which, my father told me, was changed twice a year in June and November. Light on dark evenings, when neighbours would call, was provided by a *cruiskan*, a small dish of oil with a wick in it, which usually stood on the dresser. The oil was rendered down from the flesh of seals and, at times, from that of small whales found stranded on the beaches.

Living conditions were not much better than in some parts of tribal Africa. The only education my father's parents ever received was in the church schools, where they were taught to read the Bible and the Shorter Catechism in Gaelic.

The family croft was small, as it still was in 1920, with only a few acres of pasture; and yet, lacking either grants or subsidies, my grandfather, Angus MacVicar, persevered in his own limited way and struggled to augment his meagre income by working also as a dealer. At the beginning of summer he usually bought some young cattle, grazed them on the nearby tidal islands of Baleshare or Illeray and then sold them at the autumn markets. Every August he sold his season's lambs to the more prosperous Lewis and Harris men who came looking for bargains. At the end of September he often bought old ewes from the crofters of comparatively distant Locheport and Grimsay and sold them to his neighbours, sometimes having to wait for his money for years. As a standing order, he dispatched fifty ewes annually to a farmer in Tiree.

My grandmother, whose maiden name was Isabella MacLean, was no less industrious. In the kitchen, which was her province, with its damp floor and smoky atmosphere, she cooked and washed with water from the township's common well, pedalled her spinning wheel, sewed and knitted and fashioned clothes for her son and daughter and, in winter, tended the cattle chewing and steaming at the other end of the building.

Such unremitting labour, however, did not bring many physical advantages to the children. Indian meal porridge was my father's staple diet, and only occasionally did he savour the luxury of a mutton stew or a dish of salt herrings and potatoes. From April to October he ran about barefoot. Even on a day when wind and rain swept over the comfortless flats of North Uist he had to do without an overcoat when he visited the toilet, which was the open machair.

In this primitive environment, with its cultural and material poverty, the old people of North Uist, like the MacVicars, retained a kind of dignity: a dignity supported by a long tradition of religious belief and of family history handed down by word of mouth from generation to generation. My father, however, even in his young days, recognized it as having become sad and submissive, enfeebled by a fatalism which probably stemmed from the Clearances which had occurred some fifty years before, at a time when men, women and children were herded aside to make way for sheep and when it seemed that nobody cared, neither lairds nor ministers nor government officials. There was a stirring in his head of rebellion, of a desire to throw aside the blankets of poverty, superstition and inertia under which his people cowered.

But the North Uist folk had seen happier and more prosperous times. They used them as pegs on which to hang their pride.

6. Son of the Vicar

My father was always proud of his family history, the focus of such pride being Trinity Temple (Teampull na Trionaid) in Carinish, which lies in the moorland some four or five miles south-east of Claddach Kirkibost.

As he told me on our day-long pilgrimage to its ancient ruins, Trinity Temple is one of the oldest ecclesiastical buildings in the Outer Hebrides and, next to Roidil (St Clement's) in Harris, the most important. It was founded in 1263, on the site of an old Columban dedication, by Belliag, the first Prioress of Iona, who was a daughter of Somerled, the great ancestor of the MacDonalds. It was rebuilt and repaired in the middle of the fourteenth century by Amie NicRhuari, the discarded wife of John of Islay (who called himself the first Lord of the Isles), and reconstructed in its present form during the sixteenth century. Measuring 61 feet 8 inches by 21 feet 6 inches, its walls average in thickness about 40 inches.

Never a place of public worship, except on special occasions such as Christmas and Easter, it functioned principally as a college of learning, where, according to the Clan Donald historians, young men of the Isles were trained for the priesthood. Though reckoned to be older than such highly acclaimed religious schools as those at Ardchattan, Lismore and Saddell in Kintyre, it was never so well endowed or so influential in its teaching. It had connections, however, with the Augustinian Abbey of Inchaffray in Maderty, Perthshire, and with the collegiate church of Kilmun on the shores of the Holy Loch in Cowal, Argyll.

Tradition has it that the progenitor of the North Uist MacVicars was born in Argyll and, in the late thirteenth century, went from the collegiate church of Kilmun as a teacher priest, in much the same way as a modern lecturer in Divinity at Glasgow University might move to Edinburgh on being appointed professor there. As priests of the medieval Celtic Church were untrammelled by vows of celibacy, he was probably succeeded in this hereditary office by his son (or sons), because, during the following centuries, MacVicars are recorded on the ecclesiastical and civil scene of the island as teachers and priests and also as editors and custodians of documents belonging to the Church and to the Lords of the Isles.

An act of parliament, dated 13 June 1496, ordered that 'all barons and freeholders who are of substance send their eldest sons and heirs from eight or nine years of age to the schools and remain there until they become completely educated and have perfect Latin, and thereafter remain three years at the Schools of Art and Law so that they may have knowledge and understanding of the laws.' The penalty for non-compliance was a salutary fine of twenty pounds Scots. There is no doubt that Trinity Temple and its associated schools came under the terms of this act.

According to my father, the first MacVicar of more than local importance appeared in the fifteenth century: Domhnuill Mac an Abba (Donald, son of the Abbot). Himself probably a lay abbot, he is said to have been a man of influence in both church and state affairs.

Alexander, Lord of the Isles (a grandson of John of Islay), cherished an ambition to bring Orkney and Shetland under his Gaelic rule. With the approval of the king, therefore, he organized an expedition from the Islands to Inverness, Easter Ross and Sutherland, its purpose being to persuade men in those areas to join him in a seaborne invasion of the Northern Isles. The 'public relations officers' attached to the expedition included an Irish orator, an Irish diplomat and Donald MacVicar.

Their propaganda had little effect. The people of the northern mainland turned their backs on Lord Alexander, obviously preferring a peaceful if poor existence to the danger inherent in yet another MacDonald adventure. It appears that Donald failed in his advocacy, as did many a MacVicar who came after him.

It has often occurred to me to wonder how a lay abbot such as Donald would be dressed. My father, whose knowledge of the olden days in North Uist depended in the main upon information supplied by the *sennachies* (storytellers), was vague about this detail. Recently, however, on rereading Martin Martin's *A Description of the Western Islands of Scotland*, first published in 1695, I discovered a passage which may be relevant.

Referring to a lay monk with whom he spoke in Benbecula, Martin wrote that this *brahir-brocht* (poor brother) had nothing but what was given him.

> He holds himself fully satisfied with food and raiment, and lives in great simplicity. His diet is mean and he drinks only fair water. His habit is no less mortifying than that of his brethren elsewhere. He wears a short coat, which comes no further than his middle, with narrow sleeves like a waistcoat. He wears a plaid above it, girt about the middle, which reaches to his knee. The plaid is fastened on his breast with a wooden pin, his neck bare, and his feet often so, too. He wears a hat for ornament, and the string about it is a bit of fishing line made of horse hair. This plaid he wears instead of a gown worn by lay monks in other countries. I told him he wanted the flaxen girdle that men of his order usually wear. He answered me that he wears a leather one, which was the same thing. This poor man lies upon straw. He frequently diverts himself with the angling of trouts.

I'm glad I'm not a lay abbot like some of my ancestors. The only part of their existence which might appeal to me is that they could engage in 'the angling of trouts'.

It seems that another MacVicar – another Donald, indeed – held an important though perhaps somewhat unenviable position under the Lords of the Isles. On several of their expeditions from the Hebrides to the mainland, most of them still aimed at the annexation of Orkney and Shetland, he acted as a kind of quartermaster general, responsible for the troops' food and equipment. On the transport side his worries must have been severe, with only small, insubstantial craft at his disposal to ferry fighting men across the stormy Minches.

None of the raids proved successful. This second Donald, like the first, found himself on the losing side.

A song (or part of a song) relating to one of those raids (in 1460) still lives among the islanders. I remember, vaguely, hearing it sung in the Gaelic by an old lady in Claddach Kirkibost, who had no teeth and wore a mutch (cap). The English translation begins:

> Our expedition did not have bloodshed in view,
> Our object was the cementing of friendship.
> In the land of clouds, kyles and cold winds
> They had the choice of Christian peace or blood-letting.
> The evil of the Cats, the perfidy of the Galls
> Closed our passage through *Ceolas nam Beuc*.

What a perfect example of an invader's cynical propaganda technique, echoed centuries later in communiqués from, for example, 'a peak in Darien', from Culloden, Abyssinia and Afghanistan.

Incidentally, the 'Cats' were the inhabitants of what are now the counties of Caithness and Sutherland. The 'Galls' were the progenitors of the modern Sinclair family. Ceolas nam Beuc (the 'roaring channel') lies south of the Island of Graemsay in Orkney, at the western end of Scapa Flow.

The story, if not the song, goes on to relate how the Uist men in particular retired from the operation, 'sailing off into the sun'. Their orders from the commander of the expedition were 'not to approach land until Uist would appear to the east of the dawn.' In other words they were to seek the open Atlantic because it would be safer there than in the narrow waters of the Minches.

There is irony in the fact that after so many abortive forays by the MacDonalds, Orkney and Shetland were acquired peacefully by the Scottish crown in 1468, a pledge for the dowry of Margaret of Denmark when she married James III. This would bring little pleasure to the Lords of the Isles, whose dreams had been of personal rather than national conquest.

In the mid sixteenth century, shortly before the Reformation (1560), a conference of church dignitaries and clan chiefs was convened at Dunkeld, with the object of settling the bloody disputes which constantly arose between the king and his nobles. Among those invited was the chief priest of Trinity Temple, a MacVicar, who acted as spokesman for the Church in the Western Isles. He must have made a good impression on members of the conference, because the Bishop of Elgin, who presided, commended him on his grasp of the national situation and offered him the abbacy of Scone in Perthshire. MacVicar, however, politely refused, saying that the people of the Isles were 'more peaceable than those of the Low Countries and much more amenable to reason'. In any case, he believed he could do more good among his own people in North Uist than among Lowlanders in Perthshire.

The impact of the Reformation did not reach the Hebrides for many years. When it did, it met with opposition. In some of the islands it still does.

In North Uist – so the *sennachies* told me – the main opposition came from the MacVicars. Influenced by their ancient ties with Trinity Temple, they regarded themselves as custodians of the old faith and the old customs. The reforming authorities on the mainland decided that as long as the MacVicars retained power there was little chance that the Reformation would succeed in North Uist. They hatched a plot, therefore, to break their power.

At the time, in the late sixteenth century, the greater part of the island was owned and administered by a certain Donald MacVicar (Am Piocair Mor, Big MacVicar) and his four sons. Of those sons Donald had Carinish and Claddach Carinish, Angus the pennylands of Baleloch, Balemartin and Balelone, Hector the lands of Ceolas Bernera and Bale MhicPhail, while John, the youngest, lived with his father, who held the whole island of Baleshare, together with the great hill of Eaval. Each MacVicar occupied a dun on one of the numerous island lochs to which there was access by an artificial causeway.

The remains of such duns, built originally about a

thousand years ago, possibly as places of defence against marauding strangers, can still be seen in North Uist. One of them, in Loch Una near Claddach Kirkibost, is called Dun Ban. I remember well, during that holiday more than sixty years ago, being warned by my father and grandfather not to go near it or, at any rate, not to step on to the causeway. Two boys named MacVicar had lost their lives there, and a whispered prophecy implied that a third MacVicar death in Loch Una was inevitable. (As far as I know this death has not yet occurred. So all young MacVicars, beware!)

In the autumn of 1581 Am Piocair Mor received an invitation from the Privy Council to attend a meeting in Edinburgh, ostensibly so that he might advise them on the political climate in North Uist. His wife tried to persuade him not to go, saying she had a presentiment that something evil was about to happen; but in the end Donald decided it was his duty to go.

Having got Big MacVicar out of the way, the plotters went into action.

At this period in history the MacDonalds of Sleat in Skye had, by force, occupied some lands in North Uist adjacent to those of the MacVicars. Donald Gorm MacDonald, the chief, had appointed as his factor on the island his nephew Hugh MacDonald, 'son of Archibald the Clerk'. Bribed by his uncle with promises of money and territory, and spurred to action by the reforming head of Clan Campbell, Hugh agreed to carry out a cruel plan.

Having collected a strong bodyguard in Skye, he returned to North Uist, landing at Lochmaddy. Then, in the dark and stealthily, he made for Carinish, where he found Big MacVicar's eldest son, Donald, sleeping for the night with his wife and one of their children in a hunting hut. As swiftly and efficiently as any modern hit man, he murdered them all and burned down the hut, which also contained many valuable ecclesiastical and family documents. The remainder of Donald's several children were lucky. It would seem that on the fatal night they were being looked after by servants in the family dun.

Before news of this evil deed could emerge from Carinish

Hugh MacDonald made contact with the other three brothers, offering them his hand in friendship and inviting them to a business meeting at the MacDonald headquarters in Dun an Sticir, another island fort. Guilelessly, Angus, Hector and John accepted his invitation; and that night, as they feasted, the MacDonalds drew their dirks and killed the brothers, one by one.

When Big MacVicar returned home, just before Michaelmas, he found his four sons dead and their holdings taken over by the MacDonalds. Like old MacGregor of the song, he was left 'sonless and landless'. According to the fireside tales he bowed his head and said, 'I am over sixty years of age and never thought to see such evil and wickedness perpetrated in the name of our Saviour. I fear this is only the beginning of much evil and destruction!'

Much evil and destruction did follow in North Uist, as elsewhere, in the name of religion. And Am Piocair Mor would have found no difficulty in understanding the so-called 'troubles' in Northern Ireland today.

The four brothers who died by treachery had three sisters. One of them composed a lament for the brothers, 'Oran Chlann a Phiocair', 'The Song of the Clan MacVicar'. In the original Gaelic it is a cry of agony and vengeance wrung from a woman's heart. It begins:

> Tall man from the Coolin hills,
> Light is your step, strong your blow,
> My seven curses on your foster mother
> That she did not press on you with knee or elbow
> Before you killed all the brothers.

After 1581 the MacVicars became mere tenants and eventually were integrated with the crofting communities in North Uist. They were also persuaded to become Protestants, more to conform with their neighbours' ideas than out of any deep conviction.

When my father used to tell me the story and recite the poem, he would conclude by saying, 'Our family is descended directly from Donald, Big MacVicar. I am Angus, son of Angus, son of Angus, son of Archibald, son of Donald, son of Angus, son of John, son of Donald, son of Angus, son of Donald, son of Donald, Am Piocair Mor.' And having got this proud patronymic impressed on my mind, and having reminded me that my son Jock, christened Angus John, could add two more Anguses at the beginning of *his* list, sometimes he would change the mood and become pontifical.

'A knowledge of our forebears is highly important if we are to understand ourselves and give of our best in the society in which we find ourselves. We can observe their characteristics in our own behaviour and, with luck, learn from their failures, both moral and physical. And, of course, from their successes.

'I think a proof of this argument may be found in our own family: in myself and in yourselves, my five sons and one daughter. I am a preacher. So is your brother Kenneth. Archie and Rona, they were schoolteachers. Willie commanded a ship and John is a Professor of Midwifery. You yourself write books and talk on radio and television, and your son Jock is a newspaperman. We all became teachers and preachers in one way or another, like the thirteenth century MacVicars in Trinity Temple. We all hated to leave home, like the MacVicar priest who was offered and refused the abbacy of Scone. In spite of the fact that nowadays we may all vote differently, as Socialists, Tories, Liberals and Scottish Nationalists, we are all by nature conservative, with an inbred suspicion of change, like Big MacVicar and his sons at the Reformation. And, incidentally, look what happened to them!

'In specific cases the resemblance to our ancestors is striking. Many of the old MacVicars were good shinty players.' (He did not add that many also have been fairly good at shooting a line.) 'I myself played shinty for Scotland, as you know. It came out in Willie's daughter Susan and John's daughter Marsali, who both played hockey for Scotland. Kenneth is minister of Kenmore in Perthshire, not far from Scone. Unlike his ancestor in the mid sixteenth century, he has a high regard for the people there; but he resembles him closely in his attitude to change. When offered the pulpit of a big church in Edinburgh he refused it, on the grounds that the people of Perthshire were more peaceable than those of a big city and more amenable to reason. Or words to that effect!

'What about Willie as the captain of a ship and yourself as a transport officer during the Second World War? Weren't you following in the footsteps of old Donald, who acted as a seafaring quartermaster for the Lords of the Isles?'

By this time in full spate, my father was sometimes interrupted by my mother, herself a MacKenzie from North Argyll. 'Have I no say at all in the characteristics of our family?'

'Of course you have, Mamma. But the MacVicars – well – '

'Are much more important?'

'Now, Mamma, don't you start arguing!'

'I'm not. At any rate, my ancestors fought at Culloden, which is more than yours did.'

'On the wrong side! With the blasted Hanoverians! In any case, the MacVicars were in the Navy at the time!'

But I do believe that a knowledge of one's heredity is important, if only as a measure to guide one's own performance in the exciting game of life. I do believe, also, that it is a good thing to try and break out of its smothering influence as, in fact, my father did.

One thing the MacVicars can say with authority is that they are Celts, in every ancestral direction. And about the Celts the poet Ossian wrote: 'They went forth to the battle, but they always fell.'

My father went forth to the battle; but he himself would never agree that he had even stumbled in the fray.

Out of this background of violence, poverty and sadness the Padre emerged as a vigorous, optimistic and prejudiced man.

He was vigorous in both body and spirit, perhaps because he was a product of a society in which only the fittest survived. He had powerful arms and wrists, the result of youthful digging in the fields and peat hags of North Uist and of much playing of 'the shinty'.

Long before church youth clubs became fashionable, he ran a kind of young man's guild, at meetings of which Sandy

MacCallum gave lessons in carpentry and other crafts which might prove useful to young farmers and young farm labourers. On one occasion the Padre himself produced a three-legged stool. This he presented to Maimie, the maid, who accepted the gift without marked enthusiasm. Her reservations were justified. One night it collapsed underneath her, leaving her sprawling on the kitchen floor in a flurry of skirts and starched apron, and Archie and Willie and I had to flee to the boys' room above not only to utter shrieks of private laughter but also to escape from her snorts of rage and low mutterings, '*Chiall bennachd mi!* Can some folk not stick to their own job of preaching instead of trying to do poor Sandy MacCallum out of a job!'

What I remember equally vividly about the guild were the parties held in the Manse to mark the end of each session. Games of many kinds were played, including one called 'Fire, Air, Water', a rumbustious affair at which enormous young men – enormous, that is, to my childish eyes – leaped and hurled themselves about, causing danger to my mother's furniture. Indeed, during one particularly violent scramble a sofa leg was broken off, much to everybody's dismay. Dryly my mother remarked, 'Well, let's see how good you all are at carpentry! Can't you repair it?' Sadly, my father and the other young men had to admit that Sandy MacCallum's expert hand would be required for the job.

Another ploy at the guild parties was a hand-wrestling competition, at which the contestants faced each other, elbows on a table, forearms upright, hands clasped in powerful opposition. The winner's task was to force his opponent's forearm flat down on the table. Much to the chagrin of all the agricultural strong men – and to my secret pride – the Padre always emerged as the champion, a fact which probably did as much for his Christian influence in the parish as a year's sermonizing.

It became obvious at an early stage that he wanted his children to equal him in physical fitness. Often he made us accompany him on his parish visitations, which, as a rule, entailed long walks in rough country. He insisted also that we should help him in the garden, digging, hoeing, planting potatoes and sawing down trees. Sometimes we felt considerable resentment when he left us to work by ourselves and went off, as he explained, to attend to 'parish business'. Only by slow degrees did we come to understand that sustained physical labour was not suited to his volatile temperament.

He encouraged us, too, to become athletes and was full of enthusiasm when my brother Archie won a soccer blue at his own old university and my sister Rona won a blue for lacrosse at Edinburgh. When we competed at local Highland games he shouted us on, uninhibited by false modesty; and when I won the 100 yards at the age of sixteen he boasted to his elders, 'He's even faster than I was at his age!'

He was optimistic, in face of much evidence to the contrary, that his message of Christian love was bearing fruit in Southend. Towards the end of his forty-seven years as minister of the parish he was in the habit of saying, 'Things are always getting better. Living conditions have improved beyond recognition since I was inducted here in 1910. Poverty is being eradicated. There is a concern for the old and the sick and for the well-being of children, which was conspicuous for its absence at the beginning of the century. The value of education, both theoretical and practical, is now recognized even by the most reactionary of landed proprietors. In days to come there will be even greater blessings.' In Southend, as I discovered, he had done a great deal himself, as a preacher of the Word and as a member of the Argyll County Council, to alleviate the situation of his parishioners.

On rare occasions, however, when some favourite scheme of his had crumbled to disaster, his optimism would be overwhelmed by a mood of black despair. Strangely enough, this did not result in his becoming sadly resigned like his Hebridean ancestors. On the contrary, it caused him to utter loud diatribes against those he considered guilty of wrecking his plans and to contemplate terrible revenge against them. Afterwards he would express shame for his actions, though we soon came to realize that such shame was not always sincere.

He was prejudiced against people he called 'holy willies', some of them his fellow ministers: people he described as having 'one face for the Sabbath and another for weekdays'. A Free Church minister, distantly related to himself, was one I remember who incurred his wrath. Asked to assist at a summer communion in Southend, this stout divine preached hell fire for those who drank to excess and then had three helpings of rich plum pudding at lunch, leaving my mother with none. Afterwards he called her 'a frivolous creature' because on the Sunday afternoon she took Archie and me for a walk and helped us to gather wild flowers by the riverside. 'I hate a man like that,' snarled the Padre, which said little for his Christian charity but a great deal to indicate that his roots were deeply embedded in the old Christian precepts of hospitality and tolerance.

The Rev. Kenneth MacLeod of Gigha, author of the song 'The Road to the Isles', once described the Padre and himself as being one third Protestant, one third Roman Catholic and one third pagan. There was truth in this. Steeped as they were in the traditions of the Celtic Church, which still retained traces of Druidic superstition and wasted little time in discussing fine points of doctrine, they both believed that ecumenical arguments bore small relevance to Christ's universal message: 'Love thy neighbour.' And in this context 'neighbours' indicated not only Protestants and Roman Catholics but also pagans.

It is significant that in many Hebridean islands today Protestants and Roman Catholics live in quiet harmony and, if left to themselves by their respective leaders, would worship together willingly and without embarrassment. It is significant, too, that when I was in North Uist, sixty years ago, my father told me that one old lady, speaking in the Gaelic, had asked him on the first Sunday, 'Are you going to the stones?' She meant, 'Are you going to church?' But she was echoing the question of an ancestor who had lived thousands of years ago and who worshipped with the Druids at a place marked by tall, still-standing megaliths.

He was prejudiced also against those of wealth and high position who did not support his view of Christianity. The

Dowager Duchess of Argyll and Mrs Boyd of Carskiey did not, of course, come into this category. They counted themselves among his parishioners and gave liberally to church funds, and their attitude to less fortunate neighbours was, in his opinion, sufficiently humble and sincere. But there were others, especially descendants of the great landowners who had engineered the Clearances, for whom he had an unswerving disregard.

In the early nineteenth century ancestors of his own had been dispossessed of their crofts in North Uist in order to make way for sheep, and stories recounting similar deeds of shame in Sutherland and Argyll had been told to him around the peat fire in his father's house. In the sixteenth century the Clan Donald had killed the sons of Big MacVicar and taken their lands: in his pocket book he kept a copy of the poem which recorded the tragedy, 'Oran Chlann a Phiocair'. Like a true Celt, if not a true Christian, he had no intention of forgiving and forgetting. The Church of Scotland ministers who had supported the noble lairds in their eviction plans, preaching to their people that they must submit to 'the will of God' and emigrate, were the subjects of his most virulent criticism. 'They sold their souls for a mess of potage!' he would thunder. 'They depended on the generosity of the lairds for their stipends and so put greed for money before all Christian principles.'

And yet he had no time, either, for these ministers who, at the Disruption in 1843, broke away from the Church of Scotland and founded the Free Church in order to release the clergy from such patronage. Like his ancestors who had resisted the Reformation, he had a feeling for continuity and tradition. He used to quote a saying of his grandfather, who had witnessed the clearances in North Uist and been an elder of the Church at the time of the Disruption: 'My Church, right or wrong! And in any case, ministers never made or marred it!'

The Padre was prejudiced against all false prophets. This prejudice I have inherited: and I am glad he did not live to become apoplectic about some of the most modern examples of the species. They are not ministers of the Church. They are to be found amongst politicians and amongst those who call themselves, variously, advertising agents and public relations officers.

Within recent years, the originators of a brilliantly successful publicity campaign on behalf of the American television series, 'Dallas', tried to make us all believe that a question of huge importance to every man, woman and child in the civilized world was this: 'Who tried to kill J.R.?' (J.R. was J. R. Ewing, an oil-rich villain whose style and smile we were supposed to admire and love.) Aided and abetted by ladies and gentlemen of the media terrified of missing out on a new cult – and by bookies naturally eager to prise even more money out of the pockets of the gullible – they planted the question in well-tilled fields and reaped the harvest.

Of money, that is: money, the god of modern man, to whom, as the Padre used to say, the idea of profit appears to have become more sacred than love or compassion or friendly argument. Great megaliths have been erected in its honour, labelled TUC and CBI. Governments bow down before them, apparently oblivious to Christian voices pleading: 'Love thy neighbour. Have respect for the dignity of others.' (But I don't blame the governments, entirely. *We* elected them. *We* are to blame, especially those amongst us who profess the antediluvian creed that politics and religion don't mix.)

Acolytes of the great god are the hidden persuaders, the pressure groups of various kinds. They compete fiercely against one another, and there is nothing wrong with that, just as there is nothing wrong with alcohol, provided it is used with discipline. What is becoming more and more frightening are the methods sometimes employed to achieve their ends: methods which are now so common that society appears to have become blind to their inherent hypocrisy and dishonesty.

We listen and snigger with grudging admiration and tell one another: 'It's the way of the world.' It may be the way of some people in the world; but are we all too 'wet' to understand it is not the way of Christianity?

Take the now almost forgotten Rhodesian sanction

busters. A few small firms were pounced upon; but some big multinationals got away with it, partly because they were financially too powerful even for governments to tackle and partly because pressure groups supporting them – inside and outside parliament – were able to persuade us that sanctions were against our national interests and that, therefore, a blind eye might wisely be turned upon them. The truth is now clear. Such pressure groups helped to prolong the strife in Zimbabwe for more than a decade and were, therefore, in some degree responsible for the deaths of thousands of people, both black and white.

Take the unfortunate business in 1980 of the British Lions' tour of South Africa, followed by the equally unfortunate business of the Olympic Games. The roars of indignation uttered by Colonel Bogey in the clubhouse bar at the idea of rugby players being denied their sport in a country which killed and tortured in the name of apartheid were suddenly transformed into roars from the same colonel at the idea that athletes should pursue their sport in a country which killed and tortured in the name of Communism. The cry of 'You can't bring politics into sport', uttered, for example, by the Prime Minister's husband, was drowned by a subsequent cry from the Minister for Sport, 'You can't keep politics out of sport.'

It is obvious, if our will to oppose apartheid and Communism stops short of physical warfare, that our only other weapon is sanctions, both spiritual and material. At the same time I detest the thought of idealistic young sportsmen being pressured into making sacrifices when those who continue to trade with South Africa and Russia are asked to make none. (At the time of the 1980 Olympic Games, according to Customs sources, British exporters were using Russian supply routes to ship three million pounds worth of vital goods to the Soviet side in Afghanistan. In addition to large quantities of spares and motor oil, the exports included textiles, miscellaneous metal products, clothing and food. Some 60 per cent of the goods were sent by ship to Leningrad and then taken by rail to Termez and Kushka, on the Soviet–Afghan border. The rest was air-freighted to Kabul.)

Who tried to kill J.R.? In time, all those interested received an answer.

For us today there is a more appropriate question. Who is trying to kill the Christian ethic? Are we seeking in all good faith the answer to that one?

But all this philosophizing, which I know is prejudiced and even unChristian, has run far ahead of the story of a boy growing up in a country manse. Neither radio nor television existed then, and the only newspaper I ever saw – but seldom read, except for the football results – was the *Glasgow Herald*. And yet, perhaps in childhood I had a clearer view of the springs of human behaviour than I have now in crabbed age, bemused as I am by the voices and the writings of numerous experts on the subject, so few of whom seem to agree.

There is one thing certain. The boys of sixty years ago had no worries concerning money or the employment of their leisure time. They seldom possessed even a penny to worry about; and, luckily, recreation was always free in the fields and on the shores of the Mull of Kintyre.

7. Ginger in my Genes

My father's parishioners were mainly farmers and farm labourers. It was fortunate that his own background, as a crofter's son, enabled him to talk knowledgeably about crops and cattle and relate the care of the land to his Christian message.

'He shall feed his flock like a shepherd: he shall gather the lambs within his arms, and carry them in his bosom, and shall gently lead those that are with young.' This was a favourite text of his, one which, in his view, must be in tune with the practical experience of many of his congregation. 'As your minister,' he said once, 'I am a kind of assistant shepherd. My work is to feed you in a spiritual sense and care for your immortal souls.'

His kirk treasurer at the time was Hugh MacEachran, tenant of the arable farm of Kilblaan across the river from the Manse. Brusque, red-bearded, sparing with compliments, Hugh had an Old Testament vision of Christianity which brooked no easy options for backsliders. His care of a few pennies in the collection plate was as strict as that of the Bank of Scotland in dealing with millions of pounds. After my father's pulpit flight of fancy, I overheard one hill farmer chuckle to another, 'Ay, maybe MacVicar's no' a bad assistant shepherd, but man, in ould Hughie he hes a gran' workin' doag!'

And, indeed, like a collie with straying sheep, Hugh was inclined to bully his fellow elders when, in his opinion, they failed in their duty. The spiritual aspect of his discipline must remain in doubt because of his habit of swearing, a habit of which my parents believed he was innocently unaware. There was the Sunday, at turnip-thinning time in June, when a young elder, handing round the wine at a communion service, overlooked the occupants of a long pew near the east door of the church. 'Ye stupid young bugger,' said Hugh afterwards, 'ye missed a bloody drill!' (The Padre heard; but his ear remained Nelsonian.)

In summer, Archie and Neil MacLean and I enjoyed many days out at 'the clippings'. Those were organized on a cooperative basis, with dates set aside for individual farms, when all available sheep hands in the district foregathered to shear the fleeces from hundreds of ewes and 'gimmers' in a single day.

Sometimes my father included such dates in his 'Intimations' from the pulpit. His rule was to avoid making what he called 'secular announcements'; but he had a soft spot for the shepherds and occasionally broke it in their favour. I think his carefulness in this respect stemmed from a story he once heard from a colleague in the Lowlands, a story he subsequently loved to tell at weddings and other public functions.

One day, in his vestry before the morning service, the Lowland minister was approached by one of his elders, an old farmer who was almost stone deaf. 'Minister, wad ye intimate that last nicht I lost a young cattle beast frae the laich meedow?'

'All right, John.'

'An' wad ye ask the folk tae keep a guid look oot for her?'

'Certainly.'

'An' seein' I'm a wee thing deef, wad ye gi'e the pulpit a bit dirl when ye mak' the intimation, so as I'll ken ye've done it?'

'I'll do that, John. Don't worry.'

The time for the 'Intimations' came. The minister began with an announcement that a new district nurse had been appointed. 'I hope,' he said, 'that she will receive from all of us the warmest of welcomes. Our parish has the reputation of being one of the kindest and most hospitable in the Lowlands. Let us remember this when a young and somewhat inexperienced girl enters the community.' And to emphasize the point he struck his hand hard on the pulpit board.

Sitting in the front pew, hearing nothing, old John saw the gesture and took it for the promised 'dirl'. Excitedly he rose to his feet. 'An' ye'll ken her fine if ye see her,' he told an entranced congregation. 'She's got a big broon spot on her belly, an' she's in calf!'

My father, when talking in a casual way, had a genius for messing up the punch line of a story. I have it too, much to the embarrassment of my nearest and dearest. In his case it must have been caused by the fact that he did most of his thinking in the Gaelic. When he told the story of old John and the district nurse – which he did so often that everybody in Southend knew it by heart – his listeners always waited with joyful anticipation for the denouement. Chuckling heartily to himself, he would repeat the words of old John: 'An' ye'll ken her fine if ye see her. She's got a big broon calf in her belly, an' she's – she's got a spot!' Whereupon, his audience would explode into delighted laughter and the Padre would remark to my mother, 'They fairly enjoyed that one, Mamma!'

But back to an old-time clipping in Southend.

For the individual sheep farmer and his men the day always began at first light, when the sheep whose wool was to be shorn were slowly gathered in from the hills. By breakfast time, thanks in the main to strenuous efforts by well-trained collies, the task was complete, and a dozen or more neighbours were in position on triangular wooden stools, exchanging current gossip and honing their shears in readiness for a long day's darg.

The youngest members of the party – shepherds' sons and daughters and stray adventurers like ourselves, along with a few young men of the parish on summer vacation from the university – had a special job to perform. We caught the sheep in the pens, dragged them on to the nearest vacant stool, then turned them over on their backs so that the clipper might secure their feet with special leather straps and make the first thrust with his shears into the thick wool on their bellies.

Procuring the sheep was not easy. We had to select our animal, catch it, get astride it and, with hands gripping its horns, haul it between our legs a distance of anything up to thirty yards. For a boy of eleven or twelve, no matter how physically fit, those bucking, squirming ewes, temporarily separated from their lambs, were hard to handle. Many a time, as we struggled to bring them to the waiting clippers, they would kick up their hind legs, strike our bottoms with their hard rumps and send us sprawling over their heads. Then we had to recover, dust ourselves down and chase and catch them again, while the shepherds roared with laughter and uttered ribald jokes at our expense. Often we felt bruised and battered and almost exhausted; but it was a point of honour to try and show no weakness.

Sometimes, however, on account of the numbers present, we were able to work a rota system, whereby, after the first flush of enthusiasm declined, a few of us could take time off. On those occasions we liked to sit with the collies, which were also resting, and fondle and speak to them until warned by the shepherds to leave them alone and not spoil them.

We also liked to watch the shepherds wielding their shears. (At that time each man owned his own shears, honing them and oiling them with loving care. Now they mainly use electric clippers, hired for the occasion.) The speed at which they worked astonished us. With three or four powerful cuts the underside of the sheep was done. Then they turned it over and dealt with the upper part of its body. If it happened to be nicked by the shears, the clipper bent down and, with a short stick, took a gout of Archangel tar from a tin and smeared it on the wound. In seconds, it appeared, the whole fleece was lying beside the stool and the sheep, released and bleating loudly, was being chivvied towards the pen. There, naked as a skinned rabbit, it was immersed in a long, deep trough filled with sheep dip, after which it was driven out, back on to the hillside – no doubt, considering the undignified treatment it had undergone, to its immense relief.

Meanwhile, one of the older shepherds lifted the fleece and handed it up to the man in charge of 'the bag'. This bag, about ten feet in height, was suspended from a kind of gallows consisting of two tall wooden poles surmounted by a crosspiece. To begin with, the charge hand operated from a ladder propped up against the gallows. As it gradually filled, however, he stepped from the ladder into the bag in order to stamp down the contents.

The noise was constant and exciting: the bleating of sheep, the shouting of men, the laughter when one of us boys took a tumble, the frustrated barking of collies when small boys joined them in rounding up a sheep that had tried to escape from the pens. The smells were constant, too: of sheep dip, of tar, of the sheep themselves, of sweating men. The scene was one of continual movement as bright shears flashed, as men in shirt sleeves and gallowses (braces) directed shorn sheep into the splashing dip trough, as panting boys wrestled with recalcitrant ewes. I can hear and smell and see it all even after sixty years.

At midday there was a lull while the host shepherd and his womenfolk served an outdoor lunch. This usually consisted of huge cheese and meat sandwiches washed down with equally huge glasses of whisky and water or, for the less mature, of lemonade. During this time, soon after the First World War, at a price of approximately 35p per bottle in modern money whisky was relatively cheap.

But it was when the day ended, about seven o'clock in the evening, that I enjoyed myself most. Everybody tramped into the farm kitchen, a cool, airy place with a polished stone floor and strips of dried cod hanging from the ceiling beams. We sat round scrubbed wooden tables, talking and laughing with relief at work well done. Great bowls of Scotch broth, containing coarse barley, diced turnips and carrots, shredded cabbage and fresh green peas, were set before us, followed by plates of steaming mutton stew with new potatoes. For dessert, if anyone had space left in a violently distended stomach, there might be curds and cream accompanied by stewed gooseberries. The food matched keen appetites, and our appreciation was measured by a continuous slurping and smacking as we consumed it.

Afterwards, when dusk began to gather and paraffin lamps were lit, the older men lit their pipes and over an unlimited supply of whisky began to tell the stories and the jokes which held me spellbound. It reminded me of the *ceilidh* nights in my grandfather's house in North Uist, though the talk here was generally louder, more self-assured, without the Hebridean undertone of sadness.

As a rule, the oldest man present was Archie Campbell, a tenant shepherd with the Duke of Argyll and a parish councillor. His wit was keen, and nobody ever tried to argue with him for fear of a verbal whipping. And yet he loved a joke, even at his own expense, and he was always courteous and kind to women and children. His descent was from the MacNeills, an aristocratic family in the Mull of Kintyre – no doubt connected with the kingly O'Neills of Antrim across the water – and his precise and careful speech was evidence of this.

One day my father, my brother Willie and I went visiting to Dalsmirren where Archie lived with his sister Rosie and brother Ned. As soon as we entered the house, following a traditional rule of hospitality, a bottle of whisky was placed on the table and, beside it, a jug of milk.

'And now, minister,' said Archie, 'after your long walk you will be having a wee dram?'

'Thank you, Archie.'

'And you, Angus?' pointing to me, aged ten.

'A glass of milk, please.'

Then to Willie, aged five, 'And what about yourself, *laochain*? Tell me what you'd like.'

Willie pointed at the whisky bottle.

Archie's round, white-whiskered face broke into a happy smile. 'Ah!' he said, patting my brother's head. 'There's a great future in front of *you*, my boy!'

Having tramped the hills and glens of Southend for so many years as a shepherd, Archie had a store of knowledge concerning the Bronze Age duns and the even more ancient Neolithic chambered cairns hidden away in remote corners of the parish.

After one clipping I remember listening with a strange stirring of excitement to a story he told about the big stones arranged in the shape of a heart in the hills above Dalsmirren. They lie beside a hill road leading to Campbeltown, and Archie brought silence into the kitchen as he described how, on his way home from the town on a moonlit night, he had seen shadows moving around the stones in a silent dance. 'I was not afraid,' he said. 'I stood there, watching, and felt that maybe I should be joining them, even though I knew quite well that what I was seeing must have happened five thousand years ago. Then a cloud came over the moon and the shadows disappeared. It was then that I was afraid, and a great loneliness came on me.'

Coming from anyone else around that table such a story might have caused sceptical laughter; but nobody laughed at Archie. In a dim way I understood even then the feeling he was trying to convey to us: an awareness of our links with prehistory; an awareness that people in the Neolithic Age must have been very like ourselves, their ancient settlements and places of burial clear evidence that the ideal of community existence is by no means a modern concept; an awareness that such community existence, in which people share with one another not only food but also joys and sorrows, is the mark of caring humanity as against that of the animal world which is always callously material.

It was this story, told by a jolly, down-to-earth pragmatist like old Archie, which, I think, caused my initial interest in the prehistory of my parish community: an interest which still gives me pleasure and excitement as I explore the hills at the Mull of Kintyre looking for more evidence of the men, women and children who lived in Southend long before the first pyramid was erected in Egypt. In North Uist stories concerning my family went back seven hundred years. They gave me insight into the question: 'Who am I?' Now, in my imagination, I can conjure up pictures of the wider human family which go back seven thousand years. And which add a new significance to the question.

The first human beings known to have lived in Southend – and indeed in Scotland – did so in the age described by archaeologists as Mesolithic. They were active, small-boned hunters and fishermen whose flint arrowheads and spear-heads have been found in abundance near the Mull. Not long ago one of their flint workshops, cluttered with rejected weapon heads, was discovered on a building site in Campbeltown, ten miles away. Their courage in leaving their native territory in Ireland and crossing the North Channel in boats made of wicker, hides and clay – or perhaps even of hollowed out treetrunks – was impressive, though it is interesting to discover that they always appear to have moved in tribal groups, never alone.

According to my wife's cousin, the late Andrew McKerral, who was an archaeologist as well as a noted historian, 'the discovery of a Mesolithic flint workshop in Campbeltown has disclosed the fact that this is the first known locality in Scotland to receive human colonisation'. Southend, being only eleven miles distant from Ireland at the narrowest part of the North Channel, can be likened to a pierhead for groups of adventurers moving out of Ireland into new territory.

After the Mesolithic men came the Neolithic men (*circa* 3000–2000 BC). They were farmers and probably less mobile than the Mesolithic hunters, but most of them reached Southend by sea from Ireland. It is the opinion of some archaeologists that 'between the Mesolithic and Neolithic periods there is not only a chronological but also a distinct cultural gap'. I believe this to be unlikely, because people always mix and intermarry and argue amongst themselves, so that chronological and cultural gaps are unknown in any properly researched history of human development. It seems that the Royal Commission on the Ancient and Historical Monuments of Scotland supports this view. One radiocarbon date is available for Mesolithic remains in south-west Scotland. It is 4050 BC (give or take 150 years) for a coastal site in Wigtownshire, much later than used to be thought possible; and it forces the Royal Commission to conclude that 'the Mesolithic communities were still occupying the foreshore at the head of Campbeltown Loch at much the same time as the arrival of the earliest Neolithic people in the peninsula'.

Evidence of Neolithic occupation of Southend and the surrounding district is plentiful. A paleobotanical investigation has been carried out on the Aros Moss, an area of peat bog between Campbeltown and Machrihanish, only a few miles across the hills from Southend. Pollen analyses of peat samples show that around 3000 BC, or even earlier, there was a marked decline in elm pollen and a corresponding increase in the frequency of grass and other non-arboreal pollens, in particular of ribwort plantain and similar light-seeking weeds of cultivation. The investigation suggests that in the fourth millennium BC the aboriginal forests of Scotland were being cleared and cultivated by progressive Neolithic farmers.

I can't help feeling that many a furious argument must have arisen as the Mesolithic men, probably content to be described as 'aristocratic old squires', continued to rampage after reindeer, elk and wild boar through the laboriously tilled Neolithic fields. (Is there a clue here to the reason why, in general, we Scots are a nation of inveterate poachers?)

More evidence of Neolithic occupation is provided by their ruined chambered cairns, examples of which are common in Southend. Their builders, being farmers, erected them in fertile areas, in particular the raised beach deposits and alluvial gravels. Generally comparable cairns exist in Northern Ireland, and it is obvious that those ancient grave places had a common architectural origin, conceived on a monumental scale for communal burial over many generations. No two examples are exactly alike, and several, it appears, have had a complicated history.

In their initial form, dating from the early part of the third millennium BC, they probably consisted of a single burial chamber rectangular in shape and of megalithic construction, enclosed in a round or oval cairn. But as time went by and the Neolithic inhabitants of Southend made contact with other tribes from England, Wales and Ireland, the original cairns were enlarged and improved and more than one burial chamber added. As my Neolithic ancestors absorbed outside influences they began to recognize something of the divinity in man and erected tall portal stones at the entrances to their burial grounds, thus paying a kind of tribute to the dignity of death.

Long ago my father took me to see the Neolithic cairn on

Macharioch Hill, about two miles east of the Manse. Now, on a Sunday afternoon in late spring, Jean and I often go back there to experience again the atmosphere of the place.

Peewits call around us. The whins bloom yellow, filling the air with the tang of burgeoning life. The houses of Southend are sprinkled like crumbs in the valley below – a valley which widens out to face the North Channel and the distant backdrop of the Antrim Hills. We stand in the midst of the cairn, the portal stones behind us, the open and empty burial chamber at our feet, and it becomes clear why ancient men chose this place as one where they might contemplate a new awareness of the human situation. Here there occurs a sense of being above mundane anxieties, a feeling of peace in the quiet heart of nature.

A proper uncovering of the life style of Neolithic man in Scotland has only just begun. Controlled digs of their chambered tombs have been comparatively rare. In spite of this, however, experts offer two theories about their habits which appear to be incompatible.

Some experts – those who can be described as orthodox – tell me that the Neolithic men emerged from caves. In due course they built primitive dwellings, reared animals for domestic use and practised agriculture for the first time, propagating a few useful plants like one-corn and emmer, two wild grasses known to be the ancestors of wheat. Laboriously they shaped flint and obsidian to make the crude axes and knives which clutter up museums – though some of those axes, in my opinion, are actually hoes once used for tilling the soil. The same experts tell me that the Neolithic men designed and constructed not only chambered cairns like the one on Macharioch Hill but also great religious centres like Callanish in Lewis and Temple Wood near Lochgilphead in Argyll (and Stonehenge in Wiltshire).

To me, an interested layman, it seems curious that rude and constantly busy farmers, eking out a livelihood from hitherto uncultivated ground, should have been able to spend incalculable time and effort in erecting such enormous monuments. There may, of course, have been a ruling class, among them predecessors of the so-called Druids, who were able to seduce their ignorant subjects into doing long stints of slave labour. But a mystery remains. How did the Neolithic builders suddenly become so highly trained in the dressing and mortising of stone? And how were so many great boulders, some weighing more than fifty tons, transported from distant quarries? As yet nobody has been able even to guess at the location of the quarry from which the Callanish stones were taken.

I suppose it is conceivable that men of the Neolithic Age were capable of building cairns and henges that would present problems to a contractor equipped with every kind of modern, microchip machinery. Now, however, with the publication of some recent lines of thought, mystery is piled on mystery.

Other less conservative experts, among them scholars like Professor Alexander Thom and Dr Rolf Muller, have written books which prove, to their own satisfaction and to that of many professional and lay readers, that some Neolithic monuments were built by highly skilled mathematicians and astronomers. Professor Thom has said, categorically, that 'Neolithic man had an almost incredible knowledge of geometry and astronomy'. He is also convinced that the Callanish stones and the stones at Temple Wood – and other lesser known monuments, some in Southend – were in fact lunar observatories and that their designers could 'work out results in advance that would need the help of a computer today'.

What is the answer to such apparently irreconcilable conclusions? Should the theories of Professor Thom and Dr Muller be correct, how is it that three thousand years after the Neolithic period all this advanced knowledge of astronomy and of stone building had to be rediscovered in Scotland?

I suppose that the asking of such questions is an important part of my 'Scottish' character. In certain circumstances I act like a Druid holding up poetic arms to a rising moon, in others like a boorish savage intent only upon pandering to inbuilt carnal lusts. Why? Do my Neolithic ancestors provide a clue?

Are my pagan ancestors responsible also for the love of mystery and magic so strong inside me, as it is inside so many Scots?

I believe that we Scots, lacking in the main an urban sophistication, are closer to the influences of magic than our metropolitan cousins in places, say, like London. We want to believe in it. We welcome its intrusion into a workaday life because of romantic implications foreign to Anglo-Saxon processes of thought but well understood by us (particularly well by the Celtic element in Scotland).

For example, a great many of us, in the course of our experience, have seen objects in the sky which we could not and cannot explain; but our reticence prevents us talking about them, except to neighbours in quiet corners. Like old Archie Campbell, we have seen shadows moving near the chambered cairns. Like Mary MacAulay we have seen the Fata Morgana and only with reluctance have we sought a scientific explanation for it.

Does an inborn memory of ancient magic help me to understand why I am a writer of imaginative stories and why so many of my fellow Scots (especially Hebridean Scots) are born storytellers and, at the same time, eager listeners? My Neolithic ancestors built cairns to the glory of an unknown god – possibly the sun – and to commemorate their dead. Are they still speaking, through a foggy dew of time, reminding us that there are many things in heaven and earth alien to our modern pragmatic culture and that a proper medical study of our mental as opposed to our bodily processes has scarcely even begun?

Neolithic men were succeeded by Bronze Age men, who, in turn, were succeeded by Iron Age men. That is what the archaeologists say, though I believe the statement is merely a shorthand used for chronological convenience. People don't change at the drop of a date. Their habits, philosophy and outlook on life keep developing slowly over the centuries. Future archaeologists may call us the Oil Age men, but we know that our passions and emotions are similar to those of St Ninian and St Columba, who were born on the fringes of the Iron Age but lived on into a period docketed as Early Christian.

During the millennia which followed the Neolithic Age (that is, from about 2000 BC until the dawn of the early Christian period) the story of my ancestors in Southend is one of gradual progress towards a mode of life in the Bronze Age and the Iron Age which was not much different from that which existed in most of rural Scotland less than two hundred years ago (and in the Hebrides, as I discovered for myself, less than a hundred years ago). The evidence for this comes from Bronze Age burial cairns and Iron Age duns (or forts) which are plentiful in the parish.

In time the practice of collective burials in chambered tombs was replaced by that of individual burials in cists or graves, many of which were covered by round cairns or barrows. The men and the women whose remains have been found were, without exception, of small stature (some of them less than five feet in height), and if the giants of Scottish legend ever did stride across the mountains, archaeologists have discovered nothing of their earthly existence.

Neolithic farmers with stone tools became Bronze Age farmers with bronze tools. It is said by some archaeologists that the method of making bronze was introduced to the 'savages' of Britain by Celtic immigrants from Europe. They, in centuries before, had learned the art from Sumerian and Indian smiths, whose experiments with copper and tin alloys had established the formula. On the other hand, Professor Colin Renfrew, the whizz-kid of modern Scottish archaeology, believes that the knowledge of how to produce bronze was discovered independently in European locations: for example, Czechoslovakia and Spain.

It is certain, however, that the Bronze Age farmers were also fishermen. On flat stones they found ancient cup marks – relics of unknown and even then long forgotten rites – which they used as convenient mortars for the grinding of their shellfish bait. As life became a little more prosperous, the Bronze Age ladies began to spend time on the adornment not only of their persons but also of their household and funerary utensils. Probably unwilling to be outdone in the gentler aspect of life, the menfolk began to shave.

Objects to prove all this have been unearthed in a single cairn at Balnabraid, situated near the east coast of Kintyre, on Southend's boundary with Campbeltown. They include agricultural hoes and knives made of flint, bronze fish-hooks, jet disc beads, food vessels, beakers and cinerary urns (some patterned by ropes tied tightly about them while the clay was still soft), slim and elegant pins made of bone and – the final sophistication – a razor with a bone handle and a bronze blade. I take a short breath of wonder when I realize that the Balnabraid cairn and the objects within it were already in existence long before King Tutankhamen ruled in Egypt.

In the centuries which preceded the coming of Christianity to Scotland it is fairly certain that my ancestors were sun worshippers, under the influence of the learned Druids. (In Southend's old churchyard at Keil almost every gravestone has been erected facing east and the rising sun. Only within recent years has the custom gone into abeyance.) Their fortified settlements were built on high ground above the extensive marshes which at the time bordered the rivers Con and Breckrie. I picture them as hard-working people, herding their cattle and cultivating the stony fields during the day, while at the approach of night, when 'hobgoblin and foul fiend' invaded pagan minds, and wolves, wild boar and other dangerous animals roamed the countryside, they retreated for safety behind the stone walls and thick earthworks of their duns; but the discovery of duns several acres in extent leads me to the conclusion that even at this stage the idea of tribal (or village) communities was already well rooted.

The remains of one such settlement can be seen on a hill called Cnoc Araich, above the Manse of Southend. Dating from about 600 BC to AD 400, it covers more than six acres and is the largest to have been found in Scotland. With the Royal Commission on the Ancient and Historical Monuments of Scotland I share a theory about this dun. On account of its size, may not Cnoc Araich have been the headquarters or principal village of the Epidii (horse people)? And may not the well-known family of MacEachran, still numerous in Kintyre, be the direct descendants of this ancient tribe? (The surname MacEachran has its origins in the Gaelic and means 'son of the horseman'.)

By now my ancestors in Southend had become a mixed race, deriving their blood from the small and active hunters of the Mesolithic era, from the dour, hard-working Neolithic farmers and from the warrior Celts, tall and fair, who were described by ethnologists as Goidels (or Gaels) and whose language was the original of Scots and Irish Gaelic and Manx.

During the past two thousand years the Gaels have become the dominant race of Celtic Ireland and the western lands of what is now Scotland; but the genes of the Mesolithic and Neolithic men persist. This is evident in many local families, including Jean's and my own. Jean herself and her surviving brothers are squarely built and dark. But another brother, John, was tall, with light brown hair. In the MacVicar family my brother Archie was tall and fair, like Kenneth, but Willie and John, as Rona was, are stocky and only of medium height, though their colouring remains blond.

It is clear that ancestors are of primary importance in any assessment of my 'Scottishness'; and because of this another question comes bubbling to the surface. Where did my Mesolithic, Neolithic and Celtic ancestors come from?

Few experts are pedantic about the origin of the Mesolithic men; but on the subject of their Neolithic successors prehistorians and archaeologists provide me with contradictory answers.

Professor Gordon Childe believes that they came from Spain, southern France and Sardinia, a short and powerful people, probably dark-skinned and with an oriental cast about their eyes. They were not Aryans, and prehistorians call them by a variety of names: Turanian, Silurian, Iberian. It has been suggested that they still survive as a community in the Basques, whose strange and complex speech, unlike any other in Europe, may be a development of their ancient language.

Another scholar, Dr L. A. Waddell, has written a book called *Phoenician Origin of Britons, Scots and Anglo-Saxons* which 'proves' that my Neolithic ancestors were Phoenicians.

The pillar of his argument is the Newton stone in Aberdeenshire. Standing in the grounds of Newton House, under the grey crags of Bennachie (at the back of which, according to the song, there 'rins' the river Gadie), it has two inscriptions, one in Gaelic Ogam, the other in what Dr Waddell believes is Phoenician script. He has translated both and finds that they echo each other: 'This sun-cross was raised to Bil [or Baal, the god of sun-fire] by the Kassi of Silyur of the Khilani, the Phoenician Ikar of Cilicia.' To confuse the issue further, Dr Waddell declares that the Phoenicians were descended from Aryan Hittites.

Modern archaeologists scream with horrified amusement when Dr Waddell is mentioned. But his argument appeals to my imagination.

There is not so much argument, however, about the origin of the Celts – the Gaels who gave their name to my native county of Argyll (Earradh Gael, 'the coastline of the Gael'). A widely held theory is that they came from Asian country north-west of the Indus, Aryan tribes seeking lebensraum in the west and driving before them people of the Neolithic culture. Four thousand years ago they filled and possessed the rich, arable lands of Central Europe.

Then it seems that the Huns arrived, also from Asia, and that they, in turn, drove the pioneering Celts farther to the west. Dr Agnes Mure MacKenzie writes: 'By the time the Greek tragedies were written, when Rome was becoming mistress of Italy – the fourth century before Christ – bronze-using Celts had reached as far as the Orkneys: they may have worked north from the southern part of the island, or come overseas from the Weser and the Rhine.'

Following them there came to our island another race of Celts, the users of iron. They were the Gauls, who gave the Romans such a heap of trouble. Their descendants, the Brythons, settled in Wales and Cornwall, Cumberland and the south-west of Scotland between Clyde and Solway. Their name lingers on in 'Britain' and 'Briton'; and their hatred and suspicion of continental Rome, transmitted down the echoing centuries, may be one reason for a less than enthusiastic response in those areas to the Common Market referendum.

I am, therefore, an Asian, perhaps also an African, and certainly a European with Celtic and Gaulish connections. I am also a Norseman, because of the Vikings who raided and settled in the Hebrides and Argyll in the dark ages between the ninth and thirteenth centuries. This is the extraordinary foundation of my 'Scottishness', a fundamental reason, perhaps, for the chaotic mixture in my character of weakness, aggression, superstition, practicality, suspicion, trust, timidity and adventurousness.

But I like to believe that in the main my characteristics are derived from a Celtic tribe called the Scotti. In the Iron Age, speaking the Celtic language, they began to cross the North Channel from Ireland and infiltrate the territory of the Epidii in Southend. They brought with them St Columba and a brave new religion called Christianity. They gave their name to Scotland -- and to me, a Scot.

A Scot? In a narrow sense, yes. In a wider and more humble sense, simply another member of the human race.

8. Farmers' Glaury

('Glaury', not 'glory'. The distinction will become clear.)

I know that the digression from the subject of farming at the Mull of Kintyre, in search for answers to the questions 'Who am I?' and 'Who are we all?', has been a long one. It may, however, have been necessary. Archaeology is a subject which helps to eliminate the narrow fences erected by nationalists and sectarians of every colour. I admit that I am an occasional fence-builder myself; but at any rate I hope I can recognize my errors and struggle to overcome them.

Sixty years ago, when I played hide-and-seek with other boys and girls in their parents' stackyards, most farmers were untroubled by such philosophical problems. They had too many other problems of a mundane character to worry about. They were poor, both in a material and spiritual sense; and their main concern was the wresting of a living for themselves and their families from soil inclined to be inpoverished owing to constant unscientific cultivation over centuries.

Their state was less primitive than that of the North Uist folk. Their holdings were bigger, and they lived in a less isolated situation, with Glasgow only a few hours away by coach, steamer and train. But in order to pay the high rents demanded by the Duke of Argyll and other landowners – especially for mixed arable farms – they had to work throughout almost every daylight hour, with few mechanical aids and with agricultural prices kept deliberately low by governments obsessed with the idea of industrial advancement. (In 1910, the year my father came as minister to Southend, the rent of Lephenstrath, at less than 300 acres one of the largest farms in the parish, was over £400, roughly similar to what the tenant was paying forty-five years later, when the duke sold most of his farms and, at a stroke, allowed the farmers to become landowners in their own right.)

Their education was better than that of their Hebridean neighbours; but at the same time the majority had left school at the age of twelve and their knowledge not only of the world in general but also of scientific methods of farming was rudimentary. With a few exceptions they could be classed as peasants.

The contrast between such farming conditions in Southend and those appertaining today is startling. A revolution has taken place, a revolution only partly camouflaged by the farmers' habit of continual grumbling. (They are not alone in this. When, in the past few years, has anyone heard a member of the CBI or the TUC boast of his prosperity?)

The revolution may be said to have begun soon after the First World War with the introduction of the Kentish white clover, which tended to improve the fertility of clay-based soils. Then around 1930, when milk was being sold by farmers for the pitiful price of threepence ha'penny per gallon (old money), the government stepped in with a Milk Marketing Board and began to distribute farming subsidies, loans and grants. Agricultural colleges and agricultural advisers brought new methods to bear, with beneficial results.

Of course the farmers of Southend, like farmers everywhere, protested loudly at the number of forms they had to fill in; but, in fact, since that time they have never looked back in a material sense. And when, in 1955, the impoverished Duke of Argyll was forced to sell most of his farms to the sitting tenants, the revolution was almost complete. (One farm bought by the tenant in 1955 for £2500 recently changed hands for £250,000.) Money now became plentiful for the purchase of modern mechanical implements of every kind. Great troops of farm labourers were made redundant.

The ploughing used to be done by horses and single-furrow ploughs. Weeks and even months were needed to cultivate the fields. Now heavy tractors yoked to double- and sometimes triple-furrow ploughs can do the job in days, if not hours. The day has already come when a well-heeled farmer, reclining indoors on a comfortable window seat, can press a series of buttons and direct an unmanned ploughing unit in a field half a mile away.

I remember men with wooden seed trays strapped to their chests trudging hour after hour along the furrows, sowing the oats and the barley. A sweep of the right hand, a sweep of the left: the rhythm had to be maintained unbroken, to ensure an even scatter of seed. There were the good sowers and the bad sowers; and even as a boy I formed the theory that a good sower had to be musical, with a keenly developed sense of timing. My wife's brothers, Archie and Davie, were prize-winning singers at many a music festival. They were also experts at sowing by hand. (I believe that good golfers also benefit by having an ear for music. I have played with many top-class amateurs and a few professionals; but the most elegant, most perfectly timed shots ever played against me were by Laurence Glover, the concert pianist.)

But now the hand sowers have been replaced by tractor-drawn machines which insert the seeds in inch-perfect symmetry. As for turnips, which used to be grown for cattle feed, they are seldom sown at all. Hay crops, too, have become scarce. Silage has taken over, and soaring silage towers give farm steadings the appearance of factories, which in a way they have become.

It may be interesting to record that it was a Southend man, Peter MacKay, who worked for a time as an engineer with a Campbeltown shipbuilding company, who invented the 'ruck lifter'. This was a tall contraption formed of three legs of wood mounted on castor-type wheels, which could be manoeuvred into position around and above the hay ricks. At the apex of the pyramid thus formed was a block and tackle, through which ran a wire rope with three dangling iron hooks. The hooks were inserted under the base of a rick and the wire, when pulled by a horse, lifted the whole rick into a cart, thus saving many man-hours of forking and building. Peter MacKay failed to patent his invention, with the result that though his rick lifter became a common item of agricultural equipment throughout the country, he made no profit from it whatsoever.

The harvesting of oats and barley – oats for animal feed, barley for the many distilleries then flourishing in Campbeltown – used to be a long and laborious process. Sometimes, on account of wet and stormy weather, it lasted from the end of August even into November. (Old Hugh MacEachran, the kirk treasurer, used to say, 'If ye miss the tid an' let the equinoctial gales at the en' o' September catch up wi' ye, then ye'll ha'e a late hairvest.')

The crops were cut by horse-drawn reapers and bound into sheaves by small platoons of hired harvesters, some of them tinkers, like old Danny, earning a quick penny and living in tents on the farms. If a farmer and his men happened to strike lucky and complete their harvest early, they went *en masse* to help less fortunate neighbours. Archie, Willie and I were often enlisted at weekends to help the laggards. Some farmers we enjoyed working for: at the end of a day's work, which usually consisted of tossing sheaves into a procession of carts for conveyance to the stackyard, they might slip us each a precious half-crown. Others simply took our assistance for granted; and if we complained to our mother about their parsimony she would reply, with some severity, that surely the satisfaction of doing good unto others was sufficient reward. In those days, when the idea of weekly pocket money for children had still to be conceived by budding trade unionists, such a high-minded philosophy offered us but small comfort.

I was six years old when the first binder appeared in the parish. This machine, though still drawn by horses (usually three heavy Clydesdale mares), cut and gathered the corn, bound it with special twine and spewed out the resultant sheaves into stooks which were then stacked. It caused me surprise that in spite of his old-fashioned, Old Testament vision of life, it was Hugh MacEachran who purchased Southend's first binder.

Now, of course, binders are obsolete. Combine harvesters, giant, diesel-powered mobile factories, crawl through the fields of barley and oats, cutting, gathering, threshing and filling bags with grain in one comprehensive operation. At present a harvest is sometimes completed in three days, whereas, in my boyhood, it often took three months. And no longer does a farmer need to clutter his barn with a crude threshing machine, often powered by a water wheel mounted against the outside wall and invariably equipped with dangerous flying belts and unprotected gear-wheels. Even cruder and more dangerous hand-operated machines for slicing turnips and riddling potatoes have also disappeared.

On the dairy side, farming in Southend has also undergone a dramatic change. Before the modern era of silage and lush, scientifically nurtured grass, a medium-sized farm of about 150 acres could support an average of only twenty or thirty cows. Now it is not unusual for a similar farm to have 100 milk cows, plus a full quota of younger cattle.

Before and for some time after the First World War milk was made into butter and cheese, only a small surplus being sold to the locally run creamery. Today every drop is carried away in tankers to a creamery which forms part of a multinational concern. The result is farming prosperity. It has also led to an absurd situation in which Jean and I, our bungalow surrounded by fields of munching, milk-heavy cows, have to buy tasteless pasteurized milk from the local shop: milk slopping about in slippery plastic bags which have come all the way from Glasgow. Is this 'civilization'? Or the bureaucratic ideal gone haywire? (With waves showering spray on our windows, and many varieties of marine life enjoying a carefree existence in the seas around the Mull of Kintyre, we get most of our fish supplies from Aberdeen, nearly 300 miles away!)

The people who benefit most from the dairy revolution are the farmers' wives and daughters. I remember women who slaved seven days a week at the manufacture of butter and cheese and, during their period of fertility, bore children at regular two-yearly intervals. Often they were old and bent before their time. Work, work, work. Milking the cows by hand in two-hour operations, one at five o'clock in the morning, another at five o'clock in the afternoon, each and every day, each and every week, each and every year. Moving the plunger of the butter churn up and down, up and down for hours on end, with only short intervals of rest for aching arms. Pressing the hardened curd into chisets and heaving those heavy wooden cheese containers from the dairy to the drying and maturing atmosphere of the lofts above. In the evenings knitting, sewing, darning and fashioning clothes for themselves and their children by the light of oil lamps and smouldering peat fires.

There was little or no relief from a drab existence, apart from visits to the church or to Woman's Guild meetings or to Campbeltown on special occasions. The rent had to be paid, and the menfolk had to have their days to market and evenings at the inn. Yet some of those women could smile. They could sing as they worked and could take time off to spread us a 'piece and jam' when we played with their children.

As for the wives of the agricultural workers, who lived in tiny cottages on the farms, their existence was equally hard. They helped out at 'the milkings' for 2s. 6d. per week and bonuses of butter and buttermilk, potatoes and cheese. The younger ones also worked in the fields. At turnip-thinning time I used to see them crawling along the drills, their druggit skirts ragged and stained with glaur (damp earth), while their babies slept – or sometimes howled – behind a hedge at the end of the field. And yet they, too, could be cheerful. Many a time I have stood in a steaming byre at milking time listening to them singing the old 'come-all-ye" ballads, with the local Irish flavour. (Some of those ballads I remember still and can repeat for the benefit of any youngster in the parish who shows the slightest interest. Unfortunately, such youngsters are few, and I have to depend for an audience on erudite folklorists who occasionally come to explore the outback.)

On the day of a fair or an agricultural show, it was recognized that after they had done the morning milking and churning, the ladies were free to visit Campbeltown where such exciting events were held. The farmers' wives travelled the ten miles in open, high-wheeled horse-drawn 'machines', their Sunday hats held on with woollen scarves. The agricultural workers' wives were sometimes given a lift. More often they walked.

The Southend ladies of today offer an amazing contrast. There is no need for hand-milking. Through an array of rubber tubes, pulsing machines convey milk from the cows' udders straight to enormous, clinically clean containers from which it is eventually pumped into the creamery tankers. It is never actually exposed to the air – or to human eyes, except through small glass windows in the piping system – until it emerges from the pasteurizing plant and is poured into the slobbery plastic bags which cause me so much embarrassment when I do the shopping.

A triumph for hygiene. But though we can be sure in this scientific age that milk is utterly free of tuberculosis and brucellosis, its taste has become neutral, and we cannot produce from it the lovely clotted cream which my mother used to say 'put smeddum' into us. (To a Scot 'smeddum' means virility.)

Nor do the farmers' womenfolk need to worry about their butter or cheese-making. These chores are done in the creameries, sometimes by computer. On account of subsidized farm prices, they have plenty of money to spend. All the clothes required for themselves and their children can be bought at Marks & Spencer's or at a fashionable House of Fraser store. And there is no need for eye-straining needlework by lamplight. The occasional darning of a sock is done in a blaze of electric light.

Many among them smoke, drive fast cars, enjoy a gin and tonic, use the pill and wear smart trousers, all of which would have horrified their grandmothers, whose probable reaction would have been to prophecy their imminent descent to hell. They have time in which to tend their gardens and play golf. Instead of churning and cheese-making they do flower arrangements. Instead of thinning turnips, wearing fustian clothes stained with earth, they appear on the golf course in colourful outfits straight from the advertisement pages of the *Scottish Field*.

The British Women's Amateur Golf Champion for 1981

was Mrs Belle Robertson, a farmer's daughter from Southend. She is trim, athletic, feminine, with a world-wide reputation as a gallant sportswoman. Had she been born sixty years earlier, all her gallantry might have been dissipated in a blur of milking, churning and cheese-making, and this male member of her home club in Southend might never have been able to remark, proudly, 'I have played golf with Belle at Dunaverty ever since she was a little girl.'

Many of the farmers in Southend used to keep their money in a sideboard drawer in the 'good room'. Today they employ the banks to execute financial deals more readily associated with city tycoons. But few of them are interested in accountancy, which has become as important a factor in farming as in every other trade and profession. (Including authorship, I may add, in a sour aside.) But like their fathers and grandfathers, who left difficult, finicky jobs like milking, churning and cheese-making to their wives and daughters, many of them now leave them to cope instead with the hard grind of paperwork.

In the drab days, however, there were farmers who did their best to lighten the work of their ladies.

I was often sent by my mother to collect butter and eggs from Dalmore, about a mile away along the riverside from the Manse. The tenant of this farm was nick-named Owld Yadi. Lean and loud-voiced, even at the age of sixty he presented a patriarchal appearance. His grey beard was long and straggly. His eyes, deep sunk in hollow cheeks, seemed to flash fire. He looked like the prophet Abraham pictured in the big family Bible at the Manse (in which all our birth dates were recorded); but in spite of such a holy association I was scared of him. When I encountered him in the fields or in the farmyard I walked warily, giving him a wide berth as I sought the safety of the kitchen and a warm welcome from his wife and daughter. (I was accustomed to carrying out similar manoeuvres if confronted by his Ayrshire bull.)

One day, approaching Dalmore, I was crossing the apparently deserted farmyard when a roar occurred behind me and Owld Yadi emerged from the barn, waving a knobbly walking stick in my direction: a stick which seemed to threaten dreadful pain and sorrow. Indeed, he looked so dangerous that I took to my heels and made for the fence separating the yard from the open fields beyond.

'Stop! Stop!' he bellowed.

I flung myself at the fence and had almost thrust my way through when the seat of my trousers was caught in the barbed wire. It was like a nightmare. The pounding feet came closer. I could imagine the stick raised high to add to the pain in my bottom.

'Whit are ye daein', ye stupid wee bugger?' The voice crackled like thunder.

I waited for the blows. None came. Instead, I felt his hands on my trousers, extricating me from the wire.

Roughly he clutched my arm and hauled me upright. 'Whit's wrang wi' ye? I was only gaun tae ask if ye wanted a sweetie.'

The relief was so great that I could say nothing. He took a peppermint from his pocket. It was covered with fluff and traces of glaur.

'There ye are noo. Away inside an' the wife'll gi'e ye a piece.'

Still shaking, I took the sweetie and did what I was told. It was revealed to me then what a trapped bird must feel when liberated from a garden net by a loud, enormous human being.

Owld Yadi had surprised me by betraying a glint of kindness behind a grey exterior. He surprised other farmers – and his own family – by his invention and building of a machine for stirring the cheese vat.

In the yard, just outside the dairy, he erected a stout wooden pole, some forty feet high. Through a pulley at the top he threaded a thin wire rope, with a heavy metal weight attached. At the bottom end the rope was wound round a metal shaft. This was connected, through a hole in the wall, with an intricate system of gear wheels inside the dairy. Those wheels operated a flail-like arm which, at speed, accomplished the heavy task of stirring the curd in the cheese vat.

The apparatus worked on the principle of a grandfather

clock. As the weight at the pole top was released, its slow descent caused the shaft to revolve, and the gear wheels inside initiated the movement of the stirring arm. When the weight reached the bottom of the pole, Owld Yadi simply wound it up again and continued the process until the curd had reached a proper consistency.

Once, not long after my discovery that his bellow was worse than his bullying, I asked him to show me the invention in action. He grunted with apparent annoyance at this brash request but immediately set the weight in motion. I watched and listened, fascinated, while he explained the workings in proud detail. I thought it marvellous in its simplicity and effectiveness. I still do. And have often wondered why it was not copied by other farmers.

Owld Yadi was known as one of the many Lowlanders in a Kintyre population which otherwise consisted of families of Highland and Irish descent. His people had come from Ayrshire in the early nineteenth century and since then had farmed successfully in Southend. Apparently he was a Scot of the Scots, with all the dour and abrasive qualities glibly attributed to the Lowland Scots. But, as is often the case, such tab marking camouflaged the truth of his heritage. A hundred years before his family's arrival in Southend, his forebears had come to Ayrshire from Poland, as miners in the coalfields.

We are all 'Jock Tamson's bairns'. The question arises: 'Who was – or is – Jock Tamson?'

In his youth, Owld Yadi had been a champion ploughman, handling his horse and 'high cut' plough with snarling expertise. His son Archie became a champion, too, as did his grandson Andrew. When young Andrew won his gold medal, encouraged by fiendish shouts and threats from his grandfather at the end of the rig, the old man, with pretended reluctance, agreed to have his photograph taken with Archie and Andrew. It appeared in the *Campbeltown Courier* above the caption: 'Three generations of champions.' Owld Yadi did his best not to appear too proud.

His relationship with the Padre was, on the surface, a stormy one. He was a keen but quarrelsome golfer, stumping the fairways of Dunaverty at formidable speed, using half a dozen hickory-shafted clubs tied together with binder twine and cursing the whins and his opponents with equal vigour. On his way to and from the course he often called at the Manse to discuss politics with my father. Cringing behind the door, Archie and I sometimes feared for our parent's safety as his visitor, to emphasize a point, beat his stick on the study table and uttered oaths at the pitch of his voice. It was only later we understood that far from being annoyed Owld Yadi was thoroughly enjoying the argument. As was the Padre.

On his death bed he sent for my father. The knobbly stick was laid aside. The vigorous body lay inert underneath the bedclothes. The loud voice had become a whisper.

For a while he discussed sin with the Padre, trying weakly to argue about it as if it were a political issue. (Which, of course, in a way it is.) Suddenly he caught my father's hand and said, 'Will ye – will ye christen me?'

'Christen you? Weren't you baptized, as a child?'

'No. They forgot.'

There was a cup of water on the table by the bed. The Padre used it to climax a short baptismal service in which he and the old farmer were the only participants. The General Assembly of the Church of Scotland might not have approved; but my father, descendant of the semi-pagan Columban vicars in North Uist's Trinity Temple, wasted no time in worrying about that. He had brought comfort to a dying man. Water sprinkled on the white head had submerged loud argument in meekness and peace.

I listened to the Padre tell his story to my mother soon after it happened. It conveyed to me, if only dimly at my age, that human nature is never simple and that good and evil are often relative terms.

The crude earthiness of agricultural life in Southend sixty years ago was matched by the crude earthiness of its morality.

Poverty and bad housing were prevalent: so there was malnutrition and disease. Drink was a way of escape from harsh reality: so there was drunkeness. Sex provided moments of love in an unloving environment: so, at a time when contraceptives were only known to and used by urban sophisticates, there was illegitimacy. Strangely enough, however, there was little violence, except perhaps for some horseplay among the boys and the young men. And in a small community where everyone, 'gentle and simple', knew everyone else, down to the last quirk in his or her character, habitual thieves did not exist.

In respect of robbery and violence, similar conditions prevail in Southend today. That is one reason why we struggle to retain the parish as a community, against the planners and the bureaucrats in church and state who try to submerge us in the anonymous, characterless mass of a larger unit.

In a rural backwater where organized evening entertainment was then practically non-existent – and dark barns and the moonlit 'rigs o' barley' were invitingly private – illegitimacy among farm servants was accepted as being inevitable and no great fuss was made about it, except perhaps by the 'unco guid'.

It was different for the farmers and the farmers' sons and daughters. When a middle-aged farmer with a wife and family fathered a child on one of his servants, the matter was covered up by a quick money payment and the promise of support for the girl's mother if she agreed to bring up the child. Whispers of scandal ran through the parish; but glass-house dwellers were unwilling to throw too many large stones.

When a youthful member of the farming community went astray, however, the consequences were often disturbing. As a rule, if the two young people were of equally respectable families, the situation was resolved by a hastily arranged wedding. But there were occasions, if a farmer's daughter became pregnant by a farm labourer, or a farmer's son was named as being responsible for a servant girl's expected child, scandal reached a crescendo and a small hell was let loose. In most of those cases love and not lust was concerned, but this was ignored. Marrying beneath you was not on, and many a marriage that might have proved happy was aborted, as some of the bastards were, in blood and tears.

Inevitably, my parents were involved in such situations. I remember hearing them talk together about the young people in distress, always with sad voices; and I vaguely understood they were on the side of the errants against the hypocrites who could hide behind money and respectable backgrounds.

One evening I found my mother crying. She passed it off, telling me she had a headache. I know now what she was crying about. My father had just returned from visiting a prosperous farm in the parish where a son of the house, about to become the father of a child by his mother's kitchenmaid, had drowned himself in the mill dam behind the farm.

Tragedies of this kind seldom occur today. The climate of morality in Southend has changed, as it has done everywhere else in Scotland, especially in the area of sex. Whether it has changed for better or worse is not the point. The fact remains that it has changed, as a result, in part, of the pill and, in part, of the media's efforts to present society in terms of realism. It can be argued that society now looks upon itself more honestly. But is there any evidence that such honesty is accompanied by more Christian love and compassion than it was sixty years ago?

William Hickey sniggers knowingly about love nests and love children, giving the impression that they represent normality in a 'civilized' society. Does such 'honesty', however, reduce the anguish of the innocent spouse in a divorce case? Does it improve the future lot of equally innocent children, legitimate and illegitimate, who are condemned to face life without the anchor of a stable family? They are 'liberated', of course. But from what?

Beyond the pallisades there lies the jungle; and the jungle is a lonely place, where cries for help can be smothered and remain unheard in the thickness of the undergrowth. There is no permanent escape from humanity: not even in Southend.

Harvest time was the farming season I enjoyed most. The stooks of corn and barley were thrown down so that the sheaves might become perfectly dry in the wind and the sun. Then they were loaded into high-sided horse-drawn carts for conveyance to the stackyards. There they were built laboriously, row upon row, into round, peak-topped stacks which would eventually be thatched with dried rushes.

Everybody worked happily and with a will, because this was the climax to a year of ploughing and sowing and reaping and mowing and, as long as the weather remained cool and bright, ultimate success was just around the corner.

As Neil MacLean and I grew into adolescence we could play useful parts. We were in demand for the 'forking', a job requiring more muscle power than skill, which consisted mainly of throwing the sheaves up into the carts (using a long, two-pronged fork) as they moved from stook to stook. More difficult and responsible jobs, such as leading the horses with their swaying cartloads through steep and narrow gateways, such as forking sheaves from the carts on to the growing stacks, such as the building of the stacks themselves, all these were left to our elders and betters, the expert farmers.

The danger of delegating one of these tasks to somebody less than competent was demonstrated by the experience of a small, stout farm labourer of advanced years, who, on account of a pointed nose and protruding teeth, was nicknamed the Rat by his fellow workers.

We were taking in the harvest at a farm tenanted by Jean's brother, Archie. (The farm is called Dalbhraddan, from the Gaelic, meaning 'glen of the salmon', though the stream in which the salmon once disported themselves has long since been disciplined into a tiled drain.) Owing to a shortage of labour on this particular day, the Rat had volunteered to be the stack builder.

In the present enlightened agricultural era no stacks are built. Any corn or barley that is grown is dealt with by combine harvesters, the resultant straw being baled and stored in open-sided corrugated-iron sheds. But 'in the vaward of our youth' stacks were built on a foundation of dried bracken, row upon row around a central open shaft which provided ventilation. As a rule, a bag of straw in the shaft was pulled up after him by the builder, to ensure that the size and shape of the ventilation shaft remained constant.

The Rat, however, forgot to provide himself with a straw bag, and it was only when his stack had reached a height of about fifteen feet that he decided to inspect the condition of his shaft. As he crawled inwards to look over the edge, some of the sheaves slipped. With a yell of dismay, he plunged down, out of sight, into the bowels of the stack.

'Hey, get me oot! Get me oot!' The voice was like an echo from a Frankenstein grave.

The rest of us doubled up with laughter. This was the kind of diversion which gave lightness to labour. For weeks it would provide material for jokes cracked at kirk and market: crude jokes concerning rats and rat holes. Indeed, 'the day the Rat fell doon the stack at Dalbhraddan' is still remembered by old men supping beer in quiet corners of Southend's Argyll Arms.

Soon, however, our laughter was subdued by an onset of anxiety. What if the stack were suddenly to collapse inwards upon itself and smother the Rat?

A ladder was placed against it, and Neil, who was nimble and light, climbed up to assess the situation. Gingerly, across the slippery sheaves, he approached the opening through which the Rat had disappeared. A sudden movement in the jerry-built stack caused him to scramble back, quickly, just in time to prevent himself joining the Rat in his dark and dangerous misery.

To the feebly moaning victim he shouted, 'Dinna fash yersel'. We'll ha'e ye oot in a jiffy!'

It was a promise more easily made than carried out. As a last resort we might have taken the stack to pieces, flinging off the sheaves row by row; but throughout such a lengthy operation we reckoned that the Rat would always be in imminent danger of being crushed and smothered.

As the chuckles died away, somebody had a bright idea. 'The ruck lifter! Set it up on wan side o' the stack. Put a rope through the pulley wi' a noose on the end o't. We'll lassoo the wee bugger an' haul him oot.'

We ran to the implement shed and, after some trouble,

manoeuvred the rick lifter out and into position, with the noose dangling above the hole in the stack. But the rope was light. The noose might stick in a narrow part of the shaft. We pulled the whole contraption aside, spreadeagled it and attached a 28-lb. weight to the noose. When the rick lifter was set up again, we were ready.

'Watch oot fur yer heid!' we yelled to the Rat and began lowering the noose.

Down went the weight, sliding and rustling amongst the sheaves.

'Ha'e ye got it?'

'Ay, I've got it.'

'Put the loop ablow yer oxters. We'll heave ye up.... Are ye ready?

'I'm ready!' came a stifled shout.

Four of us at the end of the rope began to pull. And eventually, like a cork being eased out of a bottle, the Rat emerged from the hole, covered with straw, squealing and kicking his legs because of the discomfort of the noose under his armpits.

Danger was past. The stack remained intact. Laughter became permissible again. We thought it a huge joke to keep the Rat dangling for a minute or two.

But finally we let him down and told him to remember to use a straw bag in future. And a tiny piece was added to the mosaic of Southend's folklore.

Working at Dalbhraddan that day, as casual hands, were Big Doser and Kleek. They no longer tried to bully Neil and me; we had grown as tall and strong as they were. In fact, on this occasion we felt a little sorry for them, because in the emergency they had stood open-mouthed and helpless, lacking in either initiative or ideas for rescue. Neil's agility and speed had demonstrated his obvious superiority, and my suggestions had been listened to by Jean's brother with respect. In the end they had obediently taken our orders and the four of us had pulled on the rope together.

I enjoyed harvesting at Dalbhraddan. But not so much as at Brunerican, where Jean, on the death of her mother, had become the lady of the house at fourteen. Even then, when I was only fifteen, we were aware of each other. I hadn't yet asked her to go out with me; but we both knew that this would happen, sooner or later.

In the middle of a harvest afternoon there was always a short break. While the rest of the hands enjoyed tea and 'jeely pieces' in the stackyard, the forkers in the field lay back against piles of sheaves in a mood of comfortable contemplation.

In the high field above Brunerican the scene was worth contemplating. It still is, on a day in September when a wind from the north renders visibility sharp and clear, a photographer's dream.

To the south, the Firth of Clyde spreads out in a blue flood, lapping the coasts of Kintyre and Ayrshire, with Ailsa Craig and Sanda causing the only breaks in a smooth expanse. To the north, beyond the mountains of the Mull of Kintyre, lie Islay's slate-grey hills and the improbable Paps of Jura. To the west, seventeen miles away across the North Channel, are the Antrim hills, with dome-shaped Slimish and Trostan, shaped like a coolie's hat, easily identifiable among them. They engender in us a feeling of romance and mystery, like silhouettes in a Walt Disney cartoon.

The hills of Ireland engender also a feeling of warmth and kinship. Here we are Scots. There they are Irish. But the constant comings and goings across the narrow sea, down through centuries, have blurred the sharp edges of nationality, and in spirit we reach across to one another as loving members of the human race.

We remember that to the people of Ireland we owe an age-old debt. Indeed, we have a common ancestry in the Mesolithic men who crossed from Red Bay to the pier head of the Mull 8000 years ago, and in the tribe of the Scotti who followed them 6000 years later.

Since then they have given us Columba, the saint whose halo, though always a little crooked, still shone with the Spirit. They have given us noble lords with their armourers and *sennachies*. They have given us fishermen and farmers, smugglers, potato-gatherers, thatchers and pedlars of linen goods, whose names and deeds, all of Irish origin, are commemorated in the songs called 'come all ye's' still sung at our local concerts. They have given us an accent subtly different from the mainstream Scots. And today they lend us, for short spells, the Irvines and the MacCambridges, the Spurs and the Kennedys, with whom we can exchange news of Antrim and Kintyre, both ancient and modern, and laugh uproariously at the same kind of jokes.

In those harvest days, sixty years ago, we watched the coastal puffers carrying whisky and coal to and from Glasgow and the Hebridean islands. We watched the great red-funnelled ships belonging to the Anchor Line passing through Sanda Sound, with 'a bone in their teeth', on their way to America.

In place of the liners, we watch the movement of huge oil tankers and container ships, all far out at sea because now they are directed by the Board of Trade to avoid the black-toothed dangers of Sanda. We watch the little grey ships searching for oil in the North Channel and the converted assault craft, also drably grey, carrying supplies to the rocket range in South Uist. We watch black nuclear submarines from the Holy Loch (yes, the *Holy* Loch) near Dunoon going about their ugly business. And in recent times we have watched furtive and sinister vessels carrying nuclear waste from Dounreay to a small, unhappy port in England. Where there was warmth and excitement before, now we experience shivers of apprehension, as if clammy, dead fingers were touching our bodies.

But when I was fifteen, enjoying an afternoon break in the high harvest field, I was less interested in the scenery than in the girl who, leaving the stackyard hands to the ministrations of a serving lass, made it her business to come up to the field alone with a thermos of tea for us and a basket of 'pieces'.

Sometimes Jean and I were able to sit together by ourselves, while the other forkers finished off their 'pieces' behind a distant stook. We looked out across the sparkling sea towards Ireland. We said little; but each of us knew that the other was seeing the Fata Morgana of a life together. This was one Fata Morgana that became, years later, a substantial vision. A vision substantial still.

9. Sportscene

After the First World War, I began to ease myself out of the serpent skin of childhood. The disciplined, protected life at the Manse was never penally irksome (and now I never cease to be grateful for it); but when I came to understand that all things interesting in life were not contained in my native parish and that Southend was not, by any means, the hub of the universe, there was a stirring in my blood and a growing desire for new sensations and new knowledge.

I know that my brother Willie was also dreaming dreams. One day, when he was only ten years old, I saw him sitting on a high branch of the copper beech tree outside the Manse. He had found an old pair of binoculars and was looking through them at the Anchor liner *Transylvania* making passage up the Clyde. In a moment of unusual candour he said to me, 'Some day I'll be captain of a ship like that.' His dream came true. He retired a few years ago as senior skipper with the Anchor Line.

I always wanted to be a writer, and my dream came true as well. It was in outdoor sport, however, that I found most of my recreational pleasures and sensations.

As boys, my friends and I rode dirt track round the Manse avenue on ancient, cannibalized bicycles. The gravel flew; we skidded and crashed into trees, and once, when we attached a go-cart to one of the bicycles and hauled it round after us at speed, with Willie in it (aged five), Maimie the maid screamed terrible Gaelic oaths at us and boxed our ears. '*Chiall beannachd mi!* Would you murder the child!'

We constructed a nine-hole pitch and putt course on the Manse front lawn, imagining the avenue as a river which had to be crossed several times during a round. We began to dig bunkers round some of the greens but were dissuaded from doing so by the awful wrath of my father (and members of the Kirk Session) at such apparent vandalism. But this did not interfere with our pleasure. We assumed the names of Vardon, Braid and Herd – and, as the years went by, of Duncan and Padgham – and played open championships as often as we could arrange them with our pals.

In summer, when we played cricket in the glebe below the Manse, we were Hobbs, Sutcliffe and Strudwick. In winter, playing football, we quarrelled as to which of us should be called Alan Morton.

Thankfully, sixty years on, I can still enjoy my sporting fantasies.

I was there at St Andrews on a sunshine day in July 1978, striding up the last fairway with a two-shot cushion to win the Open. I waved and bowed acknowledgement of the thunderous applause from 15,000 spectators on either side. My name was Jack Nicklaus.

I was there at Moscow in the summer of 1980, running for my life in an outside lane of the 100 metres (from Big Doser and Kleek?) and snatching on the tape the Olympic gold medal. My name was Allan Wells.

From Bobby Kelly, a nephew of Hugh MacEachran, I bought my first real bicycle, as opposed to a home-made one for the dirt track. Or at least my father bought it, for a pound.

I tended it with the care of a twelve-year-old, oiling and greasing and adjusting nuts. I became so expert a rider that I could speed down past the church, pedalling like a maniac without hands. I could also, like my brother Archie, kneel on the saddle and do a flying angel down a steep decline on the Kilblaan side road.

We fell, bruising our limbs; and once, when skidding off the Kilblaan track into a ditch, I sprained my left arm at the elbow. This did not worry me at the time. Now, however, I find it difficult to keep the straight left arm so necessary in a perfect golf swing. But there is a bright side. I am able to exploit my 'disability' as a subtle variant of the many excuses available to a golfer when he or she mis-hits a shot, confident in the knowledge that most of my opponents are now too young to remember – and remind me – that Ed Furgol, who won the American Open and played for America in the Ryder Cup, had a withered arm.

When I went to Campbeltown Grammar School – in the autumn following the visit with my father to North Uist – I stayed in lodgings in the town from Monday morning until Friday evening. For three years, week in, week out, my friend Boskers and I cycled the ten miles to Campbeltown and the ten miles back. (Boskers will confirm this. He is otherwise known as Lt. Col. Hamish Taylor, recently convenor of Argyll County Council.) We pedalled furiously to achieve record times, and our fastest, I remember, was twenty-five minutes, with a brisk north wind in our favour. But there were other mornings and other evenings, filled with driving rain, when we took more than an hour to do the journey.

Eventually 'scholars' buses' were introduced; but by then Boskers and I, with many hours of hard pedalling behind us, had developed leg and thigh muscles that were tough and strong: muscles which stood us in good stead when we began to take part in the local Highland Games, Boskers as a shot-putter and hammer-thrower, myself as a sprinter and jumper. By brute force and a considerable amount of ignorance I won the Grammar School Sports Championship two years in succession, and for this I give most of the credit to my bicycle. (It should be added that the Dux medal for academic distinction eluded me during the same two years.)

Boskers worked on his father's farm, for, I think, no more than his keep. I had bursaries to support me at school and, later, at the university; but my parents, on a ministerial stipend, had no cash to spare even for occasional doles. Our problem, therefore, was how to earn enough pocket money to carry us through the holidays. The Highland Games, with their money prizes, provided a solution.

We had no coaches, nobody who took the slightest interest in our leisure pursuits, except our parents in a casual way. We trained ourselves, using the glebe as a training ground.

With the prize of ten shillings which I won for a first place in the 100 yards at Southend Highland Games (when I was sixteen) I bought a book written by Harold Abrahams, and we followed faithfully all the hints on training for athletics so generously supplied by the Olympic gold medallist.

Eventually we were joined by my brother Archie and his friend, Lachie Young (retired, not long ago, as Director of Education for Perthshire), and by the late Neil John MacCallum, a son of the local blacksmith. In time Neil John outshone us all by winning the mile at the most famous of all professional athletic events, the New Year meeting at Powderhall in Edinburgh.

As we grew more confident – and a little more affluent – we toured all the Games in Argyll (Oban, Inveraray, Lochgilphead, Tayinloan, Campbeltown and Southend), first in an old T-Ford belonging to Boskers' father and then in a bull-nose Morris which I had bought for £7 10s.

Along with our athletic gear we always carried a few sliced potatoes. In those days mechanical wipers had not yet become standard equipment in cars; but when a sliced potato was rubbed against the windscreen its juice dissolved the spots of rain and allowed the driver to see clearly ahead – for a few miles at any rate, until the effect wore off and another quick rub had to be made.

In Southend a minister's son received an excellent grounding in the study of human nature. As children we tended to categorize men and women in stark black and white; but when we became adolescents and began to encounter more and more people from alien environments it was brought home to us that the predominant colour in the picture of humanity, like the colour of drapes on a stage, is grey. A grey, nevertheless – again like that of drapes on a stage – which can be the background, under lights, for memorable and sometimes inspiring characters.

Our participation in the games brought us into contact with great sportsmen like Weir of Clydebank and the Andersons of Dundee, who tossed enormous cabers, threw 56-lb. weights over high bars, sent 16-lb. hammers with long wooden shafts hurtling high into the sky and putted heavy stones (16 lb. and 22 lb.) as if they were marbles. And like Starkey and McGregor who could jump and pole vault as well as heave weights about. All were huge men, cool, calm, rough but entirely honest, who, in the heavy events, invariably competed in their kilts.

One day, at Oban, I sprinted through the tapes at the finish of a 100-yard race. As recommended by Harold Abrahams, my head and chest were thrust down at the time, and I failed to notice that directly in my line of flight stood George Anderson engaged in smearing a hammer shaft with a tacky substance which ensured a firm grip. Though I struck him at speed he remained as immoveable as a tree. I bounced back off him and landed on my bottom. Momentarily he glanced down at me, with less interest than he would have shown to a passing bumble bee. 'Get off yer arse!' he advised me without rancour.

Most of the events were adjudicated by the lairds and the sons of lairds who inhabited the district in which the Games were held. Some of them who had been in the army, and had thereby gained valuable knowledge of piping and Highland dancing, were excellent judges of those colourful events, and nobody took advantage of them. But few were expert in the conduct of athletics.

For example, their preparations for a hurdle race was to place heavy wooden bars, suspended on three-foot-high fence stobs, at intervals of about twenty yards around the circular grass track. At first, as apprentice professionals, Archie, Lachie and I used to dash off in front and try to jump those bars. In consequence, we often knocked them down, bruising our shins and falling on our faces in the process. The wily old pros dawdled behind us, with the result that they often had no jumping at all to do and could overtake and pass the halt and the maimed and the innocent down the finishing straight.

Sometimes, in the sprints, handicaps were given, each yard advantage being indicated on the track by wooden pegs with a line of sawdust or whitewash drawn between them. Here the scratch men were at a considerable disadvantage. Let me explain.

As a rule the starter was the product of an English public school where sportsmanship was taught to be among the highest virtues. He would put the scratch man on his mark and then, in a quick gabble, read out our handicaps to the rest of us. 'MacVicar, Angus, three yards. MacVicar, Archibald, five yards. Young, Lachlan, six yards.' And so on. He made no effort to check that we took our proper marks, cheating at sport being something he had been taught to believe impossible.

At our first Games we thought it impossible, too, and advanced carefully to our allotted lines. Then we began to be aware that on the command 'Get to your marks' some of the hard-bitten runners from (to us) mysterious localities like Kilmaurs, Tranent and Galashiels were creeping forward an extra yard or two, without being reprimanded – or even noticed – by the starter. For the unfortunate scratch man, crouching directly under the eyes of the young official, this kind of manoeuvre was impossible.

By hard experience we learned that honesty – particularly in the short races – simply did not pay, and as we were there for the money we played the cheats at their own game and so became cheats ourselves. After a while we suffered no pangs of conscience when taking advantage of innocent newcomers. The trouble is, I now find no pleasure in the memory.

(No doubt some questionable practices still occur at the seventy or eighty Highland and Border Games, which, each year, are held in various parts of the country. Most of these meetings, however, are now conducted under the strict rules of the Scottish Games Association, incorporated in 1946, and I should be surprised if many 'fly' men are allowed to prosper, as we were.)

But good memories of the Games are still available. The skirl of the pipes and the flutter of the kilts and tartan plaids. The neat, tight step of the dancers twirling and turning on high wooden platforms. The scent of mown grass on the running tracks and the sparkle of dew on a sunshine morning. The grunts and triumphant shouts of the heavyweights lifting the cabers high and throwing them over. The spectators moving on the sidelines in streams of changing colours and their shrieks of applause at the finish of a close race or for an athlete leaping lithely over the bar of a high jump stand. And, above all, the smell of embrocation.

Few Highland Games boasted sand pits for the long jump or for the hop, step and leap. Nor were air cushions provided for the high jumpers and pole vaulters. We landed heavily on the turf and, in consequence, were liable to frequent bumps and bruises. Most of the Games had rubbing tents, where an athlete whose legs or arms required attention was minstered to by old professionals. Their active days were over, but they loved to follow the Games and offer physical comfort and practical wisdom to those still taking part.

My favourite rubber was Jamie Ma. 'Ma' was obviously a nickname; I never did discover his real one. He had once been placed second in the New Year 130-yards sprint at Powderhall but always maintained that the officials at the tape were bent, in the pay of the bookmakers, and that he ought to have won the first prize, which in those days amounted to the fabulous sum of £100. 'Ma breist hit the tape first. Maybe the other fella's hand touched it afore I did, but that was agin the rules.' (If he was telling the truth he had a point. According to the rules of the Scottish Games Association 'competitors shall be placed as they strike the worsted and cross the imaginary line with head, breasts or legs. Competitors striking the worsted with their hand deliberately may be disqualified at the discretion of the Referee or Judges.')

Jamie Ma came from an Ayrshire village. He would be in his late forties when I knew him, about 5 feet 6 inches tall, stockily built and 'bowly' legged. He worked intermittently as a coal miner and had the dry cough and blue-pocked face so often acquired by workers in pre-Coal Board pits. As a rule he kept his false teeth in a trouser pocket, and I understood why. With them in his mouth he was so preoccupied by keeping them in position that long silences were broken only by incoherent mumblings. Without them he spoke clearly – and incessantly.

'Lie doon on the table,' he would tell me. 'On yer belly.'

From a worn and dirty canvas bag he would take a bottle

containing a pungent, white mixture. Pouring some on to his hands he would slap it on my legs and begin a thorough and sometimes painful massage. The smell of his special embrocation was so strong that before he was finished I often found myself in tears.

As he rubbed and then pummelled my thigh and calf muscles with the edges of his hands, he would offer advice and reminiscence in equal quantities, seldom stopping to receive comments from me.

'Ye're ower lang in the leg fur a sprinter. But yer muscles is no' bad. Yer thigh muscles is jeest like ma ain when I was at ma best. Lie still noo 'an let me gi'e them a hammerin'. They're a wee bit tight efter that last race. That's better. . . .

'The first time I ran in the Powderhall sprint I was on the back shift at the pit the nicht before. I hurried hame, but ma mither hadna the breakfast ready, so I had tae dae wi' jeest a cup o' tea. Then wee Sammy Pagan's owld motor broke doon somewhere ootside Edinburgh. I was late reachin' the stadium and hadna time tae get a rub. Haufway doon the track I seized up like Wee Sammy's bloody motor an' I was near last.

'Hooan'ever, that meant that next year I got a guid handicap, eicht yairds. I took bloody guid care that this time I was at the stadium early, an' Wee Sammy basted an' bashed me like a turkey, usin' the same stuff as I'm usin' on yersel'. It's a secret recipe, ye ken, invented by Wee Sammy's faither, who was a sprinter tae. I should ha'e won that day – Wee Sammy had a packet on me – but thae buggers at the tape were nobbled by the bookies an' I lost ma chance. Wee Sammy couldna afford a drink fur weeks efter't. An' neither could I. . . .

'But ach, some o' the sprinters is as bad as the offeecials. See yon big bugger frae Glesca wi' the fair hair an' the broon skin. Ye'd think he was a hauf-cast, but he's no'. Sun-ray treatment – that's why his skin's sae broon. His faither runs a gym an' a Turkish bath fur Glesca business men. Watch him on the bends, son. He'll cut across ye in the fower-forty if he gets the chance, an' it'll no worry him if he spikes ye forbye. Listen. If he comes on yer ootside on the last bend, dae whit I used tae dae. Let on ye've been tripped frae behin', fling oot yer richt airm as if tae steady yersel' an' hit him hard in the stomach. Ye'll be at the tape afore he gets his win' back. . . .

'Noo then, hoo dae ye feel? . . . That's gran'. Away oot there an' mak' me proud o' ye. I'm no' backin' ye fur the hunner yairds: yon wee nyaff frae Tranent's far quicker aff his mark as ye'll ever be. But I've a pound on ye fur the two-twenty. Wi' thae lang legs o' yours nane o' them should see ye fur dust doon the feenishin' straight. No' even the big bugger frae Glesca. Wad ye like me tae putt a pound on fur yersel'?'

This, of course, was the business end of our one-sided conversation. His usual charge for a rub was a pound. Now he was suggesting, in as friendly a way as possible, that I should give him two pounds. He knew that I knew that he had no intention of risking even a ha'penny on the off-chance of my winning the two-twenty.

But I always gave him the two pounds. One way and another I felt he had earned them.

On the way home from the Inveraray Highland Games, having won a fair amount of money between us, Archie and Lachie and Boskers and I always used to stop for a slap-up high tea at Lochgair Hotel, north of Lochgilphead. Mine host was John Sinclair, who was married to a MacVicar lady, a far-out relative of my own. John's hotel was well known throughout Scotland for real Highland hospitality.

First of all, as we sat down with mouth-watering appetites after a day's hard work in the open air, our table was supplied with home-baked scones, pancakes, cream sponge cake, shortbread, and gingerbread. Then came the teacups and the plates, the cream jugs and the sugar bowls, dishes of real butter and a squat glass jar containing some of Mrs Sinclair's special rhubarb jam. Then the toast, a laden rack for each of us. Then the tea in two huge silver pots, flanked by another silver pot of hot water. And finally an ashet (a Scots word for a large – in this case *very* large – flat dish), piled high with sizzling rashers of bacon and at least a dozen fried eggs, from which we could help ourselves.

At this point, round and smiling and sparing of words,

jacketless and with a silver watch chain draped across his bulging waistcoat, John Sinclair would come into the dining-room, ask how we had got on at the Games and then retire to a position near the doorway, where he could watch us eat. As the ashet was emptied, as the scones and the cakes and the sponges disappeared, his smile would grow broader. When the teapots and the hot-water jug had been drained and only crumbs were left on the plates he would approach us again and ask if we wanted more. We never did. We were full to bursting point. But in our awkward way we would indicate our appreciation of a marvellous meal.

He would shake his bald head. 'You've thanked me already,' he'd say. And once he added, 'The MacCrimmons didna mak pipe tunes for the money. They made them for the folk tae enjoy.'

At the time, as a beginning writer, I understood vaguely what he meant. Now I understand exactly what he meant. I still wait, with halting breath, not only for the cash my books bring in but also for the reactions of readers and critics. When I receive a letter of appreciation from a stranger or a favourable review in a national newspaper, my smile becomes as broad as John Sinclair's. Royalty cheques keep an author's body alive; but it is proven success in giving pleasure to others that nurtures his spirit.

Incidentally, I remember that for one of his famous high teas John Sinclair charged 3s. 6d.

When I took an active part in athletics, more than fifty years ago, professional runners and jumpers had a bad image. They were known as 'peds' (in the *Glasgow Herald* their doings were always recorded under the heading of 'Pedestrianism'), and high-minded amateurs would describe them as money-grubbers always prepared to cheat and steal for the sake of an odd sixpence. This description was true in some cases. But in the 1920s and 1930s, when social security was embryonic, a poor man simply could not afford to run except for money. And there were as many honest sportsmen among the professionals as among the amateurs. I know this to be true because I have run races in both categories.

And I may add that it was an amateur whose spikes caused the livid scar which decorates the inside of my left calf. (A scar which I am happy to unveil at the slightest sign of interest.)

In my young days, however, the main sponsors of many a promising young athlete were the bookmakers. As a result he often became caught up in a financial quagmire. This consisted of loans which tied him to a certain 'school', of subsidies to cover the expense of secret training, of small bribes to run poorly at certain games in order to acquire a favourable mark later in the season. If he failed to win on a certain specified occasion and thereby make a killing for his backers, he was liable to be tossed aside like an old dishcloth and left to fend for himself.

Without the support of the system this was no easy task. Archie, Lachie, Neil John and I were able to do so for a time. But in the end, refusing all offers from sly-eyed strangers, we found ourselves being handicapped so severely that the only kind of race we had any chance of winning was one in which all the competitors started from scratch. And even then it was curious how often we were knocked off our stride, early in the race, by somebody banging into us.

I suppose part of the trouble was that none of us had the talent and the courage of Eric Liddell, the greatest runner Scotland had ever produced, amateur or professional, until Allan Wells came on the scene more than half a century later.

Eric Liddell's parents were both missionaries in North China, where he was born in 1902, in Tientsin. He came to study in Edinburgh, where his athletic potential was soon recognized. A fellow student made a joke about him in the university magazine. 'Eric's early days,' he wrote, 'were spent happily chasing Chinese whippets or running against streaks of lightning, while the little Chinese boys and girls sat and held their breaths, astounded.'

At the university he worked hard, training for his chosen profession as a medical missionary. He won a rugby blue and played left wing threequarter for Scotland. But it was as a sprinter that he made his reputation.

He became my hero on a day in July 1923, when, at Stoke-on-Trent, he ran for Scotland against England and Ireland. That day he won not only the 100 and the 220 yards but also the 440 yards. And what a race that 440 was.

In the first three strides, Gillis of England knocked into him. Eric stumbled and almost fell. For the fraction of a second he seemed ready to give up. But then, suddenly, he was going after them – twenty yards behind but still going after them.

As they reached the home straight he was running fourth. Forty yards from the tape he was third, ten yards behind Gillis. He looked exhausted, pale, on the point of collapse. But he pulled himself together once again and in a desperate finish won the race by about a yard, with Gillis second.

On the track beyond the tape he fell and, for a time, lay unconscious.

Even for money, Archie, Lachie and I were not prepared to rack our bodies to such an extent, though it is possible we had the physical strength to do it. Eric Liddell did it for nothing, which shows how far his spirit soared above ours.

Incredible as it may seem today, some English sports writers had been saying he was scarcely good enough for the 1924 Olympic Games. (Perhaps not so incredible: fifty-seven years later, from their journalistic ivory towers, they were saying the same about Allan Wells.) His performance at Stoke-on-Trent, however, caused them to reconsider their judgement. He was chosen to run in Paris in all the sprints, though his own personal sights were set on the 100 metres.

When the lists were published it was revealed that the heats of the 100 metres were to be run on a Sunday. Eric said, firmly, 'In that case I'm not running. Not in the 100 metres at any rate.'

His decision was based on a principle which may now seem outdated and even illogical; but he never wavered. Afterwards he had no regrets, not even when the 100 metres was won by Harold Abrahams, a man he had already beaten, several times.

So now it was the 400 metres or nothing. (He had won a bronze medal in the 200 metres, but he considered his running in that race to have been 'unsatisfactory'.)

The favourite in the 400 metres final was the great American, H. M. Fitch, who had recorded the best time in the heats. Not only that. In 1924 there was no running in lanes, with staggered starts, and E. H. Liddell was drawn on the outside.

Just before the race started, while Eric was limbering up, an unknown man in the crowd called him over and handed him a piece of paper. As he stood there, looking at some writing on it, he was called to his mark with the others.

The pistol went. Fitch was off in front, streaking for the bend. But then, in the back straight, a white-vested figure was seen to be pounding at Fitch's heels: a chunky, powerful figure, arms flailing, head thrown back. It was Eric Liddell, the man so many had reckoned to have no chance at the Olympic Games because of his ungainly style.

As he rounded the bend into the finishing straight he was on Fitch's shoulder. And at this moment Fitch seemed to recognize that he was beaten. In front of a shouting, screaming crowd in the Colombes Stadium Eric passed him easily and broke the tape with six yards to spare. His time was 47.6 seconds, which was then an Olympic record.

Later in the same year a graduation ceremony took place at Edinburgh University. From a ruck of many names one was called: Eric Henry Liddell, Bachelor of Science. The audience rose to their feet. The building shook with their applause.

'Mr Liddell,' said the Vice-Chancellor, 'you have shown that no man can pass you but the examiner. In the name of the University, which is proud of you, I present you with this scroll and place upon your head this chaplet of wild olives.'

Afterwards, the students carried their champion shoulder high to the steps of St Giles Cathedral, where the citizens of Edinburgh let their hair down and accorded him a welcome far louder and more fervent than that given, forty years later, to the Beatles.

And the underlying cause of such a day of glory? I do not think it was altogether the fact of Eric Liddell's physical strength and courage. A clue may be found in the piece of paper put into his hand in the tense seconds before he ran the race of his life in Paris. Before he died in a Shantung Internment camp in 1946, he himself told a friend what was written on it. A text from I Samuel: 'These that honour me I will honour.'

That the character and reputation of an athlete should be judged on his standing either as an amateur or a professional has always seemed to me to be ridiculous. It has always been the case that if a person runs or jumps against a professional, whether for a money prize or not, then that person automatically receives a black ball and is branded professional, unfit to stride the track with the Eric Liddells, the Allan Wellses and the Linsey MacDonalds of this world. And to be reinstated as an amateur costs money and time and worry, none of which a young man or woman can easily afford.

Even in cricket, which I imagine to be a game of the utmost conservatism, Gentleman have regularly competed against Players. In golf, Bobby Jones, an amateur, played continually against the professionals, frequently beating them, but with never a complaint from anyone. (In one year, 1930, he won what has been called 'The Impregnable Quadrilateral': the Open Championship, the American Open Championship, the British Amateur Championship and the American Amateur Championship.) In football, the amateur club, Queen's Park, is welcomed in the professional leagues. Nowadays, in tennis, important tournaments like that at Wimbledon are all open to amateurs and professionals. It is the same with every other major sport, except athletics. (And, in a peculiarly archaic sense, rugby.)

I could never and still cannot understand why a man or woman who possesses talent as an athlete should become the subject of denigration, denied all the benefits of official support, simply because he or she can only afford to develop it by accepting money prizes. Somebody with a talent for music can play for money in an orchestra and still be regarded as a lady or a gentleman. Somebody with a talent for painting can sell canvases in a back alley and still aspire to the Royal Academy. Somebody with a talent for writing has always to endure competition from hordes of eager amateurs but is not looked upon with disfavour because he or she becomes a professional in self-defence.

In my youth I ran at the Glasgow University Sports as well as at the Highland Games and won several medals. Archie and Lachie did the same. But then somebody informed the authorities that we were, in effect, professionals, which involved us in an interrogation as ruthless, it seemed to me, as the Inquisition. Archie and Lachie applied successfully for reinstatement as amateurs, and eventually Archie won a soccer blue, which might have been denied him had he remained a professional athlete. I did not apply for reinstatement. I continued to run at the Highland Games and, though invited to return them, kept my amateur medals. I still have those medals in a box. I am proud of them. If the university or the SAAA want them back they will have to come and get them.

Surely it is time that athletics was made an open sport, like the others. Not only would it encourage young people to achieve a high standard of physical fitness and self-discipline; it would also stifle the hypocrisy which at present grows like lichen on the rules and regulations of the governing bodies.

Most of the men and women famous in athletics today are sponsored, in much the same way as the old peds were. They receive hidden expenses. They are employed by firms which give them unlimited time off. They are trained by professional coaches who are, in effect, civil servants. Every now and then a bright newspaper reporter unearths a scandal, which suggests that some notable amateur has been paid expenses far exceeding those allowed by the rules. This causes no more than a ripple on the turgid surface of the sport, because all concerned – especially the influential firms which sponsor important athletic meetings as part of their advertising campaigns – would lose a great deal of money and credibility if the inquiry were pursued to its logical conclusion. If athletes were paid openly for their skills, the organization of many an unsavoury cover-up would no longer be necessary.

I find it significant that it is the so-called purely amateur sports which often become involved in the hypocritical dealings of certain politicians.

In the midst of all this confusion of moral values – the trade mark of a dying century – I look back at my careless youth with envy. My ideals then were bright, impervious, I believed, to tarnish. The Padre taught us that life was simple and direct, a matter of good versus evil, with the good, like the US cavalry, charging in to victory at the end. I think differently now. Good does not always triumph, as TV playwrights keep reminding us, *ad nauseam*. Politicians, public relations officers and advertising agents have become highly skilled in the art of portraying evil as good. My ageing brain keeps telling me that standards do not change and that the Ten Commandments are always there, a spiritual lifebelt. But the seas are choppy, and sometimes I find difficulty in grabbing hold of it, especially when some modern apologist tugs at the line and tries to snatch it away from me.

I try to believe I am still the boy I was and find a certain comfort in the words of Shakespeare: 'You that are old consider not the capacities of us that are young: you measure the heat of our livers with the bitterness of your galls: and we that are in the vaward of our youth, I must confess, are wags, too.'

10. The Power of a Rose

This book is my first attempt at a real autobiography. In order to answer the question 'Why am I what I am?', I looked back on my childhood and tried to describe some of the influences, both human and environmental, which surrounded me more than half a century ago. But it soon became evident – to me, at any rate – that I should have to probe further, especially into the influences which had involved my father as a boy in North Uist. And when I did that, an urge came on me to dig even deeper into the past, first into the history of the MacVicar priests of the thirteenth century and then down and down into Scottish history.

I realize now, however, that all such devoted research has been largely an exercise in self-indulgence and that, once again, as a writer of autobiography I have failed. I went digging in dark peat mosses, endeavouring to prove a theory that heredity plays an important part in our personalities. Interesting artefacts were uncovered: but it seems to me that I found nothing of satisfying substance. My original question has been answered only superficially. Perhaps grains of truth have glinted momentarily in the debris, including some which I now find myself wishing had not been revealed.

Was the question worth asking in the first place? My life, my knowledge, my prejudices, are they of any importance whatsoever in a world teeming with so many million neighbours? I try to believe that my efforts to find an answer may be of some infinitesimal value in that they demonstrate that I love my neighbours – most of them, at any rate – and find happiness in recording it.

The writing of this book, too, has given me a clearer picture of the changes that have taken place in society, both material and spiritual, in the past sixty or seventy years.

Material changes have been many in Southend at the Mull of Kintyre: changes which reflect similar ones in rural communities everywhere.

In his song, Paul McCartney refers to Southend as consisting of mountains and heather, with 'mist rolling in from the sea'. The description comes mainly from Paul's romantic imagination.

In my childhood, before the development of marketing boards and social services, it shared government neglect and consequent poverty with other remote Scottish parishes. Today it is a busy and, on the whole, prosperous farming area, with undulating acres of fertile land sheltered by the mountains. Its population includes not only farmers and farm workers but also fishermen, shipyard workers, business people young and old (who commute to offices in Campbeltown), shopkeepers, hotelkeepers and a number of senior citizens who, having retired to an imagined haven of peace and quiet, now find themselves constantly active as they become involved in the kirk, in guilds, in rurals, in drama and in golf. For the young in body and heart there is a badminton club and a football club and parties and discos galore arranged by the community council. At times mist does roll in from the sea, though rain and howling gales are much more frequent. In general, however, the climate is mild (thanks, it would appear, to the proximity of the Gulf Stream) and Jean and I can harvest vegetables from our garden, without the aid of a greenhouse, as early as they can in the Channel Islands.

There is one example of material change in Southend which may serve as an example of what has been happening in my day and age.

Here, as I sit at my writing table, I look out of the window and see, beyond Dunaverty Rock, the island of Sanda, separated from the coast by two miles of water. Today the only people who live there are the on duty lighthouse-keepers, whose families and permanent homes are in Campbeltown. It has a fine sheltered harbour, a fact appreciated by the Vikings, who in the dark centuries between the time of St Columba and that of Robert the Bruce, used it as a rallying place for their invasion fleets. On old maps the island is sometimes called Avon, no doubt from the Norse word meaning 'haven'.

In the Middle Ages Sanda became an important religious centre. St Ninian's chapel, the ruins of which, situated above the harbour, are still fairly well preserved, was included in Fordun's list of ecclesiastical foundations in the Western Isles of Scotland, compiled during the second half of the fourteenth century. It also used to support a small farming and fishing community. Now the fields and farmhouse have become almost derelict.

The old chapel and graveyard are of considerable interest to archaeologists. An old man in Southend, whose father had been born in Sanda, once took me across in his boat and showed me his family burial ground. Near it lay an ancient flagstone about which he told me a strange story. In olden times, he said, when the crew of a boat were in danger at sea, people ashore used to gather round the stone, wash it with clean water and chant an incantation beseeching the person buried below to have mercy on those in danger.

'Who is buried below?' I asked.

'Nobody knows. But I can repeat the incantation, if you like.'

It was in the Gaelic, of course; but here is a rough translation:

> Champion famed for warlike toil
> Art thou silent, mighty?
> I come not with unhallowed dread
> To wake the slumbers of the dead.
> Waken now or sleep for ever,
> For thus the sea
> Shall smooth its ruffled crest for thee,
> And, while afar its billows foam,
> Subside the peace near Halcc's Tomb.

Once again the Norse connection?

Sanda used to belong to the Clan Donald; but as the centuries passed it fell into the hands of various owners. In

1929, when agricultural conditions were poor, it was purchased by the tenant farmer, Sandy Russell, for £900. (This figure and those which follow are, of course, approximate.)

Sandy Russell was successful as a farmer, even though the conveyance of his sheep and cattle to the mainland markets was often an awkward and sometimes even dangerous business. His son, Jim, was successful too. And when the latter retired to live in Southend in 1969, the island was bought by Jack Bruce, guitarist in the pop group called the Cream, for £35,000.

For the next few years Jack Bruce and his family came to the island as often as they could, living in the farmhouse. He composed a great deal of music while in Sanda, and a television film was made of his life there.

Eventually, however, he grew tired of his island hideaway, and in 1976 he sold it to James Gulliver, the well-known financier, for £75,000.

Though James Gulliver is a Campbeltown man – his father had a grocer's shop there, and he himself attended the local grammar school – he soon found that Sanda did not suit his family needs as a holiday resort. In 1979 he disposed of it to a gentleman reputed to be an Iranian for £125,000. We have never seen the new owner but he is known to us as Mr Chengezi.

Not long before this transaction took place, it had been confidently predicted by a member of the Coal Board that oil would be found in plenty below the nearby waters of the North Channel. Is it possible that in the near future great fleets will again sail into Sanda harbour – fleets not of Viking longships but of giant tankers?

In a spiritual sense, Southend is lucky in that it has been able to retain its identity as a community. This, I believe, is mainly due to its having the sea on three sides and only one good road leading out of it. A feeling of neighbourliness persists, which may be due to the fact that everybody in the parish knows what everybody else is doing – and even thinking. The ground is unfertile for public relations officers who manipulate public images and for media propagandists who preach a creed sometimes called 'liberal' but which, in effect, undermines all respect for the dignity of the individual.

For me, the cult of the anti-hero signposts a considerable change which, in my lifetime, has taken place in the mores of our society. Why is it so assiduously promoted in books, in newspapers, and on radio and television? Is it because of awareness on the part of writers and producers that in such characters we see our mirror images and can thereby side-step guilt by persuading ourselves that the whole human race is as weak and undisciplined as we are? ('Pap for the masses'?)

My generation was encouraged to have heroes and heroines. St Columba, Robert the Bruce, Joan of Arc, Lady Grizel Baillie, Eric Liddell, Barney Ross, Odette, Ben Hogan: these are but a few. They struggled, they faced hardship and disappointment, but ultimately gained a victory, not only for themselves but also for mankind.

I cannot understand why the young of today should be encouraged to admire instead – for example – amoral train robbers, Wimbledon wailers, drug-addicted pop stars and, in fiction, drunken, womanizing detectives and grotty cowboys with all the graces of barracudas. No wonder society appears to be uncaring, when loving one's neighbour is so often represented as a sign of 'wetness'. It is valid, of course, to record the doings of such unlovely people; but it is equally valid – and, in my opinion, more valuable – to record the deeds of the heroes and heroines. Because, in the end, there can be no happiness without love. Christ, the ultimate hero, died to prove it. Hitler, the ultimate anti-hero, died to prove that hate means death and destruction. And oblivion.

I suppose that something of my character is revealed in that three of the heroes on my list are sportsmen. Two of them happen to be American, one a boxer, the other a golfer.

Barney Ross's real name was Rosofsky. His father was a smalltime grocer in a Chicago slum. One day gangsters called at the shop and demanded protection money. When Rosofsky senior tried to argue they shot him dead.

Barney was only fourteen, but the family now became his

responsibility. He sold papers and worked as a shoeshine boy, all the time making Walter Mitty plans to better the family fortunes.

In due course, one of his plans came true. In 1928, as an amateur, he won a Golden Gloves title in New York. Despite his mother's disapproval, he changed his name to Ross and became a professional boxer.

Money – real money – began to come in, but his mother refused to give his new way of life her blessing. Never, she said, would she go and see him fight.

When he was twenty-five, Barney took on Tony Canzoneri for the lightweight championship of the world. After half a dozen rounds there was little between them, as far as boxing skill was concerned. In the seventh Barney seemed to be getting the worst of it, when suddenly a woman began screaming encouragement from the ringside. He glanced down through the ropes and saw his mother. After that, as one commentator wrote, 'Canzoneri was a dead duck'.

But one world championship was not enough for Barney. Or for his mother, who now realized that her son had the stability of character to be rich and famous and yet remain unspoilt.

Before a crowd of 45,000, he won the welterweight title from Jimmy McLarnin, though some of the crowd thought the referee had given the wrong verdict. But the referee's name was Jack Dempsey, and Jack Dempsey, ex-heavyweight champion of the world, could scarcely be called inexperienced.

Barney Ross retired from boxing just before the Second World War, with what a journalist on the *Washington Post* called 'an unsurpassed record of sportsmanship and gallantry'. He was over thirty now, but he volunteered for the Marines. At Gaudalcanal he won the Distinguished Service Cross for an action in which he saved three wounded comrades by holding a slit-trench single-handed against repeated attack by the Japanese.

He himself was wounded in this fight and taken to hospital, where the doctors relieved his headaches with a certain drug – an experimental drug which seemed to be effective at the time. But after the war Barney's headaches recurred. He began using the drug again, on his own account. Before he could understand what was happening, he had become an addict.

His marriage and his health broke down. He became a pathetic Skid Row figure, bleary-eyed, always searching for new supplies of the stuff that was killing him.

In his brain, however, a spark of moral sense remained alight. One day in September 1946, it flared up, stronger than usual. He stumbled into his lawyer's office in Manhattan, his clothing ragged, his hands trembling. 'I'm sick,' he muttered, with desperate humility. 'My wife has left me, and I'm ready to be counted out. Please – please help!'

Those of us who, by good fortune, have never known the spirit-sapping effect of drugs can scarcely comprehend the courage it took to make this plea. But Barney Ross was committed now. The fight was on, in the public health service hospital in Lexington, Kentucky: a fight to a sad and painful finish, according to the pessimists and the worldly wise.

But this is not a modern scenario, with a down-beat curtain. This is true. Months later a New York newspaper came out with a banner headline: 'Barney Ross KO's Drug Habit'. The champion had won his last great fight.

He left hospital cured, began courting his wife again and eventually remarried her.

A happy ending, old-fashioned, corny. Strange how the brave and battered human spirit quite often supplies one.

And Ben Hogan. Why is Ben Hogan another of my heroes?

When he came to play in the Open Golf Championship at Carnoustie in 1953 I was hoping fervently that he would be beaten by British players. At the time I knew nothing of his story.

He was born in 1912, in Dublin, Texas, a small cattle town about 75 miles from Fort Worth. His father, the town blacksmith and junk dealer, died when Ben was only nine years old, and the family, consisting of his mother, a brother, a sister and himself, moved to Fort Worth. Like Barney Ross, he worked hard, selling newspapers. Eventually he became a caddie at Fort Worth's Glen Garden Country Club.

In 1932 he began to play golf for a living, at first without conspicuous success. Two years later he married Valerie Fox, a girl he had met at Sunday school in Dublin when he was twelve. Jimmy Demaret, another distinguished American golfer, wrote of her: 'Valerie is a girl blessed with strong insight and sure knowledge of what her husband needs from her. In my opinion she has been one of his secret weapons, as fine a woman as it has been my privilege to meet.'

In spite of his wife's encouragement, however, Hogan's golf was still not good enough to win important tournaments. When he came to play at Oakland, California, in late February 1937, he had only five dollars in his pocket. For a time he and Valerie had been living on hamburgers; now the money even for these was running out. 'If I don't win here,' Ben told his wife, 'we'll sell the car and go home. I'll try to get a steady job.'

He played reasonably well for the first two days of the tournament, remaining in contention for a good prize; but his putting worried him so much that he stayed awake for most of the night before the final day. In the morning, when he and Valerie went to collect their car (which they had left in a vacant lot because they could not afford the fee for the main car park), they found it resting on its steel rims. Somebody had jacked it up and stolen the four tyres.

'I felt sick,' Ben said later. 'I thought for sure it was the end. How could I even get to the golf course?'

It was then than Valerie took charge. 'Don't be silly,' she said. 'We'll ride out to the course with somebody else. Don't get upset about it.'

They were given a lift by one of the other competitors, and that day Ben played his heart out. He finished the fourth round to make a total score of 280, good enough for a tie for sixth place. And, more important, a prize of 380 dollars. That evening there were hamburgers galore for himself and Valerie. And new tyres for the car.

The money he won at Oakland was enough to keep Hogan going on the tournament trail, for a few weeks at any rate.

But still the important prizes – the winner's prizes – eluded him.

Towards the end of the 1937 winter season, Henry Picard, then professional at Hershey, Pennsylvania, and a big money winner on the tour, was staying at the Blackstone Hotel at Fort Worth. One evening, in the corner of the lobby, he spotted Ben Hogan and Valerie, whom he had met earlier in the year during an event at Hershey. The pair seemed to be arguing.

Picard went across. 'What's the matter?' he said.

Ben replied with his usual frankness. 'I don't have enough money for both of us to make the tour, and I'm not going alone. Val wants me to go without her, but I won't do it. I'm giving up.'

Valerie, however, continued to argue. 'You can't give up the game, Ben. Not now, after all you've been through.'

Picard was a wealthy man. He was a kind and good man. He was a golfer. To him the answer to their problem was simple. 'All right,' he said. 'Let's end the argument. Ben, take Valerie with you and go out and play. If you need anything, come and see me. I'll take care of things.'

The conversation was casual. It lasted less than ten minutes. But, according to Ben himself, it saved him for golf. From that day he began to earn a steady income from the tournaments, with plenty of small luxuries for Valerie. At the end of the 1939 tour, when Henry Picard decided to accept an offer from Cleveland's Canterbury Club, Hogan was appointed professional at Hershey, which gave him a solid base from which he could work. In 1940, at Pinehurst, North Carolina, he won the North and South Open with a score of 277, a record for the event. At last he had arrived.

By the time he came to Carnoustie, thirteen years later, he had won almost every important tournament in America, including four US Opens.

In his book, *My Partner Ben Hogan*, published in 1954, Jimmy Demaret recounts a conversation he once had with Henry Picard. 'Ben and I hardly know each other, even today,' Picard told him, 'but he dedicated his book to me, and I know we are close friends. I'm the most surprised person in the world that what I said that day in the Blackstone Hotel meant so much to him. And the funniest angle of all is that I never loaned Ben a penny. He never asked for it. All I did was promise to back him up. I could see he was a fine player. It would have been a shame if he had left golf; he has been such a credit to the game.'

A little love, a little care. For Ben Hogan it worked wonders. And I like the style of Henry Picard.

After spending three frustrating years in the Army Air Corps during the Second World War, while Byron Nelson, excused national service because of a tendency to haemophilia, was ruling the American golf scene with a Midas touch, Ben returned to play in tournaments at the end of 1945. He made up for lost time by taking first place in thirteen consecutive events. In 1948 he won his first Open at the Riviera Country Club at Los Angeles. A local newspaper renamed the course 'Hogan's Alley'.

But for all his success, fate held in store for him a terrible reckoning.

On 2 February 1949, he and Valerie were on their way to inspect a new house they had bought in Fort Worth, after he had taken part in the Arizona Open. A heavy fog overlay the highway which crosses the West Texan plain. Two hundred miles from El Paso, at a place called Van Horne, Ben was carefully picking his way through the mirk at ten miles an hour. He saw the headlights of a truck approaching in the opposite lane. Then the two headlights suddenly became four as a huge Greyhound bus swerved out to pass the truck. It came thundering straight at the Hogans' Cadillac.

To Ben's right there was a deep culvert. He had no chance of avoiding a head-on collision. At the last moment he let go of the wheel and threw himself in front of Valerie, an action which saved her life – and, as it happened, his own. As the bus struck with a rending crash, the wheel of the Cadillac was hammered back, burying itself in the driving seat from which Ben had flung himself sideways a moment before. The truck jammed on its brakes and slithered sideways on the road. Another car ran into it. In the blinding fog a fifth vehicle slammed into the tangled wreckage.

Four hours after the accident Hogan was admitted to the Hotel Dieu, a hospital at El Paso. His pelvis was fractured. His left collar bone, left ankle and several ribs were broken. The doctors gave him only an outside chance of survival.

But he survived, with Valerie constantly at his bedside, willing him to live. The physical fitness he had acquired in his years as a professional golfer overcame the shock and the pain and the broken bones. On his third day at the hospital they encased him in a plaster cast from his chest to his knees and put another on his ankle. He smiled wryly. 'Now I'll beat this thing,' he told his wife. 'I'll be back playing golf real soon.'

She believed him; but the doctors didn't. The doctors were mistaken.

In three months from the date of the accident Hogan was out of hospital. With grim determination he began to learn how to walk again. Step by uncertain step he built up his strength. Then he began, stiffly, to play a little golf: pitching and putting first, finally long irons and drives. Day after day he practised. His body was often full of pain; but it also became iron hard. His hands were calloused; but his swing was back, his spirit recharged.

In January 1950, he tied with Sam Snead for the Los Angeles Open. He lost the play-off, because, in the words of Grantland Rice, the sportswriter, 'his legs weren't strong enough to carry his heart around'. But he was happy. And so was Valerie. The Hawk, as he was nicknamed now, was back in business. Indeed, that same year he won the US Open for the second time.

When he came to Scotland to play in the Open, tales of his mechanical golf and dour, unrelenting character preceded him. For some reason, however, few British golf writers enlarged upon the dramatic details which revealed the truth about his life. Jean and I, with our son Jock, then sixteen years old and unaware that the next time the Open was played at Carnoustie he would be reporting it for the *Daily Express*, were among thousands of spectators who hoped to see this arrogant American humbled.

When I saw Hogan for the first time I was surprised by

how small and frail he looked. I could even detect the traces of a limp as he walked. But there was nothing frail about the iron shots he struck, long and straight, towards his caddie, Cecil Timms, on the practice ground. And strangely, when I saw the face under the white cap, grey, gaunt and expressionless, the feeling it gave me was not one of antagonism but rather of sympathy. On one occasion, as I watched him complete a practice round, Valerie was pointed out to me among the crowd behind the eighteenth green. It occurred to me that if he could retain the love and devotion of such a beautiful woman there must be more to Hogan than appeared on the surface.

In the two qualifying rounds – though he had no difficulty in qualifying – Hogan played poorly by his own standards. On the opening round of the championship proper he scored a 73, three shots behind the American amateur, Frank Stranahan, who led the field. By this time, piece by piece and from various sources, I was learning the Hogan story, and my heart, albeit reluctantly, was warming towards this small quiet stranger with the steadfast eyes.

Jock's hero at the time was Dai Rees. Jean had taken a fancy to a young Australian with a quick smile and white shoes, who was competing in the Open for the first time: his name, Peter Thomson. As usual I was hoping that John Panton and Eric Brown would do well. In those days spectators were allowed on the course, and we were able to walk immediately behind our favourites or to sit beside some green and watch them playing through.

At the end of the second day Jock and I were overjoyed. Stranahan had stumbled with a 74. Dai Rees and Eric Brown were tied for the lead on 142. But we noted with interest that Hogan, finishing with a 71, was only two shots behind them. And we had discovered that beneath the grim exterior there was humour. To a fellow professional he had remarked, 'I understand the tees we are using here are called 'tiger' tees. I believe it. They are so far back among the heather and gorse that every time I drive I expect a tiger to jump out at me.'

The last day was cloudy, with squally showers. This meant that Jean and Jock and I did a lot of walking, because if we sat down for any length of time we felt cold and uncomfortable. We weren't surprised that Hogan played both rounds with two sweaters on top of his favourite turtle-necked pullover. What we didn't know was that he had contracted flu and spent a restless night with pains in his back. Indeed, he and Valerie told nobody about his physical condition until after the championship was over.

An added interest for us was that for his two final rounds Hogan was paired with Hector Thomson, whom we knew personally. (Ex-Amateur Champion, Hector is one of the famous golfing family of Thomsons from Machrihanish in Kintyre.) We forgot the cold and the occasional rain as we joined the crowd that followed them.

In the morning Hogan scored 70, which included a double bogey 6 on the seventeenth hole, where, after driving into a bunker, he took three putts on the green. In the afternoon he went round in 68, a record for the course, and became Open Champion. His total score of 282 beat by eight strokes the previous competitive best over Carnoustie.

I think a shot we saw him play at the fifth hole that afternoon was the one that inspired his victory. His second to the sloping green rolled back almost into a bunker. The ball was on a sandy lie, fifty feet from the pin. Using a seven-iron – I *think* – he chipped it straight into the hole for a birdie. He was shivering with flu, he had a stiff and painful back, and yet his self-control was so marvellous that he could execute to perfection the most difficult shot in golf – a short pitch off sandy turf.

I remember two interviews which appeared in a magazine after the Carnoustie Open.

One was with Hector Thomson. He had been asked about Hogan's apparent coldness. 'Why, for example,' asked the interviewer, 'did he seem so indifferent when the spectators were cheering him on?'

'He was anything but indifferent,' Hector answered. 'Every time they applauded one of his shots he'd murmur 'Thank you'. You had to be close to hear it, but it was always there.' Then he added, 'He's a fine sportsman as well as a great golfer.'

Hector should know. He is also a fine sportsman and a great golfer.

The other interview was with Hogan himself. He was neither a hypocrite nor in any way sanctimonious, yet he concluded it by saying, 'I don't think anybody does anything unless the Lord's with them. I think the Lord has let me win so many tournaments for a purpose. I hope that purpose is to give courage to all those people who are sick or injured and broken in body as I once was.'

'Intellectuals' among the media men insist that what the public should read and hear and see are slices of real life. Hands on anguished hearts, they thrust such slices at us, brilliantly depicting cruelty, sadism, selfishness, social deprivation and tragedy, everything including the kitchen sink. They have a right to do so, of course. My worry is that they would sneer at the two stories I have just told about Barney Ross and Ben Hogan and dismiss them as being beyond the pale of 'real art', simply because they tell also of courage, integrity and the triumph of the human spirit. The slices of real life which have become fashionable (though not, I believe, with the majority of readers, listeners and viewers) are true. But then are not the stories of Barney Ross and Ben Hogan, with their elements of social deprivation and tragedy, also true? A further question arises. Which are more balanced?

Old Mary MacAulay saw a fairy city in the sky. Are the media men afraid to recognize a Fata Morgana, noble and beautiful and perhaps even within our reach?

Today discipline by parents and teachers is sometimes represented as cruelty. Many children are being taught to take, seldom to give. When they become adolescents they expect the process to continue. They give nothing but keep on looking for more. And, when they fail to get more, their lack of discipline causes them to strike out in vandalism, hooliganism and even rioting. In these circumstances the cult of the anti-hero comes into its own.

It seems to me that stories about heroes and heroines are necessary to sweeten the sour flavour that has become evident in real life: stories which prove that even without discos, skateboard parks, community halls, music centres, television and trampolines, without organized games or parties of any kind, boys and girls can still become happy and fulfilled men and women.

I believe that we, the older generation, are failing our children. We are failing to provide them with an ideal. And with the knowledge that the power behind a nuclear mushroom cloud is the same as that behind the opening petals of a rose.

Index